THE EFFECT OF AN
UNCONSTITUTIONAL STATUTE

Da Capo Press Reprints in

AMERICAN CONSTITUTIONAL AND LEGAL HISTORY

GENERAL EDITOR: LEONARD W. LEVY
Claremont Graduate School

THE EFFECT OF AN UNCONSTITUTIONAL STATUTE

By
OLIVER P. FIELD

DA CAPO PRESS • NEW YORK • 1971

A Da Capo Press Reprint Edition

This Da Capo Press edition of
The Effect of an Unconstitutional Statute
is an unabridged republication of the
first edition published in Minneapolis,
Minnesota, in 1935.

Library of Congress Catalog Card Number 74-146273

SBN 306-70118-9

Copyright 1935 by the University of Minnesota

Published by Da Capo Press
A Division of Plenum Publishing Corporation
227 West 17th Street, New York, N.Y. 10011
All Rights Reserved

Manufactured in the United States of America

THE EFFECT OF AN
UNCONSTITUTIONAL STATUTE

THE EFFECT OF AN UNCONSTITUTIONAL STATUTE

OLIVER P. FIELD, M.A., LL. B., S.J.D.

AUTHOR OF

CASES AND AUTHORITIES ON
CONSTITUTIONAL LAW

1935

THE UNIVERSITY OF MINNESOTA PRESS
MINNEAPOLIS

PREFACE

I am grateful to the Social Science Research Council for a grant-in-aid which helped defray some of the expense of clerical and research assistance in the prosecution of this study. The Bureau for Research in Government at the University of Minnesota lessened that expense materially by furnishing supplies and clerical facilities. I am indebted to Dean Guy Stanton Ford 'of the Graduate School of the University of Minnesota for aid from research funds in publishing this book.

Professor William Anderson of the Department of Political Science at the University of Minnesota has read some portions of the book, and as chairman of the department did much to aid and encourage me in the completion and publication of the work. Professor Walter F. Dodd, of the faculty of the School of Law at Yale University, helped me by his kindly but critical comments upon some of the portions which were prepared while I was a graduate student at that school and which have since appeared as articles. Professors Edwin M. Borchard of the School of Law at Yale University and Dudley O. McGovney of the School of Jurisprudence at the University of California, visiting professor of law at Yale University in 1927, also encouraged me to complete the study and read some chapters while they were being prepared for publication as articles in law reviews.

Miss Marie Shattuck of the University of Minnesota Law Library rendered invaluable assistance in helping me sift through the thousands of cases that had to be read to find the few that were significant. I owe her a debt that the reader can pay better than I, but the faults of the work are mine, not hers. No materials have gone into this book which I have not read and studied, personally.

To Paul L. Sayre, now professor of law at the University of Iowa, and formerly a colleague at Indiana University, I am under a deep personal obligation, because he, more than any other, urged me to begin serious work upon this problem, and at considerable personal inconvenience published the first results of my investigation in the form of an article in the first volume of the *Indiana Law Journal*.

I am indebted to the editors of the California, Michigan, Minne-

sota, Pennsylvania, Iowa, and Harvard *Law Review* for permission
to reprint materials, or portions of materials, that have appeared as
articles, in connection with chapters 2, 3, 4, 5, 8, and 10. Reference
to the page and number of each *Review* is made at the beginning
of each of the chapters concerned.

OLIVER P. FIELD

University of Minnesota
January, 1935

TABLE OF CONTENTS

Chapter I

INTRODUCTION

For over a hundred years, state and federal courts in the United States have been declaring statutes unconstitutional, and a great deal of discussion has centered about the American doctrine of judicial review.[1] For many years prior to independence, the judicial committee of the Privy Council had attempted to establish the principle of the supremacy of parliamentary or royal acts over inconsistent enactments of the colonial legislatures.[2] The practice of judicial review is one of the oldest of American political practices.

It is a little curious that during all these years so little should have been said or written upon the effects, legal, social, economic, and political, of unconstitutional statutes and judicial review. It was apparently assumed as early as Marbury v. Madison,[3] at least, that an unconstitutional statute or section thereof was wholly void, and the reasoning of the opinion in that case is such as to warrant the belief that John Marshall assumed that the courts would not enforce laws condemned as unconstitutional.

Many years later one of the most learned of American commentators on constitutional law said, in voicing this same opinion:

When a statute is adjudged to be unconstitutional, it is as if it had never been. Rights cannot be built up under it; contracts which depend upon it for their consideration are void; it constitutes a protection to no one who has acted under it, and no one can be punished for having refused obedience to it before the decision was made.[4]

At about the same time that Cooley wrote this statement, Justice Field delivered himself, in an opinion written for the Supreme Court of the United States, of the characterization of the effects of unconstitutionality which has since become classic. He said: "An unconstitutional statute is not a law; it confers no rights; it imposes no duties; it affords no protection; it creates no office; it is, in legal

---

[1] An excellent recent discussion of judicial review is C. G. Haines, The American Doctrine of Judicial Supremacy (2d ed., 1932).

[2] Winthrop v. Lechmere, Thayer's Cases on Constitutional Law, p. 34; Schlesinger, Colonial Appeals to the Privy Council, 28 Political Science Quarterly 279, 433 (1913). See also Boudin, Government by Judiciary.

[3] 1 Cranch 137, 2 L. Ed. 60 (1803). C. J. Marshall said, ". . . a law repugnant to the constitution is void . . ."

[4] Cooley, Constitutional Limitations (7th ed.), p. 259.

1

contemplation, as inoperative as though it had never been passed." [5] Since then courts have attempted to outdo one another in stating this doctrine in a novel and incisive manner. Some have said of an unconstitutional statute that "it is an empty legislative declaration without force or vitality," [6] others have paid their compliments to legislative bodies by characterizing such an enactment as "of no more force or validity than a piece of blank paper." [7] Some have spoken of such a law as simply a statute "in form" which under every circumstance or condition "lacks the force of law." [8] Still another court has spoken of an unconstitutional statute as "fatally smitten at its birth." [9] No distinction is drawn between statutes violating some procedural technicality and those violating important substantive prohibitions; a defect in title is as fatal as is a violation of due process.

It is no exaggeration to say that this theory that an unconstitutional statute is void ab initio is the traditional doctrine of American courts as to the effect of an unconstitutional statute. As it is usually stated it is a doctrine or rule of uncompromising and general application, and from it one would little suspect the flexibility it has developed in judicial practice, or the compromises that have been made to harmonize it with judicial decisions.

It should be stated here that the doctrine, as thus broadly phrased, is not now a general or universal rule governing the effect of unconstitutionality. The rule may not even yet be as flexible as it should be, but it is no longer the sole rule on the effect of an invalid statute. In some instances all courts, federal and state, decide cases by giving effect to unconstitutional statutes, and giving effect to them directly, as such, for the case under consideration; in other instances all courts agree that effect shall be given to such statutes by use of other legal rules or doctrines, such as estoppel, de facto, or clean hands in equity. In the chapters that follow each of these statements is illustrated in detail.

I. THEORIES OF THE EFFECT OF UNCONSTITUTIONAL STATUTES

There are several rules or views, not just one, as to the effect of an unconstitutional statute. All courts have applied them all at

[5] Norton v. Shelby County, 118 U. S. 425, 6 Sup. Ct. Rep. 1121, 30 L. Ed. 178 (1886).
[6] Carr v. State, 127 Ind. 204, 26 N. E. 778 (1890).
[7] Ex parte Bockhorn, 62 Tex. Cr. 651, 138 S. W. 706 (1911).
[8] Minnesota Sugar Co. v. Iverson, 91 Minn. 30, 97 N. W. 454 (1903).
[9] Ex parte Bockhorn, *supra*, note 7.

various times and in differing situations. Not all courts agree, however, upon the applicability of any particular rule to a specific case. It is this lack of agreement that causes the confusion in the case law of the subject.

A. The Void ab Initio Theory

The void ab initio theory of the effect of an invalid statute is, as was indicated above, that the statute should be eliminated entirely from the consideration of a case. Not only is the statute eliminated from the case as law but also as one of the facts in the situation. This theory gives no weight to the fact that the statute has been enacted by the legislature, approved by the governor, and relied upon by the people until it was declared invalid by a court.

There are numerous instances in constitutional law where this rule works well and is soundly applied. For example, if a person is arrested, accused, tried, and convicted under a statute which upon appeal is held to be unconstitutional, it is usually proper to permit him to go his way, a free man, so far as this case and statute are concerned. The same holding would be justified if the statute had been held invalid prior to the commission of the act in this case.[10] This would be true though he pleaded guilty to violating the statute.[11] Some question might arise over the subsequent attempt to try him for the violation, by his one act, of another valid statute that also made it a crime, and if the void ab initio theory were applied strictly, the first trial would not be considered a jeopardy, and the subsequent trial would be viewed as the first jeopardy. Double jeopardy would not be violated, therefore, under the strict void ab initio theory.[12] To so hold might, however, raise a serious question whether such an application of the void ab initio theory would not

[10] See Norwood v. State, 136 Miss. 272, 101 So. 366 (1924); State v. Greer, 88 Fla. 249, 102 So. 739 (1924); Moore v. State, 26 Okla. Cr. Rep. 394, 224 Pac. 372 (1924).

[11] Norwood v. State, *supra,* note 10; State v. Greer, *supra,* note 10.

[12] See Barton v. State, 89 Tex. Cr. 387, 23 S. W. 989 (1921), suggesting that lunacy adjudication is not a bar to subsequent prosecution if the adjudication is authorized by an invalid act. In State v. Oleson, 26 Minn. 507, 5 N. W. 959 (1880), the members of the court apparently disagreed on the incidental question of double jeopardy if one prosecuted under an invalid ordinance were again to be prosecuted for the same act. Justice Berry said, in dictum: "As the conviction set up in bar of the indictment was under an ordinance invalid and void as respects the offense charged in the indictment, it was a conviction without any authority of law whatever — a conviction for an offense which was not an offense; or, in other words, it was not a conviction at all, and hence the defendant was not, in contemplation of law, put in jeopardy of punishment for the offense for which she is indicted, either by the so-called conviction under the ordinance, or by the prosecution which led to it." See Chapter 4, note 100.

be an unwarranted invasion of a situation to which the double jeopardy guarantee was intended to apply.

It is under the void ab initio view that the rule is properly applied that a statute, once declared unconstitutional, need not be pleaded and assailed in subsequent cases.[13] This theory is likewise properly applied by courts holding that officers may defend against an action for mandamus to compel them to act under an invalid statute.[14]

B. Presumption of Validity Theory

Another view of the effect of an unconstitutional statute is that the act is to be given some effect. It shall be given sufficient effect, under this theory, to constitute at least one of the facts of the case. When the courts apply this view, they often speak of giving effect to the presumption that a statute is valid until it is declared by a court to be invalid.[15] The exact effect of such a presumption is not clear, but that it does, when indulged, aid in giving some factual status to what under the void ab initio view would be nonexistent legally and factually, so far as the court is concerned, seems pretty clear. Courts sometimes state explicitly that they will decide the case as though the law were valid, admitting that it is not valid, because the parties have been led to assume its validity and because they were warranted in that assumption. The courts say, in some of these cases, that in these situations it would be unfair to apply the void ab initio rule.

At other times the courts emphasize the applicability of rules of mistake of law, or estoppel, and apply them in such a manner that the net result is a decision that does not formally take account of the invalid statute and is indistinguishable from one formally based upon it. It is under the de facto doctrine that the acts of the governing board of a large midwestern university and the officers, if any, appointed by it, were valid after the decision in State ex rel. University v. Chase,[16] if that decision is interpreted

[13] State v. Cormier, 171 La. 1035, 132 So. 779 (1931). See Perdue v. Maryland Casualty Co., 43 Ga. App. 853, 160 S. E. 720 (1931), not necessary to assail statute after it has been held unconstitutional, since lower courts may assume from then on that the statute is invalid.

[14] See the excellent opinion by J. Treanor in State ex rel. Test v. Steinwedel, 180 N. E. 865 (Ind. 1932).

[15] See Wade v. Board of Commrs., 17 P. (2d) 691 (Okla. 1932), board members not liable for excess salary payments made under an invalid statute, although statute said they were liable for illegal payments. For an interesting discussion of the problem of presumptions in this branch of the law, see Comment, 31 Col. L. Rev. 1136 (1931).

[16] State ex rel. University v. Chase, 175 Minn. 259, 220 N. W. 951 (1928).

as holding invalid the statute under which the board was selected. Sometimes courts disagree vigorously over the question whether such doctrines are or are not applicable, in connection with invalid statutes, but when they are applied they usually bring about decisions identical with those based upon the statute. The courts that frankly admit that they apply, in these cases, a theory giving to the invalid act itself some legal effect encounter fewer legal difficulties than do those that avowedly refuse to give such statutes any effect whatever but nevertheless attempt to evade the void ab initio doctrine by resort to other legal rules and principles. The difficulty of harmonizing some of the estoppel doctrines in this field with the usual theories of estoppel as they are applied in other branches of the law influences one to favor the more direct and simple approach of those courts that flatly deny that every unconstitutional statute is without any legal effect whatever in cases involving factual situations arising prior to the time of the declaration of invalidity. It is probably unimportant whether legal effect be given to the statute directly, or legal significance be attached to the fact of writing on the statute book accompanied by acts of reliance thereon.

The election cases fall under this heading. An election may be valid although the law authorizing or regulating it is unconstitutional, the question of its validity being determined by the law of elections, not by any doctrine of unconstitutionality. If the election be upon a constitutional object or purpose, and if in it the voter's will can be said to have been fairly expressed, then the election is valid, despite the constitutional defect in the election statute.[17] It is interesting to note that invalid congressional acts have been held to have sufficient effect to be evidence of an intention to occupy a part of the regulatory field in interstate commerce, thereby ousting the states from the field.[18]

It must be clear upon reflection that the void ab initio rule is the more doctrinaire; that the second of the rules is the more realistic. The latter view often aids in the just settlement of disputes when the facts are more complicated than in the illustrations referred to under the void ab initio doctrine. It has been developed and utilized because in some cases courts have hesitated to take the responsibility for the results that would flow from an application of the strict void ab initio rule.

[17] Adsit v. Ormun, 84 Mich. 420, 48 N. W. 31 (1891); Wiley v. Reasoner, 69 Ore. 103, 138 Pac. 250 (1914). See Griffin v. Brooks, 129 Ga. 698, 59 S. E. 902 (1907); State ex rel. Fletcher v. Ruhe, 24 Nev. 251, 52 Pac. 274 (1898).

[18] Chicago, I., & L. Ry. v. Hackett, 227 U.S. 559, 33 Sup. Ct. Rep. 308, 57 L. Ed. 966 (1912). See also Bentley v. Board, 152 Ga. 836, 111 S. E. 379 (1921), statutory remedy invalid, but other remedies excluded by it.

C. The Case-to-Case Theory

A third view of the effect of an invalid statute is that it is neither wholly valid nor wholly invalid. In accordance with this view a statute is constitutional under some circumstances, unconstitutional under others; constitutional as to some persons, unconstitutional as to others. This view will be found to be associated very closely with a view as to what parties may raise the question of constitutionality and, also, with a view as to the generality of the scope of judicial decision. The following quotation is illustrative of this view:

Perhaps, however, it may be well doubted whether a formal act of legislation can ever with strict legal propriety be said to be void; it seems more consistent with the nature of the subject, and the principles applicable to analogous cases, to treat it as voidable. But whether or not a case can be imagined in which an act of the legislature can be deemed absolutely void, we think it quite clear, that when such act is alleged to be void, on the ground that it exceeds the just limits of legislative power, and thus injuriously affects the rights of others, it is to be deemed void only in respect to those particulars, and as against those persons, whose rights are thus affected. Prima facie, and upon the fact of the act itself, nothing will generally appear to show that the act is not valid; and it is only when some person attempts to resist its operation and calls in the aid of the judicial power, to pronounce it void, as to him, his property, or his rights, that the objection of unconstitutionality can be presented and sustained. Respect for the legislature, therefore, concurs with well-established principles of law, in the conclusion, that such act is not void, but voidable only; and it follows as a necessary legal inference from this position, that this ground of avoidance can be taken advantage of, by those only who have a right to question the validity of the act, and not by strangers. To this extent only is it necessary to go, in order to secure and protect the rights of all persons, against the unwarranted exercise of legislative power, and to this extent only, therefore, are courts of justice called on to interpose.

Besides, and this is another argument leading to the same result, if a legislative act may or may not be valid according to circumstances, courts are bound by the plainest principles of exposition, as well as by a just deference to the legislature, to presume the existence of those circumstances which will support it and give it validity. For instance, if an act of the legislature appears on the face of it to be an encroachment on the rights of any persons, but would nevertheless be valid if passed with the consent of those persons, the court is bound to presume that such consent was given. And this presumption must prevail in favor of the validity of the act, until the contrary is shown, and shown too by a person having an interest in the maintenance of the rights supposed to be thus injuriously affected, and having a right to call for the interposition of the court for their support and protection, and a stranger can have no right to appear and contest the validity of the act upon such a ground.[19]

No sweeping law-making effect is attributed by this view to judicial decisions. A judgment is as to a litigated question, and as to the parties thereto, and is not a device for establishing rules of general import. A decision that a statute is invalid as between Smith and Jones in a dispute over the ownership of bank stock may or may not have any significance as precedent or as establishing a rule of law for a dispute over a public office between Doe and Roe. It may or it may not have significance in such a case. The Supreme Court of the United States has said that "a statute may be invalid as applied to one state of facts and valid as applied to another." [20] The Texas court has expressed a similar idea:

We recognize the superior authority of the Supreme Court of the United States upon this question, and in obedience to its decision we shall hold that in so far as the law of 1895 comes within the terms of the Connolly case, it is invalid; it will not support an action by the state to recover a penalty for a violation of the law, nor will it, in suits between corporations or individuals, support a defense based upon the fact that the right of action originated in a violation of the anti-trust law. But to the extent that the statute of this state is not embraced in the decision of the Supreme Court of the United States, we shall adhere to our former decision that it is constitutional and valid, and therefore enforceable.[21]

Penalties could not be recovered by the state under this holding, but corporations had their privilege to do business revoked for the violation of this unconstitutional statute.[22]

An Iowa statute was declared invalid by the federal courts as applied to national banks, but was held to be valid as to state banks.[23] State and federal decisions in the fields of interstate commerce, taxation, and due process abound with examples of this rule.

One of the clearest statements of this view of the effect of an unconstitutional statute is that of the West Virginia court in West Virginia v. Wheeling, when it said:

[19] Wellington et al., Petitioners, 16 Pick. 87 (Mass. 1834), at 96.

[20] Dahnke-Walker Milling Co. v. Bondurant, 257 U. S. 282, 42 Sup. Ct. 106, 66 L. Ed. 239 (1921). See also Yazoo & M. R. V. Co. v. Jackson Vinegar Co., 226 U. S. 217, 33 Sup. Ct. 40, 57 L. Ed. 193 (1912); Jeffrey v. Blagg, 235 U. S. 571, 35 Sup. Ct. 167, 59 L. Ed. 364 (1914). See also Rutten v. Mayor, 73 N. J. L. 467, 64 Atl. 573 (1906). A statute may be invalid as to past transactions and valid as to future ones. Harlee v. Ward, 15 Rich. Law 231 (S. C. 1868).

[21] State v. Compress & Warehouse Co., 95 Tex. 603, 69 S. W. 58 (1902).

[22] Scott v. Smelker, 280 S. W. 297 (Tex. Civ. App. 1926).

[23] State v. Bevins, 210 Iowa 1031, 230 N. W. 865 (1930).

The court may give its reasons for ignoring or disregarding the statute, but the decision affects the parties only, and there is no judgment against the statute. The opinion or reasons of the court may operate as a precedent for the determination of other similar cases, but it does not . . . repeal the statute. The parties to that suit are concluded by the judgment, but no one else is bound. A new litigant may bring a new suit, based upon the very same statute, and the former decision cannot be pleaded as an estoppel, but can be relied on only as a precedent. This constitutes the reason and basis of the fundamental rule that a court will never pass upon the constitutionality of a statute unless it is absolutely necessary to do so in order to decide the case before it.[24]

This is really a type of partial unconstitutionality, but it differs from the usual case of partial unconstitutionality in that the whole of the act, so far as its text and face are concerned, is valid, whereas in the true partial unconstitutionality case some definite portion of the text is held to be invalid; some phrase, sentence, or section is singled out and condemned.[25]

The great advantage of this view of the effect of an unconstitutional statute is that it permits of great elasticity in the law. It lends itself to the administration of justice in a case-to-case system, with a proper tempering of justice to the individual case. The great disadvantage of this rule is that it does not lend itself to the formulation of rules of law. Prediction becomes well-nigh impossible. The stable element of the law almost disappears under this technique. Due process of law, and the immunity of the agencies of the national government from taxation by the states, afford examples as extreme as the void ab initio view presents in its emphasis upon universal rule. It is this view that is embodied by congressional declaration in the National Industrial Recovery Act of March, 1933. Such a declaration does not conclude the courts, of course, but may be given weight as evidence of legislative intention, as in the case of separability clauses in partial unconstitutionality.

II. THE HISTORICAL AND DOCTRINAL BASIS OF THEORIES

The courts, in the eminently practical fashion of common law courts, have, therefore, evolved several rules or views as to the effect of an invalid statute. They did this because it was more just to do

[24] 30 W. Va. 479, 4 S. E. 635 (1887).

[25] On partial unconstitutionality, see the excellent note in Ann. Cas. 1916D 89. Partial unconstitutionality is discussed only incidentally in this study. On statutory declaration of separability of the sections of a statute and the effect upon other sections of a decision involving one section, see Sage v. Baldwin, 55 F. (2d) 968 (D. C. S. D. N. Y. 1932); Williams v. Standard Oil Co., 278 U. S. 235, 49 Sup. Ct. 115, 73 L. Ed. 287 (1929). See the warning against indiscriminate use of such clauses in Noel T. Dowling, Dissection of Statutes, Am. Bar Assn. Jour., May, 1932, p. 298.

so and because the one rule, that of void ab initio, would not have worked at all in some instances, when taken together with other established principles of law. There is in this field of the law an interesting interplay of the forces of doctrine and the forces of practical necessity and justice. It has not been easy for judges to draw the boundaries so as to mark off one group of cases to which the void ab initio theory should be applied; so as to segregate another group and presume that statutes governing them shall be given some effect up to the time when the statute is declared invalid; to set apart those cases in which neither one nor the other of these two rules should apply but in which the rule of constitutionality in terms of parties and purposes should be recognized. Sometimes the doctrinal element will prevail in legal analysis; at others doctrine will be submerged. Some doctrinal elements can, of course, be distinguished in the two other views also, but inasmuch as they are responses to the requirements of situations encountered by the courts in the practical administration of justice, whereas the void ab initio theory was largely the response to a philosophical view of government, it is in the latter view that doctrine is the greater factor.

Most of the bad law in the decisions in this branch of the law has come from the inability of some courts to free themselves from the overpowering force of the logic evidenced in the void ab initio rule, once its premises are assumed. As indicated earlier, and as will be borne out by the chapters to follow, judges have actually bewailed the fact that they were compelled by doctrine to decide the cases as they did, but have seemed quite helpless to free themselves from the premises that necessitated the logical results they felt compelled to reach. Others, acting with an eye on the realities of the situations presented to them, have found much less difficulty in adopting premises that would permit the realization of different decisions or, if admitting the logic of void ab initio, have found it possible to engraft exceptions upon it or to defeat its application in the particular case by giving effect to other applicable rules or principles. In few fields of the law is a clearer illustration afforded of the importance of the selection of premises in the judicial process, and in few fields has the selection of the premise so often been dictated by doctrinal considerations.

It was with this in mind that the writer said, several years ago, in a first exploratory study into this field, that the void ab initio rule and its power over judges can be understood only in the light of the general theory of judicial review of legislation alleged to be unconstitutional. The usual explanation of the process of judicial review is said to be that there is a body of constitutional rules and principles on the one side, and on the other a conflicting body of rules or a single rule embodied in statutory form. In the decision of a given case the courts must find and apply a rule or several rules of law. Here the court finds several competing and inconsistent rules.

The courts must apply those rules of law which the constitution says are paramount, and if other competing rules are inconsistent with those found in the constitution, judges have no choice but to reject or ignore the statutory rules and apply the constitutional rule. This judicial rejection of the statutory rule, reducing the process to its simplest terms, is what is referred to by the phrase "declaring a statute unconstitutional."

A question naturally suggested by the customary explanation of the process is, What becomes of the statutory rule? The process of judicial review, in the simple case, is not difficult to understand. It is not so easy, however, to explain just why the courts say of the results of this process that the statute is entirely abrogated, except for the formality of a repeal, as a result of this procedure. A declaration of unconstitutionality does not operate as a repeal of a statute. All courts agree upon this.

It is submitted that a factor of primary importance in causing the early courts to view unconstitutional statutes as void acts was the outline of an ideal pattern toward which they sought to make the law move, and in accordance with which the law and legal rules should be administered. This pattern had as its core the idea of the supremacy of a written constitution over the legislative branch of government. True it is that we began our state governments with legislative supremacy, but legislative supremacy soon gave way to the idea of a superior law, a constitution. No doubt the emphasis laid at that time upon guarantees against arbitrary action on the part of government contributed much to this idea, both as those guarantees related to property rights and as they related to personal rights closely associated with the idea of freedom: political and legal freedom.

The early nineteenth century, not the late eighteenth century, saw the real beginnings of judicial review in this country as an accepted governmental practice, and by the early nineteenth century, constitutions had been more clearly distinguished from ordinary legislative law, or statute law, as it is now called. Early state legislatures made constitutions and promulgated them without submitting them to a popular vote. The early state constitutions were in the nature of political codes drawn up by legislators. But by the time John Marshall had begun his epoch-making series of decisions,

American legal and political thinkers had come to think of constitutions as of a higher nature than either decisional or statutory law. Constitutional conventions came into use in the early nineteenth century, and with them the differentiation between constitutions and statutes was carried still further.

The governmental pattern in the minds of judges during the first half of the nineteenth century was that of constitutional government; of ordered government with legislatures subjected to constitutional controls. Legislatures were not to be permitted to commit some of the earlier legislative atrocities. The American idea of government came to be, and is still to a considerable degree, that of a constitutional government with three departments. Each of these departments was to have its own powers and was to do its own work. None of them should overstep the constitutional limits fixed for it. Nor should any or all of them overstep those limits that had been placed upon all government to protect individual rights. In an ideal system the balance would be kept perfectly. Excesses of power should not take place under this system, and the early judges were disposed to treat legislative excesses of power so as to obliterate the effects of the excess. So to treat them was to apply the void ab initio doctrine. Legislative excesses were to leave no effect on the law, under the void ab initio view.

The first few cases in which judicial review was exercised were such as to raise no particularly difficult questions as to the effect of an unconstitutional statute. In Marbury v. Madison the writ of mandamus was not issued, because the plaintiff had asked for it in the wrong court and in the wrong action. The statute giving the court the power to issue the writ in this proceeding was unconstitutional and therefore the writ was not issued. In the political furore surrounding, and resulting from, this decision, it is only natural to find that the problem of the effect of such a decision upon the statute was passed by or forgotten. No particular difficulty on this point was presented by the case. The statute was not enforced by the court. It was called "void" by the court without any special reference to anything but its unenforceability in the particular case and under the circumstances peculiar to it.

The political theory of the time that saw the rise of judicial review, and the circumstances of some of the first major decisions involving judicial review, were such that the void ab initio doctrine came to be readily accepted. Later, when more complications resulted from the exercise of judicial review, exceptions developed. It was with difficulty that these exceptions were established in the face of the accumulation of doctrine oft repeated. By the time judicial review came to be exercised in its modern form, and to its present extent, during the second half of the nineteenth century, commentators had helped fix this doctrine as the normal rule of decision. The breaking down of the doctrine to make room for more reasonable rules of the effect of an unconstitutional statute, or the effect of a decision on such a statute, has been a slow process. It is encouraging that it is gradually breaking down where it should break down.

III. SCOPE AND LIMITS OF THIS STUDY

The effects of an unconstitutional statute may be numerous. Some of them are easily perceived; others are more difficult to identify. A decision holding a statute unconstitutional may have, and often does have, many non-legal effects. Sometimes the legal effects are the more important, sometimes the non-legal effects. Often both types of effects are of considerable significance.

To one reform movement a decision holding a statute invalid is practically a death knell; to another it serves only to strengthen the cause and to result in an educational campaign to enlist public support for a constitutional or statutory change that is more effective than it could otherwise have been. To declare a statute invalid sometimes results in the practical ruination of the fiscal policy of a governmental area for a short time; at another time such a decision may result in serious study and subsequent action to correct weaknesses in the tax structure. A commercial policy of private business may be profoundly affected by the exercise of judicial review in a particular case. Judicial review may be effective in one case, and in another have virtually no subsequent effect upon even the work of the courts in that field.

This study has been confined to the legal effects of unconstitutionality, and decisions upon it. It does not cover even all the legal phases of the subject. A complete analysis of its legal phases would require, for example, that every case in which a state or federal statute has been declared unconstitutional be followed by a systematic search of the subsequent session laws, and of proposed and adopted constitutional amendments, to ascertain the subsequent legal problems raised in the history of the case and the disposition made of them. Subsequent decisions should also be studied in the case of every statute declared constitutional, in order that overruling decisions may be detected. The decisions preceding and immediately following overruling decisions, and the statutes also, should be scrutinized carefully to ascertain the disposition made of cases resulting from reliance upon the earlier decisions. Similarly, overruling decisions in the case of a shift from unconstitutionality to constitutionality should be studied.

General trial court records would yield much excellent material, although reported appellate court cases alone would involve prodigious effort, if they were really subjected to scholarly and exacting study. These are examples, only, of what a comprehensive legal study of the effects of unconstitutionality should include.

A study of the effect and significance of judicial review must include more than its law, however; it should reach into politics, economics, and government. To what extent is a judicial decision a deterrent or an aid to a particular movement for change in law or government? One surmises that supporters of the federal child labor legislation of a decade ago have views upon such a question. Some consideration of the economic aspects of judicial review must also be included in a comprehensive study. The effect of decisions or statutes upon private parties alone offers an intriguing subject for study, and it is of the highest significance. What are the calculable costs in some of these cases of the exercise of judicial review? Bond cases would yield a veritable mine of information of the utmost significance in public finance. What happens politically, as well as economically, in these cases? Much bad feeling has often been engendered because of the exercise of judicial review; governmental inefficiency has often been promoted thereby.

Judicial review has cost many a governmental institution large sums of money; and many a private person or group of private persons has spent thousands, and even millions, because of it. The results often seem not to justify the outlays involved. Good government has often suffered, too, because of the frictions left by its exercise, or by a failure to have it exercised. Administration is injured by the bitterness of some of the parties involved, and their refusal to cooperate with other agencies. The costs to government, and to individuals, inherent in the system under present conditions are to be contrasted with costs that should be assumed by government but are now borne by individuals who suffer because of reliance upon judicial decisions as to constitutionality, or because legislative action as manifested in statute has been relied upon.

Changes in statutes and decisions have been suggested throughout the following chapters whenever it has seemed necessary and practical to do so. Were there not so many of them, and did they not deal with so many different subjects, draft statutes would have been included in an appendix. To have done that satisfactorily would have required too much space, however, and to do it is easier if the proposals follow the discussion of a single problem, culminating in a draft statute, or a series of such drafts. Wherever possible, an existing statute has been referred to rather than a new draft suggested, because a good statute at work is worth two in draft. The citations of statutes in this study are usually for the purpose of illustration rather than for the purpose of collecting all of the statutory law of any particular subject.

Throughout the work runs the unifying thread of the effect of an unconstitutional statute, and the effect of decisions upon questions of constitutionality. Such a chapter as that dealing with mistake of law is primarily of interest not because of its private law aspects but because of its bearing upon judicial review and its legal effects. The same is true of private and municipal corporations, unconstitutionally collected taxes, or any of the other subjects dealt with in subsequent chapters. It may be that these chapters will interest some readers because of their legal materials rather than because of their governmental or political aspects. It has not always been easy to strike the balance between the two phases of any given subject.

The concluding chapter deals with the more strictly political or governmental problems of judicial review. In it various appraisals and suggestions have been ventured. They should be viewed as tentative only, but they should be of some use until more reliable data have been gathered, and more comprehensive generalizations are justified.

Chapter II

THE STATUS OF A PRIVATE CORPORATION ORGANIZED UNDER AN UNCONSTITUTIONAL STATUTE*

Suppose that A, B, and C associate themselves in a corporate form of organization for carrying on a business. They comply with all the conditions specified in the statutes as necessary to the enjoyment of corporate privileges. Ten months later the corporation files a complaint against X for having cut a cable belonging to it. X defends by asserting that the statute under which plaintiff is organized is unconstitutional and that therefore plaintiff has no corporate existence. Is there no party plaintiff if the statute is held to be contrary to the state or federal constitution?

Perhaps a subscriber for stock in a newly formed corporation becomes distrustful of the constitutionality of the statutory basis for the organization and resists an action by the corporation to collect the subscription price remaining unpaid. May he do so successfully?

What is the status of a private corporation organized under an unconstitutional statute? Is it a corporation de jure or de facto, or is it a nullity? In the following pages an attempt will be made to study the cases in which courts have been called upon to answer these questions.[1]

The order in which the various phases of the subject here treated will be taken up will be: (1) the cases themselves and (2) a consideration of the general principles utilized by the courts in deciding them, with some attempt at generalization on the basis of the decisions.

I. THE CASES

The cases involving the problem of the status of a private corporation organized under an unconstitutional statute may be divided into two large groups. There are those (1) in which there

* The substance of this chapter appeared as an article in 17 Cal. L. Rev. 327–57 (1929).

[1] In the original printing of this article in 17 Cal. L. Rev. 327 (1929), a brief summary of the views of the effect of an invalid statute was presented. It is omitted at this point. See Chapter 1.

15

have been dealings between the parties on a corporate basis and (2) those in which there have been no such dealings. Further subdivisions will be indicated within each of these larger groups.

A. Cases in Which There Have Been Dealings on a Corporate Basis

These may have been (1) between a corporation and a stranger or (2) between a corporation and one of its officers or shareholders.

1. Cases of Dealings between a Corporation and a Stranger

a) Where the corporation is the plaintiff. — Suppose that X makes a note to a bank. He fails to pay it when it is due. The bank sues him on it. X defends by asserting that the bank has no corporate existence because of a defective statute and that it is, therefore, not entitled to maintain suit. The Nebraska court had before it this question, the bank to which the note had been made having been organized under a territorial statute that was inconsistent with a congressional act.[2] State constitutions and statutes bear much the same relation to one another that congressional statutes for territories bear to statutes enacted by territorial legislatures. Therefore the case may be considered as having at least persuasive force in a situation where the state constitution is substituted for the act of Congress. The court in the Nebraska case allowed the bank to maintain the suit.

The maker of a note secured by a mortgage was permitted in a Michigan case to defeat recovery on the ground that the assignee of the note and mortgage stood in no better position than the bank to which the mortgage had been executed.[3] The bank had been organized under an invalid statute and could not have maintained the action, the result being, according to the court, that the assignee was likewise barred.

Under the void ab initio[4] doctrine no law would have existed authorizing organization in either of these two cases, and when viewed from the standpoint of that doctrine, they would seem to be in direct conflict with one another. The Nebraska court applied the de facto[5] doctrine to protect the bank, whereas the Michigan

---

[2] Platte Valley Bank v. Harding, 1 Neb. 461 (1870).

[3] Hurlbut v. Britain & Wheeler, 2 Doug. 191 (Mich. 1845).

[4] Throughout this chapter the term "void ab initio" will be used in the restricted sense indicated in the preliminary explanation in Chapter 1.

[5] The phrase "de facto," as applied to corporations, will be used throughout this chapter in the restricted sense in which it is used in Warren, Collateral Attack on Incorporation, 20 Harv. L. Rev. 456, 464 (1907). The requisites for applying the de facto doctrine as set forth by Professor Warren, as well as numerous other writers,

court refused to apply it, the situation being very much the same in the two cases. If the cases are considered from the standpoint of estoppel, it will be found that the Michigan court refused to estop the defendant from collateral attack, whereas the Nebraska court used estoppel to prevent such an attack. If the existence of a law under which organization could be had is regarded as one of the conditions precedent to the application of the de facto doctrine, it is perhaps difficult under the void ab initio view to use that doctrine in cases such as these. However, the maker of the note could in both cases have been made to repay the money he had borrowed by resorting to the doctrine of estoppel. Corporations by estoppel are perhaps only a fiction and, in the minds of many writers, an objectionable fiction, but it is not necessary here to resort to the doctrine of a corporation by estoppel. It could be said by the court that the borrower should be made to repay the loan to the organization from which he had borrowed it. To accomplish this no great objection is perceived against saying that he is estopped from using the defense of no corporate existence in the plaintiff. There may be no corporation as an entity, which is of course the view of those who lean toward the void ab initio view, and their displeasure is not incurred in this solution of the problem, since we do not say that there is a corporation, either de jure, de facto, or by estoppel. The dealings between the parties in such a case would seem to be on a corporate basis.

The Michigan court refused, unlike the Nebraska court, to give any weight whatever to the existence of the statute in accordance with which the bank was organized. No one can doubt that it was one of the facts of the case, but by applying the void ab initio doctrine and the strict view of a de facto corporation the statute and the corporation were both totally ignored.

A slight variant from the loan transaction is that presented by a corporate promisee suing on a contract to pay money on the happening of a certain specified event, the corporate existence of the promisee being challenged by way of defense. The plaintiff in Hud-

are: (1) the existence of a law under which incorporation could be had, (2) colorable compliance and organization, (3) good faith, and (4) user. The phrase "de facto doctrine" as herein used refers to the doctrine whereby courts accord associates corporate standing for purposes of applying corporate rules in deciding the case by labeling the organization a "de facto corporation." No attempt is made in these pages to settle the problem whether a so-called de facto corporation is a legal entity.

[6] 113 Ill. 618 (1885). The court seems to say, at 627, that before a suit can be maintained on stock subscription it must be shown that a legal corporation with capacity to issue stock was in existence, and that otherwise there would be a failure of consideration. It is not clear whether or not by "legal corporation" is meant de jure corporation, or whether it is meant to include de facto corporation also.

son v. Green Hill Seminary [6] was in this position, and to an action brought by the corporation a plea of nul tiel corporation was filed. A curative act seeking to validate defective incorporation was assailed as unconstitutional, but since the corporation was a foreign one, the Illinois court felt that it should be slow to pass upon the constitutionality of a statute of another state, and also that the passage of the curative act in question was evidence that in the state of its creation the corporation was recognized as having de facto existence at least. The plaintiff corporation was therefore permitted to recover.

A somewhat different question was presented in Clark v. American Cannel Coal Company,[7] where the corporation brought an action to quiet title to land and to enjoin the defendant from mining thereon. The defendant claimed that the corporation lacked capacity to take title because it was formed under an invalid statute, and that if it did not have capacity to take title it could not maintain the action in the corporate name, because of its alleged corporate nonexistence. The Indiana court decided that the plaintiff could not maintain the action because it was not a corporation. The court was of the opinion that at the time the deed to the land was given to the corporation the latter enjoyed de jure existence. Had this action been brought at that time, the defense here interposed would not have been available to the defendant. But at the time the instant action was commenced the corporation existed only by virtue of an unconstitutional statute purporting to extend the period of corporate existence.[8] The court reasoned that it was not even a de facto corporation because in order to have such a corporation there must be a law authorizing incorporation or extending corporate existence beyond the charter period. There was no law here, so there could be no de facto corporation. Collateral attack was permitted. The court also reached the same conclusion by another method of reasoning. Beginning with the premise that there was no statutory authority for the corporation after the charter period had expired, the court reasoned that the corporation must be considered as dissolved. The conclusion to be drawn from this was that a dissolved corporation could not have de facto existence. When it is pointed out that there was on the statute book another statute upon which corporate existence might have been predicated, it will be seen that this case goes very far indeed.

[7] 165 Ind. 213, 73 N. E. 1083, 112 Am. St. Rep. 217 (1905).

[8] Another case in which a statute purporting to extend the period of corporate life was held unconstitutional in Indiana was In re Bank of Commerce, 153 Ind. 460, 53 N. E. 950 (1899); rehearing denied, 153 Ind. 460, 55 N. E. 224.

In Coxe v. State of New York[9] the receiver of a corporation sued to recover money paid to the state for land purchased for drainage purposes in accordance with statutory encouragement of such projects. This policy was changed and the corporation was deprived of most of its powers by a subsequent amendment of the corporate charter. The defense was the nonexistence of the corporation. But, the court held,

It is not important to decide what provisions, if any, of the act can be upheld, since, even if the section creating the corporation should fall with the rest, it is undisputed that it organized, assumed, and exercised corporate powers under an act of the legislature, and thus it was a corporation de facto, if not de jure, and it required the judgment of a competent court or an express act of the legislature to terminate its existence.[10]

It will be seen that the court relied to some extent upon the doctrine that the state alone shall be permitted to attack the existence of the corporation, and for that reason denied collateral attack by the defendant.[11] That the New York court took an attitude inconsistent with that of the Indiana court in the Clark case seems clear despite the fact that the transactions involved in the two cases were not identical.

b) *Where the corporation is the defendant.*—The foregoing cases have involved attempts by defendants to challenge corporate existence in the plaintiff. Cases may arise, however, in which the plaintiff is the party alleging the nonexistence of a defendant corporation. For example, the plaintiff may be seeking to recover land

[9] 144 N. Y. 396, 39 N. E. 400 (1895).

[10] 144 N. Y. at 409, 39 N. E. at 403.

[11] Quo warranto is the proper proceeding for the state to institute to ascertain the constitutionality of an incorporation statute. People ex rel. Deneen v. People's Gaslight and Coke Co., 205 Ill. 482, 68 N. E. 950 (1903). In Attorney General ex rel. Mason v. Perkins, 73 Mich. 303, 41 N. W. 426 (1889), an information in the nature of quo warranto was filed by a stockholder to test the constitutionality of a statute under which a reorganization had been completed. See particularly the answer of the court to the contention that this amounted to permitting collateral attack (73 Mich. at 311–12). Statutes occasionally provide that a local prosecuting attorney may institute an action to test the legality of incorporation. Cf. In re Bank of Commerce, *supra*, note 8. In Commonwealth v. Philadelphia, Harrisburg, & Pittsburgh R. R., 23 Pa. Super. Ct. 235 (1903), the state indicted the company for maintaining a nuisance in the form of certain railroad crossings. The court held that the state could not in such a proceeding question the constitutionality of the statute under which the corporation had been formed in this case, holding that quo warranto alone was the proper proceeding in which to raise this question. See State of Kansas v. Lawrence Bridge Co., 22 Kan. 438 (1879), where quo warranto was instituted by the state to test the constitutionality of a statute extending the life of the corporation. In this case an injunction was also granted to prevent the company from continuing the collection of tolls, the highway going to the use of the public, relieved from payment of tolls.

from a corporation to which he had previously sold it, on the ground that there was insufficient statutory authority to entitle defendant to corporate standing. In Smith v. Sheeley,[12] which involved a territorial statute that conflicted with a congressional enactment, the United States Supreme Court denied collateral attack. The court expressed the opinion that the bank in that case had de facto existence and seemed convinced that one selling land to it should not be permitted later to question the existence of the vendee in an attempt to recover the land. The court relied to some extent upon the doctrine of estoppel and reached the result that the capacity of the corporation to take title could not be questioned by the vendor.[13]

A creditor's bill was filed in Georgia Southern & Florida Railroad v. Trust Company,[14] in which the plaintiff asserted that bonds given by the railroad company to third persons who sought to have a foreclosure of the mortgage securing them were void because defendant construction company was the real owner of the road and because the statutory basis for its organization was unconstitutional. The court held that the bonds were valid. In the course of its opinion the court stated its belief that "an organization assuming to be a corporation de jure but for sufficient reasons not so in fact, may be a corporation de facto when it is of such a character that it could, under existing laws, have full and complete corporate being and powers."[15] There was in existence at the time of organization another statute under which this type of corporation could have been organized, and the court seemed disposed to allow the associates the benefit of that law "so far as to enable them to be regarded as a de facto corporation." But it is to be observed that in this case

[12] 79 U. S. (12 Wall.) 358, 20 L. Ed. 430 (1870).

[13] Cf. Siegel Land Corporation v. City of Highland Park, 235 Mich. 133, 209 N. W. 51 (1926). The corporation in this case was formed for the purpose of holding land for parks in trust for city use. Plaintiff was the owner of an apartment on the edge of a park. To have a fence removed, which the city had built, an injunction suit was brought against the city. The petition was denied, and the court held that plaintiff could not question the statute under which the city, through the park-holding corporation, held the land. In Schneider v. City of Grand Rapids, 211 Mich. 399, 179 N. W. 285 (1920), a taxpayer sought to prevent the conveyance, by a holding corporation similar to that in the Siegel case, of land to the city in which the taxpayer lived. The court held that he could not raise the question of the constitutionality of the statute under which the holding corporation was organized. The court said, 211 Mich. at 402, 179 N. W. at 286, "It will be time enough to determine the validity of this statute when a conflict arises between a municipality and an association organized under the act over the right to exercise control of streets or other public places, or the state by appropriate proceedings questions the right of the association to function."

[14] 94 Ga. 306, 21 S. E. 701, 47 Am. St. Rep. 153, 32 L. R. A. 208 (1894).

[15] 94 Ga. at 316, 21 S. E. at 705.

the court seemed to derive support for the de facto doctrine, as applied to this corporation, from a valid statute and not from the unconstitutional one under which the associates organized. That the case does not furnish authority for the proposition that an unconstitutional statute may be sufficient to sustain a de facto corporation appears from the following quotation:

Our decision is not based upon the idea that the organization of these railroad companies under unconstitutional charters would make them de facto corporations, but upon the idea that the purpose for which they were organized being lawful and proper, if they had obtained charters under the general law and organized under them, which they might have done, they would, in substance, have done what they actually did; that is, they would have observed about the same forms and requirements in the one case as in the other.[16]

That the court regarded the corporation as having de facto existence is clear, but it is not so clear that they would have so regarded it in the absence of a valid law under which the associates might have organized.[17]

Corporate existence is sometimes challenged by the plaintiff when he wishes to impose partnership liability upon the associates who organize a pretended corporation under an unconstitutional statute. This was attempted in Planters and Miners Bank v. Padgett.[18] The defendants claimed to be a corporation and had made some notes to the plaintiff. These had been signed by the president and treasurer, and the mortgage that had been given as security for the loan was also made out in the corporate name and signed by the corporate officers. The plaintiff brought suit against the corporation on the notes and obtained judgment against it, and on execution sale

[16] 94 Ga. at 319, 21 S. E. at 705. In Kehler & Brother v. The G. W. Jack Mfg. Co., 55 Ga. 639 (1876), creditors sought to have a receiver appointed because of the alleged insolvency of a corporation. The creditors claimed that corporate assets had been wrongfully transferred to a partnership of which one of the chief incorporators was a member. The corporation was attacked because it had been incorporated by proceedings before a court when they should have been under legislative control. The receiver was not appointed and a temporary injunction against the Jack Mfg. Co. was dissolved, insolvency not being shown. There is in the opinion no indication that the court gave serious consideration to the question of the effect of unconstitutional incorporation in this case.

[17] The question of the effect of an existing statute under which incorporation might have been had, but under which the corporators did not organize, upon the status of a corporation organized under an invalid law is not easy to answer. In addition to the cases involving this problem that have been mentioned in this chapter, see Jennings v. Dark, 175 Ind. 332, 92 N. E. 778 (1910), holding that the existence of such statute is sufficient to support de facto existence, and City and County of San Francisco v. Spring Valley Water Works, 48 Cal. 493 (1874). See also *infra*, note 51.

[18] 69 Ga. 159 (1882).

bought in the property. The plaintiff sued to hold defendant liable as a partner for the amount remaining due. The court felt bound by a previous decision to hold that the statute under which defendants had attempted to organize was unconstitutional. The Georgia court decided that the plaintiff could not question the existence of the corporation. The defendant could not be held liable as a partner. The dealings that had taken place between the parties showed that they had been on a corporate basis. The first suit, judgment, and conduct at the sale, with the details of the loan transaction mentioned above, were held to be sufficient to estop plaintiff from questioning the de facto existence of the organization. The court seemed to place some reliance upon the fact that the members of the corporation had never agreed to enter into a business enterprise involving partnership liability.[19] The court in the Padgett case was apparently willing to decide the case either on the ground of estoppel or on the basis of the de facto doctrine. The result was that partnership liability was not imposed upon the associates.

Partnership liability was also denied in the Minnesota case of Richards v. Minnesota Savings Bank.[20] In that case a corporation was authorized to change its name and place of business, following a long period of inactivity. The plaintiff sought to hold the associates liable as partners, on the ground that this statute was invalid and did not therefore revive the corporation. It was held that, even if the statute were considered unconstitutional, it nevertheless furnished "color of law" for changing the name and place of business of the company. In this case there had been dealings on a corporate basis, and the court emphasized the apparent absence of fraud in these dealings.

In the Michigan case of State v. How,[21] suit was brought on a bill issued by a bank, the associates being made defendants because of the invalidity of the statute under which the bank had been organized. The banking law of the state made the notes null and void, and a prohibition in the state constitution made it illegal to organize a banking institution under the circumstances present in this case. The decision was that the associates were not liable as partners. In the course of the opinion, however, the belief was expressed that had the factor of positive illegality been absent, the associates should have been held to partnership liability. The court

---

[19] For a detailed consideration of the arguments pro and con on this factor, see Dodd, Partnership Liability of Stockholders in Defective Corporations, 40 Harv. L. Rev. 521 (1927); Carpenter, Are the Members of a Defectively Organized Corporation Liable as Partners? 8 Minn. L. Rev. 409 (1924).
[20] 75 Minn. 196, 77 N. W. 822 (1899).
[21] 1 Mich. 512 (1846). Accord: Green v. Graves, 1 Doug. 351 (Mich. 1844).

adopted the void ab initio view of the effect of the statute and held that the defendants could not be charged as members of a banking corporation because no such corporation existed. Although the case was decided on the ground that the attempted formation of the corporation was illegal,[22] the court dwelt at length upon the general subject of partnership liability in the absence of the element of illegality, saying:

If the act in question had had for its object the incorporation of associations for manufacturing purposes, instead of banking, the only effect of the unconstitutionality of the law would have been to make them liable for the debts of the association as general partners, instead of corporators under the act.[23]

The peculiar facts of the case resulted in the denial of both corporate and partnership liability. This result seems somewhat odd, for it places the burden of determining illegality upon those who deal with the associates, and the associates are freed from liability only if the act they proceed under is positively illegal rather than merely unconstitutional.

In Eaton v. Walker[24] the Michigan court lived up to the prophecy of the dictum in the How case and held the incorporators liable as partners. The defendants argued that they were subject only to corporate liability, but the court stated that merely acting as a corporation did not make the associates such. The statute being invalid, there was no law, said the court, and there being no law authorizing the formation of the corporation, the de facto doctrine could not be applied. For the same reason also, the court refused to apply the doctrine of estoppel to the plaintiffs. Estoppel was to be restricted to those cases in which there was actually a corporation de facto. This would merely seem to say that if a de facto corporation is made out, the plaintiff will be estopped. Why resort to estoppel when by the application of the de facto doctrine the defendants are thereby saved from partnership liability? Does not the application of either doctrine bring the same result? The

[22] The Michigan cases are sometimes distinguished by this fact. There is in some of the cases a tendency to confuse illegality and unconstitutionality, as the latter is normally understood. 2 Morawetz, Private Corporations, sec. 759 (2d ed., 1886).

[23] 1 Mich. 512, 513 (1846).

[24] 76 Mich. 579, 43 N. W. 638 (1889). In Brown v. Killian, 11 Ind. 449 (1858), a bank had been organized in the absence of any statute authorizing incorporation. The holder of a note brought an action against the person who had formed the organization, but in view of the fact that such an organization was held to be "illegal," recovery was denied, although the court in its opinion intimates that the consideration could have been recovered. For an opinion that a corporation organized in the absence of statute should be treated as one organized under an unconstitutional statute, see 2 Morawetz, Private Corporations.

lower court found that there had been dealings between the parties on a corporate basis, but the upper court thought that some evidence on this point had been erroneously excluded, and the case was disposed of as though there had been no dealing on this basis, no new trial being ordered.

While McClinch v. Sturgis [25] may be distinguished from the foregoing cases on the ground that in it the existence of a foreign corporation was being questioned, the case is nevertheless indicative of the attitude that the Maine court might be expected to take if a domestic corporation were involved. In that case a suit was brought on a contract which the defendants claimed had been entered into with the corporation they had formed, and not with them as individuals. The court did not pass upon the constitutionality of the Rhode Island statute under which organization had been completed, but the fact that Rhode Island had thus far abstained from instituting quo warranto proceedings against the corporation was emphasized as being sufficient to warrant treating it as having de facto existence. It was said that "so long as the state raises no objection, it is immaterial to other parties whether it is a corporation de facto or de jure." [26]

In McCarthy v. Lavasche [27] an action of debt was brought by a depositor in a bank against the defendant, who was a member of the banking corporation. The allegation was that the bank was insolvent and that the defendant was by statute subject to double liability under a statutory provision. It was held that the defendant should be subjected to double liability even though the statute under which organization had been perfected was unconstitutional. This decision is quite understandable, but the reasoning whereby the court reached the result is somewhat puzzling. In the first part of its opinion the court seemed to rely on the doctrine of estoppel. It was pointed out that defendant knew when he became a member of the corporation that he was subject to double liability. The very fact that shareholders in the corporation were subject to this statutory liability doubtless contributed, thought the court, to the amount of business

[25] 72 Me. 288 (1881).

[26] 72 Me. at 295.

[27] 89 Ill. 270 (1878). Dows v. Naper, 91 Ill. 44 (1878) is sometimes cited as supporting the same conclusion as that of McCarthy v. Lavasche, *supra*. But, although the court referred to the latter case in its opinion, the Dows case is clearly distinguishable from it because, although the situation was such as to justify the court in using estoppel, there was in the case an existing corporation, and the only point touching constitutionality was the one with regard to an amendment of the corporate charter. The statute of amendment seems not to have been voted on by the people, as required by the constitution. Original incorporation was, however, completed under a valid act.

that came to the bank operated by the pretended corporation. People relied upon this additional liability in depositing money with the bank. The defendant and the other shareholders increased their profits thereby, and the defendant, by holding out to the public the protection of double liability, had been partially responsible for the loss incurred by plaintiff. So reasoned the court. Therefore defendant was estopped to set up the invalidity of the statute under which the bank had been organized. The court went so far as to say that regardless of the double liability provision in the statute the defendant would be held liable for the consequences of his "illegal and unauthorized" acts and would not be permitted to escape by showing that the statute in question was invalid. The court asked rather rhetorically whether people could go to the legislature and procure the passage of a law known to be unconstitutional, organize under it, obtain money in the course of the business established, and then later escape all liabilities that may have been incurred by showing that the statute was invalid. The obvious answer, and the one given with emphasis by the court, was in the negative. Therefore, the defendant was estopped by his conduct from assailing the existence of the corporation.

Had the opinion ended at this point there would have been nothing particularly extraordinary about the reasoning. But it proceeded to a consideration of the situation of the defendant from the standpoint of partnership law. The court opened this phase of the reasoning by adopting the view that if defendant here were a partner he would be subject to statutory liability. This was clearly an unnecessary assumption, because he was liable for the statutory amount whether he was a partner or not. But, having taken the stand it did, the task confronting the court was to determine whether defendant was a partner. After much laborious discussion the court finally concluded that the associates were partners and that the charter of the corporation constituted the articles of partnership. The defendants were liable — but liable for what amount? Up to the statutory amount. That the court finally intended to dispose of the case on the basis of partnership liability is evident from the following statement:

We are therefore of opinion that, independent of all constitutional questions, each shareholder became liable under the charter as articles of partnership, as it operated as an agreement by each subscriber to be liable to creditors to double the amount each subscribed.[28]

[28] 89 Ill. at 276. In Gardner v. Minneapolis & St. Louis Ry., 73 Minn. 517, 76 N. W. 282 (1898), an action was brought by a creditor to enforce double liability on defendant stockholder. The statute consolidating several corporations into one, of

But is this consistent with orthodox partnership liability? The statute stated that "each stockholder shall be liable to double the amount of stock held by or owned by him," and this clause was interpreted as imposing several liability. But is partnership liability several as to creditors not having notice? Or could it be contended that the depositor here had notice of the limited liability imposed by statute? To him this would doubtless come as a surprise, because he had likely viewed the statutory liability as an added safeguard rather than as a restriction. But whatever the theoretical difficulties may be in the way of harmonizing the various portions of the opinion, there can be no doubt that the result reached was the correct one. One might wish, however, that the court had not felt called upon to discuss at such length both bases for its decision. The case might have been disposed of on either basis, and to have used only one of them would have been less confusing. It is difficult to know whether to classify the case as one imposing partnership liability on members of a corporation organized under an unconstitutional statute or not.[29] Perhaps the safest course is to restrict its use as an authority to the estoppel portion of the opinion, because that is clearly stated and is a commonly used basis for decision in the types of cases dealt with in this study.[30]

Another case in which statutory liability was imposed on the shareholders arose in Alabama.[31] In that case also the defense was made that the statute under which organization took place was invalid. The estoppel basis of the court's decision is well brought out in the following quotation from the opinion:

Whatever merit there may be in this contention, a sufficient answer to it is found in the fact that the defendants, who seek to raise this objection, are estopped from setting up the illegality or irregularity of their corpo-

which defendant was a member, was assailed as unconstitutional. The court said, 73 Minn. at 527, "Since its formation, in 1881, it has acted openly in all respects as a corporation. It has borrowed money, giving security therefor upon the property of the new corporation to the amount of millions of dollars, which it has presumably used for its own benefit. It has operated its road, carrying freight and passengers, and receiving large sums of money therefor. It made construction, traffic, and trackage agreements and various leases, and in all of these matters it participated in the benefits derived therefrom. To all of these things the stockholders are presumed to have consented, and to have had knowledge of such transactions, and enjoyed the fruits of them." The Lavasche case was approved, and estoppel invoked to prevent a denial of corporate status. Double liability was imposed.

[29] The Lavasche case is not listed in the group of cases found in Dodd, Partnership Liability of Stockholders in Defective Corporations, 40 Harv. L. Rev. 562 (1927).

[30] Clark, Private Corporations, 113, 121 (3d ed., 1916), cites this case as an authority on the application of estoppel.

[31] McDonnell v. Alabama Gold Life Insurance Co., 85 Ala. 401, 5 So. 120 (1888).

rate organization. They are stockholders in the company, and have undertaken to organize and hold themselves out to the public as such, and as a lawful body corporate. They have obtained credit, and issued policies on the faith of this representation, whereby they have solemnly affirmed the validity of the law under which they organized, and consequently the legality of the organization. This was an admission of the constitutionality of the amendment now assailed as void; and this admission cannot now be retracted, to the prejudice of those who have accepted policies upon the faith of its affirmed validity. To repeat in brief: All stockholders situated as are the defendants in this case must be held to be estopped to deny the constitutionality of the law under which they organized, and for eighteen years uninterruptedly carried on their business as a de facto corporation.[32]

Had it not been for the last three words of the quotation no doubt could be entertained as to the basis of the court's decision. But to introduce the phrase "de facto" injects a confusing element. It is evident that the phrase is not here used in the restricted sense. The liability imposed was incidental to membership in the corporation and was not partnership liability.

The same difference of judicial opinion relative to partnership liability is evident in the group of cases just considered as is true of cases involving defectively organized corporations under a valid statute. Much difference of opinion exists as to the propriety of imposing such liability in the ordinary case of the so-called de facto corporation, although the weight of authority probably favors its imposition.[33]

The question naturally presents itself as to whether partnership liability should be imposed upon incorporators in the case of an unconstitutional statute, or whether they should be treated differently than in the case of a defectively organized corporation under a constitutional statute. It is difficult to give a conclusive answer to this question because so much depends upon the particular facts of the case. If the associates organize a corporation in good faith under the authority of a statute believed to be valid, one instinctively objects to holding them liable as partners. On the other hand, if the associates seem, as might be true in rare instances, to have organized under a particular statute because they thought that it was unconstitutional and because they believed that they would escape all liability by so doing, one feels that they should not be permitted to "get away with it." It is very difficult to tell in the particular case whether the motives of the associates were bona fide or not, but ordinarily little

[32] 85 Ala. at 410.
[33] Magruder, A Note on Partnership Liability of Stockholders, 40 Harv. L. Rev. 733 (1927). See also the articles cited in note 19.

question could be raised on this score, because in the average case the corporators themselves are doubtless the most surprised of all to learn that they have not formed a corporation. It is doubtful, however, whether partnership liability should be imposed or denied solely on the basis of a particular view that a court may take of the effect of an unconstitutional statute. Fairness between the parties, the social and economic consequences in the particular class of cases that may follow from the adoption of a particular rule in such cases, as well as the doctrinal side, should be given weight in deciding which of the two rules shall be followed in such a case, and in most instances these factors are given some weight.[34]

2. DISPUTES BETWEEN A CORPORATION AND ITS OFFICERS OR MEMBERS

The cases thus far considered have involved dealings between the corporation and a stranger. There are also some cases in which the contesting parties are the corporation and one of its officers or members. Take, for example, an action brought by the corporation against a shareholder to recover on subscription notes, on calls, or on assessments. Three Indiana cases are of interest in this connection. In the earliest of them[35] a corporation brought an action against a city upon a subscription that it had failed to pay. Answering the contention of counsel that the statute under which the railroad company had been organized was unconstitutional, the court said that the city was estopped "by the contract to deny the legal existence of the corporation." This was dictum. One year later a similar case came before the court and the following statement was made: "Hence, if an organization is completed where there is no law, or an unconstitutional law, authorizing an organization as a corporation, the doctrine of estoppel does not apply."[36] Concerning the plea of nul tiel corporation the court said that such a plea goes not to the power to organize but only to the existence of a de facto

[34] That the courts have not always given sufficient weight to economic considerations in these situations is the opinion expressed in 1 Thompson, Private Corporations, 304 (3d ed., 1927). It is there stated that the better theory is probably that an invalid statute is insufficient to support a de facto corporation. Following this statement the author says: "But practically, and more consistent with other views relating to the doctrine of corporations de facto, the advantage is with the courts taking the opposing view; and this is certainly more consistent with sound business principles. The rule that no corporation de facto can exist under an invalid law casts upon the incorporators the responsibility of deciding the constitutionality of an act, or, at the peril of individual liability and ultimate corporate ruin, of organizing a corporation under a statute that may be declared unconstitutional. The business interests of the country cry out against such jeopardy."

[35] Evansville, Indianapolis & Cleveland Straight Line R. R. v. City of Evansville, 15 Ind. 395, 416 (1860).

[36] Heaston v. Cincinnati & Fort Wayne Ry., 16 Ind. 275, 79 Am. Dec. 430 (1861).

corporation when a de jure one could have been organized. The position of the court seemed to be that there is no estoppel unless there is at the same time a de facto corporation.[37]

In the later case of Snyder v. Studebaker [38] the plaintiff conveyed land to a corporation on account of a stock subscription. The corporation subsequently conveyed it to the defendant, and the plaintiff then sought to regain the land because, as he alleged, at the time of the conveyance to the corporation it did not have legal existence and therefore the title to the land never passed out of the plaintiff. The plaintiff was held to be estopped from raising this question. Some nice distinctions were made by the court, and the opinion initiates the discussion of the problem by stating the general rule that if one contracts with a corporation he is estopped to deny its corporate existence. But, said the court, this applies only to estoppel on fact. "Hence, if there be no law which authorized the supposed corporation, or if the statute authorizing it be unconstitutional and void, the contract does not estop the party making it, to dispute the existence of the corporation." Does this then not cover the instant case? Apparently not, because the court proceeds with its explanation that if there is a law and the question is one of compliance with it, that is a question of fact and as to it plaintiff is estopped. In this case incorporation was permitted under special act until the new constitution went into effect. Whether organization occurred before the new constitution took effect was a question of fact. As to this question the plaintiff was held to have admitted by his contract that the corporation had been organized while the law permitted the associates to do so. The net result of the case is that plaintiff was not permitted to recover the land, and as to him the associates were accorded corporate standing. The Studebaker case expressly overruled the first of the Indiana cases referred to. The two cases are distinguishable as to facts and as to the party raising the question in each of them, but the court apparently thought the differences immaterial, and properly so. The situation presented in the Studebaker case was one calculated to persuade most courts to apply either estoppel or the de facto doctrine for the protection of the holder of the land.

A Michigan case holds that a shareholder may defend against an

[37] Estoppel was also the basis of the decision in East Pascagoula Hotel Co. v. West, 13 La. Ann. 545 (1858).

[38] 19 Ind. 462 (1862). This case was a little peculiar in that the act under which the organization was completed was a special one, enacted by the legislature at the time permissible under the then existing constitution, but which was at the time of acceptance and organization forbidden by a new constitution which had been adopted in the meantime.

action by a receiver to collect an assessment by showing that the statute under which organization took place was invalid.[39] A Pennsylvania case takes a contrary view, on the ground of estoppel.[40] Estoppel has also been utilized by courts to prevent defendant shareholders from assailing corporate existence in actions to recover calls.[41] In one of these cases the court said:

He is not dealing with it as a stranger, but as a member who has participated in its organization and claimed and exercised authority under and by virtue thereof. It will not do for him now to deny the rightful existence of this company as to himself and his own stock subscription, which he has affirmed as to all others.[42]

Corporate existence is sometimes assailed by defendants in actions by building and loan associations to enforce repayment of loans made by them to members. An early Michigan case held that a mortgage given by a member to the association should be surrendered and canceled upon repayment of the amount equitably due.[43] Some years later the same court held that the corporators must sue for an accounting in equity, but that they could not sue at law as a corporation.[44] Some emphasis was placed in the opinion upon the fact that building and loan associations were not forbidden by positive law, as had been true in some of the earlier Michigan cases.[45] The estop-

---

[39] Skinner v. Wilhelm, 63 Mich. 568, 30 N. W. 311 (1886). In Krutz v. Paola Town Co., 20 Kan. 399 (1878), same case on another point in 22 Kan. 725 (1879), the company sued a member to recover money alleged to be due it. Held, the corporation had no capacity to sue as a corporation, because the statute extending the period of corporate existence was invalid. No facts were present which called for the application of estoppel, thought the court.

[40] Freeland v. Pa. Central Ins. Co., 94 Pa. 504 (1880). In this case counsel sought to show that the assessments were ultra vires. To this contention the court answered, at 513, "But how is it made out? Simply by alleging that the legislature had not conferred the power by a constitutional enactment, in other words, repeating the objections to the validity of the act. A corporation contract is ultra vires when it is beyond the powers conferred. But here the power was conferred, whether rightfully or not, and the contract in question was within the very letter of the act. It cannot be said, therefore, that it was ultra vires within the proper meaning of that expression. If the act itself was invalid in attempting to confer the power, of course the power did not exist. But this defendant cannot be heard to make that objection, and hence the defense on this ground falls." See the reference to the Freeland case in Burkhard v. Pa. Water Co., 234 Pa. 41, 42 Atl. 1120 (1912), in the lower court opinion. In another case, involving somewhat different circumstances, the Pennsylvania court had this to say in answer to a contention that a corporation had been organized under a statute invalid because of title defects: "Their corporate existence must be attacked directly and not collaterally in a proceeding for a different purpose." Commonwealth v. County of Philadelphia, 193 Pa. 236, 44 Atl. 336 (1899).

[41] St. Louis Colonization Assn. v. Hennessy, 11 Mo. App. 555 (1882); Weinman v. Wilkinsburg & L. P. Ry., 118 Pa. 192, 12 Atl. 288 (1888).

[42] Weinman v. Wilkinsburg & L. R. Ry., *supra*, note 41, at 203.

[43] Mok v. Detroit Building and Savings Assn. No. 4, 30 Mich. 511 (1875).

[44] Burton v. Schildbach, 45 Mich. 504, 8 N. W. 497 (1881).

[45] See cases in notes 3 and 21.

pel in this case seemed not to be one operating to deny attack upon corporate existence but rather one arising from recognition of the receiver by payments to him prior to the action, based in part on the receipt of money by the defendant from which he had benefited. The court felt that defendant should be compelled to repay the loan, but it seems not to have decided the case on the de facto or estoppel basis, in the sense in which these have been applied in the other cases considered in this study.

However, both the de facto doctrine and estoppel were made use of by the South Dakota court to enable the plaintiff building association to foreclose a mortgage which was given to it by one of its members.[46]

Sometimes the shareholder as plaintiff, rather than as defendant, seeks to assail the existence of the corporation. An illustration is furnished by the case of Huber v. Martin.[47] In that case a reorganized corporation had taken over some of the property belonging to a corporation of which plaintiff claimed to be a shareholder. He brought suit to have the property transferred back to the original corporation. The statute authorizing the reorganization was held unconstitutional, and the court declared that it was "not sufficient to support even a de facto corporation." The court held that the assets of the old corporation could be recovered from the pretended new one. That the whole scheme in the Martin case looked as though a small group was to benefit from the reorganization at the expense of the other shareholders was doubtless an important factor influencing the court to disregard the alleged existence of the new corporation. By filing a counterclaim against a corporation a defendant shareholder has been estopped to deny the existence of the

[46] Building and Loan Assn. of Dakota v. Chamberlain, 4 S. D. 271, 56 N. W. 897 (1893). In McLaughlin v. Citizens Building, Loan and Savings Assn., 62 Ind. 264 (1878), there is a dictum that estoppel would be applied in a case where a member of such an association attempted to defend against an action to enforce repayment of a loan. In Building & Loan Assn. of Dakota v. Chamberlain, *supra,* the court said at 283: "Any other doctrine would be contrary to the plainest principles of reason and good faith, and involves a mockery of justice. Parties must take the consequences of the position they assume. They are estopped to deny the reality of the state of things which they have helped to make appear to exist, and upon which others have relied." Another dictum on the de facto doctrine, as applied to this type of case, is to be found in Winget v. Quincy Bldg. & Homestead Assn., 128 Ill. 67, 84, 21 N. E. 12, 16 (1889): "A party who has contracted with a corporation de facto as such, cannot be permitted, after having received the benefits of his contract, to allege any defect in the organization of such corporation, as affecting its capacity to enforce such contract, but all such objections, if valid, are available only on behalf of the sovereign power of the state. . . . And this rule applies even where the corporation is organized under a law alleged to be unconstitutional."

[47] 127 Wis. 412, 105 N. W. 1031 (1906).

corporation. As to the defendant the corporation was held to have de facto existence.[48]

B. Cases in Which There Have Been No Dealings on a Corporate Basis

The cases to be considered in this section comprise a number of divergent situations; they have little in common except that all of them involve the question of the status of a private corporation alleged to have been formed under an invalid statute.

The question of corporate existence is occasionally raised by a corporation attempting to exercise the power of eminent domain. In Pennsylvania the Superior Court[49] has held that an injunction would not be granted against a corporation about to condemn land of the petitioner, who asserted the invalidity of the statutory basis for one of the corporations in a merger. The court took the position that only the state may assail the existence of the corporation. That defendant in this case was already on the land and had made some improvements may have been sufficient to differentiate this case from Etowah Light and Power Company v. Yancey.[50] There a demurrer to a petition in condemnation proceedings was sustained because the statute authorizing the incorporation of the petitioner was invalid. The New Jersey court has taken a similar view, for the reason, it is said, that the question of unconstitutionality is one of law and not one of inference or fact.[51] In the New Jersey case the attempted condemnation was characterized as "mere usurpation" because of the invalidity of the statute authorizing organization. Although there is a conflict between these cases, the two latter decisions perhaps indicate the attitude that many courts are likely to take in condemnation proceedings. Had the court been disposed to do so in the Etowah case, it could easily have applied the de facto doctrine, because there existed at the time of organization another valid statute under which the organization might have been formed.[52] That the corporations involved in these cases were public service companies does not seem to have been given any explicit consideration. The tendency seems to be to view quite strictly the exercise of the power of eminent domain by private corporations. Its exercise is regarded as an imposition upon the individual and is

[48] Black River Improvement Co. v. Holway, 85 Wis. 344, 55 N. W. 418 (1893).
[49] Yeingst v. Philadelphia, Harrisburg & Pittsburgh R. R. Co., 40 Pa. Super. Ct. 106 (1909).
[50] 197 Fed. 845 (C. C. Tenn. 1911).
[51] Sisters of Charity of St. Elizabeth v. Morris R. R., 84 N. J. L. 310, 86 Atl. 954 (1913).
[52] *Supra*, note 17.

tolerated only because of necessity, and if others than the government are to exercise this power they must be above reproach so far as the legality of their organization is concerned. This factor may be sufficient in the minds of many judges to offset any general feeling they may have that bona fide organization under a statute should be given de facto effect even though the statute should subsequently be declared invalid. On the other hand, there is of course the inconvenience that may result from a refusal to apply the de facto doctrine in such cases. There is also the question whether any different rule should be followed in condemnation proceedings in the case of a defectively organized corporation than in the case of a corporation organized in compliance with all of the requisites of an invalid statute.[53]

Somewhat similar to the situation in the eminent domain cases is that which exists when a private landowner asks for an injunction to prevent a corporation from laying tracks in a street on which the plaintiff owns lots, or in which he may own the fee, subject to a servitude. For an example of the attitude likely to be met with in this type of case mention may be made of the Maine case in which the court held plaintiff estopped to deny the status of the defendant because he had asked for an injunction against the corporation.[54] The court expressed the view that it ill befitted the plaintiff to assail the status of the very legal person against whom he was seeking relief. The de facto doctrine was also mentioned by the court as a possible basis for the decision, and the judges did not seem to feel disposed to give serious consideration to the contention of the plaintiff that his property was being taken from him without compensation. The Georgia court has taken the same attitude in a dictum and has expressed the opinion that estoppel may be used in such a case even though the facts were not such as to warrant the application of the de facto doctrine.[55]

Another situation in which corporate status has been questioned is one in which there comes before a court for construction a will containing bequests to corporations to be formed in the future or already in existence. Thus, by the terms of a will made in New York, property was given to a corporation to be formed in Ohio. The Ohio corporation was organized, and then its existence was attacked in proceedings by an executor to procure a construction of the will. The New York court was asked to hold that the statute in

[53] There is a division of authority as to the rule to be applied in cases of corporations defectively organized under valid acts, in eminent domain cases. 2 Lewis, Eminent Domain, sec. 592 (3d ed., 1909).
[54] Taylor v. Portsmouth, etc., Street Ry., 91 Me. 193, 39 Atl. 560 (1898).
[55] Brown v. Atlanta R. & Power Co., 113 Ga. 462, 39 S. E. 71 (1901).

question was contrary to the constitution of Ohio, and that therefore it could not take under the will. The court refused to take this view of the case; it held that inasmuch as the state of Ohio had not questioned the corporate status of the beneficiary by quo warranto proceedings, it looked as though the state recognized it as having de facto existence.[56] The corporation was permitted to take under the will. The de facto doctrine was also applied in a Missouri case[57] presenting a similar question, and the court said, in the course of its opinion, that

its existence cannot be questioned in a collateral proceeding if it appear to be acting under color of law, and recognized by the state as such. The question of its being must be raised by the state itself, on a quo warranto or other direct proceeding; and this, although the act incorporating it, or authorizing its incorporation, is violative of the constitution of the state.[58]

In such a case the desire to carry out the intention of the testator as manifested in the will must be balanced against the policy involved in discouraging people from forming corporations under unconstitutional statutes. There is, however, something to be said for public policy favoring the protection of persons who have bona fide relied upon legislative action.

The general problem of the effect of an unconstitutional statute on civil and criminal proceedings instituted in reliance thereon will not be dealt with in this study, but mention should be made of the case of De Bow v. People.[59] There a person was charged with forging bank notes and defrauding a bank. The defense was that the statute under which the bank had been organized was unconstitutional, and the court sustained this contention, saying that "it is utterly void, and the banking companies which have been organized under it have no legal existence." There being no statute under which the bank could be organized, the indictment charging that a *bank* had been defrauded was defective. People may have thought that there had been in existence a banking corporation with which they had done business, but as applied in a criminal case this was all a mistake. There was no bank, and therefore it could not very well have been defrauded. So the scoundrel went his way. The court in its opinion bewailed the fact that business in the state should thus be made to suffer, but it asserted that the statute was clearly uncon-

[56] St. John v. Andrews Institute for Girls, 117 App. Div. 698, 102 N. Y. S. 808 (1907).
[57] Catholic Church v. Tobbein, 82 Mo. 418 (1884).
[58] 82 Mo. at 424.
[59] 1 Denio 9 (N. Y. 1845).

stitutional and that their course in the situation was marked out for them as one of duty and could not be avoided. No attention was paid by the court, in the opinion at least, to the social consequences that might ensue from letting a man go unpunished who had committed an offense that was punishable by statute and certainly of an anti-social character. Criminal cases would appear to present a situation wherein the court might well hold that the doctrine of a de facto corporation would be applicable.[60] The South Dakota court has applied that doctrine to a case in which a cashier of a bank that had been organized in the absence of any statutory authority was indicted for accepting deposits when he knew the bank to be insolvent.[61] Surely if the de facto doctrine could be applied to a corporation that had been formed in the absence of any legal authority in a criminal case it should have been possible, even under the strict void ab initio view of unconstitutionality, to have applied it in the De Bow case.

If the use of this doctrine is ever justifiable, it certainly would be in such cases as these. A person accused of crime should be tried on the basis of the act committed and the surrounding circumstances, and not on the basis of the legal existence of the corporation to which the indictment charged that injury had been done. The depositors in the New York case probably had little consolation in the realization that it was not the bank that had been defrauded. The South Dakota case doubtless goes the limit in applying the de facto doctrine, but it is submitted that it goes no further than is desirable in this class of cases.

Doboy & Union Telegraph Co. v. De Magathias [62] was a tort case in which an action was brought against the defendant for cutting a cable belonging to the plaintiff. The ship of the plaintiff had been anchored in such a position that when the anchor was raised it caught the cable, and to disentangle it the cable was cut. The defense was that the corporation had been organized by a court when under the constitution of the state this type of corporation was to be incorporated by legislative act alone. The court decided that the incorporation proceedings under the control of a court were unconstitutional, and that hence plaintiff was not a corporation. It followed that the state of Georgia had not authorized it to lay the cable that had been cut. There being no corporation, there was, said the court, no plaintiff, because "plaintiff corporation disappears from the rec-

[60] The tendency seems, however, to be the exact contrary in the criminal law generally, when unconstitutionality is involved.
[61] State v. Stevens, 16 S. D. 309, 92 N. W. 420 (1902).
[62] 25 Fed. 697 (C. C. Ga. 1885).

ord and 'leaves not a wrack behind.' " There being no plaintiff and nobody to take advantage of the cause of action, it followed quite logically that the case should be dismissed, and the court promptly did so. That the Doboy case carries the doctrine of void ab initio to the uttermost lengths seems clear. The defendant had cut the cable. An injury had been committed for which redress could in the ordinary case properly have been obtained. The result of the case seems highly objectionable.

An interesting and somewhat curious case is Chenango Bridge Company v. Paige.[63] Plaintiff in that case had obtained an exclusive franchise to build a bridge across a river at a certain designated place; no other bridge was to be allowed within a specified distance up and down the river. Later the legislature gave permission to a corporation to build a bridge within the prescribed area. Defendant's testator had been the moving figure in organizing the venture that resulted in the second bridge. A flood carried away this second bridge and hurled it into the plaintiff's bridge, causing considerable damage thereto. The plaintiff, owner of the first bridge, brought suit against the defendant in his representative capacity to recover (1) for the damage done by the flood and (2) for tolls collected prior to the flood. The court held that there could be no recovery on the first ground, whether the bridge had been built and owned by a corporation or defendant's testator. Recovery was allowed, however, on the second ground.

The statute authorizing the incorporation of the company promoted by defendant's testator seems to have been invalid, and for that reason individual liability was imposed for the invasion of the exclusive right of the defendant to take tolls within the area designated by the act granting him his privilege. The court was apparently at a loss as to what effect the invalidity of the statute should have in this case, but it finally decided that whether defendant's testator "be considered to have acted for himself as a stockholder, or as an agent of the stockholders of the corporation, the statute furnished him no protection." The decision held defendant's testator to individual rather than to corporate liability. The court intimated in one portion of the opinion that as against others than this plaintiff the organization would be treated as a corporation. Thus, in speaking of the effect of the unconstitutional statute it was said that "that act unquestionably made it a corporation, and it had all the rights and powers conferred upon it by the act against the whole world except the plaintiff." The exact meaning of this statement is a little difficult to determine, because it departs from the usual rule as stated

[63] 83 N. Y. 178, 38 Am. Rep. 407 (1880).

in so many cases, that the corporation is valid against the whole world except the state. Just what there was about plaintiff's position that warranted special consideration in this case is not clear, unless the case be taken as authority for holding that the corporation will be considered as nonexistent for wrongs of this kind committed by its members.

These two cases seem to indicate that the courts will not hesitate to hold that corporate privileges and immunities will not be accorded individuals who organize under an invalid statute, whether the corporation is suing for a tort committed against it or whether the individuals are made parties defendant for a wrong committed by the group against a stranger. Viewed from the standpoint of doctrine as to the effect of an unconstitutional statute, this is consistent. Viewed from the standpoint of the individual associates, it means that they may not have the privileges of suing in the corporate name, but they may be held individually liable if the organized group commits a wrong. The justice of this seems a little obscure.

No case has been found squarely in point on the doctrine of de facto officers as applied to private corporations. An Indiana case contains a dictum justifying the belief that some courts would apply the doctrine to officers of private as well as of municipal corporations,[64] although the questions of public policy involved in these two situations are not identical.[65]

II. CONCLUSIONS

It is clear then that there is some confusion in the cases dealing with the status of a private corporation organized under an unconstitutional statute. Not only are the courts sometimes divided as to the results that should be reached on a given state of facts, but even when they are agreed as to the proper result, different doctrinal bases are made use of to justify or explain it. Some of the expressions and doctrines commonly encountered in judicial opinions on the subject in hand should perhaps be considered at this point.

One of the commonest of the phrases used in the opinions referred to is that of "de facto corporation." What is meant by that phrase?

[64] Bradford v. Frankfort, St. Louis & Toledo R. R., 142 Ind. 383, 40 N. E. 741 (1895). The court said, at 392, "If, conceding for the purposes of the inquiry, the act . . . was unconstitutional, and there existed no power to reduce the number of directors from thirteen to five, we must at least assert that there was colorable authority for the proceeding, and that, until the law should be declared unconstitutional, the acts of those chosen under such colorable authority for the proceeding would be the acts of de facto officers." See State ex rel. Dulin v. Lehre, 7 Rich. 234, 324 (S. C. 1854).

[65] On the status of officers chosen to fill an office created by an unconstitutional statute, see Chapter 4.

Is a de facto corporation a corporation or is it something else?[66] This question leads in the final analysis to a consideration of the nature of a corporation "de jure," so-called. What is meant by the phrase "a corporation"? Some insist that a corporation is a legal person, or at least a legal entity, apart from the natural persons who compose it. They regard it as the eleventh person, composed of the ten natural persons who form the "it," the corporation, but distinct from the ten. To say that the conception is an impossible one is to be very bold, for many persons have for a long time entertained it. Others, on the contrary, view a corporation as a group of persons considered for certain purposes as though they were one. There are other theories also, but these two views probably have the greater number of adherents in this country. Upon one thing both sides are agreed. That is that rules of law, usually stated in statutes, create or recognize the legal relations or incidents that we think of in connection with any concept of a corporation. The legal person exists by virtue of a legal rule, or, in other words, the group is treated as one because of a rule of law to that effect. This idea is often expressed by the statement that a corporation is "a creature of the law."

When such a legal creature has been created in substantial accordance with the legal requirements of statute and constitution, we refer to it as a "corporation de jure" if we follow the accepted paths of legal thought.[67] But how does a corporation de facto differ from this? Is it also a legal creature? [68] There seems to be no agreement among courts and text-writers as to the exact content of the concept "de facto corporation." Some writers attempt to clarify their exposition by stating that a de facto corporation is the same as one de jure except that its existence is subject to attack by the state because of

[66] 1 Thompson, Private Corporations, 296 (3d ed., 1927), says of a de facto corporation that "It has an actual substantial legal existence." And again, "It is essentially a body entirely separate from the individuals who compose it; it is a legal entity. . . ." In 1 Fletcher, Cyclopedia of Corporations, sec. 273 (1917), it is said that "such corporations have a substantial legal existence." Clark, Private Corporations, 97 (3d ed., 1916), "means a body which actually exists, for all practical purposes." On the other hand, Professor Magruder, in the article cited *supra*, note 33, refers to a de facto corporation as a "matter of technique," while Professor Dodd in note 77 of the article cited *supra*, note 19, says that the doctrine of de facto corporations is based on policy, and not on logic. Ballantine, Private Corporations, 74 (1927), says that the basis for denying collateral attack "is to be found in public policy and convenience in the security of business transactions and in elimination of quibbles over technicalities which are of no concern to those dealing with the corporation."

[67] For a discussion of theories as to the nature of a corporation see: Hohfeld, Nature of Stockholders' Individual Liability for Corporation Debts, 9 Col. L. Rev. 285 (1909); Canfield, The Scope and Limits of the Corporate Entity Theory, 17 Col. L. Rev. 128 (1917); Machen, Corporate Personality, 24 Harv. L. Rev. 253, 347 (1910); Laski, The Personality of Associations, 29 Harv. L. Rev. 404 (1915); Smith, Legal Personality, 37 Yale L. J. 283 (1928).

[68] See quotations, *supra*, note 66.

some default or defect in the process of organization. As to all others than the state, however, the explanation runs, a de facto corporation is just the same as one de jure. All of which is known by anybody familiar with the cases to be only partially true. If it be conceded for the sake of argument that a corporation de facto is a legal person, or entity, or a group of legal incidents, the question may still be asked, Is it created by statute or by judges? Corporations are customarily thought of as creations of statutes. Common law judges disclaimed any technique for creating corporations. But is this an exception? If judges do create corporations de facto, upon what theory is it that they do so, and for what reasons? Is it upon the theory of estoppel?

This leads us to a consideration of another doctrine often utilized in corporation cases. Most courts and writers have taken the view that corporations de facto are not dependent upon principles of estoppel.[69] At this point it should be noted that when courts speak of estoppel in this connection they use that word in a different sense than is ordinarily associated with its use. Perhaps some will be aided by the distinction between estoppel by representation and estoppel by conduct, and the explanation that the latter is the sense in which the term is used in this group of cases. But to return to the relation between the de facto doctrine and that of estoppel, as the two are utilized in settling the problem of corporate status, is there any need for resorting to the doctrine of estoppel if the de facto doctrine is applied? If one says that there is a corporation de facto in a given case, does that not mean that the associates are to be treated as though they were a corporation, whether they are or not? Are not corporate incidents automatically applied by such a decision? What then can it add to say that a person is estopped to deny the existence of the corporation? It is submitted that to say that a corporation exists de facto is to say that collateral attack is denied. Likewise, if the doctrine of estoppel is applied, it is needless to resort to the de facto doctrine. The application of either means that the case is to be disposed of in accordance with the rules governing corporate transactions.

[69] 1 Fletcher, Cyclopedia of Corporations, 547 (1917), ". . . the rules in relation to them (that is, de facto corporations) do not depend upon the ground of equitable estoppel, but may be applicable though the elements of an estoppel are not shown." Clark, Private Corporations, 109 (3d ed., 1916), "No elements of estoppel are necessary to prevent a private individual from objecting to the existence of a corporation de facto; and, as we shall see, a man may in some jurisdictions, on equitable grounds, be estopped to question the corporate character of an association that is not even a corporation de facto." Ballantine, Private Corporations, 91, note 61 (1927), "Corporations by estoppel are not based upon the same principle as corporations de facto. Estoppel may prevail when there is no color of incorporation, or where the law under which the corporation claims to exist is unconstitutional."

Some writers maintain that there cannot be a corporation by estoppel.[70] What happens when a party is denied collateral attack on the status of an alleged corporation because of the application of estoppel? Suppose that we agree that a corporation in the sense of a legal entity is not created by a court when it applies the doctrine of estoppel to deny collateral attack. Is not the case nevertheless disposed of in accordance with rules designed for corporate bodies? Is partnership liability, for example, imposed in either case? The answer would seem to be in the negative. The result is the same in either case. If it were not for the fact that writers and judges arbitrarily limit their definition and treatment of de facto corporations, it would be very difficult indeed to distinguish between the results of estoppel and those of the de facto doctrine in these cases. The only difference between the two doctrines seems to be that one is broader than the other, although a few courts tend to restrict the use of estoppel to cases in which the elements of a so-called de facto corporation are also made out. In these latter cases there is, as has been indicated, no need to invoke estoppel.[71]

Let us next consider the point of contact between these doctrines and those dealing with the effect of an invalid statute. Suppose that a corporation is organized bona fide under a statute not yet declared unconstitutional. Subsequently the statute is declared invalid. Much will now depend upon which of the two views of the effect of an unconstitutional statute the judge chooses as a premise. Let us suppose that he chooses the strict void ab initio view. From this premise he will reason that a corporation organized under this statute cannot have de facto existence. The conclusion will then be that individual liability should be imposed upon the associates. Under the strict void ab initio view the individuals cannot be saved from liability by the application of the doctrine of estoppel because the case is to be disposed of as though the parties had acted without reference to any purported statute. The charter is considered as articles of partnership, and throughout the entire process of reasoning the statute as a factor in the case, either as a source of legal relations or as a fact

---

[70] Many writers seem to be willing to hold that a de facto corporation has legal existence, but hesitate to hold that a corporation can have legal existence by virtue of the application of estoppel. Thus, for example, Clark, Private Corporations, 122 (3d ed., 1916), says that the doctrine of estoppel is unnecessary if limited to de facto corporations, but on p. 122 the same author says that "It is of course very largely a matter of public policy whether courts shall raise an estoppel when not even the elements of the de facto incorporation are present, and naturally the courts differ." This would indicate that this writer would distinguish de facto corporations in that they had legal existence as a corporation, independent of public policy. This is only typical of the vague distinctions suggested in discussions of de facto and estoppel doctrines.

[71] Supra, note 70.

upon which to predicate legal consequences, is ignored. Even the existence of another valid statute under which incorporation might have been had will not avail to save the corporation.[72] This is the result that is reached by the strict application of the void ab initio theory.

On the other hand, if the judge adopts the view that the statute should not be entirely ignored, a different result may be reached. Assuming that the existence of a law is necessary as one of the requisites for a de facto corporation, let us see what happens when we proceed to settle a case on the theory that the statute is to be given some effect in disposing of the case. There will then be a basis on which to predicate a de facto organization, because the writing on the statute book is not to be ignored. The de facto doctrine can then be applied in the case, because even the requirements of a law under which incorporation could be had is substantially, though not literally, fulfilled. The invalid law is given sufficient effect to support the application of the de facto doctrine. A court in this frame of mind will often be quite ready to invoke the aid of some other valid statute to support its position that there is good ground for treating the associates as a corporation, in view of the fact that such a statute expresses a policy favorable to the existence of the particular type of corporation involved. It is sometimes very difficult to know whether a court regards an invalid statute as sufficient to support the application of the de facto doctrine or whether the main reliance is placed upon the existence of another valid statute under which the organization might have been incorporated. There can be no doubt, however, that many of the courts utilize the existence of such a valid statute to sustain a result already decided upon. Courts adopting the void ab initio view, on the contrary, will not be influenced by the existence of another valid statute and will usually explain that the corporation must stand or fall on the statute in reliance on which incorporation was attempted.

But even if the court thinks that the de facto doctrine cannot be applied because the statute is not a law, it may treat the statute as one of the facts in the situation and apply the doctrine of estoppel, and thereby attain the same result as would be attained by using the de facto doctrine. If benefits are received, for example, the court will say that the existence of the statute, at least in the sense of some writing on the statute books, will not be disregarded, because it was,

[72] Tooke, De Facto Municipal Corporations under Unconstitutional Statutes, 37 Yale L. J. 935 (1928), has taken the doctrine applied by some courts in private corporation cases, to the effect that the existence of a valid law under which incorporation would have been possible is sufficient to prevent collateral attack, as a basis on which to explain the municipal corporation cases. See Chapter 3.

after all, one of the factors in the situation from which benefit was derived.[73] Under the void ab initio view only one result is possible, whereas under the other a different result may be attained, and it may be reached by the application of two separate doctrines, which, taken together, cover a great variety of situations.

It may then be of considerable importance for the judge to choose the premise that will enable him to reach the most desirable result in a given situation. For once the premise is chosen, the whole train of consequences is to a large extent determined. And, as has been seen in some of the cases discussed above, some courts march the full length of the logical course thus mapped out, bewailing the consequences of their decision. But that other courts, and doubtless the majority of modern courts, have been influenced in their selection of premises by the results they wished to attain in particular types of cases can admit of no doubt. This has probably been the very reason why other views than that of void ab initio have been adopted as starting points. The correct view of these doctrines, as well as those of de facto and estoppel, would seem to be that they are tools whereby the judicial surgeon may correct a maladjustment. If they are useful in that work their use is justifiable. Whether they be logical when judged by the propositions included with them may be of interest but not of much importance so far as the administration of the law is concerned. Whether or not, for example, a corporation is created by use of the doctrines of estoppel and de facto is a question of relatively little significance except for purposes of correcting and testing the validity of the components of these assumed starting points, concepts. Perhaps they are not concepts but merely words of description. What is important is that in certain types of cases associates who organize under an invalid law are treated as individuals; in other types of cases they are treated as one.

Equally important is it that courts do not agree as to the results that should be reached in a given class of cases. The examination of doctrine and theoretical explanation in this connection can serve only to indicate in what particulars courts seem to have been properly or improperly (using these words without any moral signification) influenced by them. It is quite clear that in some instances courts have attempted to decide cases in this field of the law by rules of logic, assuming as a premise one of the views with respect to the effect to be given to an unconstitutional statute. It is also clear that

---

[73] Ballantine, *supra,* note 66, says at 74 that the weight of authority sustains prevention of collateral attack when estoppel can be applied, even though the statute of organization is unconstitutional.

the number of courts that have been misled in this manner is relatively small, and many of the cases illustrating this tendency are from the past century.

Can any generalization be made on the basis of the cases herein considered? It is clear, of course, that in the first place there is some confusion in the cases and that the courts are divided over the question whether there can be a de facto corporation under an unconstitutional statute. The weight of authority seems to favor the view that there can be such a corporation in cases involving dealings between the corporation and strangers on a corporate basis. The authority is more evenly divided in the cases between the corporation and its own officers or shareholders. But if to the de facto cases are added those based on estoppel, a slight margin probably remains in favor of preventing collateral attack even there. More uncertainty is encountered in the cases in which there have been no corporate dealings between the parties; and in the eminent domain cases, as well as in those involving crimes and torts, the courts seem to be less strict in denying collateral attack, and the de facto doctrine is not often applied. Otherwise, as in the cases involving wills and injunctions, the trend seems to be in favor of applying the de facto doctrine. This doctrine is applied in cases where foreign corporations are assailed because of organization contrary to the fundamental law of the state of incorporation. If the case can be aided by the existence of a valid statute under which organization might have been completed, but under which no attempt to organize was actually made, some courts are willing to utilize the existence of such statute to support the application of the de facto doctrine, although others refuse to apply the doctrine even when such other statute exists. If one should make a count of heads covering all the situations considered in this study, it would be found that the cases in which either the de facto doctrine or estoppel, or both, are used to prevent attack on corporate status outnumber those in which the application of either

[74] 14 C. J. 216. "The great weight of authority supports the doctrine that there cannot be even a de facto corporation unless there is a valid law under which the corporation such as the one in question might exist de jure, and therefore that a corporation cannot exist even de facto under a *clearly* unconstitutional statute . . ." The addition of the italicized word (italicized by the present writer) adds nothing, because no case has been found involving private corporations wherein the court has attempted to make use of the doctrine sometimes applied in the officer cases, namely, that of clear and cloudy unconstitutionality. 1 Thompson, *supra,* note 66, says at 304 that the cases are about evenly divided. That the better view is that no de facto corporation can exist under an unconstitutional statute is the opinion of the authors of 1 Clark and Marshall, Private Corporations, 246 (1901), and 1 Fletcher, *supra,* note 66, at 564. In note 77 of Professor Dodd's article, *supra,* note 19, the following statement is made: "The de facto rule, in the form in which it is stated by some courts, may be too narrow to do justice. The rule is based on policy, and not on

or both of those doctrines is denied.[74] The general tendency seems to be to sustain the corporation in order that the case may be disposed of in accordance with rules applicable to such bodies, particularly where to do so protects rights acquired and asserted honestly and in good faith.

logic, and the theory of some courts that it cannot be applied to corporations organized under unconstitutional statutes seems to the writer unduly technical. Nevertheless, it is submitted that the courts have been guided by a sound instinct in declining to extend the de facto doctrine to all cases of invalid corporations."

Chapter III

THE STATUS OF A MUNICIPAL CORPORATION ORGANIZED UNDER AN UNCONSTITUTIONAL STATUTE *

A municipal corporation has governmental as well as proprietary functions to perform. It differs from a private corporation in that its primary functions are governmental.[1] Municipal corporations are usually spoken of as legal persons, or entities, in the same sense as private corporations are, but in studying them it must always be borne in mind that the main purpose for which most of them are created is to perform certain governmental functions.

The problem to be considered in this chapter is the status of a municipal corporation, that term being used in a generic sense, which has been organized in accordance with, or by virtue of, an unconstitutional statute. The question of municipal status may arise under various circumstances. It may be raised (1) in a case involving attack by some official representative of the state; (2) in a dispute between two municipal corporations; (3) in a contest between two persons claiming a municipal office; (4) in a dispute between a private individual and a municipality; and (5) in a dispute between two or more private individuals, the municipality not being a party. After the cases in each of these groups have been examined some indication of their general tendency will be attempted.

I. ATTACK ON CORPORATE STATUS BY AN OFFICIAL REPRESENTATIVE OF THE STATE

The legislature in each of the forty-eight states has, subject to certain state constitutional restrictions, the power to create, or to provide for the creation of, such governmental subdivisions within the state as it thinks desirable. Legal theory has it that such governmental units as exist within the state derive their powers and functions from the state government. The privilege of becoming a gov-

---

* This chapter appeared in somewhat briefer form in 27 Mich. L. Rev. 523 (1929).

[1] For definitions and discussion of the nature of a municipal corporation, see 1 Dillon, Municipal Corporations, sec. 31 (5th ed., 1911); 1 McQuillin, Municipal Corporations, sec. 122 (2d ed., 1928).

ernmental corporation is, therefore, one that the state may grant or withhold, just as it may in the case of the private corporation.

The state has a real interest in maintaining a general superintendence over municipal corporations because of the important governmental functions performed by them. If, then, such a corporation were to be formed without the authority or consent of the state, one would expect that the state could institute proceedings to oust the corporation from the exercise of its assumed powers. Suppose, however, that the corporation has been formed in accordance with a statute enacted by the legislature. The statute is not challenged for several years. The city goes along as a functioning unit for a long time, and nobody suspects that the statute has any constitutional defect. Then the attorney-general of the state institutes quo warranto proceedings to test the validity of the organization of the municipality. Can he, in such a proceeding, question the constitutionality of the statute under the alleged authority of which the city was organized?[2]

The rule is, subject to one qualification to be mentioned later, that the attorney-general may, when acting in behalf of the state, assail the constitutionality of the statutory basis of a municipal corporation in quo warranto proceedings against the city itself as a corporate entity or against the officers of the municipality in their representative capacity. If the court finds that the statute is unconstitutional, the judgment will be for the ouster of the particular officers or of the charter of the city.

Thus in a California case[3] an action in the nature of quo warranto was brought by the attorney-general against a city for usurping the franchise of a corporation. The statute under which organization was had was declared unconstitutional and judgment was given in favor of the state. A similar result is obtained when the action is against one or more of the municipal officers in their official capacity.[4] In these cases, the statute under which the city was organized having been declared unconstitutional, the city is held to have no corporate existence. As a result of this holding no office of the corporation exists either, so the officer is ousted for attempting to

---

[2] For a discussion of this problem as it relates to the law of private corporations see Chapter 2.

[3] People v. Town of Nevada, 6 Cal. 43 (1856).

[4] State ex rel. Attorney General v. Mayor etc. of Somers Point, 52 N. J. L. 32, 18 Atl. 694 (1898); People v. Maynard, 15 Mich. 463 (1867); Shumway v. Bennett, 29 Mich. 451 (1874); Territory of Washington v. Stewart, 1 Wash. 98, 23 Pac. 405 (1890); State of Washington v. Berry, 13 Wash. 708, 42 Pac. 622 (1896); State ex rel. O'Sullivan v. Coffey, 59 Mo. 59 (1875). See Judd v. State of Texas, 25 Tex. Civ. App. 418, 62 S. W. 634 (1901), where the inclusion of certain lands within the corporate limits was alleged to vitiate the entire organization.

"intrude" into an office that does not exist. He is thus placed on the same footing as a person seeking to act as the holder of an office never created by the legislature.[5]

The attorney-general may not, however, mandamus the persons holding offices under the prior valid corporation to enter upon the duties of their offices until the quo warranto proceedings have been finally disposed of. For example, a lower New Jersey court held that a city should be ousted of its charter and the officers of their offices because of the unconstitutionality of the incorporating act. From this decision an appeal was taken to a higher court. While this appeal was pending, the attorney-general asked for a writ of mandamus to compel the old officers again to enter upon the duties that were thought to have been superseded by the new order of things just declared to be without legal basis.[6] In denying the petition for the writ the court said that if the writ of error did not have the effect of staying the judgment for ouster, "anarchy would result in cases where provision is not made for the continuance of the governing body which is displaced and superseded by the void legislation."[7] The fact that no provision for continuing the old government had been made in the particular case was thought by the court to be immaterial, the principle involved being essential to the stability and safety of local government.

When quo warranto is brought to oust the officers of a municipality because of the invalidity of a statute creating municipal offices, the court may in its discretion postpone the time at which the judgment of ouster is to take effect, because, although the corporate existence of the municipality is not involved, for all practical purposes the officers of the city constitute the governing body, so far as the performance of functions is concerned. In order to insure against the cessation of the work of government in such a case the court may take into consideration, in fixing the date at which the judgment of ouster shall take effect, the likelihood of immediate action by the executive or legislative branches of the state government to provide for the continuance of the local government.[8] Courts also emphasize that the municipality may be properly organ-

[5] For a discussion of the cases involving the existence of an office alleged to have been created by an invalid statute, see Chapter 4. See People v. Maynard, 15 Mich. 463 (1867); State ex rel. Brayton v. Merriman, 6 Wis. 14 (1857).

[6] State ex rel. Attorney General v. Town of Dover, 62 N. J. L. 138, 41 Atl. 98 (1898). The earlier case is found in 62 N. J. L. 40, 40 Atl. 640 (1898).

[7] 62 N. J. L. at 144.

[8] State ex rel. Attorney General v. Beacom, 66 Ohio St. 457, 64 N. E. 427 (1902). In State v. Lindeman, 132 Wis. 47, 111 N. W. 214 (1907), quo warranto was granted, the court emphasizing that the legislature was in session and that the defective legal basis for the board could be remedied.

ized under existing valid statutes, so that no great confusion need ensue from the order of dissolution.[9]

Quo warranto proceedings by the attorney-general will also lie to test the constitutionality of a statute annexing, or providing for the annexation of, additional territory to a municipality. The proceeding in such a case may be to oust an officer representing such territory from holding office in the city government, or to oust the city from the performance of governmental functions in the area annexed.[10] A city may also be ousted from a class to which it has been assigned by an invalid statute.[11] The city officers may be ousted because the municipality is "not rightfully or legally a city of the second class." In the case from which this quotation is taken the official representative of the state was a county attorney instead of the attorney-general, but the result was the same as though the latter officer had instituted the action. Statutes in a number of states permit local prosecuting officers to initiate such actions on behalf of the state.

In Holmberg v. Jones [12] the action was by a county officer to compel a state officer to issue ballots for a county election. The court upheld the contention of the latter officer that the county had been organized under an invalid act and that therefore he was under no duty to issue the ballots.

The qualification of the rule that corporate existence may be challenged by an official representative of the state, to which allusion was made in stating the rule, is that in some states the action must be brought within a reasonable time. Attack, even by the state, will be restricted by the courts if it is made too long after the organization of the municipality. The leading case to this effect is Attorney-General v. City of Methuen.[13] In that case the court treated the proceedings as though brought by the attorney-general, although a private relator had originally instituted the action. The statute granting the city a charter was held to be invalid. The action to test the validity of the statute was not brought until two and one-half years after the time of the grant. The court said, in denying the application for the writ because of the delay of two and one-half years in bringing the action:

Whatever legal consequences may flow from the fact that the city charter of Methuen is unconstitutional must be met as and when they

[9] People v. Weiss, 215 Ill. 581, 114 N. E. 332 (1916).
[10] People ex rel. Attorney General v. Holihan, 29 Mich. 116 (1874); State ex rel. Attorney General v. City of Cincinnati, 20 Ohio St. 18 (1870). See Judd v. State, *supra*, note 4.
[11] Corporate Powers of City of Council Grove, 20 Kan. 619 (1878).
[12] 7 Idaho 752, 65 Pac. 563 (1901).
[13] 236 Mass. 564, 129 N. E. 662 (1921).

arise. Our refusal, in the exercise of sound judicial discretion, to issue the extraordinary writ of quo warranto under the circumstances, cannot affect those consequences. Those consequences may be alleviated so far as possible by taking the obvious steps to remedy the present situation, and to put Methuen upon the basis of a constitutional charter.[14]

Other cases have held that the state would not be permitted to assail the existence of a local governmental unit if too long a time had elapsed prior to the institution of the action, but they have usually been concerned with cases of irregular organization under a constitutional statute.[15] The periods of time involved in them have been from nine to twenty years, and it may be questioned whether many courts would go so far as did the Massachusetts court in the Methuen case and hold that a period of two and one-half years was sufficient to estop the state.[16] On the other hand, it is very likely that many courts would be slow to permit the state to question municipal organization following a twenty-year period of inactivity or positive recognition, even though the statute under which the organization was had should turn out to be unconstitutional. A few states would doubtless permit attack even in such an event, on the ground that the state has an interest in maintaining the regular incorporation of municipalities that could not be barred by mere inaction.[17]

An order of dissolution does not settle claims against the municipality, such questions being reserved for later adjudication when they are properly presented to the court.[18]

II. DISPUTES BETWEEN TWO MUNICIPAL CORPORATIONS

Sometimes the question of the corporate existence of a local governmental unit is raised in a case the parties to which are two municipal corporations. In one case two towns were at odds over certain territory which each claimed. In a suit by one of them to oust the other from exercising any governmental function in the territory, the defendant alleged that the plaintiff had been incorporated in accordance with an invalid statute and that an attempted reincorporation

[14] 236 Mass. at 582.

[15] Jameson v. People ex rel. Nettleton, 16 Ill. 257 (1855); State v. Leatherman, 38 Ark. 81 (1881); Soule v. People ex rel. Cullen, 205 Ill. 618, 69 N. E. 22 (1902).

[16] See, however, discussion in State ex rel. Attorney General v. Alturas County, 6 Idaho 418, 55 Pac. 1067 (1899).

[17] Query: Would the statutes of limitations to be found in some states, barring attack on incorporation proceedings after the expiration of a fixed period, be construed as to apply to actions brought by the state? Cf. State ex rel. West v. Des Moines, 96 Iowa 521, 65 N. W. 818, 21 L. R. A. 186, 59 Am. St. Rep. 381 (1896).

[18] State ex rel. Attorney General v. Board, 54 Kan. 372, 38 Pac. 559 (1893).

under a later statute was likewise ineffective. Both statutes were held to be unconstitutional, and the defendant prevailed because "it was no law, and the claim of legislative recognition for appellant as a municipal corporation is therefore without foundation and must fall." [19] The plaintiff had not even de facto existence, said the court, and that being the case, plaintiff was not entitled to relief, nor was a cause of action stated in favor of the mayor and aldermen of the plaintiff town, because they had not been joined as plaintiffs. It is very doubtful whether it would have availed the plaintiff even if these officers had been joined, because if the existence of the town was denied, the existence of the offices held by the mayor and aldermen would at the same time be swept away, and the result would have been the same.

In the case of Town of Winneconne v. The Village of Winneconne [20] the town sued to recover certain sums of license money alleged to be due to it from the village. The village defended on the ground that it had been incorporated under an invalid statute and that service had not been made on it subsequent to the passage of a curative act that attempted to remedy the defective incorporation. The court dismissed the action, holding that the village had neither a de facto nor a de jure existence. It will be noticed that this case differs from that discussed just previously in that the defendant was allowed to assert its own corporate nonexistence, whereas in the other case the legal existence of the plaintiff was challenged by the defendant. It will be remembered that the tendency in the private corporations cases is to refuse to allow defendants to set up their own nonexistence and also to deny defendants, in contract cases or other cases in which there have been dealings on a corporate basis, the privilege of attacking the validity of the plaintiff's incorporation. There had not been any course of dealings between the two towns in the two cases just discussed comparable to that referred to by the phrase "on a corporate basis." One was a suit concerning the power to govern certain territory and the other a suit for the recovery of money. These two cases seem to indicate that, as regards municipal corporations, one may deny the existence of another, or may deny its own existence, as may best suit its purpose.

[19] Town of Denver v. Town of Spokane Falls, 7 Wash. 226, 34 Pac. 926 (1893). Also Worth County v. Crisp County, 139 Ga. 117, 76 S. E. 747 (1912); Bd. of Ed. v. Bd. of Ed., 245 Mich. 411, 222 N. W. 763 (1929); Summit County v. Rich County, 57 Utah 553, 195 Pac. 639 (1921).

[20] 111 Wis. 10, 86 N. W. 589. See Dist. Twp. v. Dubuque, 7 Iowa 262 (1858). Maury County v. Lewis County, 31 Tenn. 236 (1851). Counties may sue to recover territory incorporated into another county by invalid act. Marion County v. Grundy County, 37 Tenn. 259 (1858); Bittle v. Stuart, 34 Ark. 224 (1879).

It has been said that if one county successfully challenges boundary changes so as to recover land sought to be given to another county, it is entitled to taxes due on the land subsequent to the time when the bill for injunctive relief is filed.[21]

But the existence of one public corporation may not be litigated in an action by another such corporation against a private individual, the corporation whose existence is assailed not being a party to the dispute.[22] On this point the New Jersey court has said: "It would be extraordinary indeed, if, under a claim of a right to impose taxes on private property, one municipality could question the legal existence of another municipality having at least a de facto existence, and that in a proceeding to which the latter is not a party." [23]

III. DISPUTES BETWEEN OFFICERS OR CLAIMANTS TO AN OFFICE

In Morris v. Fagan [24] a city clerk under the old city government sought to oust the clerk in a new city organization, on the ground that the new government had not been adopted in accordance with a valid statute. The court decided that the writ should not issue and that the relator should not be permitted to assail the existence of the city government, it being a de facto government in any event. In a Missouri case a sheriff of a county that had been reorganized tried to oust the sheriff of the new county by quo warranto proceedings. The statute creating the new county was unconstitutional. The defendant was ousted from office.[25]

The sheriff of a county asked for a writ of mandamus to compel the delivery of books and papers by a person claiming to be the sheriff of the county that had been superseded by the one of which plaintiff was sheriff. The statute creating the new county was held to be invalid and the petition was dismissed.[26] Another case involving a petition for a writ of mandamus was State ex rel. Horton v. Brechler,[27] wherein the certification of certain statements concerning the valuation of property for taxation in a school district was asked

---

[21] Cheatham County v. Dickson County, 39 S. W. 734 (Tenn. Ch. App. 1896).

[22] Riverton & Palmyra Water Co. v. Haig, 59 N. J. L. 295, 33 Atl. 215 (1895).

[23] 58 N. J. L. at 298.

[24] 85 N. J. L. 67, 90 Atl. 267 (1914). See also State ex rel. Haley v. Stark, 18 Fla. 255 (1881).

[25] State ex rel. Douglass v. Scott, 17 Mo. 521 (1853). See State ex rel. Oblinger v. Spaude, 37 Minn. 322, 34 N. W. 164 (1887).

[26] McDonald v. Doust, 11 Idaho 14, 81 Pac. 60 (1905). See People v. George, 3 (Hasb.) Idaho 72, 26 Pac. 983 (1891).

[27] 185 Wis. 599, 202 N. W. 144 (1925). The mandamus was not granted because the court thought the legislation would perhaps be enacted immediately, restoring the original districts.

for. The statute creating a separate school district was held invalid. The old joint district remained intact, said the court, because an unconstitutional law is not law. With respect to the argument that the people had acquiesced in the existing state of affairs for so long a time that an estoppel should be considered established, the court stated that no amount of acquiescence on the part of the people could convert an unconstitutional statute into a constitutional one. This answer seems inadequate. It may well be that no estoppel should have been applied in the case, but the reason for not applying estoppel is not based on a change in constitutionality. To apply the doctrine of estoppel in such a case is not the same as to hold that the statute is constitutional. The application of estoppel is merely one method of giving effect to an unconstitutional law. In another case, with different parties, the same court might hold the same statute to be invalid.

It appears then that, although there is some dispute over the point, the tendency is for the courts to permit claimants to office to raise the question of municipal existence if the validity of such existence is material to the case. The constitutionality of a statute creating the corporation in such a case is drawn into question incidentally, because upon its validity depends the legal status of certain officers.[28]

Occasionally the constitutionality of a statute under which proposed organization is to take place may be raised by an officer in a mandamus proceeding wherein private relators seek to compel action by him in performing certain functions requisite to incorporation. For example, the governor of Louisiana refused to issue commissions for the organization of a parish because he believed the statute authorizing organization to be invalid. Relators asked for a writ of mandamus to compel the issuance of the commissions. The governor defended by asserting the invalidity of the statute, and the court sustained his contention, denying the petition.[29] The result was that the parish was not organized.

The court to which petitions to organize municipalities must be presented may refuse for a similar reason to proceed through the various steps of incorporation, and the petitioners may wish to compel the court, by mandamus, to proceed in accordance with the statutory steps outlined for the proposed incorporation.[30] If the

[28] See pp. 79–84.

[29] State ex rel. Carey v. Sanders, 130 La. 272, 57 So. 924 (1912).

[30] In the Matter of the Incorporation of the Village of Ridgfield Park, 54 N. J. L. 288, 23 Atl. 674 (1892). Robertson v. Collins, 218 Ala. 54, 117 So. 415 (1928). See State ex rel. Atty. Gen. v. St. John, 21 Kan. 592 (1879), mandamus against governor to compel appointment of officer.

statute is constitutional, other requisites being fully complied with, the writ will issue, while if the statute is unconstitutional the writ will not issue, and the incorporation will not take place.

IV. ATTACK BY PRIVATE INDIVIDUALS

If private individuals feel that a proposed organization of a municipality is about to take place in accordance with the terms of a statute believed to be unconstitutional, they may put the matter to a test at a very early stage in the proceedings.

An order calling for an election to vote upon the question of proposed incorporation may be appealed from if the proceedings are challenged at that stage.[31] This applies also to orders of incorporation. A review of the proceedings of the board authorizing incorporation of the municipality may be had on certiorari at the instance of taxpayers or of residents.[32] Other methods of review or attack are also used.[33]

At this stage the injunction may be pressed into use also, and a restraining order issued, if the proposed organization be by virtue of an invalid statute, forbidding designated officers from proceeding further in the organization of the municipality and its government.[34] Two Tennessee cases illustrate the factors that cause the court to issue or deny the injunctions in such cases. In Bradley v. Commissioners[35] an injunction was issued to prevent the organization of a county. The court said that the private individual who had asked for the injunction need not stand by and wait until the county had been organized and then ask the court for permission to file an information in the nature of quo warranto. In stopping the proposed organization before it had gotten well under way, the court felt that it was acting in the interest of peace and order. If the organization had been perfected, much more confusion would have resulted from an order ousting it from its powers than in this case, where the proposed project was halted at an early stage. The court might have used as an additional reason in support of its decision

[31] In re Incorporation of Village of North Milwaukee, 93 Wis. 617, 67 N. W. 1033 (1896). See North v. Bd., 313 Ill. 422, 145 N. E. 158 (1924).

[32] Kenyon v. Moore, 287 Ill. 233, 122 N. E. 548 (1919), record of organization quashed; Donoghue v. Dewey, 82 Mich. 309, 46 N. W. 782 (1890) involving action of board in changing district lines; Eckert v. Bd., 7 N. J. Misc. 850, 147 Atl. 380 (1929).

[33] Drainage Dist. v. Shroer, 145 Ind. 572, 44 N. E. 636 (1896). Warren v. Mayor, 2 Gray 97 (Mass. 1864), mandamus denied to compel certification of result of election forming invalid municipality.

[34] Albershart v. Donaldson, 149 Ky. 510, 149 S. W. 873 (1912). Rowe v. Ray, 120 Neb. 118, 231 N. W. 689 (1930). See Bd. v. Crowe, 141 Ala. 126, 37 So. 469 (1904); Cleveland v. City of Watertown, 99 Misc. Rep. 66, 165 N. Y. S. 305 (1917).

[35] 2 Humph. 428 (Tenn. 1841).

the fact that in many states the private individual could not have assailed the validity of the municipality by quo warranto after the organization had been completed. For that reason, it would seem, attack on the proposed action should be permitted in an injunction suit. In Ford v. Farmer [36] an injunction was refused because the county had already been organized and was a going concern. Officers had been elected, and the injunction asked for was to prevent them from performing their functions. The court seemed to feel that too much confusion would ensue if an injunction were granted at so late a stage of the proceedings.

These two cases bring out very clearly the importance of the time element in these cases. If an injunction is asked for at one of the earlier stages in the proceedings, it will be issued with less hesitation than if the municipality has already been launched as a functioning governmental unit. The Kentucky court has, however, permitted residents and taxpayers to bring an action to stop the officers of a city from exercising their powers because the city had been organized as of the fifth class when it should have been in another class.[37] The officers in this case had been carrying on their work for two years, and the case is therefore somewhat at odds with the Tennessee cases just considered. Perhaps they can be reconciled on the ground that organization in the wrong class is not so serious as organization without any authority at all. Reorganization in a different class is, after all, only a routine matter. The defective statute authorizing organization in such a case does not constitute the only basis for organization of some kind. When, however, there is only one statute by virtue of which organization of some kind can be had, the matter is on a different basis. The question then is as between this particular organization or no organization, the latter usually meaning that the community will remain a part of some larger unit, such as a county, township, or city.

Taxpayers' actions and injunctions to stop the formation of a municipality are not infrequently asked for to restrain the officers who are about to tabulate and announce the votes of the election that is thought to have been favorable to the adoption of the new type or organization or government.[38] This applies also to cases of

---

[36] 9 Humph. 152 (Tenn. 1848). In Stuart v. School District, 30 Mich. 69 (1874), a bill was brought to stop the collection of taxes by a school district. The court held that it would not consider the question of the unconstitutionality of the statute involved, but intimated that it might have taken a different attitude had the suit been instituted immediately after the school district in question was organized.

[37] Hurley v. Motz, 151 Ky. 451, 152 S. W. 248 (1913). See Woods v. Ball, 166 S. W. 4 (Tex. Civ. App. 1914).

[38] City of Gretna v. Bailey, 145 La. 625, 75 So. 491 (1917).

annexation.[39] A defeated candidate in such an election will perhaps not succeed in attacking the legal basis of the government nor the municipal corporation itself.

It is difficult to tell in some of these cases whether the legality of the government of the city or the legality of the corporate existence of the city is being questioned,[40] and the two questions are often inextricably intertwined. The statutes providing for incorporation usually contain many provisions relative to officers, boards, and municipal functions. If one adopts the entity theory of corporations, whether private or municipal, there would in strict legal logic be a difference between assailing the corporate existence of a municipality and assailing its governmental organization. In actual practice, attack on one usually involves attack upon the other, although this is not necessarily the case. From the standpoint of the taxpayer and citizen the distinction is not very intelligible, for to him the city and its government are inseparable, so far as political organization is concerned.

The earlier that steps are taken to halt proceedings for incorporation on the ground that the statute authorizing incorporation is unconstitutional, the more likely the taxpayer or resident is to succeed. In these early stages he will not be met with obstacles phrased in terms of estoppel or of a de facto doctrine. If there is any real doubt as to the constitutionality of the proposed action, or of the statutes authorizing it, the court will be more open to argument on that score at this stage than after the municipality has been organized and in operation for days, months, or years; and, it is submitted, quite properly so.

Private individuals may, however, attempt to attack the status of a municipality after it has been formed. The various types of situations in which such attacks are usually made will now be considered.

A. Quo Warranto on Relation of Private Individuals

New Jersey has held that private relators may not invoke quo warranto to assail the corporate existence of a city,[41] and Iowa has refused to permit a private relator to test the constitutionality of an annexation statute in a similar action.[42] In a North Dakota case

[39] Warren v. Mayor of Charleston, 2 Gray 97 (Mass. 1864).
[40] See Cleveland v. City of Watertown, 99 Misc. Rep. 66, 165 N. Y. S. 305 (1917); People ex rel. Ferguson v. Vrooman, 101 Misc. Rep. 233, 166 N. Y. S. 923 (1917).
[41] State ex rel. Steckman v. Vickers, 51 N. J. L. 180, 17 Atl. 153 (1889).
[42] State of Iowa ex rel. West v. City of Des Moines, 96 Iowa 521, 65 N. W. 818, 21 L. R. A. 186, 59 Am. St. Rep. 381 (1896).

a taxpayer asked leave to file an information in the nature of quo warranto to oust several counties from jurisdiction over certain unorganized territory in which the petitioner lived.[43] He alleged that the statute authorizing the extension of county authority over the territory in question was unconstitutional. His petition was denied.

An Illinois case permits a voter to use quo warranto even though he voted in the election on the formation of the municipality.[44] Much depends upon the law of the particular state on this writ, the old common law writ being greatly modified by statute. The writ is generally restricted considerably under modern law.

The reason given by the New Jersey court for its decision in the case mentioned at the opening of this section was that "it is highly inexpedient that these municipalities, being the depositaries of a part of the governmental power of the state, should have their very being put at hazard whenever any member of the community sees fit to make the assault." [45] The confusion that would ensue from permitting private relators to raise such questions was strongly relied upon in the Iowa case, and the action was denied, although only four of the five years of the statutory period allowed for bringing informations of this nature had elapsed. Thus it will appear that the use of quo warranto is usually reserved for some official representative of the state, and private individuals must resort to some other method of testing the legality of municipal existence, if they are to be permitted to test it at all.

B. Tax Cases

An injunction to prevent the collection of a tax by officers of a municipality alleged to have been organized under an invalid statute was asked for in Campbell v. Bryant.[46] The injunction was granted, the statute being declared unconstitutional. The court said, in the course of its opinion: "We are only holding that the act attempting to incorporate the town of Madison Heights and providing for its organization and government is invalid because not passed in conformity with the constitution of the state." [47]

The court stated that if the statute had ever been valid the judiciary could not have declared it invalid because that would be an exercise of legislative power. "But whether or not there is a valid act or charter authorizing the tax complained of is a judicial question, and

[43] State ex rel. Walker v. McLean County, 11 N. D. 356, 92 N. W. 395 (1902). On quo warranto by private parties see 32 Eng. and Am. Enc. 1442.
[44] People ex rel. Cole v. Kinsey, 294 Ill. 530, 538, 128 N. E. 561 (1920).
[45] *Supra*, note 41, at 181.
[46] 104 Va. 509, 52 S. E. 638 (1905).
[47] 104 Va. at 517.

the court not only has the right but is bound to pass upon such a question whenever it is properly presented."[48] Injunctions have been granted under similar circumstances in other cases.[49] The same result, the granting of an injunction, has also been reached where territory has been annexed to a city by virtue of an unconstitutional statute and a taxpayer has resisted by injunction the collection of the tax.[50] In several of these cases there had been continuous dispute between the taxpayer and the municipality. This, coupled with the fact that the injunction was asked for immediately following the organization of the municipality, would doubtless serve to explain the readiness of the courts to pass upon the legality of the organization. Not all courts are so ready to grant injunctive relief in such cases, however.[51]

If considerable time elapses between the time the municipality was formed and the time the injunction is asked for, the courts will be more likely to find estoppel or the de facto doctrine defeating the taxpayer.[52] The acquiescence of the taxpayer and the state for a period of thirteen years, and the existence of a statute raising a presumption that the type of public corporation in question had been legally organized after it had exercised corporate powers for a period of two years, was held by the Michigan court[53] to weigh the scales against the taxpayer.[54]

A West Virginia case[55] that involved the constitutionality of an

[48] *Ibid.*
[49] Lancaster v. Police Jury, 254 Fed. 179 (D. C. La. 1917); Allen v. Board of Mayor and Aldermen of Smithville, 140 Tenn. 418, 205 S. W. 124 (1918). See Schaffner v. Young, 10 N. D. 245, 86 N. W. 733 (1901); Crawford v. Taylor. 6 Ohio C. C. Rep. (N. S.) 278 (1905); Herochbach v. Kaskaskia Is. Dist., 265 Ill. 388, 106 N. E. 942 (1914).
[50] City of Topeka v. Gillet, 32 Kan. 431, 4 Pac. 800 (1884).
[51] Clay v. Buchanan, 162 Tenn. 204, 36 S. W. (2d) 91 (1931).
[52] Ford v. Town of North Des Moines, 80 Iowa 626, 45 N. W. 1031 (1890), involving a thirty-year period of acquiescence.
[53] Stewart v. School District, 30 Mich. 69 (1874). In Graham v. City of Grenville, 67 Tex. 62, 2 S. W. 742 (1886), an injunction was sought against the collection of a tax, the petition setting out that the territory in which petitioner lived had been improperly brought within the city. The court said, refusing the injunction, "If a municipality has been illegally constituted, the state alone can take advantage of the fact in a proper proceeding instituted for the purpose of testing the validity of its charter." The court refused to permit what it called collateral attack.
[54] Other cases in which collateral attack was disapproved, injunctions to stop the collection of taxes being denied, are Chicago, St. Louis & New Orleans R. R. v. Town of Kentwood, 49 La. Ann. 931, 22 So. 192 (1897); Wright v. Phelps, 89 Vt. 107, 94 Atl. 294 (1914), strong dictum, the statute being held constitutional; Howard v. Desdemona Indep. Sch. Dist., 19 S. W. (2d) 946 (Tex. Civ. App. 1929).
[55] Kusher v. Scites, 4 W. Va. 11 (1870). Also Mattox v. State, 115 Ga. 212, 41 S. E. 709 (1902); State ex rel. Attorney General v. County of Dorsey, 28 Ark. 379 (1873); see also Frazer v. James, 65 S. C. 78, 43 S. E. 292 (1902); Judson v. Plattsburg, 3 Dill. 181, Fed. Cas. No. 7570 (C. C. Mo. 1874), bond case.

act creating a certain county turned on the point that the legislature was the final judge of the question whether the area and population of a given county complied with the requirements of the state constitution. The doctrine of "political questions" was invoked; the state government having recognized the existence of the county, the court held that it would likewise do so, and the taxpayer's petition for a restraining order was denied. The doctrines that only the state can inquire into the legality of the organization and that such corporations act under "color," "semblance," or "appearance" of law are also invoked in some of these cases.[56]

The rule may, on the basis of these cases, be stated to be that taxpayers may assail the legality of a municipal organization in injunction suits to restrain the collection of taxes if the suit is instituted before too long a time elapses after the organization has taken place. But if the taxpayer waits several years before resisting the collection of a tax he will not be permitted to challenge the validity of municipal incorporation.[57]

Taxpayers do not, however, always challenge municipal existence at so early a stage in tax cases as in injunction cases. For example, in Coe v. Gregory [58] the taxpayer sued a village marshal in replevin to recover the value of property taken by the latter to satisfy a village tax. In answer to the contention that the statute under which the village had been organized was unconstitutional, the court said that "the corporate organization of a village and the validity of its charter cannot be attacked in this collateral manner." [59] The village had been recognized by the state in several instances, and the court relied to some extent upon that fact.

The plaintiff in Ferguson v. City of Snohomish [60] brought an action against the city to have a cloud on his title to certain land, which had been sold for tax purposes, removed, claiming that the incorporation proceedings for the city were void. Without deciding that the statute was unconstitutional the court said that plaintiff

[56] Cases *supra*, note 54.

[57] The rule is not so strictly enforced in boundary disputes, the Tennessee court permitting challenge of boundary statute by taxpayers fourteen years after enactment. Cheatham County v. Dickson County, 39 S. W. 734 (Tenn. Ch. App. 1896).

[58] 53 Mich. 19, 18 N. W. 541 (1884).

[59] 53 Mich. at 22. In Bird v. Perkins, 33 Mich. 28 (1875), plaintiff brought an action of trover for taking a horse for taxes. The village marshal was made defendant, and plaintiff alleged that the village had been irregularly incorporated, although the statute authorizing incorporation was constitutional. The court decided in favor of the marshal, refusing to permit plaintiff to show the alleged irregularity in the incorporation of the village.

[60] 9 Wash. 668, 36 Pac. 969 (1894). The statute was held to be constitutional, but the court discussed the problem on the assumption that it was unconstitutional. Also, Rachford v. Port Neches, 46 S. W. (2d) 1057 (Tex. Civ. App. 1931).

could not raise that question. The court held that he was not in a position to question the validity of the incorporation proceedings because he had brought his action against the city as a municipal corporation and was, therefore, estopped by his own pleadings to deny the existence of the city.

Can a taxpayer recover money paid to a municipality that has been organized under an invalid statute? This question was argued and decided in Board of Education v. Toennigs,[61] wherein the Illinois court held that if the taxes had been voluntarily paid they could not be recovered. The following excerpt from the opinion of the court summarizes its view of the problem involved:

> The tax levies here made by the community high school board were not valid and binding on the taxpayers, but the taxes were voluntarily paid, not under compulsion or protest, and the money received on the anticipation warrants issued by the board was spent in the conduct and operation of the high school during a period for which no other tax was levied for that purpose. During that time the people of the district had the benefit of the school.[62]

If, as in Coe v. Gregory, the taxpayer cannot recover in replevin nor, as in the Toennigs case, the money paid in taxes, may he redeem land that has been sold for unpaid taxes? According to the decision in Markle v. Hart [63] he may so do. In that case the court said: "If there was no district, and therefore no indebtedness, it must follow that there could be no lien covering the indebtedness to foreclose." [64] The sale was, therefore, canceled, although the former owner was compelled to pay the amount of taxes paid out by the purchaser for taxes before recovering the property.

Sometimes the question of the validity of the incorporation of a municipality is not raised by the taxpayer until suit is brought against him to recover taxes or special assessments. The courts are not all agreed that the defense of invalidity in the incorporation statute cannot be used in such a suit, but the tendency is to deny its use, either on the ground of estoppel or on the ground that the corporation is entitled to de facto standing. Thus one court said, in a suit by a collector to recover taxes to pay off certain drainage district bonds,[65] that this being a public corporation, "the legality of its

---

[61] 297 Ill. 469, 130 N. E. 758 (1921). See Couch v. Kansas City, 127 Mo. 436, 30 S. W. 117 (1895).

[62] 297 Ill. at 474.

[63] 126 Ark. 416, 191 S. W. 24 (1916).

[64] 126 Ark. at 419.

[65] State ex rel. Coleman v. Blair, 245 Mo. 680, 151 S. W. 148 (1912); Garden of Eden Drainage Dist. v. Bartlett Trust Co., 50 S. W. (2d) 627 (Mo. 1932), defense good.

organization and the sufficiency of its corporate existence cannot be inquired into in this collateral action." [66]

In Town of Medical Lake v. Smith [67] suit was brought by the village to foreclose a lien on certain of defendant's lots abutting on a street that had been improved. The statute authorizing the improvement made the cost of the improvement a lien on abutting lots. The village had, however, been incorporated under an unconstitutional law, and for this reason the court decided in favor of the defendant, holding that there had been no legal assessment because of the legal incapacity of the city to carry on such work. In discussing the possibility of estoppel against the defendant for standing by and watching the work proceed to completion without protesting against it, the court stated that any estoppel that might exist would not inure to the benefit of the city. Whether it would be available to the person doing the work, in case of an action by him, the court did not decide, although it was intimated that he might have been able to hold the owner of the lot liable on that basis. [68]

When the taxpayer defends against an action for taxes brought against him by the municipality and his defense is based on the ground that the annexation of the territory in which his land is located is void, the tendency has been for the courts to permit the annexation statute to be assailed. This is particularly true if no public improvements have been entered upon in reliance on the tax in question. [69] But if the annexation has taken place and has not

[66] *Ibid.*, 687. The statute in this case was held constitutional, so that in a sense this is dictum. In Blake v. People, 109 Ill. 504, 31 N. E. 123 (1884), the court said that a levee district would be de facto even though the statute authorizing its incorporation be unconstitutional, which it was not. The case came up on an appeal from a judgment for taxes against the owner of land. See Chicago & N. W. Ry. v. Langlade County, 56 Wis. 614, 14 N. W. 844 (1883). In Trumbo v. People, 75 Ill. 561 (1874), a school district had been irregularly organized under a valid law. In a proceeding to collect school taxes the taxpayer was not permitted to set up this irregularity in organization, the court saying the district had de facto existence. In Town of Decorah v. Bullis, 25 Iowa 12 (1868), the town sued in its corporate capacity to recover an assessment but the court held that the officers acting for the town in authorizing the improvement were not de facto, the statute in this case being constitutional, but inapplicable to this class of cities.

[67] 7 Wash. 195, 34 Pac. 835 (1893).

[68] On this point see Wendt v. Berry, 154 Ky. 586, 157 S. W. 1115, 48 L. R. A. (N. S.) 1101, Ann. Cas. 1915C 493 (1913), permitting recovery by the contractor. See also Ball v. Eady Co., 193 Ky. 813, 237 S. W. 670 (1922), where the defense was that the city was in the wrong class, the court saying that it was a "de facto city of that class."

[69] State of Nebraska v. Several Parcels of Land, 78 Neb. 703, 111 N. W. 601 (1907), same case 80 Neb. 11, 113 N. W. 810 (1907). The case was finally decided against the taxpayer, on the ground that a statute was found to exist, which was not brought to the attention of the court in the first hearing, under which organization could have been had. In the second opinion emphasis is laid on the fact that nineteen years had elapsed from the time of the proceeding here assailed until the time

been assailed for many years, as in a Massachusetts case,[70] eighty years, that will be held to estop the defendant from questioning the proceedings, and he must pay the tax. At times the courts, taking a stricter attitude, decide that the plaintiff is to be treated as a de facto corporation and that the defendant cannot, therefore, use the plea of nul tiel corporation. This is illustrated by a Missouri case in which one of the incorporated municipal boards of St. Louis sued to recover a penalty from a contractor for not carrying out his agreement to fill in a lot that had been declared a nuisance.[71] The statement was made in the opinion that "when they entered into the obligation and signed the bond they solemnly admitted plaintiff's corporate capacity." The policy back of such a decision was doubtless that of getting work of such an urgent nature performed on time, and holding the contractor strictly to the penalty would tend to further this result.

From the cases reviewed in this section it appears that in the majority of situations most courts refuse to permit the validity of municipal incorporation proceedings to be drawn in question in tax cases unless the suit is brought very soon after the proceedings have been held. There are a few cases to the contrary, but in most of them it will be found that some particular equity caused the court to decide the case otherwise.

This general rule that taxpayers cannot evade the payment of their share of the burden of maintaining the local government by an attack on the status of the governmental unit seeking to impose the tax is sound. Governmental functions and services are being performed by the municipality and these are presumably of benefit to the people of the community. Even if the taxpayer should be permitted to evade the payment of a tax to a particular municipality, the likelihood is that he will eventually be compelled to pay for the services performed for him by the government, because in most cases some other governmental organization will assume the obligations, to defray which the tax is levied. To this organization he will normally be compelled to pay the tax. The courts have, with few exceptions, felt that to permit taxpayers to assail the constitutionality of a statute in accordance with which incorporation was had would result in too much confusion in the conduct of the affairs of local government. The receipt of benefits, the fact that the taxpayer will eventually have to pay for the services rendered, and the

when it was first questioned. See also State ex rel. Moody v. Wardell, 153 Mo. 319, 54 S. W. 574 (1899).

[70] Cobb v. Kingman, 15 Mass. 197 (1818).

[71] City of St. Louis v. Shields, 62 Mo. 247 (1876).

confusion that would result in the financial and governmental affairs of local communities are among the more important of the reasons that have caused courts to deny collateral attack in tax cases on municipal incorporation proceedings.

Legislation validating taxes imposed by defectively organized districts has been upheld under some circumstances, so the taxpayer sometimes gains less than he appears to, at first thought, in some of these cases.[72]

C. Eminent Domain

In Colton v. Rossi [73] the California court seems to hold, in effect, that the owner of land taken from him in eminent domain proceedings may recover it if the organization of the municipality taking the land is declared to have been consummated under an invalid statute. There appears to be no way, in such a case, in which the landowner can recover compensation from the municipality. He is, therefore, entitled to possession of the land itself. An interesting problem might arise if the municipality had paid for the land taken in such a proceeding and had in a subsequent proceeding been successfully attacked because of defective incorporation. Would a court then permit the former owner of the land to redeem it on payment of the sum he had received from the city? The case of Markle v. Hart,[74] previously considered, is of course only analogous to the case here put.

D. Resisting Abatement of a Nuisance

In Coast Company v. Mayor and Common Council of Spring Lake [75] the plaintiff asked for an injunction to stop the officials of the city from proceeding to tear down certain of his buildings. These buildings the officers of the municipality had declared to be a nuisance. Plaintiff proved that the attorney-general had brought an action against another municipality organized under the same statute as that under which Spring Lake had been organized and had succeeded in ousting that city of its franchise, the court having in that case declared the statute to be invalid. Reasoning from that case and arguing that the declaration of unconstitutionality in the prior case had rendered the statute null and void for all purposes, the plaintiff assailed the corporate being of the city of Spring Lake.

[72] See Blake v. People, 109 Ill. 504 (1884); Guthrie Natl. Bk. v. City of Guthrie, 173 U. S. 528, 19 Sup. Ct. Rep. 513, 43 L. Ed. 796 (1898); Chapter 11.
[73] 9 Cal. 595 (1858).
[74] *Supra*, note 63.
[75] 56 N. J. Eq. 615, 36 Atl. 21 (1896).

The court denied the injunction and permitted the city to proceed with the abatement of the nuisance, saying in the course of its opinion:

I am unable, however, to perceive in what way the decision in that case can, in this suit, introduce the question of the corporate existence of the borough of Spring Lake. The force of the judgment in the preceding case was spent when it annulled the corporate existence of the borough of Cape May Point. It is of course obvious that the decision in that case will be controlling as a precedent whenever the constitutionality of the same act arises in a shape to be passed upon. The question can be raised by an attack upon any step taken to organize a borough under the provisions of the act, by means of a certiorari allowed before the corporation has become an existing entity.[76]

But after it had become organized, said the court, the municipality was not open to collateral attack.

E. CRIMINAL CASES

Persons accused of crime sometimes attempt to defeat prosecution by assailing the validity of municipal existence. One of the early cases in which this happened was State v. Rich,[77] in which the accused moved to quash the indictment on the ground of the nonexistence of the county court. The reasoning whereby it was concluded that the court was nonexistent was that the statute creating a new county had so reduced the population of the county in which the indictment was brought that the constitutional requirement as to county population had been violated. For that reason the county was not a constitutional county, and there could be no court for a nonexistent county. The court held that the motion to quash the indictment should be overruled. It has similarly been held in a case involving a valid statute that a defendant who is being sued by a municipality to recover a penalty prescribed by statute for the violation of an ordinance may not assail the irregularity of municipal organization.[78]

[76] 56 N. J. Eq. at 619.

[77] 20 Mo. 393 (1855). In State v. Wiley, 109 Mo. 439, 19 S. W. 197 (1891), the defendant in a criminal case claimed that the county did not contain a sufficiently large population to meet the constitutional requirement on that score. The court held that whether the county had a sufficient number of people to warrant the legislature in setting up this type of court in it was a question for the legislature to settle, and the court would presume that the legislature found as a fact that the county did meet the population requirements mentioned. See State v. Leonard, 22 Mo. 449 (1856); State v. York, 22 Mo. 462 (1856); Coyle v. Commonwealth, 104 Pa. 117 (1883); Kline v. State, 146 Ala. 1, 41 So. 952 (1906).

[78] Town of Decorah v. Gillis & Espy, 10 Iowa 234 (1859).

In State v. Gardner [79] an indictment was returned against a person for offering a bribe to a city commissioner. The defense was that the statute creating the city of which the commissioner was alleged to be an officer was unconstitutional. It was contended that if there was no legal organization of the city or its government there could not be an officer of the city to whom a bribe could be offered. The court held, however, that the existence of the city or its government could not be attacked in such a case. Stress was laid on the fact that the existence of the governments of numerous other cities would also be affected by a holding that the statute was unconstitutional. The court took, in this respect, quite a different view of the effect of a decision that a statute is invalid from that voiced by the New Jersey court in the Spring Lake case.[80] It is believed, nevertheless, that both these cases were properly decided. The results reached by the two courts were identical, namely, that collateral attack was denied, although it was necessary for them to utilize different theories of the effect of an unconstitutional statute in order to reach their respective decisions. This, it is submitted, is exactly what should have been done.

The same tendency to deny attack on the validity of municipal status in criminal cases is to be found in cases involving annexation of territory. A person indicted for keeping swine within the corporate limits contrary to an ordinance was denied attack on the statute authorizing the addition of the territory in which he lived.[81] The court relied on the fact that the statute was regular in form and

---

[79] 54 Ohio St. 24, 42 N. E. 999, 31 L. R. A. 660 (1896). Justice Lauck wrote a dissenting opinion, in which he expressed the view that persons accused of crime should have the same right to assail municipal existence as taxpayers, and pointed out that the latter had, in some cases, been permitted to question the status of a municipality. The question is, of course, whether the two groups of litigants should be treated the same. There may be good reasons for permitting taxpayers to challenge corporate existence in a city by injunction at an early stage in the proceedings to incorporate the city, or immediately after it has been incorporated. On the other hand, there may be good reasons for refusing to consider such attacks when made by persons accused of crime, or by taxpayers, after the city has been organized for some time. It is believed that the decision in the Gardner case is highly desirable.

[80] *Supra*, note 75.

[81] City of Topeka v. Dwyer, 70 Kan. 244, 78 Pac. 417 (1904). See the remarks of Justice Burch in this case, on the earlier case of Atchison, etc., R. R. v. Kearney County, *infra*, note 89. He said, after stating that he considers the Atchison case wrong, that "in the present state of the law it is impossible to announce a general rule for ascertaining in all cases what acts of legislation, invalid for constitutional reasons, are sufficient to afford color of law; and until the rule against collateral attack upon municipal existence can be made absolute, the most that can be said is that there must be something apparently regular in the form of the statute, and it must fairly indicate the legislative will." Cf. Godbee v. State, 141 Ga. 515, 81 S. E. 876 (1914), where it was held that a prosecutor was a de facto officer as to territory unconstitutionally annexed to his district.

that it furnished "color of law" for the acts of the city officials. Criticism of a Kansas case discharging a person committed after a preliminary hearing on a charge of murder because of the fact that a statute attaching a township in which the committing magistrate presided to a certain judicial district was unconstitutional, is forestalled by the fact that an officer of a reorganized district stood ready to take the prisoner into custody upon his release.[82]

F. Suits to Enforce Contractual Obligations against a Municipality

Municipal status is sometimes challenged in suits to restrain the issuance of bonds or the formation of contracts,[83] but more often in actions to enforce such bonds or contracts.

Most of the cases thus far considered have involved attacks by individuals; in this section many of the cases involve a denial of corporate status by the municipality itself. Will a municipality be liable for obligations contracted by it during a period when it purported to exist as a corporate organization if its existence was predicated upon an unconstitutional statute? The cases are in conflict on this point. Some of them hold that such obligations may be enforced, the municipality being either a de facto corporation or, because of the receipt of benefits, being estopped from questioning its own status. There are, however, some cases that seem to disregard both the estoppel and de facto doctrines, with the result that the obligation is not enforced against the county, township, or city.

In Marshall v. Commissioners,[84] parties having claims against a district were unable to prevent its dissolution when it was shown that the incorporation had been under an invalid act. Some cases hold that no recovery may be had for services performed for municipalities organized under invalid statutes.[85] The cases dealing with recovery for services performed under invalid statutes generally will be dealt with in a subsequent chapter.[86]

In Brandenstein v. Hoke,[87] a California case, the holder of some levee district bonds asked for a writ of mandamus to compel the

[82] In the Matter of Wood, 34 Kan. 645, 9 Pac. 758 (1886). But see Kline v. State, 146 Ala. 1, 41 So. 952 (1906).
[83] Green v. City of Rock Hill, 149 S. C. 234, 147 S. E. 346 (1929), taxpayer failed to get injunction to halt bond issue.
[84] 313 Ill. 11, 144 N. E. 321 (1924). See also Morgan Engineering Co. v. Cache River Drainage Dist., 122 Ark. 491, 184 S. W. 57 (1916).
[85] Morgan Engineering Co. v. Cache River Drainage Dist., 122 Ark. 491, 184 S. W. 57 (1916).
[86] See Chapter 9.
[87] 101 Cal. 131, 35 Pac. 562 (1894).

officers of the district to collect taxes to pay them off. The officers of the district asserted that the statute authorizing its organization was invalid and that therefore the petition should be denied. The court refused to issue the writ, explaining that the district was not a de facto municipal corporation, because there existed no law under which organization could have taken place. The court held that an unconstitutional law is the equivalent of no law. This being true, the court said, there existed no district against which the obligation could be enforced. The case seems to have gone so far as to hold that no district capable of incurring the obligation in question had ever been formed. A distinction was drawn in the opinion between a case involving an irregularity in the incorporation proceedings under a valid statute and a case involving proceedings under an unconstitutional statute. The opinion states that there could be a de facto organization in the first situation, but not in the second. The fact that the district had received the money and had paid interest on the indebtedness for several years was held insufficient to create an estoppel. The court admitted that had this been the case of a corporation committing an ultra vires act, estoppel might have been applicable, but it distinguished such a case from the instant case by pointing out that here there was no corporation to commit an ultra vires act. There being no corporation, logic inevitably compels one to say that it could not do anything that was ultra vires.[88]

Another case deserving as severe condemnation as does the Brandenstein case is Atchison, Topeka, & Santa Fe R.R. v. Kearney County.[89] The railroad company, as holder of certain township bonds, brought an action to recover upon them. The township had been created by virtue of an invalid statute and for that reason recovery was denied by the Kansas court. The court said, "There can be no such thing as a de facto municipal organization where the evidence of its nonexistence de jure is patent from the face of the law itself." [90]

Perhaps it should be stated at this point that the defect in the statute was in its title, and that only students of legislation can fully appreciate the utter confusion existing in the rules of law that deter-

---

[88] The bonds in this case were issued in 1872. The writer is indebted to the courtesy of the clerk of the supreme court of California for this information. The statute was declared unconstitutional in Moulton v. Parks, 64 Cal. 166, 30 Pac. 613 (1883). The operative dates in the case are therefore 1872, issuance of bonds; 1883, declaration of unconstitutionality; 1894, suit to recover on the bonds. Cf. Tooke, *infra*, note 111, at 950.

[89] 58 Kan. 19, 48 Pac. 583 (1897). Cf. Speer v. Board of County Commissioners, 88 Fed. 749 (C. C. A. 8th 1898). See comment on the Atchison case in City of Topeka v. Dwyer, *supra*, note 81.

[90] 58 Kan. at 26.

mine whether the title of a statute meets any one of the various state constitutional requirements. The particular illustration selected by the court of the doctrine that the unconstitutionality of the statute appeared on its face was most unfortunate, therefore. It is practically hopeless, in the vast majority of cases, to attempt any distinction on the basis of such a doctrine. Astute lawyers and judges are often much puzzled to know whether the particular statute is unconstitutional "on its face" or in any other part of its anatomy. Such language is as futile as it is figurative. It should be eliminated, along with "color of authority," from the legal vocabulary, so far as this group of cases is concerned.

The Kansas court held, in the Atchison case, that the township had no municipal existence, and that hence "it could have no officers and could contract no debts. It had no valid scrip or warrants to be funded or redeemed when it came into existence as an organized county." One can understand that the railroads in such a case were reaping what was perhaps a deserved retribution for the somewhat "sharp tactics" they had previously used to induce local governmental units to subscribe heavily toward railway building projects; but while this may be a sufficient explanation of the result of the case, it hardly serves as a justification for it. In judging the results of such decisions as the two just considered the fact must be kept in mind that recovery on the bonds or warrants in such cases is, for most practical purposes, defeated, because curative acts are not always enacted to remedy the situation.[91]

A somewhat more reasonable case is that of Wright v. Kelley,[92] wherein the Idaho court refused to permit the plaintiff to question the validity of the organization of a new county in an action brought by him to procure the issuance of a writ of mandamus to compel the former commissioners of the old county, which had been abolished, to consider his claim for services against the old county. The new county was said to have de facto existence and, since it was not a party to the proceedings, the court would not pass upon its corporate existence. The court did not, however, foreclose the petitioner from suing the new county on the ground that it had assumed the debts of the old one, if that could be shown. The case is, therefore, not wholly fatal to the claim of the petitioner. The court rested its decision in part, also, upon the ground that it believed that collateral attack should be discouraged, for otherwise a statute

[91] Cf. Parks v. Board of Commissioners of Wyandotte County, 61 Fed. 436 (C. C. Kan. 1894); First Natl. Bk. of Lansdale v. Same, 68 Fed. 878 (C. C. A. 8th 1895). For comment on these cases see p. 92.
[92] 4 Idaho 624, 43 Pac. 565 (1895).

would be assailed every time that a new reason had been thought of for so doing, and "the decision in none of the cases would be authoritative to destroy the de facto existence and organization of the county" because the state and county would not be parties to the actions.

As previously indicated, courts have often enforced against municipal corporations the obligations incurred by them in the course of performing the various functions allotted to them by the state or demanded of them by the local community. A variety of reasons have been given by the courts to sustain their decisions that incorporation under an invalid statute cannot be assailed by the creditor or by the defendant municipal corporation. Among them are these: that the statutes in question have been free from any defect on "their face" (as objectionable here as in the cases previously considered); that there was nothing in the statute to put persons on inquiry; that the transaction was entered into in good faith; that confusion would attend a policy permitting collateral attack to be made; that the corporation enjoyed de facto existence; that there was a presumption in favor of the validity of the statute; that the statute, though invalid, was sufficient to give authority or color of authority for incorporation; that the state government has recognized the municipality in numerous ways.[93]

A case illustrating a variation from the normal situation in the enforcement of municipal obligations is that of Oswego Township

[93] School District v. Kansas, 29 Kan. 57 (1882); Riley v. Garfield Twp., 54 Kan. 471, 38 Pac. 560 (1894); Ashley v. Board of Supervisors, 60 Fed. 55 (C. C. A. 8th 1894); Riley v. Garfield Twp., 58 Kan. 299, 49 Pac. 85 (1897); Speer v. Board of County Commissioners, *supra*, note 89. In State ex rel. Harvey v. Philbrick, 49 N. J. L. 374, 8 Atl. 122 (1887), the court issued a writ of mandamus to compel the treasurer of a municipality to pay the warrant held by the petitioner, although the treasurer defended on the ground that the incorporation statute was invalid. The court said, "It matters not whether the act authorizing the formation of borough governments be constitutional, or whether the government of the borough . . . be properly organized under the act. The commissioners and treasurer were de facto officers." Abernethy v. Town of Medical Lake, 9 Wash. 112, 37 Pac. 309 (1894), went off on the ground that the creditor sought the wrong remedy. See Young v. City of Colorado, 174 S. W. 986 (Tex. Civ. App. 1915); Burt v. Winona & St. Peter R. R., 31 Minn. 472, 18 N. W. 285, 289 (1884). The following statement appears in Young v. City of Colorado, *supra:* "We did not interpret the same as a claim that the bonds were invalid as against the city which issued them and which received the benefit of the money paid to the city therefor, especially in view of the familiar rule that a de facto municipal corporation cannot urge the invalidity of its incorporation as a defense in a suit to collect a debt which it has contracted." 174 S. W. at 997. In Bow v. Allentown, 34 N. H. 351 (1857), assumpsit was brought against the town for support of a pauper. The defense was defective incorporation. The court held that this defense was not made out by showing that no charter could be found. An exercise of corporate powers for twenty years raises a presumption that the charter was lost, said the court. See State v. Henry, 28 Wash. 38, 68 Pac. 368 (1902).

v. Anderson.[94] In that case the city claimed to be a de facto municipal corporation, instead of denying it, in order to escape liability.
The people of a village organized out of a portion of a township by
virtue of an invalid statute sought to enjoin the collection of taxes,
the proceeds of which were to be used to pay off township bonds.
The bonds had been issued after the purported incorporation had
taken place. The court held that the village was not de facto but
that it must bear its proportion of the debt burden in question. The
fact that the citizens of the village had participated in township
affairs subsequently to the organization of the village could not help
but influence the court in reaching its decision. This excellent statement of the test to be applied in such cases was made by the court
in the course of its opinion:

> It is true that a corporation organized under an invalid statute is
> sometimes held to be a corporation de facto, in order that justice may
> be done to innocent parties; but to sustain the claim of the defendant
> in error, that a de facto organization and separation from the town-
> ship has been perfected, would work a legal injustice.[95]

A municipal corporation may not escape obligations incurred by
it by pleading that it disincorporated subsequent to the date when
the obligation was incurred, if the disincorporation proceedings were
had under an unconstitutional statute.[96] It has also been held that a
validating act will be ineffective to remedy the defect in these proceedings.[97]

Two cases in which the validity of municipal incorporation was
incidentally challenged remain to be considered. The first of them
is City of Albuquerque v. Water Works Company.[98] The city of
Albuquerque brought an action to compel the defendant company
to carry out a contract whereby the company had agreed to sell its
plant to the city, taking in return a specified amount in city bonds.
The company had refused to complete the transaction, and it set up
as a defense that the bonds were void and that the city itself had no
legal existence. It was contended that as a result the city was not
capable of carrying out its part of the contract. The court decided in
favor of the city, refusing to pass upon the constitutionality of the
legal basis of the city and its government. The decision was placed
on the ground that the city and its official representatives enjoyed

[94] Oswego Twp. v. Anderson, 44 Kan. 214, 24 Pac. 486 (1890). Cf. Brown v.
Millikan, 42 Kan. 769, 23 Pac. 167 (1869).
[95] Oswego Twp. v. Anderson, *supra*, note 94, at 226.
[96] Ringling v. Hempstead, 193 Fed. 596 (C. C. A. 5th 1911). See State ex rel.
Haley v. Stark, *supra*, note 24.
[97] Ringling v. Hempstead, *supra*, note 96.
[98] 24 N. M. 368, 174 Pac. 217 (1918).

de facto standing even though the statute should be considered invalid. Many of the cases involving the problem of the status of public corporations organized under constitutional statutes were reviewed in the course of the opinion, and the conclusion was stated that the constitutionality of a statute involved in such a case cannot be raised except by direct attack on the part of the state. The question could not be raised in a collateral way in the manner sought to be used here. The court stressed, also, the confusion that would attend any other course.

In such a case as this the water company would seem to be fairly well protected in accepting the bonds, in view of the weight of authority sustaining the rule that municipalities will not be permitted to deny their own corporate existence in suits to enforce obligations against them. There is, of course, some uncertainty in the matter because of the disposition of some courts to permit the municipality to escape payment of obligations incurred by it. The company would probably in any event be put to expensive litigation in collection on the bonds, should the city refuse payment because of its alleged corporate nonexistence. The particular facts of the case are not set forth in sufficient detail in the report of it to reveal the attitude of the city and company officials toward one another. Bad feeling might easily have resulted in costly litigation for the company even though it could in the end have recovered the face value of the bonds tendered to it by the city in payment for its plant. On the other hand, there may have been bad faith on the part of the company. Such facts do not appear in the official record of the case. But if they were known to the court, the decision would perhaps have been influenced somewhat by them. The case illustrates very well the various factors that may cause a court to utilize the de facto doctrine to restrain the defendant from questioning the adequacy of the legal basis of the municipal organization.

The second of the two cases referred to is that of Dunn v. Ft. Bend County.[99] Bonds were issued to the plaintiff by a road district organized under a statute that was declared to be unconstitutional by the Supreme Court of the United States.[100] Subsequent to this decision the plaintiff asked for an injunction to prevent the expenditure of any money remaining unexpended in the treasury of the road district. The injunction was denied on the ground that the petitioner had an adequate remedy at law, the district being valid under the state statutes and constitution. A state statute had remedied whatever defects in organization had been found. The decision

[99] 17 F. (2d) 329 (D. C. Tex. 1926).
[100] Browning v. Hooper, 269 U. S. 396, 46 Sup. Ct. 141, 70 L. Ed. 330 (1926).

is therefore not in conflict with the majority rule that municipal obligations may not be escaped by showing that incorporation took place under an invalid law.

The most significant phase of the case, however, is that dealing with the question of the effect of an unconstitutional statute. The case in which the Supreme Court of the United States had held invalid the statute in accordance with which this district had been organized did not involve this particular district. The federal district court for Texas said, in its opinion denying the petition for the injunction, that the right to invoke the protection of the fourteenth amendment is a personal right,

and the condemnation of a statute in a particular case as repugnant to that amendment as to plaintiff in it does not, and cannot, affect or impair the statute itself as a valid and existing law, or corporations created under it as valid and existing corporations under the laws of the state of their creation, except as to the particular person complaining, and as to the particular thing he complains of; that the district and the bonds are valid as to these plaintiffs and this suit; that plaintiff and interveners have an adequate remedy at law against a validly created and existing district.[101]

The court also pointed out that there were in this case no parties who could question the existence of the district so far as the fourteenth amendment was concerned.

The Ft. Bend case expresses a view of the effect of a decision that a statute is unconstitutional similar to that expressed in the Spring Lake case by the New Jersey court. But the Ft. Bend case suggests an additional problem, or a new view, perhaps, with respect to the effect of decisions declaring state statutes to be contrary to the constitution of the United States upon the status of the corporations formed under such statutes, when the latter are valid under the state constitution. Whether the view expressed in the Ft. Bend case will be restricted to cases under the fourteenth amendment or not is difficult to say, although the language of the opinion indicates that the decision turned primarily on the fact that the protection of that amendment is peculiar to the persons involved in the particular case.

The courts have then, with only a few exceptions, refused to permit municipal status to be called into question by private individuals or by the municipality itself, if by so doing they are enabled to reach equitable results. On the other hand, if the justice of the case demands that municipal status be inquired into, the courts tend

[101] Dunn v. Ft. Bend County, *supra*, note 99, at 332.

to disregard the de facto doctrine. Whichever view will, in the particular case, result in the imposition of liability where in justice it belongs will generally be adopted by the court. This is as it should be. A few decisions only, and they are of the last century, disregard the equities of the case and decide it on the basis of the theory that an unconstitutional statute is not law and is to be given no effect as an operative fact in the situation.

The rules on the enforceability of contracts entered into in reliance upon decisions upholding the validity of statutes authorizing bond issues will be considered in a later chapter.[102]

G. Tort Cases

In Cole v. President and Trustees of Village of Black River Falls [103] the Wisconsin court had before it a case in which plaintiff sued the village to recover for an injury alleged to have been suffered because of a defective sidewalk. The village defended on the ground that there was no such corporation as the President and Trustees of the village. They also answered that the village existed by virtue of an unconstitutional statute. The court held, however, that the village could not deny its own existence in this way and said that in any event legal existence could be predicated on another valid statute, although incorporation under it had not been attempted.

Alderman v. School Directors [104] deals with another phase of this problem. There the directors of a school district organized under a constitutional statute but did so in an irregular manner. They brought an action of trespass against defendant for breaking into the school building. The plea of nul tiel corporation was entered. The court held that the district was entitled to maintain the action through its representatives, the school directors, and said that it existed de facto although it had been organized in an irregular manner. While this case is not a direct authority on a problem involving an unconstitutional statute, it is nevertheless analogous. From these two cases one might perhaps expect the courts to refuse

---

[102] Such bonds held valid, although the court changed its mind on validity of statute in Riley v. Township of Garfield, 58 Kan. 299, 49 Pac. 85 (1897).

[103] 57 Wis. 110, 44 N.W. 906 (1883).

[104] 91 Ill. 179 (1878). Cf. People ex rel. Brown v. Blake, 49 Barb. 9 (N.Y. 1867). In City of Guthrie v. Wylie, 6 Okla. 61, 55 Pac. 103 (1896), the city was organized in 1889 when no law authorizing its incorporation was in existence. Plaintiff deposited a check with the city, as an assurance, for the privilege of running a street railway. The check was declared forfeited by the city. Now suit was brought against the city, which had later been organized under an incorporation statute which had been enacted by the legislature. The court held that the city was not liable for the torts or contracts of the prior city, it never having been a corporation.

to permit either the municipality or the private individual in a tort case to question the validity of municipal incorporation.

V. INCIDENTAL ATTACK IN SUITS BETWEEN PRIVATE PARTIES

Municipal status is sometimes incidentally involved in disputes over tax titles and the redemption of property sold at tax sale. The courts are usually slow to permit litigants in such cases to litigate the question of the existence of a municipal corporation.[105] Such decisions seem correct, and they are in accord with the view elsewhere suggested that the existence of a public corporation should not be litigated in an action to which it is not a party.

Attacks on the status of a judicial officer sometimes turn on the question whether the judicial district in which he is presiding has been created by a constitutional statute. Inasmuch as these districts are sometimes counties, townships, or cities, the validity of their incorporation may thus become of importance. The courts are in conflict as to the proper view to be taken on this question.[106] It may well be that the case would be decided differently should it arise at the present time before the highest court of the state in which it was first decided so long ago. It is to be remembered, in mitigation of any criticism of the authority permitting attack to be made in such cases, that the social consequence of permitting the attack in this type of case is not nearly so serious as in criminal cases.

VI. CONCLUSION

The general doctrinal setting of the problems arising out of incorporation under an unconstitutional statute has been considered elsewhere.[107] It need not be analyzed again. It need only be pointed

[105] Ritchie v. Mulvane, 39 Kan. 241, 17 Pac. 830 (1898). This case seems to hold that city taxes paid by the winning party in an ejectment suit growing out of a tax title claim may not be recovered, under a statute providing that if the holder of the tax deed loses the suit he should be reimbursed by the winner, to the amount of the taxes paid. The claim urged here was that the city taxes had been paid when they need not have been paid, because the territory in which the property was situated had been unconstitutionally annexed to the city. See, however, apparently to the contrary, Back v. Carpenter, 29 Kan. 349 (1883). Also the dictum in Meyer v. Sommerville Water Company, 82 N. J. Eq. 576, 579, 89 Atl. 21 (1912). In State Bank of Pender v. Frey, 3 Neb. Unoff. 83, 91 N. W. 239 (1902), in a private suit over a conveyance, it was held that a deed recorded with an officer exercising his powers over territory annexed to a county by virtue of an unconstitutional statute constituted notice, because the officer was de facto as to the annexed territory.

[106] Bellevue Water Co. v. Stockslager, 4 Idaho 636, 43 Pac. 568 (1895), holding that collateral attack would not be permitted. Contra, Lanning v. Carpenter, 20 N. Y. 447 (1859).

[107] See pp. 37–44.

out, perhaps, that there is much less place in municipal corporation cases than in private corporation cases for the strict view that in order to enjoy corporate privileges there must be a valid statute authorizing organization. Municipal corporations are primarily agencies for the performance of certain functions for the people in the community. They are corporate in their form of organization for the sake of convenience.[108] A plausible argument might be advanced that corporate privileges should not be lightly granted to private individuals and that they should be made to bear a portion of the burden of checking the legislature in granting such privileges in an unconstitutional statute. However that may be with respect to private corporations, the case would seem quite clear for upholding the corporateness of an organization purporting to be a governmental unit, and the cases evidence a strong tendency to deny attack by private parties upon municipal existence in all but very exceptional circumstances.

It may be of interest to consider at this point the steps that may be taken to remedy conditions resulting from an attack by the state or, in some instances, by private parties, on the legality of municipal incorporation.[109] In those states where courts adhere to the doctrine that an unconstitutional statute cannot be cured by a subsequent law purporting to remove the defect of the earlier act, new statutory authority for incorporation may be provided by the legislature.[110] It may be, however, that the legislature will not meet for several months, or even years, and something must be done in the meantime. Unless the earlier statute authorizing incorporation has been repealed by a valid statute, or unless the court should hold that the repealing section of an unconstitutional statute had the effect of repealing the previous incorporation law, incorporation might be

---

[108] That a municipal corporation is a separate legal entity seems to be the view of the leading commentators. See discussions referred to *supra,* note 1.

[109] See, for the history of the situation which existed in the state of Washington for some years, the following cases: Territory of Washington v. Stewart, 1 Wash. 98, 23 Pac. 405 (1890); In the Matter of Campbell, 1 Wash. 287, 24 Pac. 624 (1890); Town of Medical Lake v. Smith, 7 Wash. 195, 34 Pac. 835 (1893); Town of Denver v. City of Spokane Falls, 7 Wash. 226, 34 Pac. 926 (1893); Town of Medical Lake v. Landis, 7 Wash. 615, 34 Pac. 836 (1893); City of Pullman v. Hungate, 8 Wash. 519, 36 Pac. 483 (1894); Abernethy v. Town of Medical Lake, 9 Wash. 112, 37 Pac. 309 (1894); State of Washington v. Berry, 13 Wash. 708, 42 Pac. 622 (1896).

[110] That the later law did not validate, see Judd v. State of Texas, *supra,* note 4. See also, for cases to the same effect, Field, The Effect of an Unconstitutional Statute, 1 Ind. L. J. 1 (1926), 60 Am. L. Rev. 232 (1926), 100 Cent. L. J. 145 (1927), under subd. no. 4 of the text. See subd. no. 6, under II, of Summary in the same article. That it did validate, see State ex rel. Oblinger v. Spaude, *supra,* note 25; People v. Madison, 280 Ill. 96, 117 N. E. 493 (1917). See Chapter 11.

had under the earlier statutes, if there be any such on the books. In the event that there is no statutory authority for corporate organization the governmental unit would seem to be in a difficult situation. Some courts would doubtless exercise their discretion in issuing an order of ouster in such a case and would postpone judgment until the legislature had had an opportunity to make provision for remedying matters. This, as has been indicated earlier in this study, was what the court of Ohio did; it postponed the judgment until steps could be taken to provide for adequate municipal organization. In this connection it should be pointed out that it is only in quo warranto proceedings that a municipality can be legally ousted from its corporate powers.

But even though from a legal point of view a municipality is not ousted from the exercise of its powers in a case involving collateral attack, the practical effect of permitting such attack may in many instances be quite as serious as in the case of a judgment of ouster in quo warranto. Confusion will usually result from a policy of permitting attack, not because the city would cease to exist as a legal organization but because it would be seriously hindered in the performance of its functions if taxpayers could continually challenge its existence; if persons accused of crime could question the validity of municipal incorporation; and if persons who have entered into contractual obligations with the city could escape them on the ground that the city had not been legally organized. The propriety of the rule prohibiting the city from denying its own corporate existence and the wisdom of the rule that private parties may not assail the corporate existence of a municipality must be tested not only by the justice and equity of each case as between the immediate parties but also by such factors as the need for uninterrupted performance of governmental functions in local areas.

There may be in existence valid statutes under which defectively incorporated municipalities may be reincorporated. If such statutes exist the courts may be more ready to treat the municipality as a de facto corporation, thus enabling the city to continue its work unchallenged by private individuals until steps can be taken to incorporate under the valid statutes. It has been suggested that the existence of such a statute, or the existence of some constitutional provision recognizing in a general way the possibility of municipal incorporation, will always cause the courts to apply the de facto doctrine in municipal corporation cases.[111] Many of the cases can be

[111] Tooke, De Facto Municipal Corporations under Unconstitutional Statutes, 37 Yale L. J. 935 (1928). The doctrine utilized by Professor Tooke to explain the municipal corporation cases is seldom mentioned in the opinions of the courts in

explained upon this ground. There are a few, however, which cannot be squared with such a theory.[112] The existence of valid incorporation statutes is doubtless an important factor in these cases, but it is only one of several influencing the courts.

It has been held that the legislature may not grant corporate status to a municipality organized under an invalid statute by enacting that the municipality shall be deemed validly incorporated. Legislation recognizing organized communities as such will, however, be sustained, even though it declares such organization to be a corporation by virtue of the recognizing statute. Such a statute is said not to attempt to recognize a previous attempt to incorporate but only to recognize an existing state of affairs, namely, a group of people conducting themselves in a certain manner, the manner being that of an organized municipal corporation lacking only legal sanction. This is a very technical way of circumventing an equally technical doctrine.[113]

It is clear, then, that in the municipal corporation cases many courts refuse to apply the void ab initio doctrine to its full extent. They tend to accord some effect to an unconstitutional statute and to action taken in accordance with it. It is not entirely disregarded. A few courts adhere closely to the logical implications of this doctrine; but they are not numerous. With few exceptions the strict void ab initio view is applied in this group of cases only when it is necessary to do so in order to reach a just decision. To its application in such a case no objection can be made. It is to be hoped, and probably with some prospect of the hope being fulfilled, that collateral attack will be reserved for the very unusual case, when it seems necessary to accomplish justice not only in a particular case but in a class of cases.

private corporation cases. The doctrine has often been mentioned in the municipal corporation cases and also in the de facto officer cases, and it does serve to explain a number of apparently conflicting decisions in municipal corporations. It fails, however, to reconcile all of the decisions, and Professor Tooke seems to recognize this in his article. See Holmes v. City of Fayetteville, 197 N. C. 740, 150 S. E. 624 (1930), sustaining city electric service outside city under invalid law because a valid statute permitted it.

[112] For example, Brandenstein v. Hoke, *supra*, note 87, and comment in note 88. Cf. Tooke, *supra*, note 111, at 950. Professor Tooke seems to have overlooked the date of the bond issue involved in this case.

[113] City of Pullman v. Hungate, *supra*, note 109. See Mortland v. Christian, 52 N. J. L. (23 Vrooman) 521, 20 Atl. 673 (1890), assuming later statute might refer to districts for another purpose although they were invalidly organized.

Chapter IV

THE EFFECT OF AN UNCONSTITUTIONAL STATUTE IN THE LAW OF PUBLIC OFFICERS: THE EFFECT ON OFFICIAL STATUS *

The effect of an unconstitutional statute becomes of importance at two points in the law of public officers: (1) in connection with official status, involving the doctrines concerning de facto officers and (2) in connection with the liability of officers for action or non-action under an invalid statute. The first of these points of contact between the two fields will be the subject of this chapter.[1]

Three situations may arise with respect to the invalidity of a statute in the law of public officers. First, the statute *creating an office* may be defective. Second, the statute creating the office may be valid, but the law providing for *filling* it may be unconstitutional. Third, the statute creating, as well as that providing for the filling of an office, may be valid, *but the statute authorizing the officer to perform some particular function* may be invalid. The first and second of these situations will be considered in the treatment of official status.

I. ATTACK BY PERSONS IN AN OFFICIAL CAPACITY

A. QUO WARRANTO BY THE ATTORNEY-GENERAL OR SOME OFFICIAL REPRESENTATIVE OF THE STATE

The rule is well settled that the attorney-general may file an information in the nature of quo warranto and thus institute proceedings to test the constitutionality of the statute under which an incumbent claims to hold an office. Thus it has been held that an officer appointed by the governor when he should have been elected by the people, the statute having prescribed the former mode of filling the office, may be ejected from office by a judgment of ouster in quo warranto proceedings.[2] This is true whether the statute creating the office is unconstitutional [3] or whether the statute provid-

---

* This chapter originally appeared in 13 Minn. L. Rev. 439 (1929).
[1] The second of these problems is the subject of Chapter 5.
[2] People v. Raymond, 37 N. Y. 428 (1868).
[3] People ex rel. Bolt v. Riordan, 73 Mich. 508, 41 N. W. 482 (1889); People ex rel. Longnecker v. Nelson, 133 Ill. 565, 27 N. E. 217 (1890), quo warranto by attorney for the state, statute held constitutional.

ing the method of filling the office is invalid.[4] An officer not possessed of the constitutional qualifications for an office may be ousted by quo warranto proceedings even if no person is waiting ready to take over the duties of the office at the time.[5]

Quo warranto will lie against an officer on the ground that the statute creating the office is unconstitutional even though the existence of a municipality is involved in the same proceeding.[6] This also applies to a case involving annexation of territory to a municipality by virtue of an invalid statute, the judgment in such a case being that the officer be ousted from office or that the city be ousted from exercising any governmental power over the territory unconstitutionally annexed.[7]

Where the existence of a municipality is questioned, the court is likely to be slower to declare the statute unconstitutional than if the existence of the office, or the validity of the method of filling the office, alone is at stake. The tendency of the courts to preserve the legal status of governmental units is well illustrated by the case of State ex rel. Strimple v. McBride,[8] in which one of the circuit courts of Ohio held that the state was barred from assailing the existence of a municipality by proceedings instituted by a prosecuting attorney on behalf of the state, because the statute of limitations had run against the action. The statute contained no reference to the state but was a typical statute preventing attack on the corporate existence of the municipality after the lapse of a specified number of years. The court interpreted the statute to be as effective against attack by the state through quo warranto as against attack by an individual.

The proceedings by the state must, however, be directed against the officer whose title to the office is in question, and the attorney-general will not be permitted, under the guise of quo warranto against officer X, to test the title of officer Y, even though Y appointed X to the office and Y is alleged to hold office by virtue of an invalid statute.[9]

The officer whose title is being assailed will be permitted to per-

[4] State ex rel. Loucks v. Bradshaw, 56 N. J. L. 1, 27 Atl. 939 (1893).

[5] State ex rel. Attorney General v. Gleason, 12 Fla. 190 (1868), ouster against lieutenant governor; State ex rel. Attorney General v. Porter, 1 Ala. 388 (1840), disqualification case, but incumbent resigned before judgment of ouster could be given, so withheld.

[6] State ex rel. O'Sullivan v. Coffey, 59 Mo. 59 (1875). See the preceding chapter for additional illustrations of this topic, as well as that involved in the cases in note 7.

[7] Attorney General v. Crane, 60 Mich. 373 (1886); State ex rel. Attorney General v. Cincinnati, 20 Ohio St. 18 (1870); same v. Cincinnati, 52 Ohio St. 419, 40 N. E. 508 (1895).

[8] 7 Ohio Cir. Dec. 522 (1897).

[9] Attorney General ex rel. Fuller v. Parsell, 99 Mich. 381, 58 N. W. 335 (1894).

form the functions of the office pending the outcome of the proceedings, and the court will refuse to grant an injunction forbidding him to perform his official functions, on the theory that his acts will nevertheless be valid as to third persons, and also on the ground that quo warranto is intended not to paralyze the business of government but to oust persons from offices to which they are not legally entitled.[10]

The fact that nobody stands ready to carry on the functions of an office is, as previously indicated, not a sufficient reason for declining to give a judgment of ouster. The court may, however, in such a case delay the execution of the judgment in order that provision may be made for carrying on the work connected with a particular office or group of offices. An Ohio case illustrates the discretion possessed by courts in this matter; the court there granted a stay of three months so that the executive and legislative authorities might provide for the government of cities of the class of Cleveland, the ouster in the case being against the members of what was virtually the governing board of the city.[11]

The de facto doctrine has no application to cases in which an official representative of the state challenges title to an office on the ground of unconstitutionality, that doctrine being reserved for cases in which title is challenged by private parties acting in their own behalf or, in some cases, acting as voluntary representatives of the state in asking a court to permit the filing of an information of quo warranto in the name of the state. The state may always assail the validity of a statute creating an office or providing the method whereby incumbents are to be placed therein, subject only to such restrictions as the state may have imposed upon itself by means of statutes of limitations. The state has an interest in ousting from office all persons claiming title thereto if such claims are not founded on valid statutes.

B. Contests between Rival Claimants to an Office

It not infrequently happens that two or more persons claim title to the same office. In such a case the party not in possession of the office may proceed (1) by asking the court for permission to file an information in the nature of quo warranto in the name of the state, seeking thereby to oust the present incumbent of the office, or (2) by asking the court to issue a writ of mandamus commanding the incumbent to deliver to the petitioner the books, papers, and pos-

[10] People ex rel. Wood v. Draper, 24 Barb. 265 (N.Y. 1857).
[11] State ex rel. Attorney General v. Beacom, 66 Ohio St. 457, 64 N.E. 427 (1902).

session of the office. If, on the other hand, the incumbent wishes to take the initiative he may ask that an injunction be issued forbidding the rival claimant from taking any steps to obtain the office. The use of mandamus and injunction to try title to office is in many states narrowly restricted, but in some states they are available to test title when an unconstitutional statute is involved.

1) Information in the nature of quo warranto. — Permission has been granted in a number of cases to file an information in the nature of quo warranto in order that the conflicting claims of persons asserting a right to hold an office may be determined. If, in such a case, the statute creating the office the defendant holds is unconstitutional, a judgment of ouster will be granted.[12] The same result will follow if the statute providing the method for filling the office is invalid.[13] Where two persons claim to be the rightful holders of a judgeship, the two claiming office under different statutes, an information in the nature of quo warranto by one of the claimants is a proper method whereby to test the validity of the statute under which defendant asserts title.[14] One Ohio case takes a contrary position, holding that an official representative of the state alone can try title in quo warranto proceedings.[15]

In McCall v. Webb [16] the defendant was permitted to deny the legality of his own office on the ground that if the statute creating the office was invalid, plaintiff could not ask that defendant be ousted from it, nor could he demand possession of a nonexistent office.

A type of case not strictly within the scope of this section but sufficiently analogous to warrant consideration at this point is that in which one officer attempts to obtain the ouster of the holder of another office. For example, in Hinze v. People ex rel. Halbert,[17] the mayor of a city filed a petition seeking the removal from office of a police commissioner because of the alleged unconstitutionality of the statute creating the office. A judgment of ouster was rendered. State v. Butler [18] presented a somewhat similar situation. In that case a county attorney filed an information to test the warrant whereby a special prosecutor for liquor cases held office. The statute creating

[12] Commonwealth ex rel. Hite v. Swank, 79 Pa. St. 154 (1875); State ex rel. Reemelin v. Smith, 48 Ohio St. 211, 26 N. E. 1069 (1891); Dullam v. Wilson, 53 Mich. 392, 19 N. W. 112 (1884).
[13] Longshore v. State ex rel. Kroell, 200 Ala. 267, 76 So. 33 (1917); State ex rel. Richards v. Hammer, 42 N. J. L. 435 (1880); State ex rel. Smallwood v. Windom, 131 Minn. 401, 155 N. W. 629 (1915).
[14] People ex rel. Ballou v. Bangs, 24 Ill. 184 (1860).
[15] State ex rel. Heer v. Butterfield, 92 Ohio St. 428, 111 N. E. 279 (1915).
[16] 125 N. C. 243, 34 S. E. 430 (1899).
[17] 92 Ill. 406 (1879).
[18] 105 Me. 91, 73 Atl. 500 (1909).

the office of special prosecutor was declared invalid and ouster granted. In both these cases the controversy partook of the nature of a private dispute between officials. In neither of them did the relator act as the official representative of the state in the same manner as the attorney-general does in quo warranto cases. The form of the action was that of quo warranto, but the moving force in the entire proceeding was the resentment of one official against attempts to encroach upon the functions of his office by the creation of a new office.

Sometimes disputes arise between persons admittedly the rightful holders of their respective offices as to the functions to be performed by each of them. If a statute conferring the power to perform certain functions on one of the officers is unconstitutional, he may, at the relation of the holder of another office claiming the power to perform the functions in question, be ousted in quo warranto proceedings from the exercise of the particular duties over which there is dispute.[19] The controversy in such a case is not over title to office but as to what officer shall perform a particular function.

It is clear from the foregoing cases that the courts are quite ready to permit the use of quo warranto by one of two persons claiming title to an office or asserting that the defendant is performing functions that rightfully appertain to the petitioner's office.

2) Mandamus. — Incumbents of existing offices are sometimes unwilling to surrender the books and papers of the office to their successors or to persons asserting that they hold an office that supersedes the one in which the former is situated. In such a case mandamus may be invoked to compel the surrender of the books in dispute. If the defendant succeeds in his attack on the validity of the statute creating the office to which the petitioner lays claim, or if the statute changing the method of selecting incumbents to the office is invalid, the petition will be denied. "If the law under which he claims is unconstitutional, he has no standing." [20] In Matter of Brenner [21] it was held that the old officer could defend against a suit to obtain the books and papers of the office by showing that the certificate of the claimant had been granted in accordance with an invalid statute. The court said in this case that the petitioner must, in order to succeed in such a suit, show a good title to the office.

[19] People ex rel. Ryerson v. Kelsey, 34 Cal. 470 (1868).
[20] Fillimore v. Van Horn, 129 Mich. 56, 88 N. W. 69 (1901); State ex rel. Kinsley v. Jones, 66 Ohio St. 453, 64 N. E. 424 (1902).
[21] 170 N. Y. 185, 63 N. E. 133 (1902). In Davidson v. Hine, 151 Mich. 294, 115 N. W. 246 (1908), mandamus was denied in a petition to compel defendants to turn over the fire and police records to the petitioner, the latter claiming to be members of a bureau of public safety. The statute creating the bureau was declared invalid.

This rule, that plaintiff in a suit to obtain possession of an office must, in order to succeed, show a good title to it, is well established. It is not sufficient that defendant's title is defective. In passing upon the claim to an office the court may consider the validity of acts performed by officers other than those directly involved in the suit. To illustrate, in Pratt v. Breckenridge [22] the plaintiff offered as evidence of his title a certificate of election issued by a board of election commissioners. The defendant assailed the validity of the statute creating the board, and the court sustained his position. The board having been created by an invalid law, it followed that the certificate issued to plaintiff did not constitute prima facie evidence of title. Therefore plaintiff failed to establish his case and defendant was left in possession of the office, although in this case he held it by virtue of a prior decision of this same board, the board having later reversed its decision in a contested election and given to the plaintiff the certificate of election. This indirect method of assailing the validity of the statute creating the board is at variance with the rule forbidding such attack in quo warranto cases. [23]

The case of People ex rel. Stuckhart v. Knopf [24] presented the question whether the old assessor could defend against a petition for a mandamus compelling him to surrender books and papers to a person claiming to be a newly elected assessor by showing that he had already delivered the books to another person, believed by him to be the rightful holder of the new office which was thought to have superseded that of assessor. The petition was denied because the statute creating the new office was sustained. What the result would have been had the law been held invalid is difficult to tell.

[22] 112 Ky. 1, 65 S. W. 136 (1901). On contesting an election, see Adsit v. Osmun, 84 Mich. 420, 48 N. W. 31 (1891), mandamus to compel counting of votes, petitioner claiming to have been elected.

[23] See State ex rel. Herron v. Smith, 44 Ohio St. 348, 7 N. E. 447, 12 N. E. 829 (1886), where relator, claiming membership on a board superseded by a newly created office, sought in quo warranto to oust members of the new board because some of the members of the state senate voting for the statute creating the new board were not de jure members of the senate. The court held that the members in question were at least de facto senators, and therefore refused to grant ouster. See also *supra*, note 8. On the status of members of the state legislature, see the discussion in Parker v. State ex rel. Powell, 133 Ind. 178, 32 N. E. 836 (1892), and Sherrill v. O'Brien, 188 N. Y. 185, 81 N. E. 124 (1907). In the case last cited the court said, concerning the effect of an unconstitutional statute: "An act of the legislature, if invalid, as violating the constitution, is invalid from the time of its enactment, not merely from the declaration of its character by the courts. But though the appointment or election of a public officer may be illegal, it is elementary law that his official acts while he is an actual incumbent of the office are valid and binding on the public and on third parties." 188 N. Y. at 212. The court said that admission by one of the houses of the legislature constituted a member a de jure member, because the houses of the legislature were judges of their own elections.

[24] 183 Ill. 410, 56 N. E. 155 (1900).

The constitutionality of a statute conferring upon the governor the power to fill an office by appointment may be challenged by the person entrusted with the function of approving the official bond of the appointee.[25] In such a case the petition for mandamus to compel the approval will be denied if the statute is declared unconstitutional. This type of case does not involve a dispute between rivals for an office, but it illustrates that an officer may justify the refusal to perform an act upon the ground that it is thrust upon him by an invalid statute,[26] and also that title to office may be challenged by officers made defendants in mandamus proceedings seeking to compel recognition by them of the petitioner's title.

The courts of some states will not interfere by mandamus in disputes between subordinates and superior officers in which subordinates challenge the validity of acts performed by superiors on the ground that authority to perform them is derived from an invalid statute. The much-cited case of Lang v. The Mayor of Bayonne [27] involved this point. In that case a police officer had been removed from the city police force by a newly created board of police commissioners. The policeman petitioned for a writ of mandamus to compel his restoration to the force by the mayor, alleging in his petition that inasmuch as the statute creating the office of police commissioner was unconstitutional, the control of the force was, as it had been prior to the pretended enactment of the statute in question, still in the hands of the mayor. The petition was denied on the ground that the commissioners were de facto officers and that as to the public, including petitioner, their acts were binding. A similar decision is that of Carland v. Commissioners of Custer County,[28] in which collateral attack was denied an officer who had been removed by the board of commissioners, the claim being, upon the part of the appellant, that the statute creating and filling the office of commissioner was unconstitutional.

3) *Injunction.* — Injunction may be resorted to by the present holder of an office to prevent persons elected to a new office established by an unconstitutional statute from assuming the functions of the new office.[29] In the majority of cases, however, the initiative is

[25] State ex rel. Geake v. Fox, 158 Ind. 126, 56 N. E. 893 (1901).

[26] This is not the rule when property rights are affected by the refusal of an officer to take action enjoined upon him unless the statute turns out to be invalid when brought to a test. See for a consideration of this problem Chapter 5.

[27] 74 N. J. L. 455, 68 Atl. 90, 15 L. R. A. (N. S.) 93 (1906). Cf. Commonwealth v. McCombs, 56 Pa. St. 436 (1867), dispute between district attorney and his assistant.

[28] 5 Mont. 579, 6 Pac. 24 (1885). See State ex rel. Sipp v. Stroble, 25 Ohio Cir. Ct. 762 (1904).

[29] Malone v. Williams, 118 Tenn. 390, 103 S. W. 798 (1907).

taken by the new officer by means of quo warranto or mandamus, and in only a few cases has the old officer sought equitable relief against threatened intrusion into office or against the establishment of a new office threatening to supersede an old one.[30]

In summary of the cases reviewed in this section, it may be said that the courts are quite lenient in permitting the constitutionality of statutes purporting to create an office, or to provide a method of filling it, to be raised in contests between rival claimants or between the holders of two different offices. This leniency does not extend to cases in which inferior officers attempt to dispute the constitutional basis of their superiors' position.

With the exception of this last group of cases the courts do not apply the de facto doctrine in these contests. There are dicta to be found in many of the cases reviewed in this section that state that the acts of officers selected in accordance with an unconstitutional statute are valid as to the public. Attack being permitted under the circumstances presented in these cases, such statements are unnecessary, and they are for that reason to be regarded as dicta and nothing more. Some of them are in accord with the decision of the Lang case, holding that there may be a de facto officer even though the office he purports to hold is created by an unconstitutional statute.

II. ATTACK BY PERSONS ACTING IN AN INDIVIDUAL CAPACITY

Thus far cases have been considered in which officers acting on behalf of the state or acting in their official capacity to protect their own office or persons claiming to be rightful holders of an office have challenged by quo warranto, mandamus, or injunction the constitutional basis of some other officer or office. The next problem to be considered is: In what cases may a private citizen acting in his own behalf, or seeking to act, of his own volition, in the name of the state, challenge the title of an officer?

A. Quo Warranto

In the absence of statute private citizens will usually not be permitted to file an information in the nature of quo warranto, and statutes permitting this are not common, although they are to be

[30] Watson v. McGrath, 111 La. 1097, 36 So. 204 (1904). In this case the injunction was denied because the statute was held constitutional. Relative to the effect of an invalid statute the court said, at 1098: "A statute may be constitutional only in part, or with regard to certain persons or things, or up to a certain point of its operation, and in other respects unconstitutional. The rule is to let it have operation within the scope of its constitutionality, if the legislative intent to that effect is clear and unmistakable." And again, "Because the legislature desired that this appointee

found in some of the states.[31] Some states by statute permit individual voters to contest the election of a candidate to office.[32]

B. TAX CASES

1) Injunction. — A taxpayer will often succeed in testing by injunction the constitutionality of a statute authorizing the levy of a tax,[33] but if the collection of a tax is sought to be restrained on the ground that the officer levying the tax, or collecting it, holds office by virtue of an invalid statute, the court is likely to make use of the de facto doctrine to defeat him.[34] Here, as in the cases involving the corporate existence of a municipal corporation, public policy should cause the courts to utilize the de facto doctrine to uphold the validity of an officer's status if the statutes authorizing the tax are constitutional and if the office is one that could have been created under the constitution. The taxpayer should not be allowed to escape his share of the burden of supporting the financial structure of the government just because one of the officers engaged in the administration of the tax laws holds office by appointment, when, for example, he should have been chosen by popular election, the legislature having mistaken the rule of constitutional law on the point. If the activity is one that could otherwise have been authorized, so that the taxpayer will in the long run be compelled to contribute to its support anyway, the fact that the officer's title is defective should not be sufficient to permit him to disrupt the financial administration of the particular governmental unit that may be involved. Particularly should this be the case if injunctive relief is not sought immediately upon the taking of office by someone not entitled thereto or immediately upon the attempt to exercise the functions of an office created by an unconstitutional statute.[35]

should have the office during the whole unexpired term, and so provided, is no reason for denying to him the right to hold it at least for the term which the legislature had clear constitutional authority to give it to him."

[31] State of Nevada ex rel. Fletcher v. Osburn, 24 Nev. 187, 51 Pac. 837 (1893). In Darrow v. People, 8 Col. 417, 8 Pac. 661 (1885), the statute was held constitutional, but the court proceeded to consider the merits of the case, which was instituted by a petition by a taxpayer for permission to file an information in the nature of quo warranto. Mo. Rev. Stat. 1919, sec. 2066 (providing that an information of quo warranto may be filed by the attorney general or prosecuting attorney "at the relation of any person desiring to prosecute the same").

[32] See, for example, Minnesota statute discussed in Brown v. Smallwood, 130 Minn. 492, 153 N. W. 953 (1915).

[33] C. B. U. P. v. Smith, 23 Kan. 745 (1880); Snider v. Jackson County, 175 N. C. 590, 96 S. E. 32 (1918); Hickman v. Kimbley, 161 Ky. 652, 171 S. W. 176 (1914).

[34] Smith v. Lynch, 29 Ohio St. 261 (1876). Cf. Roche v. Jones, 87 Va. 484, 12 S. E. 965 (1891). The cases in which the existence of a municipality is involved, as well as the existence of an office, are conflicting. See Chapter 3.

[35] Ayeridge v. Town Commissioners of Social Circle, 60 Ga. 404 (1878).

In Chicago & Northwestern Ry. v. Langlade County [36] an action was brought by the railway company to set aside a tax levy because the statute under which the county had been organized was invalid. For this reason, it was argued, the officers of the county had not even a de facto status, and consequently no obligation to pay the tax rested upon the company. The statute was held to be constitutional, but the court said that even if it had been unconstitutional, the county officers would nevertheless have been de facto officers, and as such their acts would have been valid as to the railway company. While it is true that in this case the court had the added weight of the argument supporting de facto municipal corporations under such circumstances, there is no reason why the same rule should not be applied in cases where the existence of an office, or the validity of the statute providing for choosing its incumbents, is questioned on the ground of unconstitutionality, the existence of a municipal unit not being involved.

2) *Action to collect taxes.* — May a taxpayer resist an action by the tax collector or municipality on the ground that the board or officer levying the tax occupied an office created by an invalid statute or, the office being validly created, chosen to fill it in accordance with a statute suffering from a similar defect?

State ex rel. City of St. Paul v. District Court of Ramsey County [37] presented a case in which two boards attempted to carry on the same functions at the same time. One of them was declared to be without authority and its members were ousted from office. Subsequent to the ouster of the members of the board that had been created by an unconstitutional act, the city brought an action to enforce payment of an assessment for local improvements made under the direction and orders of this board. The defense was that, since the law creating the office was unconstitutional, there could be no office to fill, because the de facto doctrine applies to officers and not to offices. The court supported this contention, deciding that the assessments in question should be set aside. The court stressed the fact that the object of the statute was an unconstitutional one, that the defect was one not of form but of substance, and observed that for that reason it was "as inoperative as if it had never been passed." The earlier case of Burt v. Winona & St. Peter R. R. Co.,[38] to be discussed in detail in another section,[39] was both limited and distinguished: limited to its particular facts, involving in a civil case the constitutionality

[36] 56 Wis. 614, 14 N. W. 844 (1883).
[37] 72 Minn. 226, 75 N. W. 224 (1898).
[38] 31 Minn. 472, 18 N. W. 285, 289 (1884).
[39] *Infra*, p. 96.

of an act establishing a municipal court, the act not having received the requisite number of votes in the upper house of the legislature; distinguished because of the fact that the object of the statute in the Burt case was constitutional, for the legislature had power to establish municipal courts, whereas the object of the statute in the Ramsey County case was a prohibited one, depending upon substance instead of form or procedure. The Ramsey County case could have been disposed of, and distinguished from the Burt case, by invoking the doctrine that there cannot be a de facto officer where there is a de jure one in existence.[40] There were in the Burt case two boards, each contesting with the other for power. It is questionable, however, whether the taxpayers should be encouraged by the courts to resist payment of assessments under these circumstances and at this stage of the proceedings. They were on notice, doubtless, of the contest between the two boards, and they should not have been permitted to sit by and accept without protest improvements for their benefit and for which they would normally have to pay, when they could by injunction have protected themselves from illegal acts on the part of either or both of the boards. Would it not have been more just, under the circumstances of the Ramsey County case, to have said that the acts of the boards in question, in so far as those done by order of the one later ousted from its functions were not in conflict with those of the board subsequently declared to be the legal body, were binding on the lot owners in question? If the court wished to hold that the statute permitting the assessments and the work to be done was unconstitutional, it should have made that clear, for a justifiable case might well have been made out on that score, but it should not have decided the case on the basis of the de facto doctrine, if that was the objection advanced. Whether or not X should pay for the paving of a street in front of his lot should not depend upon the de facto or non de facto status of an officer or board, irrespective of what might be the rule in case the statute authorizing the work to be done was unconstitutional.

Two Illinois cases hold that an action to collect a tax may not be successfully resisted if the objection advanced in defense is that the officers involved were chosen in accordance with an invalid law.[41] In one of them the court said:

There are present, here, all the elements which, from considerations of public policy and for the avoiding of public inconvenience, have been recognized as going to make up the character of de facto officers, whose

[40] Dienstag v. Fagan, 74 N. J. L. 418, 65 Atl. 1011 (1907).
[41] Leach v. People ex rel. Patterson, 122 Ill. 420, 12 N. E. 726 (1887); Samuels v. Drainage Commissioners, 125 Ill. 536, 17 N. E. 829 (1888).

acts should be held valid — as officers, by virtue of an election as such, under an act of the legislature; reputation of being public officers and public belief of their being such; public recognition thereof, and public acquiescence therein; and action as such unquestioned during a series of years, with no other body ready and willing to act as the board of supervisors.[42]

They had color of title, said the court, although the statute was defective. On grounds of policy this should be the rule whether the *office* was created by an invalid statute or whether the *officer* was chosen to fill the office under a defective statute. The reasons for applying the de facto doctrine in the one case apply with equal force to the other.

C. Eminent Domain

A property owner whose property is about to be taken from him by public authorities may prevent immediate seizure of the same by obtaining an injunction, and may thus raise the question of the constitutionality of a law creating the office that the authorities pretend to occupy.[43] If the statute is declared unconstitutional, "it results that the defendants are doing acts affecting the plaintiff's rights that they have no authority of law to do, because there is no such office, the duties of which they claim to be exercising." [44]

Suppose, however, that the officers of the municipality take possession of the property of a private citizen, thinking that they have the power to do so under the power of eminent domain possessed by the city. May the owner recover the land taken from him on the ground that, although the city had the power of eminent domain, the officers who sought to act for the city in the particular proceeding purported to be the incumbents of nonexistent offices, the law creating them being invalid? This was the situation presented in Nichols v. City of Cleveland.[45] In answer to the contention of counsel that the constitutionality of the statutes creating the offices in question could not be raised in such a case because the officers enjoyed a de facto status, and that their acts could therefore not be assailed, the United States circuit court of appeals for the sixth circuit said:

[42] Leach v. People ex rel. Patterson, 122 Ill. 420, 430, 12 N. E. 726 (1887). In Town of Decorah v. Bullis, 25 Iowa 12 (1868), the town sued in its corporate capacity to recover an assessment. The town officers enacting the sidewalk ordinance were elected to office under a statute which the court held inapplicable to this town, although the statute was constitutional. Held, the officers were not de facto and judgment for the defendant.
[43] Indianapolis Brewing Co. v. Claypool, 149 Ind. 193, 48 N. E. 228 (1897).
[44] *Ibid.*, 193, 205.
[45] 247 Fed. 731 (C. C. A. 6th 1917).

This is to assert that the owner of private property may not dispute the claimed right of a municipal board to exercise the power of eminent domain. It needs no citation of authority to show that the rightful investment of such power is essential to the taking of private property in invitum. It would be a strange, and certainly an arbitrary, rule that would forbid an owner to protect his property rights through challenge of the constitutional validity of the only statute relied on to justify the exercise of such a power as that of eminent domain.[46]

The city contended, however, that inasmuch as it had possession of the property and inasmuch as a later statute had given the city the power to take property in this type of case, it should be permitted to retain the property upon making proper compensation to the owner. The court asserted on this point that title remained in the owner all the time, despite its possession by the city, but in view of the many years that had passed and of the subsequent grant of authority to the city, a conditional judgment would be given, granting the city the privilege of instituting new condemnation proceedings to acquire the property. Allowance was made, in computing the amount of the judgment, for rent, profits, and issues, compensation thus being made to the owner for the period during which he had been deprived of possession.

The distinction between the Nichols case, where recovery of property that has been taken from a person is asked, and the case where injunctive relief is asked against threatened taking is an important one, fully justifying the different result reached in the two cases. Under the circumstances of the Nichols case it would have been of little avail to have allowed the recovery of the land in question, because the city could have regained possession of it upon the institution of condemnation proceedings.

In King v. Philadelphia County [47] a bill was filed to restrain the county from maintaining gas pipes in a street that had been opened through the plaintiff's land. The board of viewers provided for by statute for assessment and street opening proceedings was assailed, the statute being attacked as unconstitutional. The pipes had been laid for two or more years, and the street had been opened to traffic. The bill was dismissed, the court saying that it would be impracticable at that late date to tear up the pipes and undo the work that had been done. "Such municipal works having been done under color of lawful authority, when no question as to the validity of the authority was raised, must be regarded as lawfully done." [48] That

---

[46] Nichols v. Cleveland, 247 Fed. 731, 739 (C. C. A. 6th 1917).

[47] 154 Pa. St. 160, 26 Atl. 308 (1893).

[48] King v. Philadelphia County, 154 Pa. St. 160, 167, 26 Atl. 308 (1893). Cf. Pittsburgh's Petition, 138 Pa. St. 401, 21 Atl. 757 (1891).

the work had been done in the regular way; that all official acts had
been in accordance with what everybody supposed to be the law;
that the defendants had not made the law; and that people had a
right to expect that the officers' acts in these proceedings were in
accordance with constitutional legislation all contributed, in the
mind of the court, to support their decision not to undo the work
of public officials, even though the constitutional warrant for their
acts or offices was defective and would, under the doctrine of the
injunction cases, have justified the court in protecting the individual
against threatened official action had application for relief only been
made earlier in the proceedings. The King case emphasizes the doctrine of the Nichols case, namely, that to obtain relief in this type of
case application to the court must be made at an early stage in the
proceedings.

D. BONDS AND OTHER CONTRACT OBLIGATIONS

The leading case on this subject is Norton v. Shelby County.[49]
The facts of this famous case were as follows:

By the constitution of Tennessee there was, in each county, but one
county court. This was composed of the justices of the peace elected in
their respective districts in the county. Under the act of March 9, 1867,
the governor was given power to appoint county commissioners who
were to take the place of this court. The county court was one of the
institutions recognized in the constitution of the state. County commissioners were authorities unknown to the constitution and previously unknown to the law of Tennessee. There was no general acquiescence in
the change nor any general recognition of the new commissioners. On
the contrary, the validity of the act was at once assailed. Within a month
after its passage, a bill was brought against the commissioners and public
opposition continued in various forms, until the case was finally settled.
While litigation to test their authority was pending, the commissioners
issued county bonds to the amount of $29,000, and the liability of the
county on these bonds became a subject of further controversy.[50]

This "further controversy" was the subject matter of the Norton
case. The Supreme Court decided that no recovery could be had on
the bonds. That this was a proper disposition of the case seems
clear. The people who purchased bonds under such circumstances
as those presented in the Norton case had notice of possible defects
in the issue and the court could, in accordance with recognized
rules of notice and estoppel, have justified the result reached. The
case was not decided on these grounds, however, but was placed

[49] 118 U. S. 425, 6 Sup. Ct. Rep. 1121, 30 L. Ed. 178 (1885).
[50] Wallach, De Facto Officers, 22 Pol. Sci. Quart. 451, 469 (1907).

on grounds relating to the doctrines of de facto officers and the effect of an unconstitutional law.

Justice Field, delivering the opinion of the court, explained at considerable length the reasons for the doctrine of de facto officers. Following this explanation he said, "But the idea of an officer implies the existence of an office which he holds." The justice then reviews the argument presented by counsel on the question whether an unconstitutional statute can create an office. In stating the position of counsel for the bondholders, Justice Field said that their position was "that a legislative act, though unconstitutional, may in terms create an office, and nothing further than its apparent existence is necessary to give validity to the acts of its assumed incumbent. That position, although not stated in this broad form, amounts to nothing else." Concerning this argument he continued:

It is difficult to meet it by any formal argument beyond this statement. An unconstitutional act is not a law; it confers no rights; it imposes no duties; it affords no protection; it creates no office; it is in legal contemplation as inoperative as though it had never been passed.

The one redeeming feature of this statement of Justice Field's is that it does not purport to be an argument but is expressly put forth as a dogmatic statement, and such it surely is. There is only one effective answer to it: it is not true. Courts have held that unconstitutional statutes have imposed duties, have granted rights, have created offices, and have some operative effect. The statement is, therefore, not an accurate statement of the rule of law in this regard. It is, and this is perhaps all that it purports to be, a statement of one view of the effect of an unconstitutional statute — a view applied by many courts in numerous situations, but applied by no court in all cases.[51] The real weakness in this portion of the opinion of Justice Field is that it assumes the very point to be decided, namely, whether an unconstitutional statute can create an office or, to phrase it somewhat differently, whether the acts of a person purporting to exercise the functions of an office created by an unconstitutional statute will be treated by a court as valid and binding on the governmental unit for which he holds himself out to act. This dictum, then, is a statement of a view, not of an argument. Perhaps it is for this reason that it has been followed by so many courts and applied in so many situations, whether such adherence and application accomplished the ends of justice or not. Had it been presented as argument other judges might have found it easier to detect its fal-

[51] See Chapter 1. See criticism of rule of this case in note, 39 Harv. L. Rev. 373 (1926).

lacy. As it is, it has exercised a profound influence in cases involving the effect of an unconstitutional statute, regardless of the situation presented to the court that called forth its enunciation.

It is interesting to notice that Justice Field says, at the close of his opinion:

It may be, as alleged, that the stock of the railroad company, for which they subscribed, is still held by the county. If so, the county may, by proper proceedings, be required to surrender it to the company, or pay its value; for independently of all restrictions upon municipal corporations, there is a rule of justice that must control them as it controls individuals. If they obtain the property of others without right, they must return it to the true owners, or pay for its value.[52]

This was not, as the justice points out, a question involved in the case. It indicates, however, that the bondholders in this case would not be remediless. They had merely brought their action on the wrong ground, basing it on the bonds. They should have demanded the return of the stock, and if the district had refused to surrender it, should then have brought an action for conversion. It is clear, then, that the case worked no more serious hardship on the plaintiffs than any case in which the wrong action is brought and the remedy for the wrong misconceived.

In City of East St. Louis v. Witts [53] an action of debt was brought against the city on some scrip issued by certain police commissioners whose offices had been created by an invalid statute. The city was held not liable, apparently on the same theory as that expressed in the Norton case.

In connection with these two cases the case of Schloss & Kahn v. McIntyre [54] is of interest. Defendants in that case were commissioners in charge of a local liquor dispensary. They purchased liquor

[52] Norton v. Shelby County, 118 U. S. 425, 454, 6 Sup. Ct. Rep. 1121, 30 L. Ed. 178 (1885).

[53] 59 Ill. 155 (1871). In Parks v. Commissioners of Wyandotte County, 61 Fed. 436 (C. C. Kan. 1894), and First Natl. Bk. of Lansdale v. Commissioners of Wyandotte County, 68 Fed. 878 (C. C. A. 8th 1895), the bonds issued by officers holding offices created by an invalid statute were held to be non-negotiable. The court seems, however, to have thought that despite this feature of the case the bonds would not have been binding obligations, because falling within the rule of the Norton case. It is often impossible to collect bonds in such a case because of the difficulty of procuring validating legislation and also because the courts in the middle western states seemed disposed in the latter part of the past century to be rather ready to find grounds for defeating recovery. This was corrected to some extent by the position taken by the federal courts, but the instant case illustrates that recovery was sometimes difficult to obtain even in those courts. The writer is indebted to the officers of the First National Bank of Lansdale, Pa., for information as to the outcome of the litigation in the instant case. The bondholders in these cases were unable to recover anything.

[54] 147 Ala. 557, 41 So. 11 (1906).

from the plaintiff for purposes of resale in the dispensary. The statute establishing the dispensary and creating the offices of commissioners was held to be unconstitutional. Suit was brought against the commissioners to hold them liable in their individual capacity. They were not in the business for profit, received no benefit from the conduct of it, and made no personal promise to pay for the stock purchased, and for these reasons the court decided that they could not be held individually liable for the debt.

In People ex rel. Bolton v. Albertson [55] the city sought to escape payment of a bill for coal sold to the police department, on the ground that a new board had superseded the one to which plaintiff had sold the coal. Plaintiff asked for a mandamus to compel the signature of warrants to pay for the coal and the court granted the mandamus, declaring the statute creating the new board to be unconstitutional.

One entering into a contract with a municipal board of trustees whose offices are created by an invalid law is bound by the contract and may not obtain rescission of it merely on the ground of the defect in the title of the trustees with whom he contracted.[56] Nor can the constitutional qualifications of a commissioner appointed by the governor to apportion the cost of building a bridge between several railroads be questioned in an action on the contract by one road to obtain reimbursement of a share in the expense paid for another road. Such an officer is entitled to de facto status.[57] It should perhaps be observed that this last case involved no question of the effect of an unconstitutional statute. It does, nevertheless, indicate the attitude that courts may be expected to take toward the acts of an officer whose title to office is challenged because of some constitutional defect in his alleged status. The case would be quite as strong for holding an officer de facto in such a situation if the defect had been in the statute providing for his appointment instead of in his qualifications for the office.

E. Torts

Suppose that an action is brought against a village to recover damages for an injury due to a defective sidewalk. The defendants are the president and trustees of the village of X. The complaint

[55] 55 N. Y. 50 (1873).
[56] Heck v. Findlay Window Glass Co., 8 Ohio Cir. Dec. 757 (1898). See Erwin v. Mayor of Jersey City, 60 N. J. L. 141, 145, 37 Atl. 732 (1897): "It is beyond doubt that his acts on matters in which the corporation attorney could act would bind the city and parties dealing with the city."
[57] Fitchburg R. R. v. Grand Junction R. R. & Depot Co., 1 Allen 552 (Mass. 1861). Cf. Shelby v. Alcorn, 36 Miss. 273, 72 Am. Dec. 169 (1858), defective title

alleges among other things that the village is a corporation, validly incorporated under the laws "made and provided" for the organization of villages of this class. The defendants file a demurrer to the complaint, claiming that there is no such corporation as The President and Trustees of the village of X. In a case of this type the Wisconsin court held that the village existed under another valid law, but that the one under which incorporation had been attempted was invalid. Furthermore, the statute regulating the selection of the officers of the village was unconstitutional. There was, then, presented to the court a case in which the office was held to be created by a valid statute, the incumbents of which had been selected in accordance with an invalid law. Were they de facto officers? [58] Could defendant deny their title to office? In answer to these questions the court said, holding them de facto: "And the fact that they are in by color of a law which is unconstitutional and void does not make an exception to the rule." The city was not permitted to deny the validity of the law providing for the selection of these officers. It is difficult to say whether a similar result would have been reached had the statute creating the offices likewise been invalid and had there been no other valid statute under which the city might have been organized.[59]

F. Civil Cases in Which Office or Title of Judicial or Clerical Officer Is Challenged

1) *Judicial officer.* — The judge trying a civil case may have been appointed or elected to office under an invalid statute. May one of the parties to the suit appeal on that ground from a judgment rendered by a judge so chosen? The rule seems to be that he cannot. A judge elected or appointed to office in accordance with an invalid statute is a de facto officer and his title to office cannot be challenged on appeal by one of the parties to a civil suit. One opinion sets forth three arguments in support of this rule: [60] 1. There is a strong public policy in favor of recognizing the acts of such judges so that judicial business may be carried on in an orderly manner, and cases settled on their merits. 2. The judge is not a party to the action and has

is good defense to action to recover money paid, the work not having been performed per contract. The title defect arose from the holding of constitutionally incompatible offices.

[58] Cole v. President and Trustees of Black River Falls, 57 Wis. 110, 44 N. W. 906 (1883).

[59] For discussion of this factor in municipal corporation cases, see Tooke, De Facto Municipal Corporations under Unconstitutional Statutes, 37 Yale L. J. 935 (1928). See Chapter 3.

[60] Curtin v. Barton, 139 N. Y. 505, 34 N. E. 1093 (1893).

no opportunity to defend the attack upon his title. It would be unfair to try a man's title to office if he was not to be given a hearing on the question. 3. This is a collateral attack, and only the state should be permitted to question the title of an officer in a direct attack, collateral attack being objectionable on the ground that continuous assaults upon official title would be made by private individuals who might have something to gain if they were to succeed in the attack. With respect to these points the following observations might be made: that the first is the real basis of the decision; that the second is at least partially unsound because even if the title of the judge were declared to be defective, that would not of necessity mean that he would be ousted from office, ouster following only upon judgment in quo warranto proceedings; and, finally, the third is not a reason but rather a statement of a rule of law. That the first reason advanced is the real basis for the decision appears from the following quotation from the opinion:

When a court with competent jurisdiction is duly established, a suitor who resorts to it for the administration of justice and the protection of private rights should not be defeated or embarrassed by questions relating to the title of the judge, who presides in the court, to his office. If the court exists under the constitution and laws and it had jurisdiction of the case, any defect in the election or mode of appointing the judge is not available to litigate.[61]

In another case, in which a writ of prohibition was sought to prevent a lower court from proceeding with the trial of a civil case, the writ was denied because, said the court, only the state could assail the title of the judge before whom the case was being tried.[62] The court said, in the course of its opinion:

Counsel argues that relator has no other available remedy for the wrong that is about to be done to him, and that, inasmuch as there must be a remedy for every wrong, therefore a writ of prohibition will lie. But the fallacy consists in the assumption that relator is threatened with any wrong. Respondent being a justice de facto, his acts are as valid as if he was a justice de jure. In fact, as to everybody except the state in proceedings by quo warranto to test his right to the office, he is, in effect, a justice de jure.[63]

There is some authority to the contrary, however, and one of the parties to a civil action in a Baltimore court obtained a writ of mandamus to compel the removal of a case to another court, the one in which it was about to be tried being presided over by a judge chosen

[61] *Ibid.;* People ex rel. Kearney v. Carter, 29 Barb. 209 (N.Y. 1859).
[62] State ex rel. Derusha v. McMartin, 42 Minn. 30, 43 N.W. 572 (1889).
[63] *Ibid.,* 30, 31. Cf. Laver v. McGlachlin, 28 Wis. 364 (1871).

by virtue of an invalid statute.[64] The fact that there existed a de jure court capable of taking and trying the case doubtless made the court less hesitant to grant the writ than it would otherwise have been. Had there been no other court to which the case could immediately have been taken and tried the result might conceivably have been different.

When the defect is in the constitution of the office instead of in the method of choice, the courts are in irreconcilable conflict, some permitting attack, others refusing it.

In Burt v. Winona and St. Peter R. R.[65] the Minnesota court refused to permit one of the parties to a civil action to question the legality of the office of the judge who was trying the case, holding that even if the statute establishing the court had failed to receive the constitutionally required number of votes in the upper house the judge would be a de facto officer. The view of the court is well summarized in the statement that "the reason given for the de facto doctrine applies as well to offices and courts as to officers." The injustice of permitting cases to be decided upon such incidental points instead of on their merits, the inconvenience and uncertainty that would inevitably follow the introduction of the doctrine that there can be no de facto office under an unconstitutional statute, and the hardship on litigants of compelling them to ascertain the legal title to office of a particular judge before daring to go to trial with a case were stressed by the court as factors causing it to refuse to permit the legal existence of the office to be questioned. The court thought that where an office exists under "color of right, that is, under color of law," the incumbent of such an office should be unmolested in his possession of it until the state takes the initiative in ousting him by means of quo warranto. A federal circuit court for the district of Minnesota applied the same rule as that laid down in the Burt case.[66]

On the other hand, the Kentucky court, in Hildreth's Heirs v.

[64] Lewin v. Hewes, 118 Md. 624, 86 Atl. 833 (1912). In Smith v. Normant, 5 Yerg. 271 (Tenn. 1833), a statute providing for the appointment of a temporary judge was held invalid, and the commission of the judge said to be "void, and he incapable of doing any judicial act," so therefore the parties in a civil suit were permitted to challenge his acts. The court said, further, that "the judgments, decrees, and orders are all void, and must be set aside, and the causes remanded to the respective courts from whence they came, to be proceeded in." *Ibid.*, 278. See also Grogan v. Robinson, 8 S. W. (2d) 571 (Tex. Civ. App. 1928).

[65] Burt v. Winona & St. Peter R. R., 31 Minn. 472, 18 N. W. 285, 289 (1884). Cf. Shafford v. Brown, 49 Wash. 307, 95 Pac. 270 (1908). See dictum in State ex rel. Smallwood v. Windom, 131 Minn. 401, 155 N. W. 629 (1915).

[66] Comstock v. Tracey, 46 Fed. 162 (C. C. Minn. 1891). This likewise was a civil case, and the statute creating the court was alleged not to have received the requisite number of votes in the upper house of the state legislature. The court held that the statute could not be assailed in this case.

M'Intire's Devisee,[67] held on an appeal from a judgment in a civil case that proceedings which had previously been taken in a "court of appeals" created as a rival of the so-called "old court" were null and void because the statute creating the new court was unconstitutional. The court pointed out that there could be a de facto officer, but that except by revolution there could not, under a constitutional government, be a de facto office.[68] The fact that the legality of the organization of the new court had been consistently resisted from the time of its establishment doubtless made the court less hesitant to pronounce its judgments totally void. A judgment of a justice of the peace in New York was reversed because the statute creating the office was invalid.[69] A similar view to that expressed in the Hildreth case was taken in Ex parte Roundtree,[70] wherein the Alabama court issued a writ of prohibition forbidding a judge to proceed with the trial of a case, the court treating both the office and the method of choice as bad. The court said, in the course of its opinion, that

The usurpation of judicial power — the holding of pretended courts — is a great public wrong, productive of uncertainty and confusion; beclouding the title to property, vexing and harassing the citizen, involving him in a conflict of duties, subjecting him to oppression, and detracting from the dignity and authority of the known and established tribunals. It would be a reproach to the law and to justice if there were not a speedy remedy to prevent such usurpation.[71]

One cannot help wondering whether the results referred to by the court in this extract from its opinion were not more sure to follow from the view expressed therein than from the view that the title of the judge should not, in such a case, be permitted to be questioned by litigants. The reasons advanced by the Alabama court are exactly those that might well be advanced to justify the doctrine of the Burt case. As to the argument that there should be a "speedy remedy to prevent such usurpation," the ready reply is that such a remedy is available: quo warranto at the instance of the state.

In Masterson v. Mathews [72] the Alabama court treated the case as one involving only the constitutionality of the method of choosing the judge, and held that in a suit on a judgment rendered by a judge

[67] 1 J. J. Marsh 206 (Ky. 1892). Frame v. Treble, 1 J. J. Marsh 205 (Ky. 1829); State v. Gillette's Estate, 10 S. W. (2d) 984 (Tex. Com. of App. 1928).

[68] This question often arises in connection with de facto governments in international law. These cases will not be dealt with in this study.

[69] Waters v. Langdon, 40 Barb. 408 (N. Y. 1863). It is not altogether clear whether this was a criminal or civil case, but it seems to have been civil.

[70] 51 Ala. 42 (1874).

[71] Ex parte Roundtree, 51 Ala. 42 at 51 (1874).

[72] 60 Ala. 260 (1877).

selected in accordance with the invalid statute the defendant would not be permitted to object that the judge's title to office was defective. The difference between the two cases lies partly in the different attitude of the court toward the statute — in the latter case the court was treated as having been validly created, whereas in the former the law of its creation was declared invalid, as well as the law providing for the selection of the judge — and partly in the time element, the prohibition in the Roundtree case having been sought early in the case, whereas the challenge of title in the Masterson case came after judgment had been rendered. It is only natural that the court should be more hesitant to disturb what has proceeded thus far, particularly when the ground of objection is so remote from the merits of the case.

That the time element is not accorded the same weight by all courts is illustrated by the decision of the California court denying a writ of mandamus to compel the issuance of an execution on a judgment given by a judge of a court created by an invalid statute.[73] The defendant was permitted at that late stage in the proceedings to challenge the existence of the court. However, if the defect goes only to the method of filling the office, the courts incline to deny attack on title. Thus in Taylor v. Skrine [74] and Neal v. Kent [75] the courts of South Carolina and Kansas, respectively, denied motions to set aside and vacate judgments, the motions having been supported in each case by the argument that the judge had been selected by virtue of an unconstitutional statute.

The courts tend to view defects in statutes increasing the number of judges in a district, or on a court, as going to the method of filling the office rather than as going to the existence of the court. In these cases the de facto doctrine is generally applied, and judgments rendered by judges under these circumstances are not open to attack.[76]

[73] Miner v. Justices Court, 121 Cal. 264, 53 Pac. 795 (1898).

[74] 3 Brev. 516 (S. C. 1815).

[75] 102 Kan. 239, 169 Pac. 1152 (1918). In Thompson v. Couch, 144 Mich. 671, 108 N. W. 363 (1906), one of the parties in a petty civil case asked for a writ of prohibition to prevent further consideration of a case by a lower court, on the ground that the statute creating the court, as well as that providing for the selection of the judge, was invalid. The court held the officer to be de facto, the office being created by a valid statute.

[76] Rude v. Sisack, 44 Colo. 21, 96 Pac. 976 (1908), two judges; should be only one. The judge whose acts were assailed had been ousted by quo warranto. People ex rel. Attorney General v. Johnson, 34 Colo. 143, 86 Pac. 233 (1905). Butler v. Phillips, 38 Colo. 378, 88 Pac. 480 (1906); Rives v. Petit, 4 Ark. 582 (1842). The same view prevails when qualifications are lacking. Mayo v. Stoneum, 2 Ala. 390 (1841); McInstry v. Tanner, 9 Johns. 135 (N. Y. 1812). As to incompatibility of offices and the effect of holding them: McGregor v. Balch, 14 Vt. 428 (1842). Cf. Clayton v. Per Dun, 13 Johns. 218 (N. Y. 1816). In McGregor v. Balch, 14 Vt. 428, 435 (1842), the court said: "It will follow from this that, either on a quo warranto

In Nagel v. Bosworth [77] the statute seems to have been considered by the court as one going to the existence of the office. At least when the Kentucky court came to distinguish it from the situation involved in the Hildreth case, the distinction between the two cases was said to be one arising out of the difference between a statute clearly invalid and one not invalid on its face. The statutes in the two cases were considered as going to the creation of the office, but the court thought that the statute in the Hildreth case was void on its face, whereas this was said not to be true of the statute in the Bosworth case. The court said, concerning this distinction:

> The act, on its face, was a palpable violation of the constitution, as the legislature was without power to create a court of appeals; but not so is the act here. The legislature has power to create a circuit court, and under certain conditions to add an additional judge. The act that it passed showed that the conditions existed which warranted it to create an additional judge.[78]

The situation presented to the court in the Bosworth case was not quite the same as that involved in the Hildreth case. The two cases did have in common, however, a statute creating an office, because an increase in the number of judges was considered by the Kentucky court as the creation of so many more offices. The circumstances were more favorable in the Bosworth case to elicit the application of the de facto doctrine than were those involved in the Hildreth case. There was absent, also, the rivalry that characterized the dispute between the two courts of appeals in the latter case. The trial of cases would be carried on by the de jure judge of the district, and when the legislature met, the difficulties of overwork could be alleviated. It is then perhaps not accurate to say that the two cases are in conflict with each other, but the attitude of the court in the Bosworth case on the question whether an invalid statute could create an office was nevertheless somewhat different from that manifested in the Hildreth case.

or in any suit to which Merrill was a party, when he attempted to act, or to justify his acts, by virtue of and under his commission as a justice of the peace, it might be replied that he was incapable of holding that office, and, as to him, he would be treated as having no authority whatever to act, or justify his acts, as such justice, while he held the office of postmaster under the authority of Congress." But, the court said, where he was not a party, the question could not be raised, thus extending the de facto doctrine to this situation.

[77] 148 Ky. 807, 147 S. W. 940 (1912). This case is apparently not one involving a civil proceeding in which one of the parties to the suit was attacking the title of the judge. It is impossible to tell from the report of the case exactly what the nature of the action was, but it appears to have been a suit relative to compensation. The parties and some statements in the opinion lead to this conclusion.

[78] 148 Ky. 807, 809, 147 S. W. 940 (1912).

Occasionally the title of a judge is assailed because he is said not to possess the constitutional qualifications required for the office. The same is true with respect to the holding of two incompatible offices. Attack in these cases is usually unsuccessful, the de facto doctrine being extended to support the validity of the acts of the judges.[79] But when an office has been abolished altogether, there remaining no legal warrant for the court, the de facto doctrine will not be applied.[80]

Special judges provided for by invalid statutes have been held not to be entitled to de facto status, and their acts may be assailed by parties to the litigation.[81]

2) Clerical officer. — Cases sometimes arise in which the title of one of the clerical officers of a court is assailed in a civil case in which the officer is not one of the parties. In State Bank of Pender v. Frey[82] an officer exercising authority over an unconstitutionally annexed portion of territory was held to be de facto, and recording a deed with him had the usual effect of notice.[83] But when a mortgage has been acknowledged before a judge of a court created by an unconstitutional statute, it has been held that there is "no basis on which to rest an application of the rules saving the acts of de facto officers."[84] For this reason a mortgage attempting to convey title to land was held to be ineffective. In Crowley v. Southern Ry.[85] an attempt was made to remove to a federal district court a case begun in a state court. The statute creating the judicial district and the office of deputy clerk was declared invalid by a state court. Because of this decision the federal district court refused to take the case, on the ground that a suit cannot be removed from a nonexistent court. There being no office, there could be no de facto officer, according to the views expressed by the court. The decision worked an injustice to the plaintiff, as the court recognized, because the statute of limitations had run on the cause of action in consequence of this delay;

[79] *Supra,* note 76.
[80] Ayres v. Lattimer, 57 Mo. App. 78 (1894), court abolished; Daniel v. Hutcheson, 4 Tex. Civ. App. 239, 22 S. W. 278 (1893), same.
[81] Caldwell v. Barrett, 71 Ark. 310, 74 S. W. 748 (1903). The court said: "It would be beyond all precedent to term the judge presiding in a court which is not a court at all a de facto judge." A number of Arkansas cases are reviewed in the opinion. Van Slyke v. Trempeleau, etc., Ins. Co., 39 Wis. 390, 20 Am. Rep. 50 (1876). "Here Mr. Cole was not in possession of the office of judge, and did not claim it." The court declared that all that the appointee had accepted was some of its functions. Cf. discussion *infra,* p. 113, of Nagel v. Bosworth, 148 Ky. 807, 147 S. W. 940 (1912); Smith v. Normant, 5 Yerg. 271 (Tenn. 1833).
[82] 3 Neb. Unoff. 83, 91 N. W. 239 (1902).
[83] Cf. Cocke v. Halsey, 16 Pet. 71, 10 L. Ed. 890 (U. S. 1842), effect of filing trust deed after court had adjourned, no question of constitutionality being involved.
[84] King Lumber Co. v. Crow, 155 Ala. 504, 46 So. 646 (1908).
[85] 139 Fed. 851 (C. C. Ala. 1905).

but although the court felt that justice was being sacrificed, it felt it could not overturn the majority view that there can be no de facto officer where there is no de jure office.

In these cases there is to be found the same division of opinion as in those discussed in the preceding sections, some of the courts permitting the judge's title to be challenged by private litigants if the statute creating the office is invalid, whereas if the method of choice is defective, the de facto doctrine is applied.

G. Criminal Cases Challenging the Existence of a Court or the Title to Office of a Judge or Clerical Officer

1) Attack on title of judge. — One of the leading cases on the question whether the defendant in a criminal case can attack the title of a judge on the ground that the statute providing for his selection is unconstitutional is that of Brown v. O'Connell.[86] In this case an action of debt was brought by the treasurer of Hartford on a recognizance given by the defendant in the police court of the city. The constitutionality of the law providing that police justices should be appointed by the council was assailed. The court held that the statute was invalid, but said that the justice was nevertheless a de facto officer, occupying the office by "color of appointment."[87] "He was not a usurper. He had color of appointment by the common council of Hartford, and they had color of delegated authority from the general assembly." His acts, said the court, were all performed under "forms of law," and for that reason color was derived "from the law." State v. Carroll[88] involved a situation in which a person accused of petty crime challenged the constitutionality of a statute permitting a temporary vacancy to be filled by appointment. The court decided, however, that even though the statute were defective, the acts of the temporary appointee would be binding on the plaintiff, the accused below. For that reason the validity of the law was not settled. For the same reason the statement of the court to the effect that a person chosen to a de jure office by virtue of an invalid statute was a de facto officer, was dictum.[89]

The rule enunciated in the O'Connell case is well established and

---

[86] 36 Conn. 432 (1870).

[87] Brown v. O'Connell, 36 Conn. 432, 450 (1870).

[88] 38 Conn. 449 (1871).

[89] "A definition sufficiently accurate and comprehensive to cover the whole ground must, I think, be substantially as follows: An officer de facto is one whose acts, though not those of a lawful officer, the law, upon principles of policy and justice, will hold valid so far as they involve the interests of the public and third persons, where the duties of the office were exercised . . . Fourth, under color of an election or appointment by or pursuant to a public unconstitutional law, before the same is adjudged to be such." State v. Carroll, 38 Conn. 449, 471 (1871).

has been applied in several states.[90] In one of these cases it was stated that "the true doctrine seems to be that it is sufficient if the officer holds the office under some power having color of authority to appoint; and that a statute, though it should be found repugnant to the constitution, will give such color." [91] Another court has expressed the opinion that judges should have notice that their title is being assailed and an opportunity to be heard on the question before they lose their offices.[92] This argument is open to the same objection that is available to it in the civil case [93] — that is, that officers do not lose their offices, even though the statute is declared unconstitutional, in the absence of quo warranto proceedings by the state. The court perhaps expressed a more sound reason for its decision when it said that it would recognize the acts of the judges in this case because "under due forms of law they hold their offices by title regular on its face." [94] The rule has been applied in a situation in which a statute legislating out of office one circuit judge, but providing for the selection of another, so as to uphold the acts of the latter although the statute was invalid.[95] The doctrine applies whether the judicial officer whose title is assailed is a justice of the peace or a justice of the state Supreme Court.[96]

On the other hand, it seems equally well settled that the accused may challenge the existence of the court or of the office of the judge, and if the statute creating them is unconstitutional, the de facto doctrine will not be applied. The pettiness or magnitude of the crime of which the defendant is accused seems to be immaterial. If any difference in attitude is discernible in the opinions, it will perhaps be found to favor leniency in permitting challenge in cases involving the more serious offenses.

The question of the validity of the law creating the court may be

[90] Campbell v. Commonwealth, 96 Pa. St. 344 (1880); Walker v. State, 142 Ala. 7, 39 So. 242 (1904). See People v. Sassovich, 29 Cal. 480 (1866); State ex rel. Bales v. Bailey, 106 Minn. 138, 118 N. W. 678 (1908); Ex parte Bassitt, 90 Va. 679, 19 S. E. 453 (1894); Town of Lewiston v. Proctor, 23 Ill. 533 (1860); State v. Bartlett, 35 Wis. 287 (1874).

[91] Ex parte Strang, 21 Ohio St. 610 (1871). The statute here was not declared unconstitutional, but the court decided that the result would not be affected even though it had been invalid. In Parks, Petitioner, 3 Mont. 426 (1880), the de facto doctrine was applied to deny attack on a judge by the accused in a trial for assault and battery. The statute providing for the selection of the justice of peace was contrary to the organic act of the territory.

[92] Campbell v. Commonwealth, 96 Pa. St. 344 (1880).

[93] *Supra,* pp. 94–101.

[94] Campbell v. Commonwealth, 96 Pa. St. 344, 347 (1880).

[95] State v. Douglass, 50 Mo. 593 (1872).

[96] State v. Cochran, 55 Or. 157, 105 Pac. 884 (1909), the constitutionality of a statute providing for the addition of two justices to the supreme court of the state. The court decided, the two justices whose title was involved not sitting, that their

raised, it seems, in any stage of the proceeding, for it may be effective to quash an indictment,[97] on the one hand, and to obtain freedom from imprisonment after conviction, in habeas corpus proceedings,[98] on the other.

In People v. Toal [99] the California court, while admitting the soundness of the general doctrine that collateral attack should not be allowed on a de facto officer, held that this rule did not apply when the existence of the office itself was in question. Counsel argued in this case that the de facto doctrine should be applied to give validity to the acts of judges in criminal cases because of the difficulties that would result in the effective administration of the criminal law if attack on the existence of the court were permitted. To this contention the court answered that it realized that a few criminals might escape, but that the number would not be large. Furthermore, the judges were convinced that the statute in question was so clearly unconstitutional that, arguments based on policy to the contrary notwithstanding, they must hold it invalid. There was, thought the court, a stronger countervailing policy in favor of enforcing explicit constitutional limitations on legislative procedure, the act in this case having been in the form of a resolution instead of in the form of a statute, as required by the constitution.

In the course of its opinion in the Toal case the court said that most of the criminals in the city in which this particular court functioned would be brought to trial subsequently in the other courts in the city. It therefore hesitated less than it would otherwise have done in discharging the prisoner. Suppose, however, that a person had been convicted of a serious crime, such as assault to commit murder, which was the crime involved in the Toal case. Could he, subsequent to his discharge following an appeal on which the statute creating the court was declared unconstitutional, be again brought

acts would be binding on litigants, because they would at any rate be justices de facto. The statute was, however, held to be constitutional. See Coyle v. Sherwood, 1 Hun 272 (N.Y. 1873), justices of peace.

[97] State v. O'Brian, 68 Mo. 153 (1878).

[98] Ex parte Babe Snyder, 64 Mo. 58 (1876).

[99] 85 Cal. 333, 24 Pac. 603 (1890). Cf. People v. White, 24 Wend. 520 (N.Y. 1840); People ex rel. Sinkler v. Terry, 108 N.Y. 1, 14 N.E. 815 (1888); State v. Fritz, 27 La. Ann. 689 (1875). See Ex parte Reilly, 85 Cal. 632, 24 Pac. 807 (1890). A number of cases hold that the de facto doctrine does not apply when a person performs some of the functions of an office not yet in existence. State v. Shuford, 128 N.C. 588, 38 S.E. 808 (1901); In re Manning, 139 U.S. 504, 11 Sup. Ct. Rep. 624, 35 L. Ed. 264 (1890). The same result follows if a court has been abolished. Gorman v. People, 17 Colo. 596, 31 Pac. 335 (1892). Also if no statute establishes the court. In re Norton, 64 Kan. 842, 68 Pac. 639 (1902). Cf. State ex rel. Henderson v. County Court, 50 Mo. 317, 11 Am. Rep. 415 (1872); Caldwell v. Barrett, 71 Ark. 310, 74 S.W. 748 (1903); In Matter of Quinn, 152 N.Y. 89, 86 N.E. 175 (1897).

to trial, this time in a different court? Could he not successfully plead that this constituted double jeopardy? [100] If his trial in the "nonexistent" court should be held to be one jeopardy, the situation would then be that of a person accused and convicted of a serious crime going unpunished. Even if such a trial should be held not to constitute one jeopardy, there is another factor to be considered: the effect of such decisions releasing persons guilty of crime on the efficiency and zeal of law enforcement officers. While not conclusive, this consideration should at all times make a court hesitate to discharge a person accused and convicted of serious crime on grounds so far removed from the merits of the case.

Why should the accused in such a case be permitted to assail the existence of the office of a judge? Does the fact that he is appointed by the city council instead of by the governor, or that he was elected in accordance with a statute that did not meet the title requirements of the state constitution or was not read three times in the upper house, make the judge any more incompetent or prejudiced in the trial of a case? Is the grand jury indictment or the information of the prosecuting attorney likely to be more defective or biased in one or the other of these cases? The accused is given a fair hearing and is tried before an impartial jury. If he is found guilty in a trial conducted in the regular manner, it seems as though he should be treated as are all other persons convicted of the same crime. The state has, of course, an interest in enforcing the constitutional limitations upon legislative power so that the machinery of government may be established in an orderly manner and on a sound constitutional basis. It should be permitted, and is permitted, to challenge the existence of a court. It should be observed, however, that when a judge is ousted by quo warranto proceedings, this in no wise affects the status of the persons accused of crime whose cases may be on the docket of the court for trial. It is therefore submitted that persons accused of crime should not be permitted to question the existence of the court before which they are being tried.[101]

The fact that there is an irregularity in the constitution of a judicial district in which a court is held is not sufficient to invalidate the acts of a judge sitting in that district.[102] This applies to a case in

[100] No case has been found in which this precise question was raised. Courts disregarding entirely a statute which has been declared invalid, in the strict ab initio sense, might hold that trial before such a court did not constitute a trial for legal purposes. Other courts might in a more realistic vein call it one jeopardy. Cf. McGinnis v. State, 9 Humph. 43, 49 Am. Dec. 697 (Tenn. 1848), holding that if accused person acquiesces in trial under invalid statute defining a crime, he cannot subsequently be tried under a valid statute. See Chapter 1, note 12.

[101] See *infra*, pp. 113–18.

[102] Clark v. Commonwealth, 29 Pa. St. 129 (1858).

which the boundaries of a district,[103] or its population, do not meet the requirements of the constitution.[104] In one case dealing with a constitutional population requirement, the court said, in holding the judge to be a de facto officer, "A judge de facto assumes the exercise of a part of the power of sovereignty, and the legality of that assumption is open to the attack of the sovereign power alone." [105] Any other rule, thought the court, would ruin the administration of the criminal law. Some courts take the view, in these population cases, that the legislature is the final judge of whether a judicial district or a county has sufficient population to satisfy the constitutional requirement relative thereto, putting these cases in the category of those said to involve "political questions." [106]

The constitutional qualifications of judges,[107] as well as the holding of incompatible offices by them,[108] are not open to question by persons brought before them for trial. The de facto doctrine extends to judges in these situations.

2) Attack on title of officers attached to court. — Persons accused of crime sometimes seek to impeach the title of prosecutors, policemen, or other officers engaged in the work of law enforcement. State v. Poulin [109] is doubtless the leading case on the question whether the title of a criminal prosecutor can be impeached by a person brought to trial on an indictment procured and signed by a prosecuting attorney whose office has been created by an unconstitutional law. The Maine court held, in an elaborate opinion, that this could not be done, and that the prosecutor was a de facto officer despite the fact that the statute involved went to the existence of the office itself. The court expressed the opinion that the same reasons which would cause it to hold that an officer was de facto when a statute providing for his selection was unconstitutional should cause it to hold likewise when the statute creating the office was invalid. The fact that many fines had been imposed in prosecutions insti-

[103] Kline v. State, 146 Ala. 1, 41 So. 952 (1906); Speck v. State, 7 Baxt. 46 (Tenn. 1872).

[104] Coyle v. Commonwealth, 104 Pa. St. 117 (1893); In re Ah Lee, 5 Fed. 899 (D. C. Or. 1880). Contra, holding de facto, Barber v. State, 143 Ala. 1, 39 So. 318 (1905).

[105] Coyle v. Commonwealth, 104 Pa. St. 117 (1883).

[106] Ex parte Renfrow, 112 Mo. 591, 20 S.W. 682 (1892); State v. Leonard, 22 Mo. 449 (1856); State v. York, 22 Mo. 462 (1856); State v. Wiley, 109 Mo. 439, 19 S.W. 197 (1891). For additional cases see Chapter 3.

[107] State v. Blancett, 24 N.M. 433, 174 Pac. 207 (1918); Thomas Sheehan's case, 122 Mass. 445 (1877); State ex rel. Kiernan v. Recorder, 48 La. Ann. 1375, 20 So. 908 (1896).

[108] Commonwealth v. Kirby, 2 Cush. 377 (Mass. 1849).

[109] 105 Me. 224, 74 Atl. 119 (1909). Note, 8 Mich. L. Rev. 229 (1910). See also Donoghue v. Dewey, 82 Mich. 309, 46 N.W. 782 (1890); Thompson v. Couch, 144 Mich. 671, 108 N.W. 363 (1906).

tuted by this prosecutor, and that people had not only submitted to his authority but had expected him to enforce the law by performing the functions of his office, influenced the court to treat his acts as valid and to hold that their legality could not be questioned in this collateral way.

In accordance with the view expressed in the Poulin case the Georgia court has held that a person indicted for murder whose prosecution was carried on by an attorney performing the functions of his office in a district a part of which had been included by virtue of an invalid statute could not for that reason assail the title to office of the prosecutor. The de facto doctrine was applied to protect the acts of the state's attorney from attack, so far as they had taken place with respect to cases in the wrongfully annexed territory.[110] A mandamus will lie at the instance of the attorney-general to compel a judge to restore to the docket for trial a criminal case that has been removed because the indictment was returned by a grand jury held under a judge in a district created by an invalid law.[111] People ex rel. Brown v. Blake [112] is difficult to justify. In that case a policeman arrested the relator. The officer had been appointed to office by the town board of trustees. The members of this board had been appointed to office. The statute authorizing their appointment was invalid, election being the constitutionally provided mode of filling the office. This board of trustees had caused the relator's arrest by making a complaint before a justice of the peace. The accused petitioned for a writ of habeas corpus and was awarded the writ, receiving his discharge. The decision is contrary to the weight of authority from whatever angle it is viewed. In the first place, it is out of line in holding that the acts of an officer engaged in enforcing the law may be challenged by the accused when the constitutionality of the statute providing for the filling of a de jure office is involved. In the second place, the decision is contrary to the majority rule, which denies attack on a statute under which a municipality is organized. The statute in this case also provided for the incorporation of the village. The court gave little attention to this phase of the case. In the third place, if the trustees are eliminated from the case, the objection may be advanced that the relator was permitted to challenge the title to office of the appointors of the officer who had arrested him. Attack on the title of an official directly concerned with

[110] Godbee v. State, 141 Ga. 515, 81 S. E. 876 (1914).

[111] Ex parte State, 142 Ala. 87, 38 So. 835 (1904). In Lask v. United States, 1 Phinney 77 (Wis. 1839), prosecutor held a de jure office, but held two incompatible offices, contrary to the organic act of the territory. Held, a de facto officer.

[112] 49 Barb. 9 (N. Y. 1867). See criticism of this case in In re Ah Lee, 5 Fed. 899 (D. C. Or. 1880).

the proceedings is sufficiently objectionable, but it is much more objectionable to permit this "running back" along the line of appointing authority in search of some constitutional break in the chain.

H. Cases of Crimes Involving Official Status

Suppose that X is indicted for extortion. He defends by asserting that he is not an officer because the statute creating the office he purported to hold is unconstitutional. In New Jersey X was permitted to set up his defense and to obtain his freedom thereby. After stating that "an official character, either de facto or de jure, is essential" to constitute the crime of extortion, the court stated:

These defendants were never the officers they are charged to have been, and therefore could not as such have extorted. This inexorable legal conclusion is the result of the unconstitutionality of the statute which created the office of license commissioners in certain counties, which offices the defendants are charged with using for extortionate purposes.[113]

One wonders how inexorable this conclusion is when reading the case of State v. Gardner,[114] involving an indictment for offering a bribe to a city commissioner, in which the Ohio court held that the commissioner was a de facto officer although the statute that was assailed not only created the office of commissioner but was the source of the corporate existence of the city itself. The Gardner case presented a somewhat stronger situation for the application of the de facto doctrine than did the New Jersey case because of the policy favoring the denial of collateral attack on municipal corporations. In the Gardner case both the office and the municipality were involved, whereas in the New Jersey case only the office was in question. The attitudes of the two courts were, however, quite at variance.

Whether the New Jersey court still adheres to the rule of this case is not clear. The opinion seems to rely to a considerable extent on the case of Flaucher v. Camden,[115] an earlier New Jersey case. There defendant set up a license granted to him by a board as a defense to a prosecution for selling liquor without a license. The state assailed the validity of the statute creating the board from which defendant had received his license. The statute was declared invalid. The court held that because of this invalidity the license afforded no defense,

[113] Kirby et al. v. New Jersey, 57 N. J. L. 320, 322, 31 Atl. 213, 214 (1894).
[114] 54 Ohio St. 24, 42 N. E. 999 (1896).
[115] Flaucher v. Camden, 56 N. J. L. 244, 28 Atl. 82 (1893).

and the convictions was affirmed. This decision is criticized in Lang v. Mayor of Bayonne [116] and is expressly overruled in the course of the opinion in that case. Does an express statement that the case is overruled have its full apparent effect, however, when the situations in two cases are as different as they were in these? The Lang case involved a dispute between an inferior and a superior officer. The Flaucher case involved a prosecution for selling liquor without a license. Perhaps instead of saying that one case overruled the other, it is more accurate to say that the attitude of the court in the Flaucher case toward the problem of the application of the de facto doctrine to cases involving offices created by unconstitutional statutes was disapproved in the Lang case.

There is some authority for the New Jersey view in the early case of People v. Albertson,[117] in New York. That case goes so far as to hold that a person is not guilty of perjury if he testifies falsely in a trial before a justice of the peace who holds a de jure office but is chosen to fill it in accordance with an invalid law. In view of the overwhelming weight of authority to the effect that in other types of situations the de facto doctrine will be extended to give binding effect to the acts of officers whose title to offices de jure is defective, a different result from that in the Albertson case might well be reached if the situation presented in that case should come before a court at the present time.

III. COMPENSATION

The decisions regarding the effect of an unconstitutional statute on the right to compensation of an officer selected in accordance therewith are not harmonious.

In Meagher v. County of Storey [118] plaintiff sued the county to recover compensation for services rendered as magistrate. He had held the office of recorder in a city, and a statute had conferred on the holder of that office the power to act also as a magistrate. The

---

[116] 74 N. J. L. 455, 68 Atl. 90 (1906). The court said in the Flaucher case that "The only case which I have found which gives countenance to the view that there can exist a de facto officer without a de jure office, is that of Burt v. Winona & St. Peter R. R." 31 Minn. 472, 18 N. W. 285, 289 (1884).

[117] 8 How. 363 (N. Y. 1853). In Herrington v. State, 103 Ga. 319, 29 S. E. 931 (1898), the defense to an indictment of extortion was the nonexistence of the office. The county board had attempted to create the office, but had no statutory authority to do so. Held, indictment quashed. In Morford v. Territory of Oklahoma, 10 Okla. 745, 63 Pac. 960 (1901), the defendant was accused of perjury. It appeared that the judge before whom the trial in which the perjury was alleged to have been committed lacked the statutory qualifications for office. Held, the judge was de facto, and the accused could not assail title to office.

[118] 5 Nev. 244 (1869).

Supreme Court of Nevada held that no recovery could be had. The court said that he had no authority to serve as a magistrate, hence his services were gratuitous, "for the right to the salary depends upon the title to such office, and cannot be recovered by one who is simply an officer de facto." The acts of the plaintiff were, nevertheless, said to be valid as to third parties, although "the considerations which support and validate the acts of an officer de facto do not go so far as to require the payment of fees to such officer for services so performed." [119]

The case of Reddy v. Tinkum [120] involved a mandamus to compel the payment of a warrant against a county, the warrant being drawn in favor of the plaintiff. The county as constituted by statute included some territory belonging to, and located in, the state of Nevada. The county was, for that reason, defectively organized, said the court in denying the petition for the writ. The warrant was not a claim against this county, and plaintiff was not a de facto officer of any governmental organization.

On the other hand, the New Jersey court held in Erwin v. Mayor of Jersey City [121] that a city attorney could recover compensation for services rendered by him in his official capacity even if the statute authorizing the board of commissioners to appoint him to office was invalid. The New Jersey court took the view that the plaintiff had rendered services, therefore he should receive his compensation. This is a quite different view from that adopted by the Nevada court, which maintained that salary was due an officer only because of his title to office.

A group of New York cases have also involved this question. The earliest of them is Morris v. People.[122] The suit in that case was brought by the prosecutor for the state, on the relation of a judge, to recover a statutory penalty for refusal to audit a claim against the county for salary. The statute creating the court was assailed as unconstitutional, and it was contended that therefore the judge was not entitled to compensation. That being so, counsel argued, it followed that the defendants had properly refused to audit the claim. The legislature had by statute made the salary of these judges charges against the county. The court held, Senator Lott speaking for the majority, that the penalty was recoverable; that even if the

[119] Meagher v. County of Storey, 5 Nev. 244, 251 (1869). State ex rel. Egbert v. Blumberg, 46 Wash. 270, 89 Pac. 708 (1907).

[120] 60 Cal. 458 (1882).

[121] 60 N. J. L. 141, 37 Atl. 732 (1897).

[122] 3 Denio 381 (N. Y. 1846). See also Brennan v. Mayor, 1 Hun 315 (N. Y. 1874), 62 N. Y. 365 (1875), permitting recovery, some emphasis on acquiescence on part of public employees.

statute was unconstitutional, the judge was an officer de facto whose title could not be collaterally impeached in a proceeding to which he was not a party. The services were rendered by the judge, and the legislature had the power to make this a county charge; that being the case, the defendants had no alternative but to audit the claim or pay the penalty.

People ex rel. Kingsland v. Bradley [123] is the second of the New York cases. There a mandamus was granted to compel the treasurer of a county to pay a salary claim, although the statute authorizing the appointment of the person to whom the salary was due was invalid. This case is perhaps not so strong an authority as the Morris case in support of the doctrine that such claims can be enforced, because the court treated the case as one involving legislative ratification through subsequent appropriations to pay the claims. Legislative recognition of the claim was also an element in the Morris case, but less clearly so than in the Bradley case. The case is perhaps an authority for legislative appropriation of money to pay claims of officers whose title to office is defective. The Bradley case differs from the Morris case also in this: that in the latter the statute that was defective was one creating the office, whereas in the former the statute involved was one providing for the filling of the office.

In Demarest v. The Mayor,[124] the third of the New York cases, the court held that a city may defeat an action for salary by a de jure officer by showing that the money had been paid to a person holding a certificate of election, though the election had been held under an invalid statute. The case was distinguished by the court from that of Norton v. Shelby County [125] on the ground that a de jure office existed, whereas in the Norton case this was not true.

Where the statute creating an office was invalid, the Illinois court refused to permit the claimant to the office to recover money deposited with the city and alleged to belong to him, the basis of the claim being that the city had no right to retain the money, it having been obtained by means of a nonexistent office.[126] This is a proper holding, because if the city was not entitled to it, by the same reasoning the claimant would also be denied recovery.

[123] 6 Barb. 228 (N.Y. 1872).

[124] 147 N.Y. 203, 41 N.E. 405 (1895). The court in this case treated the office as validly existing, saying at 209, in answer to a contrary contention: "Unless the office did not exist by law, how could the plaintiff and his associates base their present claim to have been elected to it? This very demand and suit are an ample concession that aldermanic offices existed to be filled."

[125] 118 U.S. 425, 6 Sup. Ct. Rep. 1121, 30 L. Ed. 178 (1885).

[126] City of Chicago v. Burke, 226 Ill. 191, 80 N.E. 720 (1907). Where no law authorized office, see Ward v. Cook, 78 Ill. App. 11 (1898). See Saxby v. Sonnemann, 318 Ill. 600, 149 N.E. 526 (1925).

A series of Minnesota cases illustrate into what tangled situations courts are sometimes led as a result of conflicting claims to the salary of an office.

From 1912 to 1915 one Windom was the municipal judge in the city of Duluth. On April 6, 1915, an election was held at which one Smallwood was elected to the office of municipal judge. Windom retained the office, however, until May 3, because of a contest of Smallwood's election. Smallwood took possession of the office on May 3 and performed the duties of municipal judge until July 30. On this latter date the Supreme Court decided that Smallwood was not entitled to the office because of the unconstitutionality of the preferential voting statute in accordance with which he had been elected.[127]

Thereupon Windom brought an action to obtain a writ of mandamus to compel the canvassing board to issue a certificate of election to him. In this action he was successful.[128] He assumed the duties of the office on July 31 and performed the judicial functions attached thereto until September 13. On September 13 the governor of Minnesota appointed Smallwood to the office of municipal judge of Duluth. This appointment was made on the theory that the office was vacant in consequence of the alleged unconstitutionality of a statute entitling Windom to act as a hold-over judge. On December 17 the Supreme Court of the state decided that Smallwood was entitled to the office by virtue of the executive appointment, the hold-over statute being unconstitutional, and a judgment of ouster was rendered against Windom in an action of quo warranto in which Smallwood was the relator.[129]

The city had paid Smallwood the salary attaching to the office during a part of the time that Windom had performed the duties of the office. To recover this money either from the city of Duluth or from Smallwood, Windom brought an action against the city, joining Smallwood, for such sums as had been paid to the latter. Windom claimed that he had been the de jure judge during the period up to September 13, when the executive appointment was made.

The Minnesota Supreme Court decided that Windom was entitled to compensation for the time he had served as judge despite the fact that he was a hold-over judge under an unconstitutional statute.[130] Smallwood, on the other hand, was said to be entitled to compensation for the period during which he had performed the

[127] Brown v. Smallwood, 130 Minn. 492, 153 N. W. 953 (1915).
[128] State ex rel. Windom v. Prince, 131 Minn. 399, 155 N. W. 628 (1915).
[129] State ex rel. Smallwood v. Windom, 131 Minn. 401, 155 N. W. 629 (1915).
[130] Windom v. Duluth, 137 Minn. 154, 162 N. W. 1075 (1917).

duties of the office. He, too, then, received his compensation, despite the fact that he performed his functions by virtue of an invalid statute.

The court declined to decide whether de facto status should be accorded both the incumbents, each for the period during which he served. The city was willing to pay whoever was entitled to the money, and the court said that all that needed to be decided was how much of the money should be paid to each of the contestants. The opinion in the case intimates that Smallwood would be required to pay over to Windom the moneys received during the period in which Windom was performing the functions of the office.

However, the court did stress, in the quo warranto case,[131] the de facto status of both judges during the period each had possession of the office. At all times, said the court, there existed a de jure office, because in none of the litigation was the *existence* of the *office* of municipal judge challenged. The case involved not the existence of the office but the validity of the methods whereby it had been filled. It is submitted that the Minnesota court decided the last of these cases correctly — and that is the only one of interest at this point — in giving to each of the incumbents his salary for the period he had served.

It appears then that the courts are divided not only on the question whether salary shall be recovered where the statute creating the office is invalid but also where the statute filling the office is invalid, the office being de jure. The courts will probably be more hesitant to allow recovery where the existence of the office is questioned than where only the validity of the title to an admittedly valid office is involved. But there may be some tendency, on the part of those courts who regard service rendered as the basis of the recovery, to permit recovery even if the defective statute goes to the creation of the office itself. Certainly the legislature can by subsequent legislation provide for the payment of salary claims, and such legislation will not be open to the objection that it appropriates public moneys to private uses. Courts adhering strictly to the void ab initio theory may be expected for some time still to refuse to permit recovery in the absence of such legislation. The inequity of this should cause

---

[131] State ex rel. Smallwood v. Windom, 131 Minn. 401, 155 N. W. 629 (1915). "To avoid useless controversy or litigation it is proper to say that the official acts of the relator and the respondent in their various incumbencies of the offices are valid. All the time there has been a de jure office of municipal judge. All the time there has been a de facto judge filling the office. The acts of a de facto judge, actually occupying the office and transacting business, are valid. . . . In the actual incumbencies since the April, 1914, election, the official acts of the incumbent, whether Judge Windom or Judge Smallwood occupying the office and exercising its functions, are valid." 131 Minn. at 420–21. See text to note 65, *supra*.

them gradually to adopt a less severe rule.[132] A few states have adopted statutes regulating the conditions under which payment of salary may be made to one of the contestants for an office.[133] The matter of compensation should be regulated by statutes in all the states, in order that the government may know to whom to make payments and that equity may be done between the claimants.

IV. SUMMARY AND CONCLUSIONS

A brief statement of the generalizations that may be made from the cases thus far considered may aid in an analysis of the points of contact between the doctrines concerning the effect of an unconstitutional statute and the theories underlying de facto status in the law of officers.

1. Persons acting in an official capacity for the state may assail the legal basis for an office. In granting judgment of ouster in such cases the courts may use their discretion in delaying the execution of the judgment in order that the functions of government may not be seriously interrupted.

2. Official status may be questioned in disputes between claimants for an office as well as in disputes between two independent officers who may be contesting each other's authority to perform specific functions. An inferior officer is not ordinarily permitted to assail the official status of one of his superiors.

3. Private individuals may not, in the absence of statute, invoke quo warranto to question official status. In other cases they are similarly restricted if the defect in official status is one going to the mode of filling an office instead of a defect in the constitution of the office itself. However, although there is some respectable authority to the contrary, the decided weight of authority is that a private individual may question the existence of an office, in disputes with officers purporting to hold such offices, if the statute establishing the office is unconstitutional. This is true in tax, eminent domain, bond, tort,

---

[132] In People v. Toal, 85 Cal. 333, 24 Pac. 603 (1890), the court said at 338, in holding the court to have been created by an invalid statute: "And the emoluments of the office to which they were not entitled will probably compensate the judges for all liabilities incurred by them by reason of having acted without authority of law." Query: Could the state recover the money paid to the officer as salary? In Nagel v. Bosworth, 148 Ky. 807, 147 S. W. 940 (1912), the court said that "a de facto officer is not entitled to the emoluments of the office, and so Judge Hodge is not entitled to any salary as circuit judge." Cf. Hubbard v. Martin, 8 Yerg. 498 (Tenn. 1835).

[133] Cal. Pol. Code (Deering, 1923), sec. 936. "When the title of the incumbent of any office in this state is contested by proceedings instituted in any court for that purpose, no warrant can thereafter be drawn or paid for any part of his salary until such proceedings have been finally determined; provided, however, that this section shall not be construed to apply to any party to a contest or proceeding now pending

and criminal and civil cases generally. It applies to judicial as well as to clerical officers. There is perhaps a tendency in the more recent cases to apply the de facto doctrine in order to prevent private individuals from questioning official status even though the existence of the office is involved, but the weight of authority is still to the contrary.

In presenting this analysis of the present state of the rules of law as to the effect of an unconstitutional statute on the status of a public officer, it has been thought best to omit detailed considerations of theory except as they were necessarily involved in the approval or criticism of particular cases or classes of cases. Some care has been taken also to avoid dwelling on landmark dicta, some of which have been of controlling importance in this branch of the law.

Is there a sound basis for the distinction that the courts draw between cases involving the existence of an office and those involving the method of filling it? A consideration of the reasons that have been advanced in support of the rule denying collateral attack may be helpful in answering this question. Four reasons have been suggested in the cases for refusing to permit a private individual to question official status when the office is de jure and only the method of filling it is defective.

a. The title of a person to office should not be tried in an action to which he is not a party. There is some merit in this reason, al-

or hereafter instituted, who holds the certificate of election or commission of office and discharges the duties of the office; but such party shall receive the salary of such office, the same as if no such contest or proceeding was pending."

Sec. 937. "As soon as such proceedings are instituted, the clerk of the court in which they are pending must certify the facts to the officers whose duty it would otherwise be to draw such warrants or pay such salary, except in the cases included in the proviso to the foregoing section."

Mo. Rev. Stat. 1919, sec. 13, 329. "Whenever any office, elective or appointive, the emoluments of which are required to be paid out of the state treasury, shall be contested or disputed by two or more persons claiming the right thereto, or by information in the nature of a quo warranto, then no warrant shall be drawn by the auditor, or paid by the treasurer, for the salary by law attached to said office, until the right to the same shall be legally determined between the persons or parties claiming such right: Provided, however, and it is hereby further enacted, that in all cases when the persons to whom the commission for such office shall have issued shall deliver to the party contesting his right to such office a good and sufficient bond, in double the amount of the annual salary of such office, conditioned that if, upon final determination of the rights of the contestants, it shall be decided that the obligor is not, and that the obligee therein is entitled to the office, in controversy, he shall pay over to the obligee the amount of salary therefor drawn from the date of the receipt of each installment received by him, then, and in such case, notwithstanding the provisions of this law, a warrant may be drawn by the auditor, and paid by the treasurer to the person holding the commission aforesaid, for the amount of his salary, as the same shall become due. It shall be the duty of any person contesting the election of any such office to give notice of such contest to the state auditor, and no such contest shall be heard or determined until he shall satisfy the tribunal trying such contest that such notice has been given."

though it is perhaps less weighty than would seem to be the case at first glance. The officer is not personally given an opportunity to enter a defense in many cases, but it often happens that the state or some other governmental division is an interested party. The state's attorney in such a case would in effect then be pleading the case of the officer. So, too, for example, in the case of a civil proceeding in which the title of a judge is challenged. The party who is to lose by the successful attack on the status of the judge may be expected to defend the status of the officer with varying degrees of diligence. It is true, however, that in some cases there may not be adequate presentation of the case of the officer whose status is assailed. On the other hand, it must be remembered that ouster does not follow an inquiry into status in any but quo warranto proceedings, so unless the state proceeds to oust him the officer may continue the performance of his functions. Against this, in turn, must be balanced the possibility that private individuals would continue to challenge the authority of the officer to such an extent that for all practical purposes his work would be seriously hampered or even completely stopped by repeated inquiries into his official status.

b. Some courts say that the status of an officer cannot be questioned in certain types of situations because he is a de facto officer. At other times the reason given is the rule that collateral attack will not be permitted on a de facto officer. This assumes the point to be decided, and is a statement of a rule but not of a reason.

c. The reason most commonly urged in support of treating an officer as de jure to all others than the state is that confusion in the work of government will ensue from a policy of permitting attack on official status. There is much soundness in this position, despite the fact that it may be mitigated to some extent by curative and validating legislation and that, as previously pointed out, actual ouster takes place only when attack is by the state. Cases should be settled on their merits, and the work of government should be disrupted as little as possible by private litigants.

d. In cases involving the status of judges the peculiar situation is presented of persons passing upon their own status. It is true that a higher court may with propriety pass upon the status of a lower one. But what of the Oregon case where the status of some of the members of the Supreme Court of the state was involved? The court in that case took jurisdiction, the two justices whose status was in question not participating in the decision, and held that their status was unassailable.

The question that naturally suggests itself at this point is whether these reasons are not equally applicable to a case involving the existence of an office. It would seem that the same reasons of public policy apply to the one as to the other. There is, perhaps, this observation to be made concerning the two problems: It may be a more serious matter to have an office created by an unconstitutional statute than to have a particular officer selected in accordance with an invalid law, because a statute creating an office defines and authorizes the performance of certain governmental functions. In the case of the defective statute authorizing the selection of the officer the problem is as to the method of choice; the functions are in any event to be performed by somebody. It is quite probable that this has been the basis of the distinction drawn by the courts between these two classes of cases, and it must be admitted that it is not without considerable weight.

But when the problem is viewed from the standpoint of the private individual dealing with the officer, or from that of the officer whose compensation may be denied because of the nonexistence of the office, or from that of the public at large whose primary interest is, in such a case, to have the work of government carried on in an orderly fashion, it seems clear that there is also some soundness in the contention that the state alone should be permitted to challenge the usurpation by officers of the powers and functions of government.

The problem in all these cases is really one concerning the effect of an unconstitutional statute. The de facto doctrine is involved only as a medium whereby to give to an unconstitutional statute sufficient effect to accomplish the ends of justice and government. All courts seem to agree that the doctrine should be invoked to give effect to an invalid statute providing for the selection of officers. When, however, the courts have before them a statute that purports to create an office, they refuse to give it any effect if the enactment is unconstitutional. For this reason they do not apply the de facto doctrine in such a case. Sometimes this refusal to apply it is due to the view that an unconstitutional statute is not law and should be given no effect whatever in the disposition of the case. At other times it is due to the belief that a valid statute is an essential prerequisite to the application of the de facto doctrine.[134] The fact that some courts have regarded the de facto doctrine as one method whereby to accord some effect to an unconstitutional statute, and that other courts have looked upon the doctrine as an independent rule or principle, to be applied only in certain situations in which specified factors are present, has

[134] For attempts to generalize on the cases in terms of the de facto doctrine, see Tooke, De Facto Municipal Corporations under Unconstitutional Statutes, 37 Yale L. J. 935 (1928); Wallach, De Facto Officers, 22 Pol. Sci. Quart. 451, 469 (1907).

caused a different rule to be formulated with respect to the situation in which the invalid statute is one purporting to create an office from that relating to the situation in which the defective law purports to fill that office.

In the greater number of cases reviewed in this study, justice would have been served by giving some effect to the invalid statutes involved. That the decisions in many of them were rendered on the assumption that an invalid statute authorizing the performance of governmental functions could have no effect was usually due to a failure to distinguish cause from effect. It may be that in some classes of cases no effect should be given to an unconstitutional statute. If this is true, it should be because justice is not served by giving the law any effect, and not because of some assumed rule of constitutional law. It cannot be too strongly emphasized that there is no general rule of constitutional law that requires that an unconstitutional statute be given no effect.[135]

When this is realized and when the courts again have occasion to reconsider the question of attack on official status, the views expressed in State v. Gardner,[136] Burt v. Winona & St. Peter R. R.,[137] and State v. Poulin [138] will doubtless gain an increasing number of adherents.[139] The opinion in the latter case contains the following statement, which has become the classic brief exposition of the view that official status cannot be assailed even though the office involved has been created by an unconstitutional statute:

The de facto doctrine is exotic, and was engrafted upon the law, as a matter of policy and necessity, to protect the interests of the public and individuals, where those interests were involved in the official acts of persons exercising the duty of an office without being lawful officers. It would be unreasonable to require the public to inquire into the title of an officer, or compel him to show title, and these have become settled principles in law. To protect those who deal with officers apparently holding office under color of law, in such manner as to warrant the public in assuming that they were officers and in dealing with them as such, the law validates their acts as to the public and third persons, on the ground that as to them although not officers de jure they are officers in fact whose acts public policy requires to be construed as valid. This was not because of any character or quality conferred upon the officer, or attached to him by reason of any defective election or appointment,

---

[135] For some situations in which an unconstitutional statute is given some effect, see Chapter 1, and, generally, all of the chapters of this book.
[136] 54 Ohio St. 24, 42 N. E. 999 (1896).
[137] 31 Minn. 472, 18 N. W. 285, 289 (1884).
[138] 105 Me. 224, 74 Atl. 119 (1909).
[139] See People v. Emmerson, 333 Ill. 606, 115 N. E. 217 (1929), suggesting that invalid nominating statute will not be fatal to title to office if election statute valid.

but as a name or character given to his acts by the law for the purpose of making them valid.[140]

As to the rule with respect to the effect of an unconstitutional statute, in its bearing on this problem, the court said:

Declaring a statute unconstitutional does not necessarily render it void ab initio. It is an axiom of practical wisdom, coeval with the development of the common law, founded upon necessity, that de facto acts of binding force may be performed under presumption of law. There is another rule so uniform in its application that it, too, has become a legal maxim, that "all acts of the legislature are presumed to be constitutional." [141]

After all, legislative acts are facts and should be factors in the decision of a case, even though as law they are not entitled to full force and effect. People act in reliance on such laws, and until their unconstitutionality has been judicially declared, those so relying upon them should be protected.[142]

[140] 105 Me. 224, 229, 74 Atl. 119 (1909). A note writer in 8 Mich. L. Rev. 229, 236 (1910) says: "It is the writer's opinion that the beneficial result accomplished by these recent cases will not only justify the reasons supporting their decision, but also win followers." The note disapproves the doctrine of the Norton case. The writer argues for a similar rule with respect to officers as that which obtains in the municipal corporations cases. Cf. Jewell v. Gilbert, 64 N. H. 13, 5 Atl. 80 (1885).

[141] State v. Poulin, 105 Me. 224, 228, 74 Atl. 119. The courts often say that the de facto doctrine is not for the benefit of the officers themselves, but is for the public welfare. So it has been held that de facto officers cannot act so as to validate own defective position. People ex rel. Ferguson v. Vrooman, 101 Misc. Rep. 233, 166 N. Y. S. 923 (1917).

[142] The foregoing discussion of the de facto doctrine has not attempted to go beyond the judicial exposition of the doctrine. What would be the effect of such a statute as the following, taken from N. Y. Cons. Laws (Cahill, 1923), Chapter 41, sec. 1820, following a section making the performance of official duties prior to the taking of oath, or the filing of required security, a criminal offense, is problematical: "The last section must not be construed to affect the validity of acts done by a person exercising the functions of a public office in fact, where persons other than himself are interested in maintaining the validity of such acts."

Chapter V

LIABILITY OF PUBLIC OFFICERS FOR ACTION OR NONACTION*

INTRODUCTION

The question of the liability of an officer for acting or failing to act under an unconstitutional statute may arise in a variety of situations.

1) Injunction. — Injunctive relief is often sought to prevent an officer from taking threatened action under a statute alleged to be invalid. If the court decides that the law is unconstitutional the decree will issue, and such a suit is not one against the state because the officer is being restrained in his private instead of in his official capacity. He is said to be stripped of his official character and consequently to be subject to injunctive restraint.[1]

2) Mandamus. — A writ of mandamus may be asked for by a private individual to compel the performance of some act that the officer asserts is imposed upon him by an unconstitutional statute. The question whether the officer may set this up as a defense is a troublesome one, and the courts are divided upon the answer to it.[2] Some courts refuse to permit the unconstitutionality of the statute to be used as a defense and will issue the writ if the relator makes out a case that otherwise entitles him to it.

* This chapter originally appeared in 77 U. Pa. L. Rev. 155.

[1] Astrom v. Hammond, 3 McLean 107, Fed. Cas. No. 595 (C. C. Mich. 1842); Commissioners of Wyandotte County v. Kansas City, Ft. Scott & Memphis R. R., 5 Kan. App. 43, 47 Pac. 326 (1896); Lynn v. Polk, 8 Lea 121 (Tenn. 1881); Board of Liquidation v. McComb, 92 U. S. 531, 23 L. Ed. 623 (1875). Bonnett v. Vallier, 136 Wis. 193, 116 N. W. 885 (1908); Rockaway Pac. Corp. v. Stotesbury, 255 Fed. 345 (D. C. N. D. N. Y. 1917); Mich. State Bk. v. Hastings, 1 Doug. 225 (Mich. 1844). See 4 Pomeroy, Equity Jurisprudence (4th ed., 1919), sec. 1819. Other cases on this point involving tax questions appear in Chapter 10, dealing with tax recovery.

[2] State ex rel. Mueller v. Thompson, 149 Wis. 488, 137 N. W. 20 (1912); Bd. of Commrs. of Newton County v. State, 161 Ind. 616, 69 N. E. 442 (1904). For a discussion of this question, with citations of cases pro and con, and a consideration of the reasons for decision advanced by the courts, see Rapacz, Protection of Officers Who Act under Unconstitutional Statutes, 11 Minn. L. Rev. 585 (1927); comment, 15 Minn. L. Rev. 340 (1931); note, 34 Harv. L. Rev. 86 (1920). Apparently a judge may raise the question if he is a defendant in a proceeding to compel him to issue a warrant. McClellan v. Stein, 229 Mich. 203, 201 N. W. 209 (1924).

The author inclines to the view that an officer should be permitted to raise the issue of constitutionality, whether the duty be ministerial or discretionary, on the ground that the validity of the statute should be tested as early as possible unless some weighty reason exists for not doing so, and such doctrines as that of "political questions" are then available to save the courts from settling them. This view does not depend entirely on liability or non-liability, or on interest as a party, but upon the broader ground of policy here involved. Much can be said for discontinuing the existing policy of permitting constitutionality to be raised so freely by everybody, but if the question is to be raised by anybody, an officer who is a defendant in a mandamus case should be considered as having a sufficient interest to raise it.[3] An officer acting under mandamus is protected, even though the statute imposing the duty be subsequently declared invalid.[4]

Administrative officers are sometimes said not to be entrusted with the power to decide questions of constitutionality.[5] If this is understood to mean that such officers do not have the final disposition of constitutional questions, the statement is accurate, but if it is taken to mean that administrative officers may never pass upon these questions, it is manifestly erroneous. This is not to say, however, that an administrative officer may pit his own judgment against that of a court. He may not do so. If the court has adjudicated the question, he must abide by its decision. So, if an order of mandamus is issued compelling a county clerk to extend certain tax levies upon the assessor's books and he refuses to do so, he may not defend against proceedings in contempt to punish him for the violation of the order by showing that the tax is invalid. The quotation from People ex rel. Attorney-General v. Solomon,[6] sets forth the reasons for this rule.

The law under which this additional tax was imposed had passed the legislature under all the forms of the constitution, and had received executive sanction, and became, by its own intrinsic force, the law to you, to every other public officer in the state, and to all the people. You assumed the responsibility of declaring the law unconstitutional, and at once determined to disregard it, to set up your own judgment as superior to the expressed will of the legislature, asserting, in fact, an entire independence thereof. This is the first case in our judicial history in which a

[3] For an excellent statement of this problem, and a proper solution of it, see State ex rel. Test v. Steinwedel, 180 N. E. 865 (Ind. 1932).
[4] State v. Clements, 217 Ala. 685, 117 So. 296 (1928).
[5] Marmon Motor Car Co. v. Sparks, 87 Ind. App. 591, 161 N. E. 647 (1928).
[6] 54 Ill. 39 (1870). See also statements on the danger of independent judgment by officer, in Huntington v. Worthen, 120 U. S. 97, 7 Sup. Ct. Rep. 469, 30 L. Ed. 588 (1886).

ministerial officer has taken upon himself the responsibility of nullifying an act of the legislature for the better collection of the public revenue — of arresting its operation — of disobeying its behests, and placing his own judgment above legislative authority expressed in the form of law.

To the law every man owes homage, "the very least as needing its care, the greatest as not exempted from its power." To allow a ministerial officer to decide upon the validity of a law would be subversive of the great objects and purposes of government, for if one such officer may assume infallibility, all other like officers may do the same, and thus an end be put to civil government, one of whose cardinal principles is subjection to the laws.

Being a ministerial officer, the path of duty was plain before you. You strayed from it, and became a volunteer in the effort to arrest the law, and it was successful. Had the property owners who were subjected to this additional tax considered the law unconstitutional, they could, in the proper courts, have tested the question, and it was their undoubted right so to do. Your only duty was obedience. The collected will of the whole people was embodied in that law. A decent respect to them required that all their servants should obey it. Your disobedience being the cause of your inability to obey the mandamus, cannot, as we have said, make a justification in this proceeding, and in full accordance with this view is the case of The People ex rel. Dox v. The County Judge of Johnson Co. et al. 12 Iowa 237.

3) Criminal prosecution against an officer. — The state may bring a criminal action against an officer for failing to perform some duty with the performance of which he is charged by statute, the non-performance of which is by the same or another statute made a criminal offense. State v. Godwin [7] was a case of this type. There an indictment was returned against a justice of the peace for failing to make a report required by statute, an omission that constituted a statutory crime. A subsequent statute purported to relieve the justice of the peace from the performance of this duty and to provide for its performance by another officer. This second statute turned out to be unconstitutional. The justice was then indicted for his omission to make the report. The theory of the indictment was that the second statute, being unconstitutional, had no effect in transferring the duty to make the report referred to, nor did it affect the duty of the justice to make it. The court decided that the justice was not guilty. The opinion emphasizes the presumption that a statute is valid until it is declared invalid. This presumption should protect the officer as well

[7] 123 N.C. 697, 31 S.E. 221 (1898). Texas Co. v. Arizona, 31 Ariz. 485, 254 Pac. 1060 (1927), state may not collect tax from collecting dealer in excess of that imposed by statute, the governor's veto of the statute increasing the tax having been declared invalid.

as insure for the statute the benefit of any doubts that the court might entertain as to its constitutionality. The decision was also influenced by the manifest injustice of requiring the justice of the peace to be wiser, with respect to the possible unconstitutionality of a statute, than the legislature and the people. To fine an officer for obeying what appeared to be the law seemed too illogical a result for the court to reach. A strict adherence to the void ab initio theory [8] might have led to a contrary decision, but the case illustrates that that doctrine will not be carried to its logical conclusion in a case of criminal prosecution of an officer for failing to perform his duty, the officer having been relieved of the duty by what turned out to be an invalid act.

4) Action for damages against an officer. — An action for damages may be brought against an officer who acts under an unconstitutional statute, by a party claiming to have been injured thereby. A similar action may be instituted against the officer by a private individual who alleges that he has been injured by the refusal of the officer to take certain action under a statute that the latter believes to be unconstitutional.

In one of the senses in which the term *liability* is used it is perhaps correct to say that the officer is liable in the first three situations just considered, to a suit for an injunction, to a proceeding in mandamus, or to criminal prosecution. As used in this study, however, the term *liability* is narrower in meaning. By it is meant liability to an action for money damages, such as was mentioned in the fourth group of cases referred to above.

In considering the cases on the effect of an unconstitutional statute on the liability of an officer, three types of situations are easily distinguishable: (1) cases in which an action is brought because of a refusal of the officer to act; (2) cases of direct action by the officer, in the absence of an intervening judicial process; and (3) cases involving judicial process or judicial proceedings. The problem of the protection of officers acting under invalid statutes will be considered after a review of the cases. Unless expressly stated to the contrary, all the situations discussed in this chapter involve official action or nonaction under an unconstitutional statute or ordinance.[9]

[8] The phrase void ab initio as used here refers to the view taken by some courts that an unconstitutional statute should be entirely eliminated in the decision of a case, as explained in Chapter 1.

[9] An officer is of course liable for action taken in the absence of a statute when such action is contrary to a constitutional prohibition which operates upon individuals. Robinson v. Bishop, 39 Hun 370 (N.Y. 1886) (liable on bond issued in excess of constitutional authority); Milligan v. Hovey, 3 Biss. 13, Fed. Cas. No. 9, 605 (C. C. Ind. 1871) (General Hovey, in the famous Milligan case of the Civil War period, held liable for false imprisonment, in exceeding his constitutional authority).

I. REFUSAL TO ACT

In Clark v. Miller [10] a road had been laid over the plaintiff's land. The first assessment of damages was $185. On reassessment this sum was raised to $355. The defendant, a town supervisor, presented the amount of the first assessment to the board for allowance, refusing to present the claim for $355 on the ground that the statute under which the reassessment had been held was unconstitutional. The plaintiff, refusing to accept the award of $185, brought an action against the supervisor for refusing to present the reassessment figure to the board. The supervisor defended with the plea that he was under no duty to act in accordance with a statute he believed to be unconstitutional. The court held for the plaintiff, allowing a recovery of $355. In sustaining this decision the court said, in the course of its opinion, that "honest ignorance does not excuse a public officer for disobedience to the law." [11] Disobedience in such a case was said to be at the peril of the officer, and inasmuch as the plaintiff had an interest in the performance of this function, he was entitled to recover what he had lost by the refusal of the supervisor to perform the same. The attitude of the court is set out in the following quotation from the opinion:

That the defendant thought the law unconstitutional, and that this view was shared by the town officers, and that his refusal to obey the statute went upon that ground is, in a legal point of view, of no consequence.[12]

The court said further:

In my opinion it ought to be deemed settled in the law of this state that a ministerial officer, charged by statute with an absolute and certain duty, in the performance of which an individual has a special interest, is liable to an action if he refuses and omits to perform it.[13]

With respect to the amount of recovery, counsel contended that interest only should be allowed and that only for the period until the claim could again be presented and allowed. The court held, however, that the gist of the wrong was the refusal to present the claim for $355. Therefore that amount with interest should constitute the amount of the judgment. On the question of damages the court said:

In respect to the rule of damages, I have no doubt that the defendant is answerable for the whole amount which, by his refusal to perform his duty, the plaintiff has been unable to obtain. The law will not limit his

[10] 54 N. Y. 528 (1874).   [12] 54 N. Y. 532.
[11] 54 N. Y. 534.   [13] 54 N. Y. 534.

recovery to anything less than the amount of the reassessment; for such a limit would drive him to a succession of actions, in none of which could he, if the defendant's position is correct, recover more than interest. It cannot be assumed that the defendant would be taught by the result of one action and proceed to do his duty, and thus avoid another. The plaintiff is not thus to be put off. The defendant's misconduct has deprived him of obtaining his money, and the defendant must answer to the whole injury which he has occasioned.[14]

One cannot help feeling that the court does not make allowance enough for the respect usually accorded its judgments when it says that it cannot be assumed that the defendant would be taught by the result of one action. Is not that exactly what one would reasonably expect: that the defendant would learn by one action and shape his behavior accordingly?

In Morris v. People [15] a New York statute provided for a penalty of $250 for refusal on the part of members of the board of supervisors to audit claims against the county. A claim for salary was presented to the board by a person purporting to be a judge in the county. The state legislature had provided that the judge's salary should be a charge against the county. The defendants, as members of the board of supervisors, refused to audit the claim. They alleged that the statute creating the court of which the plaintiff claimed to be judge was unconstitutional because in effect it appropriated public money for a private purpose. They concluded, therefore, that he was not entitled to his salary. In an action of debt brought by the prosecuting attorney, at the instance of the person claiming to be judge, to recover the penalty of $250, the court held that the defendant supervisors were liable. The court admitted that the statute creating the court was defective, but it held that the legislature could nevertheless provide for the payment of services performed as judge. To do so was not, said the court, diverting public money to a private use.

In Norwood v. Goldsmith [16] the treasurer of a county refused to pay a warrant that had been drawn for the repayment of taxes alleged to have been paid under an unconstitutional statute. In the opinion of the treasurer the statute under which the taxes had been paid was constitutional. A board of commissioners to whom the claim had been presented thought differently, however, and allowed the claim. No court had declared the statute to be either constitutional or unconstitutional. Following an ineffectual application for

[14] 54 N. Y. 535.
[15] 3 Denio 381 (N. Y. 1846). The majority opinion was delivered by Senator Lott.
[16] 168 Ala. 224, 53 So. 84 (1910).

a writ of mandamus, the plaintiff, as holder of the warrant, brought a statutory action against the treasurer and his sureties, under a statute authorizing judgment for the amount of the claim if its payment had been refused. The court found for the plaintiff. In answer to the argument that a proper proceeding should first have been instituted to have the statute declared invalid, the court said that the treasurer had passed on its constitutionality in refusing payment of the warrant, and the board had passed on the same question when they allowed the claim, and the two judgments being in opposition to each other, this was a proper proceeding in which to settle the matter.

The view of the court with respect to the privilege of an officer to pass upon the unconstitutionality of a statute is well expressed in the following statement:

All persons or officers are of necessity required to pass upon the validity of all acts or proposed statutes under which they are required to act or to decline to act. In so acting or declining to act under such proposed statute he must necessarily pass upon it for himself. He may do so with or without advice from attorneys or other sources of information. But courts are the one source from which he can get no information, in advance, as to whether he should, in any particular instance, observe or decline to observe the requirements of the proposed act or statute. Every executive officer, or every person as for that matter, is presumed to know the law — a presumption often violent but always necessary. Hence, every man is his own constructionist. If two differ as to the construction of a given act, and it is acted upon or declined to be acted upon by the one, to the hurt or injury of the other, and the one is sued in the courts by the other for so acting or declining to act, and in the decision of the cause it becomes necessary to pass upon the validity of the act in order to determine the rights of the parties in that suit, the court will then — but not until then — pass upon the constitutionality of the act; and it is then only passed upon by the court in so far as the rights of these particular parties to the particular suit are concerned. When so decided by the highest court of the land all people, including executive and judicial officers, ought and usually do consider that particular question as settled and binding; but this is only so by the rules of policy, propriety, and common consent, and the credence which the people have in the opinions of such courts.[17]

[17] *Ibid.*, 234, 53 So. at 87; cf. Sessums v. Botts, 34 Tex. 335 (1870). The court in that case said, at 349: "We are not willing to indorse the proposition, in its broadest sense, that a ministerial officer has the right or power to decide upon the constitutionality or unconstitutionality of an act passed with all the formality of law. It is the duty of such officers to execute and not to pass judgment upon the law, and we are of the opinion that the clerk of the district court should have refused to issue execution in violation of what appeared to be a valid and binding law, until the same had been declared void by the tribunal properly constituted for that purpose."

It is difficult to reconcile some other portions of the opinion rendered by Justice Mayfield with the views expressed in this quotation. The court adopted without qualification the sweeping dictum of Justice Field in the case of Norton v. Shelby County,[18] stating that an unconstitutional statute is exactly as though it had never been enacted.

Norwood v. Goldsmith [19] and Clark v. Miller [20] are distinguishable on this ground: that in the former a statutory action was involved, whereas in the latter a common law action was permitted. In the former case the officer was subject to the penalty because of the statute, as interpreted by the court. In the latter the court arrived at the same conclusion in the absence of statute. One may well question the wisdom of interpreting a statute, such as that involved in the Norwood case, to cover a refusal to pay a warrant because of doubt as to the constitutionality of the statute that purported to authorize the claim for which the warrant was issued. Suppose that Goldsmith had paid out the money on the warrant and that subsequently the county had brought an action against him to recover it. Could the treasurer defend by saying that he paid the warrant because he thought it his duty to do so although he had private doubts with respect to its constitutionality? The Declaratory Judgment Act would be available to permit the parties to obtain a judicial decree settling the question if it were in force, and such a case as this illustrates the need for such an act.[21] The treasurer, on one side, and the warrant holder, on the other, could have litigated the matter so that the treasurer would have been protected, and the warrant holder would, as a result, have obtained his money if he was entitled to it.

In considering the justice of the results of the Norwood and Clark cases, the possible use of the writ of mandamus must be taken into account. The Alabama court denied an application for a writ of mandamus in the Norwood case, on the ground that a legal remedy was available in the form of the statutory action which was subsequently brought and which has just been considered.[22] The cases are not agreed that the existence of a statutory action is sufficient to bar the application for the writ, although if the action is summary and effective the tendency would perhaps be to deny the application.[23]

[18] 118 U. S. 425, 6 Sup. Ct. Rep. 1121, 30 L. Ed. 178 (1886).
[19] *Supra,* note 16.
[20] *Supra,* note 10.
[21] Alabama has no declaratory judgment act at the present time (1933).
[22] State ex rel. Norwood v. Goldsmith, 162 Ala. 171, 50 So. 394 (1909).
[23] 38 C. J. 568; 18 R. C. L. 136.

In Clark v. Miller [24] the case is more difficult with respect to mandamus. The writ will not issue in most cases unless there has been a default, that is, a demand and a refusal, and in this case the supervisor could not be said to be in default until the time for presenting the claim had passed. To have obtained the writ after the adjournment of the board would have been fruitless. There is authority for the view that in exceptional cases mandamus will issue even though the time for performance has not yet arrived.[25] A common law action for damages is hardly to be considered in the same class as the statutory action in the Norwood case, the former being much more uncertain in outcome. For that reason it might well have been held, in Clark v. Miller, that not only was the legal remedy so ineffective that the writ would issue in the discretion of the court but also that it would issue notwithstanding that the time for performance had not yet arrived. No application for a mandamus seems to have been made in the case, but counsel contended that it, rather than the common law action, should have been brought. In disapproving of this contention the court made the following observation:

That remedy exists, in general, only where the law affords no other, to prevent a failure of justice. But, as we have seen, in this case the plaintiff makes out a right to his action at law, and in such cases it can never be necessary to resort to a mandamus, even if that remedy happens to be legally available. In this case that remedy would not have been available to the plaintiff and effectual to procure payment of his claim. It could not have been applied for until the defendant was in default; and that default could not have been ascertained to exist until the last moment for presenting claims for audit. That late period would have rendered an application for a mandamus, if granted, practically ineffectual to afford the plaintiff the relief he was entitled to.[26]

The opinion of the court leaves unanswered the question whether mandamus would be denied because of the existence of a legal remedy or whether a legal remedy should be denied because of the existence of the remedy of mandamus. The court seems to have reasoned that legal relief should be permitted because of the fact that mandamus was not available. The possible use of mandamus in cases involving questions of constitutionality will be considered in a subsequent section.

[24] *Supra,* note 10.
[25] People ex rel. Hotchkiss v. Smith, 206 N. Y. 231, 99 N. E. 568 (1912); see 18 R. C. L. 122; 38 C. J. 581.
[26] Clark v. Miller, 54 N. Y. 528, 534 (1874). There is some conflict on this point, however, and the courts seem to have considerable discretion in refusing or granting the writ, in cases in which an action for damages would lie, on the ground that it is often an inadequate remedy, and not sufficiently specific to do justice. See cases collated in 38 C. J. 563; 18 R. C. L. 133.

These two cases serve to indicate that the officer acts at his peril in refusing to perform functions in accordance with statutory requirements. If the statute turns out to be unconstitutional, he is safe. If it turns out to be constitutional, he is liable to an action for damages. On the other hand, as will be shown in a subsequent section, the officer may not safely rely on a statute in the performance of the functions enjoined upon him by it.

In State ex rel. Ballard v. Goodland [27] an officer was removed from office for refusing to levy a tax in accordance with a statute he believed to be unconstitutional. Later the statute was declared unconstitutional and the order of removal was reversed on appeal. The removal in this case was construed to be not an administrative act but, because of the phraseology of the statute, a quasi-judicial act. The law having been declared unconstitutional, the sole ground for removal failed, because "an unconstitutional law imposes no enforceable legal duty, but the duties of the office remained defined by existing valid laws and as if such unconstitutional law had never been enacted." [28] The court applied the void ab initio view of the effect of an unconstitutional statute and by so doing reached the proper result. This case illustrates that there are situations to which this theory should be applicable, but the number of such situations is small.

Members of a board of registrars who refuse to register a person as a voter, basing their refusal on an unconstitutional statute, are liable in an action in tort.[29] If the statute existing prior to the enactment of the unconstitutional law upon which the officers rely provides for the imposition of a penalty in cases of discrimination against an eligible voter, such a statute constitutes the basis for recovery.[30] The right to vote is more highly prized in these cases than the size of the vote in most elections would lead one to expect.

The cases considered in this section illustrate how severely officers have been dealt with in the past for refusing to act because they guessed a statute to be unconstitutional when it was not. It may be

[27] 159 Wis. 393, 150 N. W. 488 (1915).
[28] 159 Wis. 395, 150 N. W. 489.
[29] Kinneen v. Wells, 144 Mass. 497, 11 N. E. 916 (1887). The court said, at 504 (this does not appear in 11 N. E.): "It is not contended by the defendants that the action cannot be maintained, unless the statute in question is constitutional." Cf. Lincoln v. Hapgood, 11 Mass. 350 (1814); Meyer v. Anderson, 238 U. S. 368, 35 Sup. Ct. Rep. 932, 59 L. Ed. 1349 (1915).
[30] Meyer v. Anderson, *supra,* note 29, 238 U. S. at 382, 35 Sup. Ct. Rep. at 936: "The qualification of voters under the constitution of Maryland existed and the statute which previously provided for the registration and election in Annapolis was unaffected by the void provisions of the statute which we are considering." The court felt that unless this were true the self-operative effect of the fifteenth amendment would be nullified.

that the courts of today would be more lenient than those of the past century, but modern cases on this problem are rare. This is due to the development of methods of preventive justice and to the fact that in the greater number of cases involving official action and non-action amicable settlements or suits are possible. These suits, if settlement without a suit is either impossible or undesirable, usually take the form of an application for a mandamus or injunction, as the case may be. For these reasons suits for damages against the officer are at the present time relatively infrequent.

In all these cases involving official responsibility for action or nonaction under an unconstitutional statute, the courts are faced with the problem of determining where the cost of legislative error shall be placed. Shall the citizen or the officer suffer? In the cases involving refusal to act the courts have chosen to hold the officer more often than the citizen.

II. DIRECT ACT WITHOUT THE INTERVENTION OF JUDICIAL PROCESS

A. Collection of Tax under an Unconstitutional Statute

Money paid to an officer as a tax under an unconstitutional statute may be recovered if the payment was involuntary and under protest.[31] Suppose that the taxpayer brings suit against the officer as an individual to recover the money and the latter says in defense that he has paid the money into the state treasury. Will he be compelled to make restitution out of his own pocket? The case of Dennison Mfg. Co. v. Wright [32] presented this question. The Georgia court there held that the taxpayer would prevail. In explaining the decision the court pointed out that when the defendant illegally collected the tax in this case he acted in an individual, not in an official, capacity, because the statute was unconstitutional. The payment was involuntary and was made under protest, and was therefore not subject to the ordinary rule with respect to the recovery of payments made under a mistake of law. The protest should put the officer on notice that a suit would probably be brought to recover the tax, and for that reason the money should not have been turned over to the state treasury. The court comforted the officer with the remark that the legislature would doubtless reimburse him for his loss.[33]

[31] This subject will be treated more fully in Chapter 10, dealing with the recovery of illegal and unconstitutional taxes.

[32] 156 Ga. 789, 120 S. E. 120 (1923). For other cases in accord see note, 48 A. L. R. 1395 (1927).

[33] The legislature of Georgia seems not to have lived up to the judge's prediction. See also Rushton v. Burke, 6 Dak. 478, 43 N. W. 815 (1889) (illegal tax, though constitutional).

The court said in the Wright case that the collector was to be treated exactly as though he had made the collection in the absence of statute, as a trespasser. With respect to this liability the following dictum is to be found in Woolsey v. Dodge,[34] in which case an injunction was sought to prevent a series of trespasses by a county treasurer to collect a tax under a statute alleged to be unconstitutional: "There is no axiom of the law better established than this. A void law can afford no justification to anyone who acts under it; and he who shall attempt to collect the illegal tax, under the law referred to, will be a trespasser."[35] The state cannot be sued without its consent in these cases, so it is imperative that the officer be prevented from proceeding with the illegal collection, reasoned the court.

B. DESTRUCTION OR INVASION OF PROPERTY

The cases on this subject are in conflict. Some courts permit an unconstitutional statute to be used as justification by the defendant officer, whereas others refuse him this protection.

Dexter v. Alfred[36] was a New York case in which trespass was brought against the defendant for entering upon plaintiff's land, in laying out a road, and cutting trees. The defendant answered that he had been ordered to do so by the commissioner of highways. The plaintiff assailed the constitutionality of the statute under which the acts had been performed. The statute was held unconstitutional, but the court held that despite that fact it would constitute sufficient justification to defeat the action. In the opinion of the court, "it was no part of the duty of the commissioner of highways to decide whether the law in question was or was not constitutional. His duty was to execute the law as he found it."[37] Compare this with the statement of the court in the Norwood case,[38] quoted above, to the effect that "all persons or officers are of necessity required to pass upon the validity of all acts or proposed statutes under which they are required to act or to decline to act." Referring to the rule that ignorance of the law is no excuse, the court stated that this case constituted an exception to the rule.

In Shafford v. Brown[39] an action was brought to recover in

[34] 6 McLean 142, Fed. Cas. No. 18,032 (C. C. Ohio 1854). See San Francisco & N. R. R. v. Dinwiddie, 13 Fed. 789 (C. C. Cal. 1882); Smith v. First Natl. Bank, 17 Mich. 479 (1869).

[35] Woolsey v. Dodge, *supra*, note 34, 6 McLean at 146, Fed. Cas. No. 18,032 at 607. See 4 Pomeroy, *op. cit. supra*, note 1, secs. 1805, 1819.

[36] 64 Hun 636, 19 N. Y. S. 770 (1892).   [37] 64 Hun 636, 19 N. Y. S. at 771.

[38] *Supra*, note 16, 168 Ala. at 234, 53 So. at 87.

[39] 49 Wash. 307, 308, 95 Pac. 270 (1908).

trespass for the destruction of apples by "defendants while assuming to act as county fruit inspector and state commissioner of horticulture, respectively." It appeared that the county inspector had looked at the apples in question and pronounced them infected, and had thereupon ordered the owners to destroy them. On appeal to the state commissioner the latter inspected them and sustained the decision of the county inspector. The actual destruction of the fruit was done by, or under the immediate direction of, the state commissioner. The statute creating the office of county inspector and authorizing the incumbent to perform the acts in question was unconstitutional. A demurrer was interposed to the defense that they had relied on the statute. The demurrer was overruled, apparently on the theory that the state commissioner was not liable because of valid statutory authority for his acts, and the county inspector was not liable despite the unconstitutionality of the statute authorizing him to act. The ground for exempting the latter officer is not explicitly stated in the opinion. It is perhaps not without significance that it seems that he did not actually destroy the fruit. The exact rôle played by the inspector is not clear from the report. But the following statement by the court indicates that even though he had destroyed the fruit, he would not have been held liable:

Respondent Brown was acting in good faith under a statute of the legislature. He doubtless supposed it to be a valid statute. The owners of the fruit evidently supposed the same. They recognized Brown as county fruit inspector by appealing from his decision to the state commissioner of horticulture.[40]

The court here seems to accord de facto status to Brown.[41] The rule of liability is the same for both de facto and de jure officers in these cases. The status, whether de jure or de facto, of an officer is immaterial in liability cases, the gist of the action being injury under an unconstitutional statute. It is the performance of an act, rather than the existence of a status, that is important in liability cases.[42]

A third case which, by dictum at least, supports the view that an officer is not liable for action under an unconstitutional statute is that of Dunn v. Mellon.[43] In that case the plaintiff did not sue the officer but brought trespass against his landlord for evicting him from a building. The defendant set up by way of defense an order received from a city officer to move the house because the city proposed

[40] 49 Wash. 309, 95 Pac. at 271.
[41] See Chapter 4.
[42] Vanderberg v. Connoly, 18 Utah 112, 54 Pac. 1097 (1898); Laver v. McGlachlin, 28 Wis. 364 (1871).
[43] 147 Pa. 11, 23 Atl. 210 (1892); cf. Dunn v. Burleigh, 62 Me. 24, 38 (1873).

to open a street through the lot. The landlord was notified by the city officer that if he did not remove the building within a specified time the city would proceed to do so at his expense. The statute was declared unconstitutional in another case, and as a result this action of trespass was brought. The court treated the landlord as an agent of the officer, acting under his direction, and decided that he was not liable. The process of reasoning whereby the court reached this result was as follows: If an officer had done the act complained of he would not have been liable; therefore a citizen acting under the proper officer's order should not be liable. If anybody was accountable, it was the city, according to the court. On this point the court said:

> If he had refused to obey it and the proper officer of the city had removed the building, undoubtedly the city would be liable for the consequences to any person injured, if the law under which the act was done was a void law. But it is just as undoubted that the officer who obeyed his orders in removing the building would not have been liable for his acts of obedience to his orders.[44]

In opposition to these cases is Hopkins v. Clemson Agricultural College.[45] In a suit against the college for damages resulting from the building of a dike the court held that if on a new trial it was shown that damages resulted from the act in question, they should be allowed, because the statute authorizing the college to perform the act complained of was unconstitutional. A decree ordering the removal of the dike was refused on the ground that this amounted to a suit against the state, the school being a governmental institution.

In a New York case [46] an injunction was granted, in addition to damages, to prevent certain state officers from interfering with the plaintiff's possession of land and to compensate him for past interferences with the property. The officer sought to justify his acts under a statute that had been enacted subsequently to the acts complained of, but he failed because the statute ratifying his acts was declared invalid.

The officers of a levee district organized under an unconstitutional statute were held liable for damages for authorizing a dam to be built in a location that resulted in the overflow of the plaintiff's land.[47] An injunction forbidding the maintenance of the dam was also granted in this case.

[44] 147 Pa. 17, 23 Atl. at 210.
[45] 221 U. S. 636, 31 Sup. Ct. Rep. 654, 55 L. Ed. 890 (1911).
[46] Saratoga, etc., Corp. v. Pratt, 227 N. Y. 429, 125 N. E. 834 (1920).
[47] Moulton v. Parks, 64 Cal. 166, 30 Pac. 613 (1883).

Several cases have held officers liable for the destruction of animals under the authority of an invalid ordinance or statute.[48]

It is impossible to say that in cases involving the invasion of property rights the weight of authority protects the officer or refuses to protect him. The courts are not agreed as to the rule to be applied in such cases.

C. Interference with Personal Liberty in the Absence of a Warrant

The cases in this section are to be distinguished from those involving arrest on a warrant, to be considered in a subsequent section. Only those cases involving arrest *without* a warrant will be dealt with at this point.

With the exception of one dictum the cases are in accord in holding that an officer is liable for an arrest without a warrant under an unconstitutional statute.[49] In Tillman v. Beard [50] the president of the village ordered the village marshal to arrest the plaintiff for violating an ordinance prohibiting the operation of popcorn wagons on the streets. Other facts, immaterial so far as the action for the arrest was concerned, appeared in the case, but among the various grounds of action alleged by the plaintiff was that of assault and battery in making the arrest. It appeared that the ordinance was void, whether because it was contrary to a statute or the state constitution is not clear. The court held that the arrest was illegal, saying that, in view of the fact that no felony had been committed and there was no likelihood of immediate escape, "by ordering the arrest, he made himself responsible for it, and liable for all its consequences." [51] Sumner v. Beeler [52] is also to be included in this group of cases, for

[48] Loesch v. Koehler, 144 Ind. 278, 43 N. E. 129 (1895); Waud v. Crawford, 160 Iowa 432, 141 N. W. 1041 (1913); Carter v. Colby, 71 N. H. 230, 51 Atl. 904 (1902).

[49] Some of these cases also involved suits for malicious prosecution. This phase of the problem will be considered in the next section, dealing with acts concerning judicial proceedings. These cases, with the exception of Gross v. Rice, *infra*, note 54, involve ordinances, but if Sumner v. Beeler, *infra*, note 52, be viewed as an arrest without a warrant case it should be classified as involving a statute. Cf. Restatement on Torts (Am. L. Inst., No. 3, 1927), sec. 148, special note.

[50] 121 Mich. 475, 80 N. W. 248 (1899).

[51] 121 Mich. 477, 80 N. W. at 248. Barling v. West, 29 Wis. 307 (1871), involved an arrest without a warrant by the president and marshal of a village for the alleged violation of an ordinance which was contrary to a state statute, and perhaps (although not entirely clear) unconstitutional. Held, a verdict for $50 was affirmed. Cf. Hofschulte v. Doe, 78 Fed. 436 (C. C. Cal. 1897), on the first count of the complaint.

[52] 50 Ind. 341 (1875). In Chapman v. Selover, 172 App. Div. 858, 159 N. Y. S. 632 (1916), it was held that an ordinance of a city, which was ultra vires under the statutes of the state, did not afford justification to a police officer who made an

the court treated it as if it presented a case of arrest without a warrant, although it is impossible to tell from the report of the case whether this was the fact or not. In Williams v. Morris [53] one of the inferior courts of Ohio said in dictum that the officer should not be held liable. The reason advanced by the court for this view was that the presumption of the validity of a statute should serve to protect the officer making an arrest under it.

A literal false imprisonment was involved in Gross v. Rice.[54] Gross was committed to prison following conviction for crime. A statute provided that the number of days spent in solitary confinement should be excluded in computing the term. In accordance with this statute the defendant (the warden) kept Gross in prison sixty-eight days longer than the commitment called for, leaving out of view the days spent in solitary confinement. Upon his release Gross sued the warden for trespass to the person and false imprisonment. The statute under which the warden had acted in computing the period for which Gross should have been confined was held to be unconstitutional. The Maine court allowed recovery against the warden. In answer to the contention that the warden should be protected as to acts performed prior to the time when the statute had been declared invalid, the court made this reply:

> We do not comprehend the logic of a statute having effect as if constitutional, when not so; to be a law for one purpose and not another; a law for one man and not another. It must be either valid or invalid from the beginning, or from the date of the constitutional provision affecting it.[55]

Yet, as illustrated by numerous cases,[56] many courts are doing, in other branches of the law, exactly what the Maine court here thought impossible: holding a statute constitutional for one purpose, though not for another. The court in the Gross case was looking at the situation through the spectacles of doctrine on the effect of an unconstitutional statute instead of looking at the doctrine through the facts in the case.

With respect to the question of damages, the court thought that punitive damages should not be allowed, that only actual damages should be recovered. In accord with the Norwood case [57] is the statement of the court that "the warden is only liable to the perils that

arrest under it without a warrant. See Judson v. Reardon, 16 Minn. 431 (1871), dictum, that officer liable for arrest of person under unconstitutional ordinance.

[53] 14 Ohio Cir. Ct. (N. S.) 353, 358 (1911).
[54] 71 Me. 241 (1880).
[55] 71 Me. 252.
[56] For some illustrations of this, see Chapter 1.
[57] *Supra*, note 16.

more or less follow official stations. He had no warrant of court that could protect him." [58] The legislature of Maine subsequently made an appropriation to indemnify Rice for the amount of the judgment and the expenses of the suit.[59]

A dictum in a Texas case suggests that an officer would be liable for taking personal effects from the custody of one being entered in an asylum, if the statute authorizing this to be done was invalid.[60]

In the cases dealing with direct and positive acts of officers under an unconstitutional law, there seems to be a greater tendency for the courts to permit the statute to be used as a justification by the officer in situations involving the violation of a property right than in those involving the violation of personal liberty. The courts are apparently more severe on the officer if the case is one of false arrest or false imprisonment than if it turns on a trespass to land or other property.

III. ACTION CONNECTED WITH JUDICIAL PROCEEDINGS

A defendant who feels aggrieved because action has been brought against him in a court, with resulting arrest, seizure of goods, or trespass to land, may choose one or all of several parties against whom to bring his suit. The cases to be taken up in the several sections of this division illustrate the rules with respect to the various persons who may be made parties defendant, and the extent of their liability, if any, for participating in the proceeding at one of its several stages.

A. Liability for Making Complaint or Filing Affidavit

The first step in an action for violating an ordinance or statute is often that of making a complaint or filing an affidavit. Is an officer liable to an action for damages for filing an affidavit that results in the arrest and punishment of the plaintiff? The rule is well established that he is not. In Goodwin v. Guild [61] the mayor procured another officer to make an affidavit that the plaintiff had violated a city ordinance which was contrary to a statute of the state. In an action against the mayor and the officer neither of them was held liable. The mayor was entrusted by statute with the duty of enforc-

[58] *Supra,* note 54, 71 Me. at 252.

[59] Me. Resolves, Chapter 22 (1881). "Resolved, that the sum of two hundred and sixty-three dollars, be and the same is hereby appropriated out of the state treasury, to be paid to Warren W. Rice, the same being for moneys paid by him as damages, costs, and expenses, by reason of a suit brought against him by Darrius Gross, an ex-convict, for false imprisonment."

[60] Worsham v. Vogtsberger, 129 S. W. 157 (Tex. Civ. App. 1910).

[61] 94 Tenn. 486, 29 S. W. 721 (1895).

ing city ordinances; there had been considerable dispute between the various officers of the city concerning the validity of the ordinance; and no ill will had been shown on the part of the defendants; so, according to the court, there was no ground for imposing liability upon them. In Trammell v. Town of Russellville [62] a similar result was reached in a case involving an ordinance that was unconstitutional. Another case to the same effect contains this statement: "A party in good faith making a complaint for the violation of any law or ordinance is not required to take the risk of being mulcted in damages if courts afterwards hold it unconstitutional." [63] The same court also asked why the officer making the complaint should be liable when he would not be liable for serving the warrant.[64] This assumes that the officer serving the warrant is not liable, which, as will be pointed out later, is not entirely settled.

An officer who institutes proceedings against a person for the violation of a statute does not act without probable cause merely because the statute turns out to be unconstitutional.[65] Probable cause is not dependent on the validity of the statute under which the prosecution is instituted. The rule is the same whether complaint is made leading to the issuance of a warrant for arrest or one for search and seizure.[66] One case contains a dictum that if the functions of complainant and magistrate are both entrusted to the same officer, the issuance of a warrant under such a statute, if it is invalid, will subject the magistrate to liability.[67] The magistrate in such a case acts as a complainant, however, and in so doing should not be held liable, even though the statute is unconstitutional. There is no reason

[62] 34 Ark. 105 (1879).

[63] Tillman v. Beard, *supra,* note 50, 121 Mich. at 477, 80 N.W. at 248. See Hallock v. Dominy, 69 N.Y. 238 (1877), where the court said, at 241: "Process regularly issued upon this judgment, as was the execution upon which the plaintiff was imprisoned, was a protection to the officer executing it, and to the parties at whose instance it was used and served."

[64] Tillman v. Beard, *supra,* note 50, 21 Mich. at 477, 80 N.W. at 248: "If the officer is protected in the service of the warrant, in which act he is performing a duty imposed upon him by law, why should he not be equally exempt where he is in the performance of his duty in making complaint for the violation of an ordinance of his municipality?"

[65] Birdsall v. Smith, 158 Mich. 390, 122 N.W. 626 (1909). The complaint in this case was filed on the order of a superior officer. Suit was, however, also brought against the local inspector who procured the bottle of milk for purposes of chemical analysis. The court held neither of the officers liable. The court said in dictum that if the officers had known the statute to be unconstitutional the result would have been different. The case would then have been similar to that referred to in dicta in some of the cases; that liability would attach if bad motive were shown. *Infra,* note 70.

[66] Anheuser Busch Brewing Co. v. Hammond, 93 Iowa 520, 61 N.W. 1052 (1895) (statute contrary to federal statutes on interstate commerce).

[67] See Clark v. Hampton, 163 Ky. 698, 701, 174 S.W. 490, 491 (1915).

why the rule as to the complainant should be different in this last case from those involving complaints by other officers under invalid statutes. In fact, there is the more reason for exempting the magistrate in such a case because not only does the rule as to complainants tend to exempt him but the tendency of the cases is also to exempt him, as magistrate, for issuing the warrant, on the ground that he exercises a judicial function in so doing. If liability would not attach when these two functions were entrusted to two persons, there is no reason for imposing it when the two functions are combined in the same person.

The same doctrine is applied to private individuals who make complaints or file affidavits that an ordinance or statute is being violated.[68] But if the statute authorizing the issuance of an attachment is unconstitutional, the individuals procuring it will be liable,

[68] Bohri v. Barnett, 144 Fed. 389 (C. C. A. 7th 1906). The court said, at 392: "Any other rule would be harsh in the extreme—imposing on one who had witnessed a violation of a local ordinance the responsibility of knowing whether, as a matter of law, the ordinance itself was valid, or of remaining silent." And in Barker v. Stetson, 7 Gray 53, 54 (Mass. 1856), the court said: "The authorities are conclusive that, when a person does no more than to prefer a complaint to a magistrate, he is not liable in trespass for the acts done under the warrant which the magistrate thereupon issues, even though the magistrate has no jurisdiction." In commenting on a charge to a jury, given in the court below, it was said in Wheeler v. Gavin, 5 Ohio Cir. Ct. 246, 253 (1890): "But the charge of the court was in effect saying to the jury that whenever a magistrate issues a warrant, or a person files an affidavit for an arrest, they must not only be sure that there is a statute or ordinance warranting such proceedings, but they must be certain of its constitutionality and validity. In so charging the jury the court below erred, and for that error the judgment will be reversed." Cf. Vanderberg v. Connoly, *supra,* note 42; Fenelon v. Butts, 49 Wis. 342, 5 N. W. 784 (1880) (commissioner before whom supplemental proceedings were had was appointed for two counties, contrary to the constitutional requirement of one for each county); Rush v. Buckley, 100 Me. 322, 61 Atl. 774 (1905) (ordinance never went into effect, because not published). It has been held that where there is room for an honest difference in belief as to constitutionality of a statute malicious prosecution will fail. Cobbey v. State Journal Co., 77 Neb. 626, 113 N. W. 224 (1907) (rival printer got injunction against plaintiff, the statute on which defendant relied being invalid). In Scott v. Flowers, 60 Neb. 675, 84 N. W. 81 (1900), an action for malicious prosecution was brought for causing plaintiff to be taken into custody and put into a state girls' school, the statute under which commitment was procured being defective in that the age fixed in it as the maximum was higher than permitted by the state constitution. Plaintiff recovered damages for malicious prosecution. On rehearing, 61 Neb. 620, 85 N. W. 857 (1901), the statute was held constitutional, the court deciding to give effect to it within the limits of the age provided for by the constitution. This caused a reversal of the case, but it is to be noted that the court did not, on rehearing, abandon its position that liability would attach for malicious prosecution. The court seemed influenced by a showing of ill will. If the case is to be taken as authority on malicious prosecution it is contrary to the other cases cited or considered thus far. In accord with the general rule is Gifford v. Wiggins, 50 Minn. 401, 52 N. W. 904 (1892), where Mitchell, J., said at 405, 52 N. W. at 905: "Under any other doctrine a person would never feel safe in making complaint of the commission of a public offense until the validity of the statute creating the offense had been passed upon by the court of last resort."

and for this purpose a city is in the same position as a private litigant.[69]

The main reason for denying the liability of officers as well as of private individuals is that any other rule would impede the administration of justice. The possibility of an action for damages should not be hung over the officer's head as a deterrent. In many instances considerable reliance is placed on the initiative of private individuals in the enforcement of laws. For this reason they too should be free from such a deterrent. Although no case has been found that involves the question of malicious complaint by an officer under an unconstitutional statute, there are many intimations and dicta to the effect that if meddlesome interference, bad motive in making the complaint, or active direction in making the arrest by the officer were present, liability would attach.[70] Such a case would turn, however, not on the effect of an unconstitutional statute but on the presence of some other factor that causes the court to impose liability.

B. Liability of Magistrate for Issuing Warrant, Trying, or Sentencing a Person under an Invalid Statute

The early cases on the liability of a justice of the peace or other inferior magistrate who issued a warrant or tried a person accused of petty crime under an unconstitutional statute held the magistrate liable.[71] The later cases have relaxed this rule; now, although the rule is presumably the same in the states in which the earlier cases were decided, several states have adopted a contrary rule.[72] A numerical count of either the states or decisions reveals the weight of authority to be in favor of exempting the inferior magistrate for

[69] Zimmerman v. Lamb, 7 Minn. 421 (1862); Merrit v. St. Paul, 11 Minn. 223 (1865), where the court said, at 231: "It follows that the appellants who instructed the sheriff to make the particular levy complained of, under the warrant in question, acted without authority or jurisdiction, and were, therefore, trespassers." Cf. Hayes v. Hutchinson, 81 Wash. 394, 142 Pac. 865 (1914).

[70] Supra, note 65. In Barker v. Stetson, supra, note 68, 7 Gray (Mass.) at 54, this statement was made: "If the complaint is malicious and without probable cause, the complainant may be answerable in another form of action." See the following from Goodwin v. Guild, supra, note 61, 94 Tenn. at 490, 29 S. W. at 772: "If he took advantage of his official position to oppress the plaintiff, either from ill will toward him, or because of any other improper motive, he would be liable."

[71] Kelly v. Bemis, 4 Gray 83 (Mass. 1855); Barker v. Stetson, supra, note 68; Ely v. Thompson, 3 A. K. Marsh 70 (Ky. 1820); cf. Heller v. Clarke, 121 Wis. 71, 98 N. W. 952 (1904). A justice of the peace was held liable for false imprisonment for putting the plaintiff in jail until trial, when he had no jurisdiction over the case, as a statute had given jurisdiction over this class of cases to a city court.

[72] Cottam v. Oregon City, 98 Fed. 570 (C. C. Or. 1899); Hofschulte v. Doe, 78 Fed. 436 (C. C. Cal. 1897); Brooks v. Mangan, 86 Mich. 576, 49 N. W. 633 (1891); McDaniel v. Harrell, 81 Fla. 66, 87 So. 631 (1921); Trammell v. Town of Russellville, 34 Ark. 105 (1879). See infra, note 79.

action taken in accordance with an unconstitutional statute or ordinance, and the same rule is followed if the ordinance is contrary to the statutes of the state.

Two early Massachusetts cases, Barker v. Stetson [73] and Kelly v. Bemis,[74] adopt the rule imposing liability on the magistrate. In the first case a magistrate issued process authorizing an officer to seize plaintiff's liquor, the process being issued in accordance with a section of a statute later held to be unconstitutional. An action was brought against the magistrate as well as the officer, and both of them were held liable. The court said that inasmuch as the statute conferring jurisdiction to issue the process was invalid, the magistrate had no jurisdiction and for that reason was liable in trespass. The second case decided that a magistrate was liable in trespass for issuing a warrant on which the plaintiff was arrested, the statute authorizing the issuance of the warrant being invalid. The reason given for this result was that our government was one of limited powers; none of the departments of government could exceed the power given to them by the constitution; therefore the attempted grant of power to the judicial branch, being in excess of the legislature's power, was ineffectual. There being no statutory grant of jurisdiction, it followed that the court had none. It therefore followed that the justice who attempted to exercise jurisdiction when he had none was liable in trespass.

Ely v. Thompson,[75] decided in 1820 by the Kentucky court, was an action of trespass, assault and battery, and false imprisonment against the justice of the peace and constable who had, respectively, sentenced the plaintiff to thirty lashes and had administered the punishment. They were held liable, the court observing that the constitution was higher than the law:

It is an instrument that every officer of government is bound to know and preserve, at his peril, whether his office be judicial or ministerial; and he cannot justify an act against its provisions, even with the authority of the legislature to aid him, however much that may mitigate his case.[76]

This case is affected somewhat by the fact that the action taken here was in direct violation of a constitutional provision and did not involve a typical case of permissible action, so far as the constitution is concerned, being taken under a statute that in some phase of form or substance is not in accordance with the constitution. A recent

[73] *Supra*, note 68.
[74] *Supra*, note 71.
[75] *Supra*, note 71.
[76] *Supra*, note 71, 3 A. K. Marsh (Ky.) at 76.

dictum by the Kentucky court tends to support the view of the two Massachusetts cases adverted to, but in the same case in which the dictum was uttered it was held that the magistrate was not liable for denying bail, because that was done in the exercise of a judicial function.[77]

These are the only cases found by the author that have held the magistrate liable for acting in accordance with an unconstitutional statute. The federal courts have taken the opposite view and have refused to impose liability.[78] They have stressed the fact that inferior judges are within the reason of the rule exempting superior judges from liability for mistakes in judgment as to the constitutionality of a statute or, for that matter, for mistakes of law in general. That the justices have general jurisdiction over the type of subject matter involved in the particular case has also been looked upon as a factor supporting the rule of exemption. There being jurisdiction, the case becomes one of excess of jurisdiction rather than one involving an exercise of jurisdiction where none exists at all.

The state courts stress similar reasons and factors to support the rule as to exemption, giving them more elaborate statement in many cases. The existence of jurisdiction in general; the presence of good faith; the absence of bad faith; an existing jurisdiction over the person; that the mayor or recorder had in addition to his judicial functions the general oversight of the administration of law in the village; a statutory duty to issue the warrant; that issuing the process and sentencing the accused are judicial acts, in which the constitutionality of the statute or ordinance was passed upon; that exempting inferior judges from liability is necessary to an impartial and effective administration of justice — all these factors have been stressed in greater or lesser degree by the courts adopting a rule contrary to that of the early Massachusetts cases.

The rule exempting magistrates is applied where the ordinance is invalid because it is contrary to a statute,[79] where county regulations are in excess of the power of the supervisors,[80] and where an ordinance is in excess of the statutory powers granted to a city by the state.[81] The rule has been carried so far that a magistrate escaped liability even though the ordinance under which action was taken had never gone into effect.[82]

[77] See Clark v. Hampton, 163 Ky. 698, 701, 174 S. W. 490, 491 (1915).

[78] Cottam v. Oregon City, Hofschulte v. Doe, both *supra,* note 72.

[79] Goodwin v. Guild, *supra,* note 61; Calhoun v. Little, 106 Ga. 336, 32 S. E. 86 (1898); Wheeler v. Gavin, *supra,* note 68.

[80] Hallock v. Dominy, 69 N. Y. 238 (1877).

[81] Henke v. McCord, 55 Iowa 378, 7 N. W. 623 (1880).

[82] Rush v. Buckley, *supra,* note 68, in which notice of the ordinance was not published as required by statute. The court stressed the fact that the justice had

In view of the definite trend away from the early Massachusetts rule, it is perhaps accurate to say that the rule is becoming well established now that petty judicial officers are being accorded the same standing as judges of courts of general trial jurisdiction with respect to liability for acts done in reliance not only on an unconstitutional statute, but on an invalid ordinance. This rule is essential to effective work by inferior judicial officers, and it should become firmly embedded in judicial doctrine with the interest now being taken in the improvement of these petty courts.

C. Liability of Officer Serving Process

The authorities on this subject are about evenly divided, but many of the cases holding that the officer serving a process under an unconstitutional statute is liable were decided before or about the time of the Civil War. Several of the cases adopting the contrary rule have been decided within the last half century. While it is true that the cases are about evenly divided, it is perhaps more significant to say that the trend of the recent cases is away from such liability. This is, as previously indicated, in keeping with the trend of the courts with respect to the liability of magistrates, although in the latter cases it is more pronounced than in the cases of ministerial officers.

Early cases in Massachusetts,[83] Kentucky,[84] and Minnesota [85] and later decisions in Wisconsin,[86] Maine,[87] and Texas [88] hold the officer liable. This unsatisfactory statement is found in the early case of Fisher v. McGirr:

The law relied on for a justification, being void, gave the magistrate no jurisdiction and no authority to issue the search warrant, the officer

general jurisdiction in the city and over this type of subject, and that the mistake in thinking the ordinance was in effect was an error in judgment and for such errors the judge, though inferior, could not be held. A dissenting judge said, 100 Me. at 336, 61 Atl. at 780: "I think the majority opinion holds doctrines impairing the right of personal liberty and subversive of long established rules of law in this state." In Clark v. Spicer, 6 Kan. 440 (1870), a justice was held not liable for trying a man with a six-man jury.
[83] Fisher v. McGirr, 1 Gray 1 (Mass. 1854); Barker v. Stetson, *supra*, note 68.
[84] Ely v. Thompson, *supra*, note 70.
[85] Guerin v. Hunt, 8 Minn. 477 (1863); Zimmerman v. Lamb, *supra*, note 69. Both of these cases involved attachments. In the first, Guerin v. Hunt, *supra*, the court said, 8 Minn. at 487: "This would make the defendants trespassers as to the taking of the property from the plaintiff's possession, even although it should be found that the assignment . . . was fraudulent, as against the creditors of the assignors." The goods had been taken from the possession of the assignee in this case.
[86] Campbell v. Sherman, 35 Wis. 103 (1874). See 12 Harv. L. Rev. 352 (1898).
[87] Warren v. Kelley, 80 Me. 512, 15 Atl. 49 (1888).
[88] Beavers v. Goodwin, 90 S. W. 930 (Tex. Civ. App. 1905).

cannot justify the seizure under it, and therefore an action lies against him for the taking.[89]

Few of the cases holding the officer liable add very much to this statement in support of the rule. In Campbell v. Sherman,[90] however, it was added that a process is not fair on its face when it shows that it was issued on a maritime lien, because that would indicate that a state court would not have jurisdiction to issue the process.

The Campbell case also stated the doctrine that ignorance of the law does not excuse violation of it, justifying the statement by asserting that if it were an excuse everybody would plead it as an excuse, and the administration of justice would be hampered. The most substantial reason advanced in favor of imposing liability is that the officer may protect himself by the simple device of taking a bond before he acts. The court said, relative to this: "If the act which the writ commanded him to do was a trespass, he was not required to perform it. Nor would he be liable in that case to the plaintiff for refusing to execute a process void for want of jurisdiction." [91]

If this prediction were a correct statement of the rules of law, the officer would not be in such a serious plight, for he could then protect himself, either by taking bond or by refusing to act if the act would be a trespass, in which case he would also be protected, because to act would be a trespass. The cases hitherto considered involving the question of damages for refusal to act leave this matter in some doubt, however, and it is not at all certain that the result indicated by the Wisconsin court would be reached by all courts. The taking of bond is quite common in practice, but in small cases it might cause more delay, inconvenience, and trouble than is justified. In the larger cases a bond of indemnity could be taken by the officer. That only means, however, that the officer protects himself. The citizen will then have to bear the loss, a result not very much more desirable, though somewhat less objectionable, than to have it fall on the officer.

The liability of officers and of private individuals who assist an officer in the execution of a search warrant or other process, or in the asportation or destruction of property, is not well settled, but there is some authority for believing that they will be held liable in some

[89] *Supra,* note 83, 1 Gray (Mass.) at 46.

[90] *Supra,* note 86. In this case a sheriff who seized a ship on process issuing out of a state court in the enforcement of a maritime lien was held liable for damages for the burning of the ship while it was in his possession. The sheriff's deputy had actually executed the process. A case on almost all fours, except that the sheriff seems to have acted directly, rather than through a deputy, was that of Warren v. Kelley, *supra,* note 87. The result was identical, liability being imposed.

[91] Campbell v. Sherman, *supra,* note 86, 35 Wis. at 110.

states if they act under an invalid statute,[92] although there is authority to the contrary also.[93]

The many recent congressional investigations, with attendant commands from the two houses that various individuals appear to testify before them or their committees, make the case of Kilbourn v. Thompson [94] of increased interest at the present time. The facts of that case are so well known that they do not need to be repeated here. The phase of this famous case to which attention is called in this connection is the suit for damages brought against the sergeant-at-arms of the House of Representatives for having arrested and falsely imprisoned the plaintiff by virtue of a warrant issued by the speaker of the House, the warrant being issued in excess of his constitutional power. The first trial resulted in a verdict of $60,000. A new trial was had and the verdict then returned amounted to $37,500. A remittitur of $17,500 was filed and the award then stood at $20,000. This amount was paid by Congress, in addition to an appropriation to compensate Thompson for his expenses and attorney's fees in connection with the case.[95] Here, as in the Gross case [96] in Maine, the legislature came to the rescue of an officer who had acted to his injury in reliance on action by a legislative body, such action having been in the form of a statute in the one case, in the form of a warrant of arrest in the other.

The cases refusing to hold the officer liable [97] argue that the process is fair on its face, taking issue on this point with the cases in which liability is imposed. They insist that unconstitutionality is not shown on the face of a warrant, for example, and that it is a fiction to speak of a line between clear and palpable unconstitutionality and any other kind. They point out, too, that the administration of

[92] Beavers v. Goodwin, *supra,* note 88; cf. Cartwright v. Canode, 106 Tex. 502, 171 S. W. 696 (1914).

[93] See Henke v. McCord, *supra,* note 81 (one officer aiding another).

[94] 103 U. S. 168, 26 L. Ed. 377 (1880). The case involving suit for false imprisonment and false arrest is by the same name, in MacArthur & M. 401 (D. C. 1883).

[95] 23 Stat. 446, 467 (1885). The appropriations were: to Kilbourn, $20,000 plus $143.17 interest and costs; to Thompson, $5,000 for expenses, labor, and attention with respect to the case; to Thompson's attorneys, $3,000 for professional services.

[96] *Supra,* note 54.

[97] Cottam v. Oregon City, *supra,* note 72 (ordinance); Hofschulte v. Doe, *ibid.* (ordinance); Trammell v. Town of Russellville, *ibid.* (ordinance); Bohri v. Barnett, *supra,* note 68 (ordinance); Tillman v. Beard, *supra,* note 50 (ordinance contrary to statute); Henke v. McCord, *supra,* note 81 (ordinance in excess of city's statutory powers); Rush v. Buckley, *supra,* note 68 (ordinance had not gone into effect); Anheuser Busch Brewing Co. v. Hammond, *supra,* note 66; cf. Sandford v. Nichols, 13 Mass. 285 (1816); cf. also Am. L. Inst., Restatement of the Law of Torts, Tent. Draft No. 3 (1927), sec. 149-3 (7), (8). It seems that the Restatement does not provide for cases wherein the statute other than the one conferring jurisdiction is unconstitutional, so far as arrest with a warrant is concerned.

justice will be hampered by the introduction of a rule of liability in such cases, because the officers will be slow to act; it might be added also that, even though bonds of indemnity be taken where property is involved, such a practice tends also to slow up the already dilatory processes of the law. To ask the ministerial officer to be a judge as well as an "executioner" seems to some of the courts to be too high a requirement to impose upon constables, sheriffs, and other police and process-executing officers. The process appears to be regular in these cases. The justice or clerk issuing it does so in accordance with statutory provisions that have all the appearance of law and that may have been on the statute books of the state unchallenged for many years. The presumption is in favor of the validity of legislative enactments. All these factors combine to cause the courts of a number of states, in the later cases, to refuse to hold the officer liable. No distinction is made, in the cases pro or con on this subject, between those involving unconstitutional statutes, those involving unconstitutional ordinances, and those involving ordinances contrary to general state statutes. The policies causing a court to go one way or another on this point apply with equal or nearly equal force to all three types of case.

Whether or not an officer is liable for serving a warrant or other process under an unconstitutional statute, the person upon whom it is served is not justified in forcibly resisting the execution.[98] Nor is a private individual liable for turning over goods to an officer upon the showing of a warrant, even though he be a bailee and even though the warrant is issued in reliance on an invalid statute.[99]

D. Liability of the City or Governmental Unit for Which the Officer Acts

In Trescott v. City of Waterloo [100] suit was brought against the city to recover damages for the enforcement of an unconstitutional ordinance. The lower federal court before whom the case was tried denied recovery. In support of this decision the court observed that the police regulations of the city were not made for the city alone and that they were made in a public capacity instead of in a corporate capacity; phrased in more customary language, that they were exercises of the governmental power of the city as distinguished from exercises of private or proprietary powers. Some stress was also laid on the fact that the fine was small; for that reason the plaintiff

[98] State v. McNally, 34 Me. 210 (1852); cf. State v. Skinner, 148 La. 143, 86 So. 716 (1920).

[99] Southern Express Co. v. Sottile Bros., 134 Ga. 47, 67 S. E. 417 (1910).

[100] 26 Fed. 592 (C. C. Iowa 1885); Cottam v. Oregon City, *supra*, note 72.

should have paid it under protest or, if he had wished to appeal, he could have resisted the payment of the fine in that way. But as it happened in this case, the plaintiff preferred to go to jail. While these factors are not conclusive, they nevertheless seemed to influence the court in its attitude toward the case.

The state cases follow the same rule. Thus in Trammell v. Town of Russellville [101] the court denied recovery in a suit against the city, saying, "then, for neither the act of the council in passing the ordinance, the acts of the mayor in issuing the warrants, nor those of the marshal and his deputy in making the arrests, was the town liable to the plaintiff." [102]

IV. PROTECTION OF OFFICERS ACTING OR REFUSING TO ACT UNDER AN UNCONSTITUTIONAL STATUTE

A brief summary of the rules concerning officers' liability may serve to emphasize the need for some program of protection.

1. Officers are liable for refusal to act if the statute authorizing them to act turns out to be constitutional and if some private individual has been injured thereby.

2. Officers are liable for taxes collected under invalid statutes if they were paid under protest and their payment was involuntary. The fact that the officer has paid the money into the state treasury will not be a defense to such an action.

3. There is a conflict of authority as to whether an officer is liable for the destruction or invasion of property under an unconstitutional statute.

4. Officers are liable for interference with personal liberty if such interference is justified solely on the ground of an invalid statute.

5. Officers are not liable for making complaints under invalid statutes.

6. The weight of authority holds that magistrates are not liable

[101] *Supra,* note 72.

[102] *Supra,* note 72, 34 Ark. at 109. See also City of Albany v. Cunliff, 2 N. Y. 165 (1849); Easterly v. Town of Irwin, 99 Iowa 694, 68 N. W. 919 (1896); City of Caldwell v. Prunelle, 57 Kan. 511, 46 Pac. 949 (1896); McFadin v. City of San Antonio, 22 Tex. Civ. App. 140, 54 S. W. 48 (1899); Taylor v. City of Owensboro, 98 Ky. 271, 32 S. W. 948 (1895); cf. McGraw v. Town of Marion, 98 Ky. 673, 34 S. W. 18 (1896); 6 McQuillin, Municipal Corporations (2d ed., 1928), sec. 2811; Williams, The Liability of Municipal Corporations for Tort, 37–39 (1901). In Goodwin v. Guild, *supra,* note 61, suit was brought against the city, the city council, mayor, and board, which had let the contract under which the work was being done. The city, mayor, councilmen, and board were all held not liable. In Kilbourn v. Thompson, MacArthur & M. 401 (D. C. 1883), the members of the House who had participated in the proceedings resulting in the issuance of the warrant were held not liable.

for issuance of process or committing a person under an unconstitutional law, but a few cases impose liability.

7. Officers executing process under an unconstitutional law are held liable in some states but not in others, although the tendency seems to be to exempt them and to treat them as executing "fair" process.

This is the distribution by the courts of the risk of error in the operation of government, due to official action under an unconstitutional statute. The rule obtaining in all the states that the government cannot be sued without its own consent has prevented the courts from including it among those to share the burden. Consent to suit in ordinary tort cases has not been given by the states generally, and in the case of the national government only a beginning has been made. With respect to local governments the problem is complicated by distinctions between proprietary and governmental functions. The courts have, therefore, attempted to place the burden either upon the officer or upon the citizen. The result has been, as has been indicated in the summary, that the officer has been forced to carry an undue share of the burden.

Viewing the problem as one of judicial distribution of risk, can anything be done by judicial decision to make the rules more equitable? The rule which could probably be improved by this method is that concerning refusal of officers to act. Here the courts might well have held that if the private individual knows that the officer is refusing to act, he should be compelled to resort to mandamus rather than be permitted to bring an action for damages. In a mandamus proceeding many courts would permit a determination of the constitutionality of the statute under which the officer was asked to act, and all courts should permit this, for the officer would not be liable to an action for damages if he acted pursuant to the writ.[103] If this is done the matter can be settled in many cases without any greater inconvenience than the delay incident to the hearing in mandamus. This would be a distinct step forward, and it could be accomplished by the application of well-settled legal principles.

There are some cases that cannot be disposed of by the use of mandamus. There may not be time enough to wait for even this

---

[103] "But the weight of authority sustains the allowance of a defense of this character on the ground that an unconstitutional statute is not a law and binds no one." 38 C. J. 922. For review of the cases, and the arguments in favor of raising the question of constitutionality in mandamus proceedings, see State v. Candland, 36 Utah 406, 104 Pac. 285 (1909); Rapacz, Protection of Officers Who Act under Unconstitutional Statutes, *supra,* note 2; Field, Effect of an Unconstitutional Statute, 1 Ind. L. J. 1, 60 Am. L. Rev. 232 (1926), 100 Cent. L. J. 145, note 41 (1927).

summary procedure. It may be that the private individual does not know, and could not under the circumstances be expected to know, that the officer is refusing to act, and in the meantime the rights of the individual may be adversely affected. For example, if X goes to the register of deeds with a mortgage and leaves it for recording, and the officer, saying nothing, says to himself, "I will not record this mortgage because the statute authorizing it is unconstitutional," X can hardly be held to know that the officer is refusing to record the mortgage, at least for several days. In such a case it may be only fair to say that an officer should notify the private individual of his intention not to comply with the statute because of the belief that it is unconstitutional, and, failing this, he should be liable for the loss occasioned by the failure to perform the duty.[104] These two suggestions, if embodied in judicial decision, might aid in distributing more equitably the burden of loss in these cases.

In most of the other situations embraced by the rules in the foregoing summary, the citizen rather than the officer should bear the burden. The normal situation should be that the officer acts in compliance with and reliance on statutes as if they were constitutional. The effective functioning of the administrative branch of government requires this. But although it may be somewhat more desirable for the individual citizen to suffer in these cases than to impose the burden of paying for the mistakes of the legislative branch of government upon the officer, to leave the burden with the private citizen is also unfair. For this reason the possibilities of solving the problem by means of judicial administration are very limited. The problem is, in the final analysis, one for legislative consideration.

The first aid that the legislature of a state could give is the enactment of the Declaratory Judgment Act. Many of the states have this act now and many others will doubtless adopt it in the near future.[105]

The next step that legislatures should take is to provide for the state's consent to suit in some regular tribunal, either a special court such as the federal Court of Claims, its jurisdiction being extended

---

[104] The writer is indebted to Professor Dudley O. McGovney for this suggestion.

[105] On the declaratory judgment see the following articles by Professor Edwin M. Borchard: The Declaratory Judgment—A Needed Procedural Reform, 28 Yale L. J. 1, 105 (1918); The Uniform Act on Declaratory Judgments, 34 Harv. L. Rev. 697 (1921). On government liability and responsibility in tort see Borchard, Government Liability in Tort, 34 Yale L. J. 1, 129, 229 (1924); Government Responsibility in Tort—A Proposed Statutory Reform, 11 Va. L. Reg. (N. S.) 330 (1925), 11 Am. B. A. J. 495 (1925); Government Responsibility in Tort, 36 Yale L. J. 1 (1926); Theories of Government Responsibility in Tort, 28 Col. L. Rev. 734 (1928). See also Borchard, Convicting the Innocent; Watkins, The State as a Party Litigant, Chapters 2–4, 7, 8, 10 (1927).

to include cases in tort, or one of the regular courts in the existing judicial system of the state. If the legislature enacts a statute it has no power to enact, or does so in a manner forbidden to it, the inferior officers in the judicial and administrative branches of the government should not pay for the mistake. Neither should the citizen. The loss occasioned by the error should be borne by the people of the state as a group. No single individual should be held liable on the sole ground that the statute was unconstitutional. Officers should be liable for malicious exercise of power, or other abuse of their authority, in accordance with the established rules of torts; but neither the officer nor the citizen should be made to bear the burden of a legislative error on the sole ground that the legislature exceeded some constitutional limitation resting upon it, and that the officer or individual acted in accordance therewith.

The matter is less difficult in the national government. There the risk can be spread over a large number, and the burden on each person is very small. When we come to the states, the difficulties are more numerous. The states carry on many of their functions through county, township, and municipal officers. These officers perform some functions for the state and others for the local community. In some instances the ordinances authorizing them to act will be unconstitutional, or perhaps contrary to the general statutes of the state. In other cases state statutes authorizing them to perform some function will be invalid. But since state statutes may authorize the performance of a local function, the source of authorization cannot be made the dividing line between those cases for which the state as a whole should be liable and those for which the local unit should be liable. Larger cities and the more populous counties could perhaps bear the burdens of mistakes made in their behalf, but in the case of the small cities and villages the imposition of liability on the unit is not very much more effective than to spread the loss over a few personal sureties, or a surety company, in addition to the officer. The solution appears to be the establishment of a fund in state custody, to which all governmental units would make annual contributions and against which judgment should be rendered.

In addition to the problem of dividing responsibility, there is the question of the type of tribunal that shall be used to handle these cases. The elimination of the jury is a first requisite, because, in the light of the experience in cases like Kilbourn v. Thompson,[106] the states or other governmental units could not be expected to consent to having cases against them tried before juries in this branch of the

---

[106] *Supra,* note 94.

law. These cases might be provided for in some more comprehensive scheme of government liability in tort, with special tribunals, such as courts of claims, or more general administrative courts.

Should there first be a trial against the officer, and then a suit by the officer against the state or other responsible unit? Or should the entire matter be settled in one claim, the governmental unit being represented by counsel in the suit against the officer? If the latter method were to be adopted, the suit would probably be in one of the regular courts of the established judicial system of the state instead of in a court of claims. These are some of the problems that would have to be solved in any proposal looking to government responsibility for acts of officers under unconstitutional statutes. Perhaps the most important step to be taken is the establishment of some regular systematic administration of these and other tort cases wherein the government is for one reason or another the party defendant. With that step taken, experimentation with limited jurisdiction as to the size of claims to be entertained, the retention of legislative control over the cases involving larger amounts than those entrusted to the tribunal, and the single trial of a case to establish liability may not be so costly but that the advantages to be gained thereby will far outweigh remote possibilities of raids on the public treasury.

The practice of foreign countries in dealing with government responsibility is suggestive, but it is merely analogous, because action under an unconstitutional statute does not occur in many countries other than the United States. Such action differs from the ordinary case of tort on the part of the officer because he acts in accordance with a statute or ordinance, and in reliance thereon. The practice that obtains in some foreign countries of compensating for injury due to the operation of government regardless of whether such injury constitutes a tort or not is more nearly analogous to the responsibility here proposed for action under invalid statutes than is the practice with respect to responsibility in tort. Some injury and loss is likely to be occasioned by the normal routine operation of any enterprise conducted on so large a scale as government, in its governmental as well as in its private activities. For these the citizen should not be compelled to pay directly if the loss should in a given case fall upon him, but should be compelled to pay only indirectly, through contribution to the common fund, which should be provided for by legislation. Unconstitutional statutes will continue to be enacted. Injury will continue to be done under them. The group instead of the individual should take up the loss, regardless of whether the injury would constitute a technical tort or not.

Chapter VI

RES ADJUDICATA, STARE DECISIS, AND OVERRULED DECISIONS IN CONSTITUTIONAL LAW

The effect of unconstitutionality may be considered from two points of view: (1) from the point of view of the effect of the unconstitutional statute or (2) the effect of a decision declaring the statute to be unconstitutional. Such phrases as *res adjudicata, stare decisis,* or *the permanence of constitutionality* refer primarily to the second of these aspects, and it is with that aspect that the following discussion deals.

The idea expressed by the phrase *the permanence of constitutionality* is more general than that expressed by *res adjudicata* or *stare decisis* and includes both of them. Fifty years ago the more inclusive phrase would not have been used in such a discussion as this, but the doctrines of res adjudicata and stare decisis would very likely have been referred to frequently.

The idea of permanence or stability in legal doctrine, and particularly in a case-to-case system such as that of the common law, supplemented as it was until recently by statute,[1] applies to two different types of situations. In one the parties to a litigation attempt to avoid the decision rendered by a legally established tribunal having jurisdiction finally to settle the dispute, by asking the court to consider the case again. The parties are the same, the issues to be settled are the same, the sources and rules of law applicable to the case are the same, and it is in all respects the same case. It is not peculiar to English and American judges to feel that disputes once settled must remain settled, and therefore to feel the need of formulating the rule that, in the absence of overwhelming reasons for not doing so, the final decision shall be treated as really final as between the parties. This is only a natural human reaction to a situation of this kind.[2]

---

[1] Instead of, as at present, being a system of statutes, supplemented by decisions. Generally, see Moschzisker, Res Judicata, 38 Yale L. J. 299 (1929), for discussion of res adjudicata.

[2] This general idea of precedent and finality of decision is deeply rooted in human nature. It explains why administrators and administrative tribunals tend toward it, although they were not intended so to do, and explains why continental courts follow precedent more than the treatises suggest, despite code provisions against it. Degree only separates this tendency from the formulation of it into a rule of rela-

The second situation suggested by this idea of permanence in the effect of judicial decision is one in which different parties in a subsequent case, involving similar facts, similar sources of the applicable rules of law, and similar rules of law, contend that the court should decide their case without feeling bound by the decision in the earlier case. The doctrine of precedent, or stare decisis, has it that the court *should* feel bound to apply the rules as they were applied in the earlier case unless the sources of those rules or the rules themselves have changed, or the conditions in which they operated have altered, so much that a different decision should be reached.

The doctrine against collateral attack is often spoken of in connection with stare decisis and res adjudicata. It is a slightly different doctrine, however, and more often refers to the attack by C upon a judgment given in an action by A against B, in a case in which C is later suing either A or B or some other party. It is also used to designate a situation in which A when suing C or being sued by C, attempts to assail the judgment given in a prior case between A and B.

The idea underlying the doctrine of precedent is that of stability, just as it is in that of res adjudicata, but it is more generalized in stare decisis. Both these doctrines are founded upon a public policy favoring stability in the legal system.

Res adjudicata seems to be followed with reasonable fidelity both in England and the United States. The doctrine is not without qualifications, however, and these will be examined.

Stare decisis also seems to be quite strictly adhered to in England, but in the United States it has much less compelling force in actual decision than in England. Professor Goodhart, in a very convincing manner, has shown that several powerful factors have operated in the United States to break down the force of the doctrine of precedent.[3] One of these factors, to mention only one, is the influence that constitutional decisions, and decisional techniques, exert on the decisional process in private law. The doctrine of stare decisis is less compelling in the field of constitutional law than in that of private law, but this very relaxation in the field of public law tends to weaken it in the field of private law. The same judges decide both types of questions, and inevitably an interplay of influences and techniques results. The methods of the private law influence constitutional decision, to the disgust of many; constitutional law methods influence private law decision, to the disgust of others. The fact re-

tively compelling authority. Professor William Robson makes this point in his Justice and Administrative Law. Note the French case law on the responsibility of the state, as evidence that precedent is important in the civil law.

[3] Essays in Jurisprudence. 50. Same essay also found in 15 Cornell L. Quart. 173 (1930).

mains, however, that whether we like it or not, stare decisis is not the factor in American constitutional decision that it is in English law. To the writer it seems inevitable and desirable that the rôle of statesmanship in constitutional cases be recognized. A slavish adherence to precedent would make it too difficult for judges to do in constitutional decisions what they must do under our system, that is, decide cases as lawyers and statesmen, not as lawyers alone. Law improperly obstructs government only if judges insist upon deciding constitutional questions as questions of private rather than public law.

I. EXCEPTIONS TO RES ADJUDICATA

Certain exceptions have been made to the rule that an adjudication between the same parties on the same cause of action is binding as to those parties unless it is appealed to a higher court. Some of these exceptions apply to cases in which decisions have been rendered on the assumption that the applicable statutes are constitutional — the question of constitutionality not having been expressly raised. Or the situation may be one in which the question of constitutionality has been expressly raised and considered, only to be subsequently raised and considered again, in another case. In either type of case an attack on the first judgment by one of the parties may occur.

Criminal cases often present this type of question. For example, X is accused and tried for a criminal offense, and is convicted and sentenced to serve a term in jail or prison. No question as to the validity of either procedural or substantive statutes has been raised in the various courts passing on the case. Later, while X is serving his term, Y is accused and tried under the same statutes for the same offense; in the course of the proceedings the constitutionality of one of the statutes is assailed, and the statute is declared invalid by the court. X immediately asks for a writ of habeas corpus to gain his freedom. Will the court release him?

Or suppose that without the subsequent decision X's attorney asks, after six months of the term have been served, that habeas corpus be issued to obtain a decision on the constitutionality of the statute applicable to the crime for which X was found guilty. Will the court issue the writ and determine the question?

The courts are not agreed as to the answer that should be given to these two questions, but the majority of them would apparently hold that the writ should be issued and the question of constitutionality be determined, and that freedom should be granted on the authority of a subsequent decision that holds the statute to be invalid. The United States Supreme Court,[4] the District of Columbia courts,[5] the lower federal courts,[6] and the majority of state courts [7] will determine constitutionality under such circumstances. The texts approve the majority rule.[8] The office of the writ of habeas corpus is said to be to liberate "those who are imprisoned without authority of law." [9] Commitment under an unconstitutional statute is equivalent to commitment under no law at all if the void ab initio theory is applied. Therefore "the courts must liberate one suffering imprisonment under it just as if there had never been the form of a trial, conviction, and sentence." [10] Sometimes the same idea is expressed by saying that the writ is to correct jurisdictional excesses, and that exercise of jurisdiction under an invalid statute is such an excess of jurisdiction and consequently should be corrected.[11] Not all courts agree with this explanation, but it is commonly accepted. Special reasons for substituting the writ of habeas corpus for that of writ of error are sometimes required, however, even by courts that grant the writ of habeas corpus in such cases. So, too, courts hesitate to issue the writ before trial in the lower court.[12]

[4] Ex parte Yarbrough, 110 U. S. 651, 4 Sup. Ct. Rep. 152, 28 L. Ed. 274 (1884); Ex parte Siebold, 100 U. S. 37, 25 L. Ed. 719 (1880). Sometimes, if the state supreme court has not been asked to pass upon the question of the validity of state statute assailed in habeas corpus, appeal is a method of handling case. 3 Am. & Eng. Ann. Cas. 581 (annotation).

[5] Stoutenberger v. Frazier, 16 D. C. App. 229 (1900).

[6] 3 Freeman, Judgments (5 ed., 1925), sec. 155; 3 Ann. Cas. 581 (annotation); Stockton Laundry Case, 26 Fed. 611 (C. C. D. Cal. 1886).

[7] Ex parte Sparks, 120 Cal. 395, 52 Pac. 715 (1898); Ex parte Rosenblatt, 19 Nev. 439, 14 Pac. 298 (1887); Kelley v. Meyers, 124 Or. 322, 263 Pac. 903 (1928); Ex parte Hollman, 79 S. C. 9, 60 S. E. 19 (1907); Ex parte Heyman, 45 Tex. Cr. 532, 78 S. W. 349 (1903); Ex parte Bornee, 76 W. Va. 360, 85 S. E. 529 (1915); Servonitz v. State, 133 Wis. 231, 113 N. W. 277 (1915). See Barton v. State, 89 Tex. Cr. 387, 23 S. W. 989 (1921); Moore v. Wheeler, 109 Ga. 61, 35 S. E. 116 (1900), statute held invalid in subsequent case to which petitioner not a party; Ex parte Messer, 87 Fla. 92, 99 So. 330 (1924), stressing need for writ after conviction. Some courts refuse to grant the writ if the lower court has not passed on the validity of the statute. Ex parte Selicow, 100 Neb. 615, 160 N. W. 991 (1916). See In re Harris, 47 Mo. 164 (1870).

[8] 3 Freeman, Judgments, *supra,* note 6; Black, Judgments (2 ed., 1902), sec. 257. See void ab initio doctrine as to judgment of lunacy given under invalid statute, in Barton v. State, 89 Tex. Cr. 387, 23 S. W. 989 (1921).

[9] Ex parte Hollman, *supra,* note 7.

[10] *Ibid.*

[11] Ex parte Rosenblatt, *supra,* note 7. See Ex parte Newcomb, 56 Wash. 395, 105 Pac. 1042 (1909), that if statute goes to procedure only, and not to jurisdiction, habeas corpus will not issue.

[12] Glasgow v. Moyer, 225 U. S. 420, 32 Sup. Ct. Rep. 753, 56 L. Ed. 1147 (1912); Johnson v. Hoy, 227 U. S. 245, 33 Sup. Ct. Rep. 240, 57 L. Ed. 497 (1913); Ex parte Little, 23 Okla. Cr. 305, 214 Pac. 932 (1923); Ex parte Hanemar, 134 Wash. 51, 234 Pac. 1018 (1925). This problem is often complicated by the problem of use of the writ by the federal courts to control state courts.

Personal liberty is a right too highly prized to be defeated by the technicalities of res adjudicata and habeas corpus when it has been infringed upon under an invalid statute. This seems the proper attitude for the courts to take, and this exception to the ordinary doctrine of res adjudicata seems a sound one in both the situations considered. It is a greater disregard of the doctrine, of course, to permit the question to be reopened in the absence of subsequent decision, but if private parties are ordinarily to be permitted to assail statutes as unconstitutional, they might well be permitted to do so at any time, in view of the casual and unsystematic manner in which judicial review of legislation is practiced.[13] These observations are intended to apply to courts within state and national systems rather than to the relations between them.[14]

All would doubtless agree that when a statute is declared invalid, freedom should be granted to those imprisoned under it and still serving terms; such disregard of res adjudicata seems proper. The question may also be raised in the absence of a second decision, the rational justification for allowing it to be raised being that res adjudicata applies only to questions specifically raised and considered in the first case.[15] This is simply a refusal to apply the doctrine of res adjudicata and an extension of the writ of habeas corpus beyond what was originally intended, but it seems a sensible extension, for otherwise the unconstitutionality of the statute would be determined only when some subsequent defendant would raise it. In other words, the early settlement of the question should be encouraged, in order that all coming under the statute will be treated alike, and that the raising of the question should not be the basis for discriminating against one group of offenders and favoring another. The objection might be made that this encourages raising the question of constitutionality, and that to do so is unwise; but such an objection disregards the fundamental right of every person, under our system of judicial review, to raise the question unless he is disqualified for some special reason, and the fact that the early determination of constitutionality is desirable for the preservation of stability and justice in this branch of the law. Habeas corpus is also justified

[13] Judicial review is casual compared with administrative supervision, because it is exercised from case to case, and because its results are always somewhat uncertain. The court declares statute X unconstitutional. Does that automatically affect all statutes like statute X? Another decision is required. Judicial review is not supervision by general rule or continuous regulation, but is sporadic. See Chapter 12.

[14] See note 12.

[15] See Drinkard v. Oden, *infra,* note 35, for this idea, as expressed in a different kind of case. The courts do not often place these cases squarely on this ground, but are apparently influenced by this idea, and as seen later in the text, rely upon it also in stare decisis decisions.

in this type of case on the ground that force cannot legally be used to escape from confinement.[16]

When the question is raised and decided in the first case, res adjudicata would seem clearly to prevent its being raised again, but the operation of the rule that permits the most recent decision to prevail in situations still remediable cuts off the normal application of the rule of res adjudicata.

This exception has been extended to cover a case in which a fine was due but not yet paid, on a default judgment, so that when the statute was held unconstitutional subsequent to the original judgment but before the action to collect the fine was brought, the judgment imposing the fine was defeated, being subject to collateral attack.[17]

Res adjudicata has occasionally been weakened in its application to judgments under unconstitutional civil statutes also. On appeal, of course, a judgment rendered under such a statute will be reversed,[18] but in some cases it may be attacked collaterally as well. Tax judgments based on an invalid statute have been collaterally assailed,[19] although courts have not been equally lenient in permitting this type of defense, some having vigorously denied it.[20] Recovery of a tax has been denied because of a judgment of a state court, from which no appeal was taken, that the statute was valid, and that the tax must be paid, although at a later date the statute was held invalid by the United States Supreme Court.[21] Some of the inferior courts in New York have even gone so far in applying res adjudicata in tax cases as to extend it to cases of assessment of inheritance taxes, despite the fact that such proceedings are not final judgments.[22] Such an extension is certainly incorrect.[23] A quibble

---

[16] Kelley v. Meyers, 124 Or. 322, 263 Pac. 903 (1928). See State v. Skinner, 148 La. 143, 86 So. 716 (1900). Cf. Cooley, Constitutional Limitations (7th ed.), 259, note 2, citing Strong v. Daniel, 5 Ind. 348 (1854), not a criminal case.

[17] International Harvester Co. v. Commonwealth, 170 Ky. 41, 185 S. W. 102 (1916).

[18] Yellow Pine Lbr. Co. v. Randall, 145 Ala. 653, 39 So. 565 (1905). Stromberg Allen Co. v. Hill, 170 Ill. App. 323 (1912); People v. Schraeberg, 347 Ill. 392, 179 N. E. 829 (1932). Appeal does not contradict the doctrine of res adjudicata, it is perhaps needless to say, because judgment below is not final, so far as this doctrine is concerned, while appeal is pending.

[19] In Matter of Bd. of Administrators, 34 La. Ann. 97 (1882), decision seems based on nullity of statute and lack of citation.

[20] Harmon v. Auditor, 123 Ill. 122, 13 N. E. 161 (1887); Mo. Kan. & Tex. Ry. v. Bd., 62 Kan. 550, 64 Pac. 56 (1901); Haskett v. Maxey, 134 Ind. 182, 33 N. E. 358 (1893).

[21] Beck v. State, 196 Wis. 242, 219 N. W. 197, cert. denied 278 U. S. 639, 49 Sup. Ct. Rep. 34, 73 L. Ed. 555 (1928). Cf. Sperry Hutchinson Co. v. Blue, 202 Fed. 82 (C. C. A. 4th 1912), state court judgment in tax suit binding in federal courts, when not brought on appeal.

[22] See Chapter 10.   [23] See discussion of this problem in Chapter 10.

as to the interest section of a tax statute was brushed aside when in the first suit general statutory validity was considered,[24] the binding force of the first judgment being sustained in the following language:

The legality of this tax was the question involved in the original injunction suit, and within the issue there framed the constitutionality of these sections, and of other laws bearing on the legality and validity of such tax, was involved, and could have been there litigated and determined.[25]

The interest and penalty were said to have become part of the tax, and therefore its recovery was concluded by the decision on the validity of the tax. The dissent would have left the question open for later decision, saying that "the court should decide cases upon the merits as presented by the attorneys, unless there appear to be questions of a jurisdictional nature which preclude it from so doing." [26]

Objection to the constitutionality of a divorce statute was in one case raised successfully after the divorce had been granted, the case having involved a later distribution of property.[27]

A judgment of a probate court was also assailed with success in Finders v. Bodle,[28] wherein it was held that the validity of the statute might be re-examined in ejectment proceedings instituted after the original probate decree was entered. An Illinois case takes a contrary position, however.[29] So, too, an administrator has been held to be without adequate defense in a suit against him for moneys paid out under a probate court order which assumed the validity of a statute later declared invalid.[30]

In election contest cases,[31] in suits upon private bonds,[32] in actions on partnership account,[33] and in homestead decrees,[34] res adjudicata or the doctrine preventing collateral attack has been applied to deny attempts to evade or reopen judgments, even if they have been given under invalid statutes. As to the parties concluded by the decision when first given, the first decision was final and not open to subsequent attack.

[24] Mo. Kan. & Tex. Ry. v. Bd., *supra,* note 20.
[25] 62 Kan. at 552.
[26] 62 Kan. at 553.
[27] In re Christensen's Estate, 17 Utah 412, 53 Pac. 1003 (1908).
[28] 58 Neb. 57, 78 N. W. 480 (1899). Cf. Reed v. Wright, 2 Greene 15 (Iowa 1849).
[29] Buckmaster v. Carlin, 4 Ill. 104 (1841).
[30] Boales v. Ferguson, 55 Neb. 565, 76 N. W. 18 (1898).
[31] People ex rel. McCarty v. Wilson, 6 Cal. App. 122, 91 Pac. 661 (1907).
[32] Cassell v. Scott, 17 Ind. 514 (1861).
[33] Fuqua v. Mullen, 76 Ky. 467 (1877).
[34] Brandhoefer v. Bain, 45 Neb. 781, 64 N. W. 213 (1895).

An interesting case illustrating the same doctrine is that of Drinkard v. Oden.[35] Plaintiff brought detinue to recover some hogs seized by defendant for whose seizure defendant previously had been awarded damages. The validity of the statute had been assumed in the first case, though it had not been specifically raised and considered. In the second case it was raised, and the court was asked to consider it. The court refused to do so, saying that "the inquiry is, not what the parties actually litigated, but what they might and ought to have litigated."[36] If counsel failed to raise the issue when they could have done so, that failure would be counted against their client under this decision; only in cases involving new parties and new issues could the question be raised.

Both federal[37] and state[38] courts have denied bills of review in cases that have been settled on the assumption that governing statutes were valid. A Tennessee case[39] refused, in mandamus proceedings to compel the levy of taxes to pay a judgment against a city, to reconsider the question of the validity of the bonds upon which judgment had been rendered. Similarly, the Illinois court properly held that taxpayers were concluded by decision of an injunction suit from later questioning the validity of municipal bonds involved in the injunction action.[40] Said one court: "We think there must be an end of litigation and that, after the validity of the bonds has been twice adjudged by this court, it is too late to ask to open up that question again."[41]

State courts have held that a decision on a federal question is binding between the parties when the judgment has not been appealed from, even though a United States Supreme Court decision in another case should later settle the question differently.[42] The same rule was applied to judgments under the legal tender acts by state courts relying on Hepburn v. Griswold.[43]

Res adjudicata is usually applied in the constitutional field, but there are some exceptions to it in this field. It is only when the courts feel that overwhelming considerations demand its relaxation,

[35] 150 Ala. 475, 43 So. 578 (1907).
[36] *Supra*, note 35.
[37] Hoffman v. Knox, 50 Fed. 484 (C. C. A. 4th 1892).
[38] Harrigan v. County of Peoria, 262 Ill. 36, 104 N. E. 172 (1914).
[39] State v. Mayor, 109 Tenn. 315, 70 S. W. 1031 (1902).
[40] Harmon v. Auditor, 123 Ill. 122, 13 N. E. 161 (1887).
[41] State v. Mayor, *supra*, note 39. The same rule has been applied to private bonds when a judgment enforcing it has been given under a statute later held invalid. State v. Ark. Constr. Co., 201 Ind. 259, 167 N. E. 526 (1929).
[42] People ex rel. Bank v. Russell, 283 Ill. 520, 119 N. E. 617 (1918); Beck v. State, 196 Wis. 242, 219 N. W. 197 (1928).
[43] Miller v. Tyler, 58 N. Y. 477 (1874).

as in habeas corpus, that they should permit exceptions to this doctrine to be established.[44] The few instances in which courts have abandoned the doctrine in civil litigation are not convincing, but generally illustrate the need for res adjudicata rather than the justification for its abandonment. The doctrine should have been adhered to in most of these cases.

II. STARE DECISIS AND RES ADJUDICATA

In considering stare decisis, the problem first suggesting itself is the power of courts to overrule constitutional decisions. Much argument may take place over the question whether courts *ought* to do so in a particular case, or in general, but the question of power is settled by the numerous instances in which it has been exercised. The Supreme Court of the United States as well as those of the states have overruled previous constitutional decisions of their own. Cases as far apart as the Legal Tender cases [45] and Fox Film Corporation v. Doyal [46] suggest themselves immediately in this connection. In both of them, overruling Hepburn v. Griswold [47] and Long v. Rockwood,[48] respectively, cases were overruled that had been decided only a few years earlier. The reversal of the Supreme Court's position upon the admiralty jurisdiction also comes to mind.[49]

The power being assumed, the problem is to determine in what situations it is or should be exercised.

To separate a case of res adjudicata from that of stare decisis normally is not a difficult task, but at times the line between them becomes narrow and indistinct. Consider, for example, the case wherein a plaintiff water company sues a customer for the price of water furnished. The contract for service and the city ordinance construed as applicable to the case are interpreted and made the basis for decision. Three months later the same water company sues the same customer under the same ordinance and contract. The claim is for the water furnished subsequent to the first decision. In this case the constitutionality of the ordinance is raised and objection is entered that since no such question was raised in the first case the ordinance was assumed to be valid and therefore must be assumed to be so now. The only distinguishing features in the two

[44] See, for general discussion, Wells, Res Judicata and Stare Decisis; note, 42 Yale L. J. 779 (1933), and articles there cited.

[45] 12 Wall. 457, 20 L. Ed. 287 (U. S. 1871).

[46] 286 U. S. 123, 52 Sup. Ct. Rep. 546, 76 L. Ed. 1010 (1932).

[47] 8 Wall. 603, 19 L. Ed. 513 (U. S. 1869).

[48] 277 U. S. 142, 48 Sup. Ct. Rep. 463, 72 L. Ed. 824 (1928).

[49] The Genessee Chief v. Fitzhugh, 12 How. 443, 13 L. Ed. 1058 (U. S. 1851), overruling The Thomas Jefferson, 10 Wheat. 428, 6 L. Ed. 358 (1825).

cases are (1) that the claim for water covers a different period from that covered in the first case and (2) that the validity of the ordinance is specifically challenged in the second case. Under these circumstances it was held that the validity of the ordinance was open for consideration in the second case.

In the Geiger case the pleadings did not present and the court did not determine the question of the constitutionality of the ordinance as applied in that case and as sought to be applied in this. In a case like this, in which the suit is upon a different demand, it is not to be held that a question was determined by necessary implication, which question the pleadings did not present, and under a long and firmly settled rule, is not raised for determination unless it is so presented.[50]

Stare decisis, rather than res adjudicata, governs an attack upon defendant's title to office by plaintiff, even though the same plaintiff challenged the title of the same defendant to the same office during a preceding term.[51] The reasoning in support of this decision is given in the following quotation:

But it is said that the decision in the case of The People ex rel. Lawson et al. v. Stoddard et al., reported in 34 Colo., at page 200, based on the authority of the Johnson case, where the title of the relators to the office of county commissioner was determined in favor of them and against the respondents, the then board of supervisors of the city and county of Denver, is res judicata upon the like question here. The contention is not sound. There is no privity between the respondents here and the relators in the Lawson case. These respondents are serving for a separate, independent, and distinct term of office, to which they were elected at a different time and under different conditions and circumstances from those which surrounded the relators in the Lawson case, their predecessors in office. There is and can be no privity of interest in title to an office between a predecessor therein and one elected at a different time, to a different term, thus holding an independent, separate, and unrelated title. The thing determined in the Lawson case was the title of law of that case, and is res judicata upon that question between the parties to that suit and privies to that title, but it has no binding force as to the right and title of some subsequent claimant, asserting claim under a separate and independent title, obtained at another and different election. Nor does it matter that some purely abstract question of law was determined in a former case, which might be applicable to a later one, and by the application of which the question of the right to an office in the later case might be determined, with a like result to that reached in the former. Whatever force there may be in the contention for such application depends solely on the principle of stare decisis, not of res judicata. Mere abstract questions of law cannot be made the sub-

[50] State ex rel. St. Joseph Water Co. v. Eastin, 278 Mo. 672, 213 S. W. 59 (1919).
[51] People ex rel. Atty. Gen. v. Cassidy, 50 Colo. 503, 117 Pac. 357 (1911).

ject of litigation, so that, when once determined, such determination must be applied in all subsequent litigation between other and different parties, simply because the same question of law may be involved. Where, in the determination of a case, legal principles are invoked and conclusions thereon reached by the court, whether such conclusions shall be followed in other cases, without further investigation, depends on the rule of stare decisis, not of res judicata. The thing determined in the particular litigation becomes res judicata, and may not be challenged afterward between the parties, even though the question of law by which the decision was controlled is determined thereafter to have been incorrectly decided and applied, but such decision and application is not necessarily binding on the court in other litigation. The question is squarely settled in the case of State ex rel. Kennedy et al. v. Broatch et al., 88 Neb. 687, where a situation precisely like the one here was presented, discussed, and a conclusion reached exactly contrary to the contention of these respondents, and in full accord with the views here expressed. This action and the Lawson case are wholly disconnected, both as to parties and subject matter.

In the Lawson case the right and title of the relators therein to the office of county commissioner for the city and county of Denver for a particular term, long since expired by limitation, was adjudicated. In the case at bar, respondents are required to show by what authority of law they now claim the right to hold and exercise the duties of that office for another and different term than the one involved in the Lawson case. The court is at liberty to determine their title to this particular office, and it is its duty to do so, according to their lawful rights, upon principle and authority, as applied to the facts in this case, not of some other case, and not by the application of the doctrine of res judicata, as the situation not only does not call for such application but does not even permit it.[52]

A further illustration of the importance attached to the fact that different, though similar, causes of action are involved, is to be found in a decision that a judgment for one month's salary of an officer does not conclude the question of the constitutionality of his appointment to the office, in a subsequent suit for salary for another month in the same term.[53] The court refused to utilize the doctrine of estoppel in this case, and justified its consideration of the question of constitutionality in the second suit by pointing out that it had not been raised in the earlier decision and could therefore be considered when raised, because the question was not one of res adjudicata but apparently one of stare decisis. The court said:

But this estoppel in actions upon a different cause of action only extends to matters actually litigated and determined, and not to questions

[52] 50 Colo. at 522.
[53] Freeman v. Barnum, 131 Cal. 386, 63 Pac. 691 (1901).

involved and defenses which might have been but were not made. This applies to the question as to the constitutionality of subdivision 36 of section 25 of the County Government Act of 1893. It is true that matter was necessarily involved and must have been determined before judgment could have been entered in the former suit. But it does not appear from the record that such question was raised and litigated. This being a different action upon a different cause of action, the defendant is not estopped from raising the objection.[54]

A decision that certain securities are tax exempt for one year is binding for that year only, and if the question of constitutional exemption be litigated again the next year, the principle of stare decisis, not that of res adjudicata, governs, even though the parties and the securities are the same, if the statute governing during the first year has been declared invalid in another case before the suit for the second year is begun.[55] The general rule in the law of judgments, that a decision as to one year governs for following years as to the same parties and identical causes of action, was said by the court to be subject to the qualification that when changed conditions intervene and such a change of conditions may be a change in judicial view as to the validity of an applicable statute, the general rule will not apply.

Other cases also present nice distinctions between the two doctrines, and sometimes what looks like a res adjudicata case is labeled stare decisis.[56] The tendency seems to be for the courts to classify cases so as to subject them to the application of stare decisis, because it permits a re-examination of the questions not expressly considered earlier or a re-examination of the point of law involved in the earlier decision if a new cause of action is involved, although even by stare decisis, if strictly applied, the earlier judgment should be followed if the cause of action differs only with respect to the period covered and is in all other points identical with the earlier one. More justification for the use of stare decisis, so as to avoid its binding precedent phase, is to be found when conditions have materially changed. The courts here feel that stare decisis binds them less than res adjudicata.

[54] 131 Cal. at 389. See Freeman, Judgments (5 ed., 1925), sec. 711, for approval of result reached, and criticism of reasoning used, in this case.

[55] Security Savings Bank v. Connell, 198 Iowa 564, 200 N. W. 8 (1924). See generally on res adjudicata in taxation, note, 33 Col. L. Rev. 1404 (1933).

[56] Bd. of Commrs. v. State, 155 Ind. 604, 58 N. E. 1037 (1900), same parties, different form of action; held, classified under stare decisis and earlier decision overruled; Bond Debt cases, 12 S. C. 200 (1879), decision on validity of five bonds followed on stare decisis, not res judicata in action on others; Allardt v. People, 197 Ill. 501, 64 N. E. 533 (1902), good discussion. On the interesting relation of stare decisis to rehearings, see State v. Packer Corp. 17 Utah 500, 2 Pac. (2d) 114 (1931).

III. STARE DECISIS

In discussing stare decisis in its relation to constitutional law care must be taken to distinguish several different situations, all or some of which are often referred to in a general sense by the phrase.[57] For purposes of study distinctions need to be drawn between them.

1) Between coordinate courts of one judicial system. — There is the situation in which one court in a jurisdiction is asked to follow the decisions of coordinate courts within the same jurisdiction.[58] One general trial court may be asked to follow the previous decision of another general trial court in another district within the same state. Courts are not required to adhere to the decisions of other courts on the same level in the court system, but they often do so.[59] A somewhat similar case is presented when a court of criminal appeal is asked to follow a decision of a court of civil appeal within the same state, each court having final appellate jurisdiction within the state over certain types of cases. Here, too, what is called stare decisis is often applied,[60] although it is not strictly binding.

2) Between courts of different jurisdictions. — A quite different situation confronts a court when it is asked to follow a decision of a court in another jurisdiction. The court in Minnesota, for instance, may be asked to follow a Nebraska decision if there is no Minnesota precedent. Here the doctrine of precedent is admittedly of persuasive force only. The Minnesota court may follow the Nebraska decision, but it is not obliged to do so. When the Minnesota court is called upon, as sometimes happens, to decide a case depending for disposition upon Nebraska law, stare decisis merges with conflict of laws and with constitutional doctrine in full faith and credit. State courts have usually refused to declare the statutes of other states to be contrary to the constitution of the state from which the statute comes,[61] but presumably there is no reason why, if need be, this

[57] On this subject, Boudin, Stare Decisis in Our Constitutional Theory, 8 N. Y. U. L. Quart. 589 (1931); Wells, Stare Decisis, Chapters 43, 46; Davidson, Stare Decisis in Louisiana, 7 Tulane L. Rev. (1932); L. Sachs, Stare Decisis and the Legal Tender Acts, 20 Va. L. Rev. 856.

[58] The term "jurisdiction" is used here to denote area, for purposes of establishing courts, such as a state. The state is the jurisdictional unit, in this sense, containing various levels or ranks of courts, often organized by districts.

[59] People ex rel. Metz v. Dayton, 120 App. Div. 814, 105 N. Y. S. 809 (1907). But see Charles v. Arthur, 84 N. Y. S. 284 (1903).

[60] Lyle v. State, 80 Tex. Cr. Rep. 606, 193 S. W. 680 (1917). So, too, as to the relation between equity and other courts. See U. S. Sav. and Loan Co. v. Miller, 47 S. W. 17 (Tenn. Ch. 1897).

[61] Shelden v. Miller, 9 La. Ann. 187 (1854). That one state should follow courts of sister state on questions of constitutionality of statute of sister state, see Am. Print Works v. Lawrence, 23 N. J. L. 590 (1851); Cotton v. Brien, 6 Rob. 115 (La. 1843).

could not be done. So, too, it is conceivable that the Minnesota court might find it necessary to declare a Nebraska statute invalid because it conflicts with the constitution of the United States.[62]

3) Between superior and inferior courts of the same judicial system. — The relations between courts of different grades within a given system, such as the Supreme Court and the district courts of a state, or those of the national government, are often described by reference to stare decisis. Strictly speaking, however, a circuit or district court follows a Supreme Court decision within the same state because the latter is superior in the judicial hierarchy and because it would, on appeal or other method of review, compel the lower court to adhere to its determination. This assumes that decisions make rules of law, and assumes that the rule clearly was applicable to the case in hand. This is not stare decisis but a rule of administrative superiority within the judiciary.

4) Between the national and state courts. — Closely allied to this is the relation between the state and national courts. Two distinct phases of this relationship should be noted: (a) that in which a federal question is involved, wherein stare decisis does not of itself, as a legal principle, give to the federal courts their superiority, since in this situation their power arises because of appeal or other corrective devices; (b) that in which questions involved may be decided by either state or federal courts independently of each other. Here the national courts may follow the state decisions, or the state courts may follow national court decisions, but neither is compelled to follow the decisions of the other. This rule may be modified by statute, as has been done in certain classes of diversity of citizenship cases. The statute, then, not stare decisis, is the basis for the rule that state decisions will be followed.

Notice should be paid also to the situation in which federal courts apply what looks like a rule of stare decisis when they insist in certain cases (often classified under obligation of contracts, such as Gelpcke v. Dubuque) [63] upon adhering to state decision; upon examination, however, it will be found that the federal courts really *refuse* to follow the latest state decisions in these instances, and do not in any way directly compel the states to apply stare decisis to

---

[62] Under the full faith and credit clause, sister state statutes must be given effect in certain types of cases involving those statutes which arise in other states, and under the reasoning of the "supreme law of the land" binding state as well as federal judges, presumably state courts would not be bound by full faith and credit to apply sister state statutes which are contrary to the United States constitution. County, not obligatory rule, compels the practice of not exercising this power if its exercise can be avoided.

[63] 1 Wall. 175, 17 L. Ed. 520 (U. S. 1864).

their own decisions. They merely say that, as federal courts, they will choose the rule to apply and will refuse to apply the latest state rule if to do so will defeat bondholders who have relied upon prior state decisions. This group of cases has sometimes been said to force upon the states a rule of stare decisis,[64] but of course they do nothing of the kind. They do not compel the state to apply its earlier rule. If suit is brought in the state courts to recover on the bonds, the state courts may overrule an earlier decision holding the bonds valid and proceed to hold them invalid. The federal courts will not interfere with such a decision.[65]

5) As applied to decisions by the same court. — Finally, one court may be asked to follow one of its own decisions in a case thought to involve the same considerations as were operative in the former case. It is this type of case that will be considered here under stare decisis, the type wherein the New York Court of Appeals, for example, is asked to follow or overrule its own decisions.

Before discussing the case in which a court is asked to follow or overrule one of its own decisions based upon identical circumstances, some consideration should be given to the problem of overruling decisions under changed circumstances. It is one thing to be asked to overrule a decision because the reasons given in support of it are thought to be unsound or because important considerations were overlooked, and another to be asked to change the rule because of changed circumstances. The usual phrasing of the doctrine of stare decisis includes the qualification that precedent is to be followed *unless* conditions have so changed as to make the rule unwise or inapplicable.

Judicial decrees dealing with public utility rates will need to be changed when conditions have altered sufficiently to make unreasonable the rates fixed therein. Such decrees are binding until they are changed, but, as was said in Smyth v. Ames,[66] "of course, the

[64] See Larremore, Stare Decisis and Contractual Rights, 22 Harv. L. Rev. 182 (1908). Mr. Larremore says: "By the recognition of the right to appeal to the Supreme Court of the United States the moral obligation of stare decisis, which state judges always admit, practically becomes a legal obligation." See discussion of relation of stare decisis to obligation of contracts, in Thomas v. State ex rel. Gilbert, 76 Ohio St. 341, 81 N. E. 437 (1907). See Swanson v. Ottumwa, 131 Iowa 540, 106 N. W. 9 (1906); Land Co. v. Hotel, 134 N. C. 397, 46 S. E. 748 (1903).

[65] These state court decisions reversing the earlier ones are not treated by the federal courts, if brought to the latter after first having been settled in the state courts, as impairing the obligation of contracts. Central Land Co. v. Laidley, 159 U. S. 103, 16 Sup. Ct. Rep. 80, 40 L. Ed. 91 (1895). See Douglass v. Pike County, 101 U. S. 677, 25 L. Ed. 968 (1879). Dodd, Impairment of the Obligation of Contracts by State Judicial Decision, 4 Ill. L. Rev. 155, 327 (1910). See Tidal Oil Co. v. Flanagan, 263 U. S. 444, 44 Sup. Ct. Rep. 197, 68 L. Ed. 382 (1923).

[66] 171 U. S. 361, 365, 18 Sup. Ct. Rep. 888, 43 L. Ed. 197 (1898). See also 169 U. S. 466, 550, 18 Sup. Ct. Rep. 418, 42 L. Ed. 819 (1897).

reasonableness of a schedule of rates must be determined by the facts as they exist when it is sought to put such rates into operation." The same idea is expressed by another court when it says that a judgment that a rate is not confiscatory is binding only so long as conditions remain the same.[67]

A striking example of this rule that a decision may become inapplicable when conditions change is afforded by the situation involved in Vigeant v. Postal Telegraph Company,[68] a Massachusetts case. In this case a Massachusetts statute regulating the liability of telegraph companies for injuries caused by poles and wires was upheld as constitutional. Many years later the constitutionality of the statute was assailed on the ground that it was discriminatory, other companies similarly situated not being subjected to the same rules of liability. Other utilities had come into existence since the statute had been passed, and to them it had not been extended. The court quite properly decided that the statute was unconstitutional. The reasoning of the court merits extended quotation.

The provisions of said section 42 first appeared in St. 1851, ch. 247, section 2. When enacted, its constitutionality was beyond question. At that time the telegraph was the only known instrumentality for transmitting intelligence by electricity or for transmitting electricity at all. Since that time inventive genius has placed other instrumentalities in the same general category as the electric telegraph as to the use of poles, wires, and apparatus. A law, valid in its operation when applicable to only one instrumentality, has become unequal in its operation because the ingenuity of the human mind has added to science and industry other instrumentalities falling within the same general classification as to material construction and support of structures in public ways and the use of electricity as a main agency. The statute as drawn was specifically directed to the conditions existing at that time. It was rigid, not flexible, in terms. It was not framed to broaden in its scope with changing conditions. It has become too narrow because of the advance in the art of transmitting intelligence and electricity.

It is nothing new in constitutional law that a statute valid at one time may become void at another time because of altered circumstances. A rate for a public utility corporation sufficient to afford fair return on capital invested and hence valid at one time may become confiscatory by increase in costs of production and hence invalid at another time. Newton v. Consolidated Gas Co. of New York, 258 U. S. 165. The adoption of a constitutional amendment may nullify laws whose constitutionality theretofore was not open to attack. Neal v. Delaware, 103 U. S. 370. Ex parte Virginia, 100 U. S. 339, 346, 347. National Prohibition Cases, 253 U. S. 350, 386, 387. Leser v. Garnett, 258 U. S. 130. Numerous other statutes

[67] Kings County Lighting Co. v. Nixon, 268 Fed. 143 (D. C. S. D. N. Y. 1920).
[68] 260 Mass. 335, 157 N. E. 651 (1927).

may become inoperative because of the enactment by Congress of some statute within a field in which it is supreme under the constitution, although until Congress acts that field may be open to legislation by the several states. Commonwealth v. Nickerson, 236 Mass. 281, 292, 296, 302–305, and cases there collected. A change in economic conditions may render void a statute valid at its enactment. Chastleton Corp. v. Sinclair, 264 U. S. 543.[69]

Emergency rent statutes were upheld during and after the World War, but were declared invalid when the emergency ended.[70] This type of case may arise oftener as time goes on, as readjustment following the war continues. Many types of legislation are likely to be sustained as emergency measures, since the present concept of due process of law recognizes the need for relaxing the more ordinary or normal standards during an emergency. This will be the more true if there is a continuation of the present tendency to study constitutional restraints, rather than constitutional enumerations of power, in testing for congressional power.[71]

That due process affords these possibilities is illustrated not only in rate and utility cases but also by the case of Abie State Bank v. Bryan.[72] A state bank guaranty statute had been sustained as a police power measure shortly after its enactment. Approximately twenty years later the validity of the statute was assailed again.[73] Objection was made in argument that the question had been foreclosed by the earlier decision. In reply, the court said, in the course of its opinion:

As to the first objection, it is sufficient to say that the Bank Guaranty Law was sustained by this court as a police regulation (Shallenberger v. First State Bank of Holstein, *supra;* Noble State Bank v. Haskell, 219 U. S. 104, 575), and that a police regulation, although valid when made, may become, by reason of later events, arbitrary and confiscatory in operation. Smith v. Illinois Bell Telephone Co., 282 U. S. 133, 162; Ablen v. St. Louis, Iron Mountain, & Southern Railway Co., 230 U. S. 553, 555, 556; Lincoln Gas & Electric Co. v. City of Lincoln, 250 U. S. 256, 268.

[69] 260 Mass. at 342.

[70] Block v. Hirsch, 256 U. S. 135, 41 Sup. Ct. Rep. 458, 62 L. Ed. 865 (1921); Chastleton Corp. v. Sinclair, 264 U. S. 543, 44 Sup. Ct. Rep. 405, 68 L. Ed. 841 (1924); Peck v. Fink, 2 F. (2d) 912 (App. D. C. 1924), cert. denied, 266 U. S. 631, 45 Sup. Ct. Rep. 197, 69 L. Ed. 478 (1924), emergency ended.

[71] The day has passed when people ask whether Congress has been given a power, and the first impulse even of lawyers seems to be, just as in the case of state legislative power, to inquire whether the power has been taken away, or has been restricted, by constitutional provision. The natural result is to permit the exercise of powers in emergencies, not because they are granted, but because due process does not prevent it.

[72] 282 U. S. 765, 51 Sup. Ct. Rep. 252, 75 L. Ed. 690 (1931).

[73] The parties were different in this case from those in the earlier ones. The earlier cases are discussed in the opinion in the Abie State Bank case.

In the Shallenberger case, the suit was brought immediately upon the enactment of the law, and that decisions sustaining the law cannot be regarded as precluding a subsequent suit for the purpose of testing the validity of assessments in the light of the later actual experience.[74]

In Missouri Pacific Railway v. Norwood [75] the Supreme Court of the United States implied again that had the plaintiff shown to the satisfaction of the court that the conditions had so changed as to make full-crew laws arbitrary and unduly burdensome, they would have been held invalid despite prior decisions sustaining their constitutionality.

Due process and interstate commerce furnish most of the illustrations of the doctrine that the courts will change decisions on the constitutionality of statutes where changed conditions go to constitutionality itself. Constitutionality itself, under modern conceptions of case-to-case decision, is dependent upon the facts or conditions in these branches of the law.[76]

Another interesting aspect of constitutionality in these fields is exemplified in the cases which hold that a statute is valid as applied to one group of persons and one group of facts, while at the same time it is invalid as applied to another group of persons and another set of circumstances. Tax phases of due process afford some interesting examples of this doctrine.[77] The tax may be valid as to one, but invalid as to another. This is partial constitutionality in one sense, but not in the sense that a section or portion of the statute is invalid. It is partial in the sense that the whole of the statute is valid as to some persons, but wholly invalid as to others.[78] Here, too, the facts are important, because it is the facts or circumstances that make the statute unreasonably discriminatory as to some, but reasonable as to other groups.

Stare decisis here does not mean that if the statute is held to be valid, it must be held valid as to everybody. In these cases stare decisis means only that as to persons in those conditions involved in the first decision, the statute is constitutional, but as to persons not

[74] 282 U. S. at 772.

[75] 283 U. S. 249, 51 Sup. Ct. Rep. 458, 75 L. Ed. 1010 (1931). Here, too, should be studied such a case as the Genessee Chief v. Fitzhugh, *supra,* note 49.

[76] St. L. I. M. & So. Ry. v. Wynne, 224 U. S. 354, 32 Sup. Ct. Rep. 493, 56 L. Ed. 799 (1912), statute invalid on railroad liability for killing stock; Kan. City So. Ry. v. Anderson, 233 U. S. 325, 34 Sup. Ct. Rep. 599, 56 L. Ed. 983 (1914) held valid. Stevenson v. St. Clair, 161 Minn. 444, 201 N. W. 629 (1925), invalid as to women but valid as to children.

[77] Gast Realty & Invest. Co. v. Schneider Granite Co., 240 U. S. 55, 36 Sup. Ct. Rep. 254, 60 L. Ed. 523 (1916); Schneider Granite Co. v. Gast Realty Co., 245 U. S. 288, 38 Sup. Ct. Rep. 125, 62 L. Ed. 292 (1917).

[78] See, for an excellent discussion of types of partial constitutionality, State v. Bevins, 210 Iowa 1031, 230 N. W. 865 (1930).

in that situation it may be held to be invalid. This reduces considerably the utility of stare decisis in the constitutional field.

These cases are not without dissents, and some courts refuse to enter upon such an uncertain case-to-case technique. Several courts have agreed with that of Nebraska, which has said:

> It is possible that with other railroads . . . the difficulties shown here do not exist and the act might be enforceable, but we cannot draw a line and say the act is enforceable as applied to one railroad and invalid as to another, or as to shipments in one direction and not to shipments in the other direction.[79]

The cases on stare decisis to be discussed next are those in which courts *say expressly* that they either overrule or refuse to overrule particular decisions. Those cases which critics may believe to have overruled earlier cases, but which include an express statement by the judges that no such overruling took place or no statement at all about overruling, will not be discussed in this section. The discussion in the Pollock case,[80] involving the income tax, is significant in connection with stare decisis and constitutional law, but the decision itself will not be considered as overruling previous decisions because the court said that none of them was overruled, but that they were distinguished.

A question that naturally suggests itself in this connection is whether stare decisis applies differently to constitutional than to statutory decisions. A Missouri opinion [81] concludes that stare decisis should have less force in the constitutional than in the statutory field. The reasoning deserves to be presented in the language of the court.

> In support of its first contention plaintiff asserts the proposition: "After a statute or constitution has been settled by judicial construction, the construction becomes, so far as rights acquired under it are concerned, as much a part of the statute or constitution as the text itself, and a change in the decision of the courts is, to all intents and purposes, the same in effect on contracts, as if made by legislative enactment or a constitutional convention." Without the interpolated words about the constitution and a constitutional convention, this statement is substantially and almost literally the language of Chief Justice Waite in Douglas v. County of Pike, 107 U. S. 687. The doctrine thus stated is almost universally accepted as applied to decisions construing statutes, especially where there has been a long line of decisions on the question, but even then the doctrine of stare decisis has not been followed where a palpable

[79] Davison v. N. W. Ry., 100 Neb. 402, 160 N. W. 877 (1916).

[80] Pollock v. Farmers' Loan & Trust Co. 157 U. S. 429, 15 Sup. Ct. Rep. 912, 39 L. Ed. 1108 (1895).

[81] Mountain Grove Bank v. Douglass County, 146 Mo. 42, 47 S. W. 944 (1898).

wrong or injustice would be done, or where the mischiefs to be cured far outweigh any injury that might be done in the particular case by overruling prior decisions. A distinction has also been drawn where only one decision is relied on as establishing the doctrine. Butler Van Wyck, 1 Hill. 462; Leavitt v. Blatchford, 17 N. Y. 533; Pratt v. Brown, 3 Wis. 609; Callendar's Administrator v. Insurance Co., 23 Pa. St. 474; State v. Silvers, 47 N. W. Rep. 772. Whether the doctrine applies to the construction of the constitution is a question that has been differently decided in different jurisdictions. The Supreme Court of the United States enforces the principle. Taylor v. Ypsilanti, 105 U. S. 1 c. 71–72; Greene Co. v. Conness, 109 U. S. 104. Some of the text writers also lay down the rule that there is no difference in the application of the doctrine to decisions upon the constitution and upon statutes. Endlich on the Interpretation of Statutes, section 529; Sutherland on Statutory Construction, section 317. The last-named author says: "The two grounds of justification in departing from even a single decision which has become a general rule of property within a certain line of dealing, are, first, the necessity of preventing further injustice; second, the necessity of vindicating clear and obvious principles of law." On the other hand, in Boyd v. State, 53 Ala. 608, and Willis v. Owen, 43 Texas 41, it was held that this doctrine did not apply to cases construing the constitution. And in O. V. and S. K. R. R. v. Morgan Co., 53 Mo. 158, while the court refused to overrule its prior decisions, it said: *"It is true that constitutional questions are always open to examination."* It may not be amiss to remark that in most of the jurisdictions where the doctrine has been applied to decisions interpreting constitutional provisions as strictly as it has to those construing statutes, their reports are not without instances where the rule announced has not been observed, but that prior decisions have been overruled, from such considerations as Sutherland says justify such a course, or upon the broader ground that a further adherence to such prior cases would do more mischief to the public generally than it would do harm to a few people.

There is another reason for a distinction between decisions construing statutes and those construing the constitution. If the people are dissatisfied with the construction of a statute, the frequently recurring sessions of the legislature afford easy opportunity to repeal, alter, or modify the statute, while the constitution is organic, intended to be enduring until changed conditions of society demand more stringent or less restrictive regulations, and if a decision construes the constitution in a manner not acceptable to the people, the opportunity of changing the organic law is remote. Moreover, no set of judges ought to have the right to tie the hands of their successors on constitutional questions, any more than one General Assembly should those of its successors on legislative matters.[82]

[82] 146 Mo. at 52. See "The rule of stare decisis has not been held to apply with the usual force and vigor to decisions upon constitutional questions." Robinson v. Schenck, 102 Ind. 307, 1 N. E. 698 (1885).

The dictum on this point in Pollock v. Farmers' Loan & Trust Company,[83] referred to above, is equally interesting. The Supreme Court there said: "Manifestly as this court is clothed with the power, and entrusted with the duty, to maintain the fundamental law of the constitution, the discharge of that duty requiring it not to extend any decision upon a constitutional question if it is convinced that error in principle might supervene." [84]

The opinion in the Legal Tender cases,[85] in so far as it refers to the problem of stare decisis, is explicit. "In so holding," said the court, "we overrule so much of what was decided in Hepburn v. Griswold as ruled the acts unwarranted by the constitution so far as they applied to contracts made before their enactment." Again, "The questions involved are constitutional questions of the most vital importance to the government and to the public at large."

And finally, "And it is no unprecedented thing in courts of last resort, both in this country and in England, to overrule decisions previously made. We agree this should not be done inconsiderately, but in a case of such far-reaching consequences as the present, thoroughly convinced as we are that Congress has not transgressed its powers, we regard it as our duty so to decide and to affirm both these judgments." [86]

Sometimes the courts are not so explicit in their decision or their reasons, but a fair construction nevertheless leads to the conclusion that previous cases are overruled and are meant to be so treated. Consider the following: "Upon full consideration and after a reargument, we cannot think this extension of the exemption referred to, if intended to apply to oil sold after arrival in the state, to be justified either in reason or authority, and to this extent the opinions in the cases cited are qualified." [87]

Cases thus far referred to which have overruled earlier decisions involving constitutional questions have dealt with the power of Congress over money, the extent of admiralty jurisdiction, state taxation in relation to interstate commerce, and state taxation of royalties from patents and copyrights.

Some decisions have overruled cases on the validity of municipal incorporation; [88] others have refused to do so.[89] Cases affecting

---

[83] 157 U. S. at 429 (1895).   [84] 157 U. S. at 576.
[85] 12 Wall. 457, 20 L. Ed. 287 (1871).   [86] 12 Wall. at 554.
[87] Sonneborn Bros. v. Cureton, 262 U. S. 506, 520, 43 Sup. Ct. Rep. 643, 67 L. Ed. 1095 (1923); Terral v. Burke Constr. Co., 257 U. S. 529, 42 Sup. Ct. Rep. 188, 66 L. Ed. 352 (1922).
[88] See the cases discussed in Lanning v. Carpenter, 20 N. Y. 447 (1859). See also People ex rel. Cole v. Kinsey, 294 Ill. 530, 128 N. E. 561 (1920); College of City of New York v. Hylan, 120 Misc. Rep. 314, 199 N. Y. S. 634 (1923).
[89] People ex rel. Atty. Gen. v. Alturas County, 6 Idaho 418, 55 Pac. 1067 (1899); Malin v. Housel, 105 Neb. 784, 181 N. W. 934 (1921).

officers, their compensation and official duties, have likewise been overruled.[90] In one of these decisions the following explanation occurs:

On the other hand, we must remember that the nature of our government is such that the constitution is necessarily committed into the keeping of this court; and, when this court has erroneously interpreted that instrument, and no harm can follow the correction of such erroneous interpretation, its plain duty is to do so, and thereby enable the express will of the people to be carried into effect. Especially is this true when the erroneous interpretation has restricted the people in the exercise of a right which they have expressly reserved to themselves.[91]

In another case stress is laid on the fact that property rights were not involved and that stare decisis is meant to be a guide to, but not an enslaver of, the courts.[92] Tax decisions have also been overruled by both state and federal courts.[93]

Stare decisis did not prevent the Indiana court from reversing itself on the question of the validity of a legislative apportionment statute.[94] Tax cases [95] and criminal law cases have been treated similarly.[96]

Property cases, however, are said by most courts and writers to be the class in which stare decisis is binding as a principle of decision in constitutional law. "Ordinary legislation," even though it may involve constitutional questions, may not be so strictly subjected to stare decisis, so the exposition goes, but vested rights, property rights, are peculiarly susceptible to stare decisis treatment. As one court said: "A construction placed upon a section of the constitution prescribing the mode of amending laws is not a rule of property, within the principle that the supreme court ought not to overrule former decisions which constitute a rule of property, but only a rule of legislation." [97] Yet a dictum in another case affecting property says that "where the error of a previous decision is recognized, the question whether the rule of stare decisis shall be fol-

[90] State ex rel. Collins v. Jones, 106 Miss. 522, 64 So. 241, 469 (1914); State v. Lewis, 69 Ohio St. 202, 69 N. E. 132 (1903); Virtue v. Bd., 67 N. J. L. 139, 50 Atl. 360 (1901).
[91] State ex rel. Collins v. Jones, 106 Miss. at 576.
[92] State v. Lewis, *supra,* note 90.
[93] See, for example, cases discussed in Bank of Ky. v. Stone, 88 Fed. 383 (C. C. Ky. 1898); Farmers Loan & Trust Co. v. Minn., 280 U. S. 204, 50 Sup. Ct. Rep. 98, 74 L. Ed. 371 (1930).
[94] Denney v. State, 144 Ind. 503, 42 N.E. 929 (1896).
[95] Willis v. Owen, 43 Tex. 41 (1875); Penn. Co. v. State; 142 Ind. 428, 41 N. E. 937, 42 N. E. 37 (1895).
[96] McCollum v. McConnaughy, 141 Iowa 172, 119 N. W. 539 (1909).
[97] Greencastle So. Turnpike Co. v. State, 28 Ind. 382 (1867). On property factor, see also Grubbs v. State, 24 Ind. 295 (1865). Also Menges v. Dentler, 33 Pa. St. 495 (1859), overruling former title decision.

lowed becomes a simple choice between relative evils." [98] The one evil is to overrule [99] and unsettle; the other to let a judicial mistake stand.

One of the best discussions of stare decisis as it is applied in cases involving property is that found in Willis v. Owen, a Texas tax case.

We cannot, however, regard the rule of stare decisis as having any just application to questions of the character involved in these cases. This doctrine grows out of the necessity for a uniform and settled rule of property, and definite basis for contracts and business transactions. If a decision is wrong, it is only when it has been so long the rule of action, as that time and its continued application as the rule of right between parties demands the sanction of its error. Because, when a decision has been recognized as the law of property, and conflicting demands have been adjusted, and contracts have been made with reference to and on faith of it, greater injustice would be done to individuals, and more injury result to society by a reversal of such decision, though erroneous, than to follow and observe it. But when a decision is not of this character, upon no sound principle do we feel at liberty to perpetuate an error into which either our predecessors or ourselves may have unadvisedly fallen, merely upon the ground of such erroneous decision having been previously rendered.

The questions to be considered in these cases have no application whatever to the title or transfer of property, or to matters of contract. They involve the construction and interpretation of the organic law, and present for consideration the structure of the government, the limitations upon legislative and executive power, as safeguards against tyranny and oppression. Certainly it cannot be seriously insisted that questions of this character can be disposed of by the doctrine of stare decisis. The former decisions of the court in such cases are unquestionably entitled to most respectful consideration, and should not be lightly disregarded or overruled. And in case of doubtful interpretation, a long-settled and well-recognized judicial interpretation, or even legislative or executive construction within the sphere of their respective functions, might be sufficient to turn the balanced scale. But in such case the former decision or previous construction is received and weighed merely as an authority tending to convince the judgment of the correctness of the particular inclusion, and not as a rule to be followed without inquiry into its correctness.

An additional reason why we do not feel at liberty to dispose of these cases on the authority of the decision to which we have referred in similar cases is that we do not think the most vital objection to the right to collect the tax in question has been discussed or passed upon by the court in any of these cases. Indeed, if all the points discussed in the

[98] Prall v. Burckhardt, 299 Ill. 19, 132 N. E. 280 (1921).
[99] Storrie v. Cortez, 90 Tex. 283, 38 S. W. 154 (1896).

previous opinions were conceded to be correctly decided, it is, in our view of the matter, susceptible of demonstration that the judgments are erroneous.

That our views in relation to the authority to levy and collect a school tax may not be misunderstood we deem it proper to say that while we do not by any means concur in all of the positions assumed in the opinions of the court in these cases, neither do we dissent from some of the most important of them. And while it is unnecessary for us at present to indicate particularly those with which we agree and those from which we dissent, we desire to be understood as expressing an opinion only in reference to those to which we may have occasion to make direct reference.[100]

A similar unwillingness to depart from stare decisis is shown in some of the cases wherein business practice has long been established in reliance on the earlier decision. In the words of the Wisconsin Supreme Court, in Kneeland v. Milwaukee, "The question in such cases is not whether the first decision was correct, but whether a decision has been made, and business conducted on the faith of it." [101] The court continued after discussing stare decisis:

But where a decision relates to the validity of certain modes of doing business, which business enters largely into the daily transactions of the people of a state, and a change of decision must necessarily invalidate everything done in the mode prescribed by the first, there, when a decision has once been made and acted on for any considerable length of time, the maxim becomes imperative, and no court is at liberty to change. Take a case involving the validity of certain modes of executing deeds or wills. A decision is made, and the people act upon it for years, executing all such instruments in the manner prescribed. After that someone raises the question again and contends that the first decision was erroneous. Admit it to have been so, would the court be justified in overruling it? Every man, whether lawyer or layman, would answer, No!

It is true that as to such questions it was more a matter of indifference how they were first decided than as to one like the present, involving a constitutional principle designed to secure so just an end as equality in taxation. And I admit that this fact makes some distinction between the cases and might justify a struggle to regain the lost ground of constitutional justice, even at the expense of some inconvenience and hardship. But it is equally as true in this case as in those supposed that the decision constituted a business rule, involving the validity of the entire revenue transactions of the state, and of all the thousands of pri-

---

[100] 43 Tex. 41 (1875). See also Malin v. Housel, 105 Neb. 784, 181 N W. 934 (1921). See this from Greencastle So. Turnpike Co. v. State, 28 Ind. 382 (1867): "It is sufficient answer to this to say that the construction of this section of the constitution is a rule of legislation, and not a rule of property."
[101] 15 Wis. 497, 517 (1862).

vate contracts growing out of them; and having been acquiesced in and acted on for such a length of time, the error had passed beyond the reach of judicial remedy. No case can be found where any court ever changed a decision once made, conceding that the change must have such an effect. On the contrary, there are many cases which would almost sustain the proposition that the practical construction of mere administrative officers which has been acquiesced in for a long time, without any judicial decision whatever, should in such cases be followed, though in conflict with the constitution. I think that doctrine has been carried too far; but where there has been a judicial decision, the reason upon which it is based then becomes unanswerable.

It is said that in looking at the consequences of a change, to see whether we are at liberty to make it, we are setting aside the constitution upon grounds of policy. Such a charge might be excusable in a layman; I think it is not in a lawyer. The maxim stare decisis, it is true, rests upon grounds of policy. But it is equally as true that the constitution itself intended that that maxim should exist in the judicial system which it established, and should be applied to decisions relating to its own construction as well as to those relating to any other legal questions.

The court, therefore, which follows a decision once made upon a constitutional question, in obedience to this maxim, is no more open to the charge of setting aside the constitution upon grounds of policy than if, in obedience to the same maxim, it should follow a decision upon a statutory question contrary to its own views, it would be open to the charge of disregarding the law on grounds of policy. The court is as clearly bound to enforce the law as it is the constitution. But in giving due effect to the maxim of stare decisis, though its own views would be different, it disregards neither the constitution nor the law, for both intended that this maxim should have due effect in the judicial system which they established. The question is, did the constitution itself intend that each judge should for all time decide upon its own interpretation according to his own views, as though no decision had ever been made, or did it intend that such (695) decisions once made and acted on by the people so that change would overthrow all the transactions of the past, should be followed by succeeding judges? Obviously the latter. It is not to be expected that any express provision should be found in the constitution enjoining obedience to this maxim. But it was an established, unquestioned principle in the English and American law, and every constitution must be assumed to have contemplated its existence, and to have intended its enforcement. The judge, therefore, who follows a decision once made and so long acted on that a just application of this maxim forbids a change, although his own views of the question, if new, would have been different, is not disregarding the constitution but obeying it according to its true intent and meaning.[102]

[102] 15 Wis. 521–24.

The majority of cases in which a prior decision involving contracts has been made adhere to the earlier decision, on the same theory that underlies property cases.[103] As previously noted, not all contract cases come under the federal rule on following state cases sustaining the validity of statutes under which contracts have been made, even though the state decisions have been changed, because state courts themselves may get the cases in the first instance and reverse the former holdings, and the obligation of contracts clause does not apply to these judicial decisions by state courts that hold invalid the statutes previously upheld.[104] The statement in a Missouri case is typical: [105] "It is true that constitutional questions are always open to examination, but practically the courts must regard precedents, on the faith of which people have acted for years, especially where there can be a doubt concerning the matter decided."

Thus far the situations discussed under this section have been those in which one decision on the constitutionality of a statute was arrived at, after arguments pro and con, in the usual manner in which judicial decisions are reached, and then in a second case involving the same or a similar statute, with different parties, the court was asked to decide the constitutional question differently. In this situation courts are slow to decide differently, but they will occasionally do so. They have done so oftener than is commonly supposed even by the bench and bar.

There is, however, another situation that has given rise to even greater theoretical and practical difficulty. It is the case in which the court in the first decision assumes the statute to be valid, though it has heard only a part of the argument or perhaps no argument at all on it, or has dealt with only some aspects of the question in its opinion in the case. If the court is asked at a subsequent date to consider the question of constitutionality, is the question subject to the rule of stare decisis? Has the court decided anything with respect to constitutionality, and if so, how much has it decided? Neither the courts themselves, nor the lawyers, nor the professors, nor the philosophers, nor the logicians, seem able to agree.

The courts differ over the question whether they are bound by a previous decision in which constitutionality was assumed, just as

[103] Willoughby v. Holderness, 62 N. H. 227 (1882); Shoemaker v. Cincinnati, 68 Ohio St. 603, 68 N. E. 1 (1903); Hall v. Madison, 128 Wis. 132, 107 N. W. 31 (1906); Maddox v. Graham, 59 Ky. 56 (1859); Hart v. Floyd, 54 Ala. 34 (1875); O. V. & S. K. R. R. v. Morgan County, 53 Mo. 156 (1873). See Allison v. Thomas, 44 Ga. 649 (1872). Also Fisher v. Horicon Iron Mfg. Co., 10 Wis. 351 (1860), eminent domain; Amoskeag Mfg. Co. v. Goodale, 62 N. H. 66 (1882).

[104] On relation of stare decisis to obligation of contracts, see Thomas v. State ex rel. Gilbert, 76 Ohio St. 341, 81 N. E. 437 (1907).

[105] O. V. & S. K. R. R. v. Morgan County, 53 Mo. 156 (1873).

they differ over the question whether they are bound by one in which constitutionality was argued, considered, and decided. An Alabama criminal case opinion contains the following statement:

We are aware that with more or less unanimity the statute declared above to be unconstitutional has been by this court held to be constitutional and valid in three several decisions. In those cases the constitutional question above discussed was neither present nor considered. We regret the necessity we are under to depart from the rulings of our predecessors. We regret it all the more because those several decisions have no doubt been relied on by the appellant as authorizing him to do the act for which he was convicted. The relief is not with us.[106]

The Nebraska court said in one opinion that "a statute may be upheld as against an attack made by one party claiming it to be invalid upon one ground, and still it may be declared unconstitutional in a later attack by another litigant for reasons not called to the attention of the court, or not shown to exist, on the first attack."[107] Said the Illinois court: "To sustain the constitutionality of a statute against a particular contention is not decisive of its validity against subsequent attacks upon different constitutional grounds."[108]

The theory underlying this view that unless it is raised a question is not settled, and that only so far as it is raised is it settled, is well stated in a case from one of the New York courts.

It is elementary that constitutional questions will not be considered unless they are raised, and raised, too, in the court of first instance, and it must follow that, when a constitutional question is not so raised, neither the doctrine of res adjudicata nor the rule of stare decisis can be applicable, as the constitutional point was not only not necessarily involved, but could not properly have been considered.[109]

This doctrine has even been carried so far that a statute authorizing a bond issue and assumed by the court to be valid was later declared invalid when its constitutionality was assailed in a later case.[110] In this case the court stated:

[106] Boyd v. State, 53 Ala. 601 (1875). See City Council v. Fowler, 48 S. C. 8, 25 S. E. 900 (1896).
[107] Sandhill Land & Cattle Co. v. Chicago, B. & Q. Ry., 101 Neb. 24, 161 N. W. 1053 (1917). Also Davidson v. Chicago & N. W. Ry., 100 Neb. 462, 160 N. W. 877 (1916), assume statute on speed of livestock trains to be valid, later held invalid on other grounds.
[108] People v. Bruner, 343 Ill. 146, 175 N. E. 400 (1931).
[109] College of City of New York v. Hylan, 120 Misc. Rep. 314, 199 N. Y. S. 634 (1923). See also Gribble v. Wilson, 101 Tenn. 612, 49 S. W. 736 (1899), taxing costs statute; Sturges & Burn Mfg. Co. v. Pastel, 301 Ill. 253, 133 N. E. 762 (1922), police power, factory regulation; Freeman v. Barnum, 131 Cal. 386, 63 Pac. 691 (1901).
[110] Debnam v. Chitty, 131 N. C. 657, 43 S. E. 3 (1902).

We see no way of deciding upon their validity before the question is presented to us, and this question can be, and frequently has been, presented and decided before the issuing of the bonds. . . . If parties prefer to take the risk of buying the bonds before the determination as to their legality, they cannot complain of the consequences.[111]

When property rights are involved, however, different decisions and opinions generally prevail, just as in the case where the question of constitutionality was specifically raised. In commenting upon the problem as it arose in a case wherein the constitutional aspects of it had not been presented, the Texas Court of Civil Appeals said in its decision:

This recognition of its constitutionality by the Supreme Court and by the Court of Civil Appeals is authority for its validity. It must be presumed that the Supreme Court, before vesting property rights upon an act of the legislature, first determines its constitutionality.[112]

So, in another case, a Kentucky court refused to permit constitutionality to be raised a second time, saying that "that question presumably having been considered on the former appeal," it should be permitted to rest there.[113] A California decision is in accord with this view, in refusing to reopen the question of validity when in a previous decision a quiet title statute had been assumed to be constitutional.[114]

That this view is not restricted to property cases is clear from a Virginia case in which a court held, in a case of police power regulation, that "all objections to the constitutionality of the statute are concluded by the Bowman case, whether brought to the attention of the court in that case or not." [115] Another opinion from the same state contains this statement:

It is a grave mistake to suppose the case is not in point. It is wholly immaterial that the attack upon the statute in that case was "upon entirely different grounds." Whenever a statute is enforced by a judgment or decree of a court, it is a judicial determination that the statute is a valid enactment and is free from *all constitutional objections*. If unconstitutional for any reason whether assigned or not, the statute is void.[116]

A court really has its eyes on two things when it decides a case between private parties in which one element of the legal rule is a constitutional provision. It has one eye on the constitutional provi-

---

[111] 131 N. C. at 682.

[112] Cockrell v. Work, 17 S. W. (2d) 174 (Tex. Civ. App. 1929).

[113] Bell County Coke & Impr. Co. v. Pinesville, 19 Ky. L. Rep. 789, 42 S. W. 92 (1897).

[114] Lacy v. Gunn, 144 Cal. 511, 78 Pac. 30 (1904).

[115] Miller v. State Entomologist, 146 Va. 175, 135 S. E. 813 (1926).

[116] City of Portsmouth v. Weiss, 145 Va. 94, 133 S. E. 781 (1926).

sion. The other eye is focused on the parties and the dispute between them. The situation becomes even more complicated when the meaning of the statute, as well as that of the constitution, is in dispute. The problem is thus stated by one court:

> It is argued, however, that the decision in the case of Morton Bliss & Co. v. Comptroller-General is confined to the five bonds there considered, none of which are under consideration here. This, we think, is an entire misconception of the effect of that decision. What is said in that case in regard to confining the remedy there applied for to the particular bonds mentioned in the pleadings manifestly was not intended to have, and could not have, the effect of confining the operation of the decision of the various constitutional questions there discussed to the five bonds there in issue. A court of justice, when called upon to administer a remedy under a statute which is alleged to be unconstitutional, must first determine whether the statute is liable to the objection urged against it, and, having determined that question, it then proceeds to inquire whether the parties in the case have shown themselves entitled to such remedy. The two inquiries are entirely distinct and separate. Whether the objection urged against the constitutionality of the act is well founded is one thing, and whether the parties in the particular case have shown themselves entitled to the remedy which the act purports to give rise to is quite another thing. The decision of the one question was an authoritative construction of a particular clause of the constitution, which necessarily affects everyone, while the decision of the other question could only affect the parties then before the court. The decision of the various constitutional questions raised in the case must necessarily be conclusive whenever the same questions arise in any other case, though the application of the remedy claimed as following from such decision must be confined to the particular parties who had shown themselves entitled to such remedy.[117]

When stare decisis, and not res adjudicata, is involved, overruling a decision means that the construction placed upon a constitutional provision in the earlier case is changed. It may be changed in a sweeping and general sense, or it may be changed only as applied to the particular type of case presented. Whether it is a broad or restricted change can be ascertained only from the language of the opinion as applied to the facts of the case, and from the subsequent conduct of the court in later decisions. A deviation from stare decisis involves no change in the status of the parties to the earlier litigation.

When res adjudicata is involved, and a change is made, it involves the parties as well as the particular dispute between them which was thought to have been finally settled in the earlier case.

[117] Bond Debt cases, 12 S. C. 200 (1879).

Occasionally a court expressly overrules a "principle" said to have been established by a previous decision, although the parties, statute, and fact situations are different. It is hard to appraise the exact effect of such an overruling decision. Presumably, under such circumstances, this type of statement is dictum, and only an expression of an opinion that as to the future the rule may be different.[118] In a recent opinion of the Supreme Court of Montana the statement is made that a rule is changed for the future, but as to the case before the court the old rule will be applied.[119] This has been held by the Supreme Court of the United States to be no denial of due process of law.[120]

Professor Goodhart has correctly described the American practice with respect to stare decisis in constitutional law. Many cases could be cited here, and might have been cited earlier, to prove that stare decisis is a powerful doctrine in this field of the law, and no informed person would deny that its efficacy is great in this as well as in other branches of American law. Instances can be cited where judges have held an earlier decision to be unsound and have written dissenting opinions, but have nevertheless felt that once the earlier case was decided by a majority vote in the court the question was settled. They therefore express the belief in the later case that the earlier decision should be followed.[121]

At the same time it is clear that the strength of the doctrine of stare decisis is not nearly so great in this field of the law as it is usually thought to be, and the influence of the doctrine is certainly less powerful in constitutional law than in private law. The test of its power is really to be found in its breach, in a very real sense. Most courts would probably agree with that of Washington when it said, in State ex rel. Clithero v. Showalter:

A court should not allow the facts of the particular case to influence its decision on a question of constitutional law, nor should a statute be construed as constitutional in some cases and unconstitutional in others involving like circumstances and conditions. Furthermore, constitutions do not change with the varying tides of public opinion and desire. The will of the people therein recorded is the same inflexible law until changed by their own deliberative action; and therefore the courts should

[118] For examples, see Mayor v. Klein, 89 Ala. 461, 7 So. 386 (1889); Lang v. Mayor, 74 N. J. L. 455, 68 Atl. 90 (1907); Greencastle So. Turnpike Co. v. State, ex rel. Malot, 28 Ind. 382 (1867).

[119] Sunburst Oil & Ref. Co. v. G. N. Ry., 91 Mont. 216, 9 Pac. (2d) 927 (1932).

[120] G. N. Ry. v. Sunburst Oil & Ref. Co., 53 Sup. Ct. Rep. 145 (U. S. 1932). See discussion, in note, 42 Yale L. J. 779 (1933).

[121] A case of this kind is Force Handle Co. v. Hisey, 179 Ind. 171, 100 N. E. 450 (1913). See also Statement in Williamson v. Richards, 158 S. C. 534, 155 S. E. 890 (1930).

never allow a change in public sentiment to influence them in giving a construction to a written constitution not warranted by the intention of its founders.[122]

The fact that most courts would be willing to make such a statement should not be permitted to obscure the fact that in actual decision they do not hesitate to depart from the principle therein enunciated whenever they are convinced that it is in the interests of wisdom and sound public policy to do so.

[122] 159 Wash. 519, 522, 293 Pac. 1000 (1931), from State ex rel. Banker v. Clausen, 142 Wash. 450, 253 Pac. 805 (1927).

Chapter VII

RELIANCE UPON DECISIONS AND THE EFFECT OF OVERRULING DECISIONS IN CONSTITUTIONAL LAW

Judicial change of decision as to the constitutionality of statutes gives rise to problems that are most vexing. The question of the amount of legal protection to be given to persons who have acted in reliance upon, or with reference to, judicial decisions that hold statutes to be constitutional or unconstitutional has been presented to the courts in numerous instances. In a sense this problem of reliance is common to all cases involving the effect of unconstitutional statutes, whether the statutes have been the subject of judicial decision or not, and in a general sense the whole of such a study is concerned with the concept of mistake of law, in the more general significance of that phrase.

"Mistake of law" has come to have a more technical meaning in Anglo-American law, however, and for that reason those cases that fall under technical mistake of law will be considered in a separate chapter. Some of the cases to be considered there will also be discussed in this chapter, but the emphasis here will be chiefly upon problems arising out of overruled decisions, though some attention will be given to cases involving reliance on judicial decisions that have not been so overruled. Cases involving mistake of law need not necessarily deal with prior judicial decisions in their facts, but the cases discussed here have this in common, that in all of them reliance has been placed upon judicial decision as well as upon statute.

We are concerned at this point, as in the preceding chapter, not so much with the effect of an unconstitutional statute as with the effect of judicial decisions concerning statutes, whether they be constitutional or unconstitutional. Still more particularly, attention now will be given to the effect of such decisions, and of acts done or left undone in reliance upon them, where decisions serving as the basis for reliance have later been overruled. The effect of the first and second decisions must therefore be examined in some instances.

181

I. CRIMINAL CASES

Criminal cases present some of the best examples of the difficulties that result from change of decision on constitutionality, because in them is clearly exhibited the conflict between legal logic and the desire for ethical bases of justice.

Consider the situation involved in Ingersoll v. State.[1] A person was accused of the crime of violating a statute thought to have been repealed by a subsequent statute. An equally divided state Supreme Court had in effect (because of the lack of a majority to reverse lower court decisions) sustained the validity of the repealing act. After several terms of court the repealing act was finally held to be invalid. This left the prior statute in effect; defendant was convicted of having violated it, the alleged violation of the statute having taken place prior to the time of the second or, more accurately, the final decision. Should he be held guilty? The Indiana court decided that he should not be subjected to punishment, saying that he should be protected in his reliance on the judicial decisions that had held the statute to have been repealed. This decision has been criticized severely,[2] but defenders of it are not entirely lacking.[3] Some weight was given by the court to the fact that the legislature was in session at the time the last decision was handed down, but this was in connection with the general problem of constitutionality rather than with reference to Ingersoll's status. The legislature could not have altered Ingersoll's status, but it could of course have enacted whatever legislation was necessary to accomplish the repeal of the earlier statute if such repeal had still been considered desirable. Executive clemency alone could have aided Ingersoll had the court decided that he should have been held responsible for his violation of the statute mistakenly supposed to have been repealed.

Boyd v. State,[4] an Alabama case, presented a somewhat similar problem. The case is technically distinguishable, as will be indicated later, but the views expressed in the opinion differ greatly from the views of the Indiana court. Boyd was convicted of operating a lottery in violation of statute. He defended by pleading another statute that authorized the lottery. This authorizing statute had been passed upon by the Alabama courts before, as had the prohibiting statute, and in several cases the authorizing statute had been assumed to be in force. The difference between the Ingersoll and Boyd cases was that the statute in the latter was never expressly

---

[1] 11 Ind. 464 (1858).
[2] Sedgwick, Interpretation of Statutes, 338.
[3] Endlich, Interpretation of Statutes, sec. 529, note 187.
[4] 53 Ala. 601 (1875). See the quotation from this opinion set forth in Chapter 6.

declared invalid. The distinction is not so important as it might seem to be, however, because of the view of many courts that an assumption of this kind is tantamount to a decision on the constitutionality of the law, as was pointed out in the preceding chapter, and because in actual effect in life, and in law, such decisions are considered as judicial recognition of the validity of the statute concerned. For the purposes under consideration here the two situations should be treated the same, and they often are so treated by the courts.

The next step in the Boyd case was that after the alleged violation of the prohibitory statute, the authorizing statute was held invalid. The Supreme Court of Alabama upheld Boyd's conviction. The court expressly referred to its previous decisions and voiced regret over the necessity under which it felt constrained to change those decisions. The Supreme Court of the United States, on appeal, comforted the unfortunate Boyd by saying that "if he has been misled by previous adjudications of the state courts, his relief from the present judgment must be sought from the clemency of the executive." [5] The court did not feel, however, that any federal question was raised by this reversal of opinion on the part of the Alabama courts.

In such cases as these the federal courts apply the same rules as are applied to the bond or contract cases. Technically viewed, the Boyd case was decided by the United States Supreme Court in conformity with the obligation of contract decisions, because, as now understood, the rule is that contracts are not protected against overruling decisions either, if the case is brought to the Supreme Court after having proceeded through the state tribunals.

Results such as those accomplished in the Boyd case do not conflict with "ex post facto" or "cruel and unusual punishment" provisions of federal and state constitutions, although suggestions that they should be considered violative of such provisions have been made.[6]

State v. O'Neil [7] is perhaps the best known of the cases involving the general problem being considered in this section. In it an Iowa statute which had previously been held unenforceable because it conflicted with congressional control was held to have gone into effect again by virtue of a subsequent federal statute permitting the

[5] Boyd v. Alabama, 94 U. S. 645, 24 L. Ed. 308 (1876).
[6] See Boyd v. Alabama, *supra,* note 5; State v. O'Neil, 147 Iowa 513, 126 N. W. 454 (1910). Judicial decisions are held not to be "law" generally within ex post facto clause prohibitions. Ross v. Oregon, 227 U. S. 150, 33 Sup. Ct. Rep. 220, 57 L. Ed. 458 (1913). Cf. State v. Longino, 109 Miss. 125, 67 So. 902 (1915).
[7] 147 Iowa 513, 126 N. W. 454 (1910).

states to exercise such powers as those exercised through the Iowa statute. O'Neil was accused of, and tried for, the violation of the statute, the offense having been committed after the state law had been held unenforceable and before it had again been declared enforceable. Here again the problem arose as to whether legal logic should be tempered with justice; the Iowa court decided that it should, holding that O'Neil should be released. The reasoning of the court merits extended quotation.

It is, of course, well settled that a statute which has been held unconstitutional either *in toto* or as applied to a particular class of cases is valid and enforceable without re-enactment when the supposed constitutional objection has been removed, or has been found not to exist. That was the holding in McCollum v. McConaughy, *supra,* and is not now questioned. See also Pierce v. Pierce, 46 Ind. 86. And the conviction below was proper, unless some benefit is to be given to defendant of the fact that, when the acts were committed, the latest announced decision of this court was to the effect that the statute was unconstitutional, and therefore not enforceable. It is only by analogy, applying the rule of precedent and not of adjudication, that the decision in one case becomes in any sense the law in another case. The analogy may be so complete that the reasoning of the one case necessarily points out the conclusion to be reached in the other, and, if so, the court feels bound to bow to its previous decision, unless it is made to appear that it is so manifestly erroneous that it should be overruled. If overruled, its force as a precedent ceases, and the later decision becomes a precedent. The analogy, however, may be incomplete, and then it is for the court to determine in the subsequent case whether the reasoning of the prior case is applicable under circumstances in some of which the cases are similar, and in others dissimilar. It is not the function of a court to lay down the law for future cases, but to announce the law for the case which it is deciding. It is an important function of an appellate court to so announce its reasons for decision that they may be understood and applied with reference to subsequent cases which are likely to arise, but no court can attempt to anticipate by announcement what the law will be found to be in a case in some respects dissimilar which may subsequently arise. Therefore, as has often been said, there is no vested right in the decisions of a court, and, under the clause in the federal constitution prohibiting any state from passing any law impairing the obligation of contracts, the Supreme Court of the United States has uniformly held that the change of decisions of a state court does not constitute the passing of a law, although the effect of such change is to impair the validity of a contract made in reliance on prior decisions. National Mut. B. & L. Assn. v. Braham, 193 U. S. 635 (24 Sup. Ct. 532, 48 L. Ed. 823); Central Land Co. v. West Virginia, 159 U. S. 103 (16 Sup. Ct. 80, 40 L. Ed. 91). And see Storrie v. Cortes, 90 Tex. 283 (38 S. W. 154, 35 L. R. A. 666); Swanson v. Ottumwa, 131 Iowa 540; Lanier v. State, 57 Miss. 102.

It is also quite clear that the change in the decisions of a court of a state does not violate the prohibition found in the same clause of the federal constitution against the making of ex post facto laws.

From the conclusion that in a constitutional sense there is no vested right in reliance on decisions of the court as precedent, and that one who is brought into court for a violation of law cannot sustain himself on the mere plea that in some other case which he thought to be analogous the court rendered a decision which, if applied as he thought it would be applied, would result in exculpating him from wrong, it does not necessarily follow that the court cannot take into account as a controlling consideration in reaching the conclusion as to the justice of a case that the party charged with wrongful conduct relied reasonably and in good faith upon decisions of the courts in determining whether a wrong was committed. . . .

This again is but an illustration of the effort the court will properly make to do justice in a broad sense. In criminal cases, where the life or liberty of an individual is involved on one side, and the enforcement of law in the interest of the public welfare on the other, no private right of contract or property being imperiled by liberality of construction, the courts go further than in civil cases to recognize the common judgment of humanity as to what is right and just, and they allow many exceptions to statutory definitions of what shall constitute a crime. For instance, in this state, although there is no statutory recognition of a coverture as a defense on the part of a married woman for a crime committed in the presence of her husband, we have said that the common law exception in that respect is applicable. State v. Fitzgerald, 49 Iowa 260; State v. Kelly, 74 Iowa 589; State v. Harvey, 130 Iowa 394. . . .

In this connection it is to be noticed that the decisions of courts as to the constitutionality of a statute stand on somewhat different ground than those relating to the common law or the interpretation of statutes, as applied to particular cases. The function of determining whether a statute is invalid because in excess of the legislative power is one peculiar to our system of government, and unknown in other jurisdictions in which the common law prevails. It is true that such an adjudication is made in a particular case. Although the power to be investigated is that of the legislative department itself, which cannot be a party so as to be bound by any judicial decision, nevertheless the courts discuss such question when it arises, and decide the matter not only for the purpose of determining the rights of particular parties, but with reference to the effect of the decision upon the law of the state. A statute unconstitutional properly remains on the statute books as a part of the written law, but those who are bound to obey the law may, we think, reasonably take into account the decisions rendered by the courts in the exercise of their peculiar function of passing upon the constitutionality of the statutes in determining what the law of the state really is. To the ordinary mind it would smack of absurdity to say that defendant ought to have known that the statute was constitutional, and would in case he violated it be enforced against him, although the Supreme Court of the state had fully considered the validity of the statute as against the claim that it was unconstitutional, and had unanimously held that it was in excess of state legislative power as to its entire subject matter, and therefore invalid. Under such circumstances, it is plain that there should be some relief to defendant from punishment, for the very purpose of punishment is defeated, if unreasonably and arbitrarily imposed. Respect for law, which is the most cogent force in prompting orderly conduct in a civilized community, is weakened if men are punished for acts which according to the general consensus of opinion they were justified in believing to be morally right and in accordance with law. If we should sustain the conviction, we would do so in the belief that the case was one in which executive clemency ought to be exercised. But is it quite fair to throw upon the executive the responsibility of relieving from punishment on account of the very nature of the act committed which is made apparent to this court, and its nature as being innocent or guilty appears to depend upon the effect to be given to the decisions of this court? We think we would be shirking our responsibility if we should leave it to the executive to do what we believe to be manifest justice in this case, and should stigmatize the defendant with a conviction for crime when as it appears he was innocent of any real wrong. We think the real question as to the guilt of defendant is to be settled by referring to the doctrine of criminal intent, which has always been held to be of the essence of a crime. . . .

That our conclusion in this case may not be misapprehended and relied upon in support of propositions to which we have no disposition to yield consent, we desire to emphasize the following controlling conditions. This is a criminal case, and therefore involves no conflicting claims as to contractual or property rights. The defendant may be presumed to have acted with knowledge of the fact that the statute now invoked as rendering illegal an act not otherwise wrongful or immoral had been expressly held by this court in cases prosecuted under public authority to be unconstitutional because in excess of legislative power.[8]

A statute, such as New York has,[9] protecting persons who have acted in reliance on judicial decisions should be enacted in every state to cover criminal cases, so that formal recognition may be granted to the ethical basis of the O'Neil and Ingersoll cases. Statutory enactment should make certain that this protection would not be denied upon logical grounds, derived from the premise that deci-

[8] 147 Iowa at 519. See also State v. Longino, 109 Miss. 125, 67 So. 902 (1915), holding would not convict person of crime included within statutory definition by judicial decision, which had by prior decisions been held not to be included within the definition.

[9] N. Y. Code Civ. Proc., sec. 1961. See 32 L. R. A. N. S. 788 (annotation); Hollaman v. El Arco Mines Co., 137 App. Div. 862, 122 N. Y. S. 852 (1910). The statute does not cover change of opinions by the Court of Appeals itself, however. It should also cover this point.

sions are only declaratory of the law, not sources of legal rules, and that unconstitutional statutes are void ab initio. The need for protection in criminal cases against retroactive overruling decisions is particularly great, because personal liberty seems unable to exert the same influence in molding the course of logical judicial thought that often is true of contract and property considerations.[10]

II. CIVIL CASES

A. CONTRACT CASES

A Kansas case growing out of the cases and statutes surrounding the enactment of the Wilson Act (which also gave rise to the O'Neil case) will serve to introduce the problem of retroactive overruling in contract cases. A salesman for a liquor house sold goods for his employer in Kansas at a time when the courts of that state had declared to be invalid a state statute prohibiting such sale. Later a federal decision held the statute valid, on the ground that in the light of subsequent federal legislation it did not contravene federal power over interstate commerce. Suit having been brought by the salesman to recover commissions on sales made prior to the federal decision, the employer defended on the ground that the sale transactions had been in aid of a crime, and that to permit recovery of the commissions would be to put the stamp of judicial approval upon plaintiff's acts. The Kansas court denied recovery, stressing the unexecuted feature of the transaction, and following the line of reasoning just alluded to.[11] The court said:

In considering this subject the rule of stare decisis has sometimes been confounded with the constitutional provision inhibiting laws impairing the obligation of contracts. Under this rule courts will not overrule decisions which have settled property rights where greater mischief would be caused by departing from the decisions than by following them, but will leave the correction of a possibly erroneous interpretation to the legislature. This, however, is only a rule of policy, and has no application here. The legislature has already enacted this law, and the court is under no legal or moral obligation to perpetuate an erroneous construction placed upon it through an imperfect understanding of the views of the federal Supreme Court. Courts do not and cannot change the law by overruling or modifying former opinions. They only declare it by correcting an imperfect or erroneous view. The law itself remains the same, although the interpretations may have differed. . . . An erroneous ruling may in some circumstances become the law of the particular

[10] This is believed to be true generally, despite the United State Supreme Court's attitude in the Boyd case.

[11] Crigler v. Shepler, 79 Kan. 834, 101 Pac. 619 (1909).

case, but this will not prevent the court in another action from holding to the contrary. A person who is not a party or privy in the action cannot acquire a vested right in an erroneous decision made therein.[12]

Here, as in the Boyd case cited in the preceding section, the court reached a manifestly unjust result by adopting the premise of the declaratory nature of judicial decisions. Also, the doctrine of res adjudicata was confused with that of reliance, and, as will appear more clearly later, the two are not necessarily connected.

Presumably the salesman could have recovered if he had brought his action prior to the time of the federal decision. To deny him relief because he brought his action after the federal decision seems manifestly unjust. He sold the goods and earned the money as agreed upon by the liquor house and himself. At the time he did so the courts told him, in effect, that his claim for services of this kind was not contrary to public policy and that the state statute making it contrary to such policy was invalid. Congress by statute sought to permit the state to condemn this policy, and the Supreme Court of the United States sustained this congressional action. As to future transactions one would expect, of course, that the courts would aid the state in enforcing its policy, but as to past transactions, legal at the time the rights accrued, one would expect it to lend its aid to the enforcement of the bargain as made between the parties, so far as it had been relied upon to the detriment of one and to the benefit of the other. It is to be remembered that this retroactive feature resulted from judicial decision, and so was the result of judicially initiated policy, voluntarily entered upon, and not the result of a legislative enactment expressly retroactive in terms. The court should certainly have hesitated to adopt the retroactive rule here, although it might have permitted the legislature to impose such a retroactive operation of a statute.

Compare this case with the much more just decision in Thomas v. State, ex rel. Gilbert,[13] wherein recovery was permitted for the work done up to the time of the overruling decision in the trial court. Here also the work had been done pursuant to a contract entered into while decisions made it seem that the statute relied upon was valid. Later the statute was declared to be invalid. The court was unwilling to grant recovery for work done after the overruling decision, apparently on the theory that when it was decided in the first instance the case constituted notice that the work should be halted.

[12] 79 Kan. at 842.
[13] 76 Ohio St. 541, 81 N. E. 437 (1907).

This decision is to be commended, so far as it goes in permitting recovery, the only real question being whether it should have stopped there. Other Ohio cases indicate that the rule in that state is that contracts entered into in reliance on statutes held to be valid at the time of the formation of the contract will not be affected adversely by a change of judicial opinion on the validity of the statute. Just as bonds may be paid, so work contracted for should be performed and paid for, even though the process is not entirely completed at the time of the overruling decision.[14] This rule has been applied even though the previous decisions are on a similar, but not on an identical statute.

An example of a contract enforced under circumstances similar to those just alluded to is that of a promissory note given by a city to a person enlisting in the army, such note having been sustained by the current of judicial decision at the time, though a later decision held such promises to be unconstitutional, and therefore unenforceable so far as notes given in the future were concerned.[15] This is in sharp contrast with the liquor commission case discussed above.

It is with this type of case that the bond cases, such as Gelpcke v. Dubuque,[16] are to be grouped. As noted previously, these cases are no longer explicable on grounds of obligation of contracts, because change of judicial decision, even though impairing the obligation of contracts, is not an impairment by "law," and has been held to present no question under the contracts clause of the federal constitution when brought to the Supreme Court of the United States from the state courts.[17] State courts themselves tend to the rule that bonds issued when the authorizing statute, or type of statute, has been held constitutional are valid and binding obligations despite later holdings that the statute is invalid, though the later decision be handed down before the bonds are due.[18]

[14] Price v. Toledo, 4 Ohio Cir. Ct. Rep. N. S. 57 (1903); Lewis v. Symnes, 61 Ohio St. 471, 56 N. E. 194 (1900), modifying Tone v. Columbus, 39 Ohio St. 281, 48 Am. Dec. 438 (1883); Shoemaker v. Cincinnati, 68 Ohio St. 603, 68 N. E. 1 (1903). See Storrie v. Cortez, 90 Tex. 283, 38 S. W. 154 (1896).
[15] Willoughby v. Holderness, 62 N. H. 227 (1882).
[16] 1 Wall. 175, 17 L. Ed. 320 (U. S. 1864).
[17] Central Land Company v. Laidley, 159 U. S. 103, 16 Sup. Ct. Rep. 80, 40 L. Ed. 91 (1895); Tidal Oil Co. v. Flanagan, 263 U. S. 444, 44 Sup. Ct. Rep. 197, 68 L. Ed. 382 (1923). On obligation of contracts, see Dodd, Impairment of the Obligation of Contract by State Decisions, 4 Ill. L. Rev. 155, 327 (1911).
[18] Maddox v. Graham, 59 Ky. 56 (1859); Hall v. Madison, 128 Wis. 132, 107 N. W. 31 (1906); State v. Mayor, 109 Tenn. 315, 70 S. W. 1031 (1902); O. V. & S. K. R. R. v. Morgan County, 53 Mo. 156 (1873). Some state courts have confused stare decisis and obligation of contracts, and put these cases on obligation of contracts grounds. See Harmon v. Auditor, 123 Ill. 122, 13 N. E. 161 (1887); Storrie v. Cortez, 90 Tex. 283, 38 S. W. 154 (1896).

A few cases [19] go so far as to hold that recovery on bonds will be permitted in the federal courts, in diversity cases, even though state courts hold the authorizing statute invalid, if the public thought the statute valid and if that belief was not proved to be unwarranted by decision for a considerable period following the issuance of the bonds, even though there had never been actual decisions upholding the particular authorizing statute.[20] The state courts have not usually taken this step, the contrary rule denying recovery in the absence of reliance on sustaining judicial decision being common, but, as pointed out elsewhere, this rule could be changed and brought into line with the suggestions in the federal diversity cases just mentioned by judicial initiative in the states if the state courts desired to do so.[20] Statute should accomplish this change if the courts do not make it soon, and perhaps legislative enactments generally should be resorted to immediately to correct the rule, in order to forestall the difficulties attending judicial reversal of so well established a rule.

With the steady expansion of the due process concept it is also conceivable that the Supreme Court will in due time incorporate the idea of protection to those who have acted in reliance on judicial decisions and who have purchased bonds or entered into contracts as a result of such reliance.[21] Recent developments make this seem less startling than it would have been a few years ago.[22]

The overruling of Hepburn v. Griswold [23] by the Supreme Court of the United States gave rise to several state cases involving contracts and payments made under the Hepburn case. State courts held that payments made in accordance with court order,[24] or in reliance on the Hepburn case,[25] were, in the absence of intervening

[19] Taylor v. Ypsilanti, 105 U. S. 60, 26 L. Ed. 1008 (1881); Folsom v. Ninety-Six, 159 U. S. 611, 16 Sup. Ct. Rep. 174, 40 L. Ed. 278 (1895); Great Southern Fireproof Hotel Co. v. Jones, 193 U. S. 532, 24 Sup. Ct. Rep. 576, 48 L. Ed. 778 (1903). In the Folsom case it was said: "There not being shown to have been a single decision of the state court against the constitutionality of the act of 1885 before the plaintiff purchased his bonds, nor any settled course of decision upon the subject, even since his purchase, the question of the validity of these bonds must be determined by this court according to its own view of the law of South Carolina." It is surprising how generally in these cases the federal courts find that the state law permits recovery, irrespective of state court pronouncements to the contrary.

[20] See 3 Willoughby, Constitutional Law (2d ed.), sec. 778, for discussion of these cases.

[21] On this point see note, Constitutionality of Judicial Decisions in Their Substantive Law Aspect under the Due Process Clause, 28 Col. L. Rev. 619 (1928).

[22] See the discussion on decisional law and due process in Chapter 10, dealing with tax recovery.

[23] 8 Wall. 603, 19 L. Ed. 513 (U. S. 1869).

[24] Doll v. Earle, 59 N. Y. 638 (1875); Miller v. Tyler, 58 N. Y. 477 (1874); In re Dunham, 9 Phila. 451, Fed. Cas. No. 4146 (D. C. N. J. 1872).

[25] *Supra*, note 23.

order, final, not recoverable, and not to be disturbed, although the Legal Tender cases[26] changed the rule of the Hepburn case.[27] Contracts made in reliance on the earlier decision were also held to be valid and enforceable even after the change.[28] Speaking of reliance on the Hepburn decision, the New York Court of Appeals said in Harris v. Jex: "The plaintiff had a right to repose upon the decision of the highest judicial tribunal in the land. It was, as applied to the relations between these parties and to this case, the law, and not the mere evidence of the law."[29] This is a gratifying refusal to adhere to the declaratory theory of judicial decision, and deals with such decisions and people's attitudes toward them in a sensible manner. The Legal Tender cases did not operate to divest rights or undo transactions founded upon the Hepburn case, although they properly did change the rule as to contracts entered into before the Hepburn decision, sought to be enforced for the first time after the Legal Tender cases.[30] These cases will be analyzed at greater length elsewhere with respect to their bearing on payments and contracts made or entered into under mistake of law.[31]

B. PROPERTY AND MISCELLANEOUS CASES

Payment of taxes in accordance with a contract of lease, and in compliance with the then applicable decisions, is protected despite subsequent change of decisions.[32] The lessor may not, as a result of the changed rule, recover from the lessee the sums paid by the latter in reliance on the earlier cases. Also, it has been held that the difference between a statutory rate paid for public utility service and a lower reasonable and therefore constitutional rate cannot be recovered from the customer by the utility, although it furnished the service at the lower price only because of an injunction based upon a statute later covered in effect by a contrary decision.[33] Res adjudi-

[26] 12 Wall. 457, 20 L. Ed. 287 (U. S. 1871).

[27] *Supra,* note 23.

[28] Troy v. Bland, 58 Ala. 197 (1877); Woodruff v. Woodruff, 52 N. Y. 53 (1873).

[29] 55 N. Y. 421 (1875).

[30] Proctor v. Heaton, 114 Ind. 250, 15 N. E. 23 (1887). On the various confusions resulting from these two cases in the United States Supreme Court, see Bedford v. Woodward, 158 Ill. 122, 41 N. E. 1097 (1895).

[31] See Chapter 9.

[32] Rutland R. R. v. Central Vt. R. R., 63 Vt. 1, 21 Atl. 262 (1890). So, a taxpayer may rely on a decision against him for taxes, and after paying the amount of the judgment may not again be sued for more merely because the city mistook its rights and did not sue for enough. Phila. v. Ridge Ave. Ry. Co., 142 Pa. 484, 21 Atl. 982 (1891).

[33] Mpls. St. P. & S. S. M. Ry. v. Washburn Co., 40 N. D. 69, 168 N. W. 684 (1918).

cata defeats recovery in such a case, said the court. The later decision operated prospectively, not retroactively. In the lease case referred to above, the Vermont court said:

It is an elementary principle that a contract valid under an existing law, and payments made upon it, will not be invalidated by subsequent legislation or subsequent judicial interpretation of the law. The decision of a court of competent jurisdiction upholding the validity of an existing law validates everything done under it, so long as such adjudication remains unchanged. . . . The subsequent change in the decisions of the United States Supreme Court is only operative prospectively, and all acts done in obedience to the former decisions are valid and cannot be disturbed.[84]

This is not an accurate use of the concept of res adjudicata, but courts often use this phrase in a general sense to express the idea of reliance that should be protected.

A commercial transaction, entered into in reliance on a decision holding a bulk sales statute invalid, was a sale of goods made without reference to such a statute, although a later bulk sales statute was subsequently held valid.[85] An attempt to set aside the sale because of noncompliance with the statute failed.

Property cases afford some interesting studies in the problem of reliance. For example, in Cassel v. Scott [36] a judgment given by an Indiana circuit court on a bond required by a statute then held to be valid was held binding, although subsequent to the execution of the bond the statute was held invalid. Jurisdiction existed in the court to render the judgment at the time it was rendered, and that saved the judgment, despite the change of decision concerning constitutionality. The overruling decision did not disturb the prior judgment, nor the rights under it.

In Brandhoefer v. Bain,[37] the Nebraska court held that homestead rights accruing from court action based on statute would not be affected by a later declaration that the statute was invalid. The case is weakened somewhat by the probable existence of power, independent of this statute, to set aside these homestead rights anyway, but the case illustrates again the willingness to let rest acts done in reliance upon judicially applied statutes.

Suppose a statute governing the descent of property is held to be constitutional by the courts. Property thereafter descends in accord with its terms. Later the statute is held invalid. Will the rights vest-

[84] Rutland R. R. v. Central Vt. R. R., *supra*, note 32.
[85] Dauchy Co. v. Farney, 105 Misc. Rep. 470, 173 N. Y. S. 530 (1918).
[36] 17 Ind. 514 (1861).
[37] 45 Neb. 781, 64 N. W. 213 (1895).

ing under the statute be disturbed? Christopher v. Mungen [38] says that they will not. Rights to vest in the future will be governed by other law, but those already vested under the statute while the first case stood untouched by subsequent decision will be governed by what seemed to be the law at the time of the vesting, especially since the courts, too, thought that the law seemed so. The opinion of the court should be quoted at length because of its eminent soundness. The court said:

Where a statute is judicially declared to be unconstitutional, it will remain inoperative while the decision is maintained; but if the decision is subsequently reversed, the statute will be held to be valid from the date it first became effective, even though rights acquired under particular adjudications where the statute was held to be invalid will not be affected by the subsequent decision that the statute is unconstitutional.

And again:

As the appellee inherits under the act of 1866, the fact that such act was in 1899 held to be unconstitutional, in a case where the appellee was not a party, does not deprive the appellee of her right to inherit under the act of 1866, when it is declared to be a valid act as originally adopted, and the decision declaring the act to be unconstitutional is disapproved and not followed, the doctrine of stare decisis not being justly applicable. The decision overruled does not vest rights in those not parties to the suit.[39]

In Finders v. Bodle [40] it was held that a person buying title in reliance on a law thought to be applicable because another apparently applicable statute had been declared unconstitutional could not be divested of title by a curative statute enacted after the purchase and declaration of invalidity. Thus some courts protect the buyer who relies upon a decision relative to validity even against legislative attempts to disturb the property rights that have vested in the meantime.

Bona fide purchasers tracing title in reliance on judicial decision were protected by the Pennsylvania court against those tracing title through purchases made in reliance upon subsequent overruling decisions.[41] The court stated that "in strict law the title remains, but in equity it is lost; and this is a sort of equity which the courts alone can properly declare and administer," in speaking of logical rule on title and equitable rule on title, referring to logical rule as being the rule tracing through the overruling decision, and equitable

[38] 61 Fla. 513, 55 So. 273 (1911).
[39] 61 Fla. at 532.
[40] 58 Neb. 57, 78 N. W. 480 (1899).
[41] Menges v. Dentler, 33 Pa. 495 (1858).

rule as being that traced through the first decision upon which the bona fide purchasers relied.

Again, the court said, in commenting on the general problem of reliance: "Men naturally trust in their government, and ought to do so, and they ought not to suffer for it." The court emphasized the need for care on the part of judges to prevent unnecessary injury when a deviation from the usual rule of stare decisis becomes necessary.

Pierce v. Pierce,[42] an Indiana case often cited in discussions of reliance and overruled decisions, does not hold that rights vested in dependence upon a judicial decision touching the validity of a statute are divested when that decision is later overruled. The court took pains expressly to reserve that question. The sequence of significant events in the Pierce case may be stated briefly. A statute of 1853 amended an 1852 act so as to change some of the rules governing descent of property. The members of the Indiana bar generally assumed that the amendatory act was invalid, and the state Supreme Court so declared in 1854. Pierce died in 1862. The distribution was made in accordance with the act of 1852 — the decision of 1854, which held the 1853 act invalid, being relied upon. In 1867 the state Supreme Court decided that such acts as that of 1853 were valid. Just prior to this decision the state legislature repealed all acts not in conformity with the 1854 decision and limited to three months the period during which actions arising under such acts could be brought. A sale of the property apparently took place *after* this overruling decision, and a dispute arose over the division of the proceeds of the sale. The court decided that the proceeds should be divided in accordance with the law of 1853. In the course of its opinion the court said: "It was not the overruling of the cases which gave validity to the statutes; but the cases having been overruled, the statutes must be regarded as having all the time been the law of the state." [43] The 1853 act was therefore to be deemed valid; the testator having died while it was in force, and the sale and distribution having still to be made after the overruling decision had been handed down, it was to govern the distribution of the proceeds of the sale.

As noted above, the court expressly reserved the question of the rule that should be applied to acts done while the first decision was still in force, prior to the overruling decision. The case seems to have been decided on the theory that overruling decisions have prospective effect only, but the language in the opinion could easily

[42] 46 Ind. 86 (1874).
[43] 46 Ind. at 95.

mislead one to the opposite conclusion. For example, the court says that "where a statute has been held unconstitutional by the Supreme Court it is inoperative while such decision is maintained, but a later decision sustaining such statute gives it vitality from the time of its enactment and it is to be treated as having been constitutional from the beginning." Such a statement is to be taken to refer to theory only, not to the case involving acts done in reliance upon the first decision. In theory, nothing in the case existing to prevent justice being done by so viewing it, the statute is valid from the beginning if the last case holds it constitutional. But that theory does not apply if the equities of reliance in good faith dictate that it should not apply, and still in the general sense of this quotation the theory remains valid, even though not applicable. Presumably the court would have protected acts done in reliance on the earlier decision, and the case has been referred to on that assumption, by many other courts.

C. Personal Liability of Persons Acting in Reliance on Court Decisions or Orders

This question in so far as it relates to officers has been discussed elsewhere.[44] The writer feels that the cases holding officers liable under such circumstances are wrong in theory and mischievous from the standpoint of policy.

The question arises, however, though somewhat rarely, in other branches of the law. Boales v. Ferguson,[45] a Nebraska case, affords an example. There the administrator of an estate distributed it in accordance with a decree issued on the assumption that the statute was valid. The act was later declared invalid. The Nebraska court held the administrator liable for distribution otherwise than by the terms of the valid law, validity being determined in the light of the subsequent decision. Considerable stress was placed in the opinion on the defendant's failure to have heirs and amounts judicially determined. This suggests that he would have been protected had he litigated the question instead of taking the decree at its face value, and suggests further an indefensible distinction, so far as liability is concerned, between litigated case determinations and unlitigated orders and decrees. To compel litigation as a condition precedent to protection to those relying upon court orders is often to defeat the very purposes to be served by the procedures involved. It is no answer to say that such court orders are prepared, as a rule, by the

[44] See *supra*, Chapter 6. See also State v. Clements, 217 Ala. 685, 117 So. 296 (1929), that officer making payment under mandamus is protected.
[45] 55 Neb. 565, 76 N. W. 18 (1898).

interested parties, for that is true of other orders as well; and in any event they are officially the order of the court, and if commonly signed as a matter of course should nevertheless be taken seriously — if need be at the cost of having them more carefully scanned by the signing judges.

The court in the Boales case was misled by the sweeping statement sometimes made to the effect that an unconstitutional statute is void ab initio, and it overlooked the effect normally given to honest reliance on judicial orders or judgments rendered under such statutes before they have been declared to be invalid. To quote the following is to show the court's overstatement of the proposition sought to be established in the opinion. The court, speaking of the statute, said:

It was never in force, and the decision of this court in Trumble v. Trumble (holding the statute invalid) was a mere judicial declaration of a pre-existing fact. The court did not amend the statute, for it was already lifeless. It had been fatally smitten by the constitution at its birth.

A good portion of this book has been devoted to an analysis of the many cases denying the legal validity of such a statement. It has a limited validity, to be sure, but when used as it is in the Boales case such a proposition decides the case by its statement. Statutes may be smitten at birth by the constitution, but many feel that courts have something to do with wielding the fatal weapons and with dealing the fatal blows. Sometimes statutes should be so treated, but if so it should be for some good reason of law or policy. Other rules of law or considerations of policy may lead to the conclusion in many cases, however, that for purposes of disposing of the case the statute should be treated as valid. If not valid, in these cases it should nevertheless be treated as though it were valid. The law is full of just such sensible rules. This case, it is submitted, should have been decided on the theory that invalid statutes, when applied in judicial decision, or in court order, prior to a judicial declaration of unconstitutionality may furnish sufficient protection to persons who have acted in reliance upon such judicial action to forestall the imposition of liability because of deviations from the rules of law that would have been applicable had the defendant and the courts known or decided that the supposedly valid statute was unconstitutional.

A more satisfactory decision is that of Forest Lumber Company v. Osceola Lead and Mining Company,[46] wherein the Missouri court

[46] 222 S. W. 398 (Mo. 1920).

denied collateral attack on a judgment confirming a lien, and thereby denied liability on the part of the party removing articles under authority of the judgment, though the lien statute was declared invalid in another case decided subsequent to the time when the judgment had been entered. The same is true of a recent Oklahoma decision in which the title acquired by a purchaser in good faith at a tax sale, the sale having been confirmed by the court and the purchase price having been paid into court.[47] This should be the rule even though the procedural or taxing statute is held invalid later, unless overwhelming equitable considerations dictate a contrary decision.[48]

The majority of cases hold that such protection should be afforded and, in the opinion of the writer, all of those herein discussed which denied that protection under circumstances such as those just alluded to were wrongly decided. Retroactive operation may in some instances be given justly to an overruling decision, and in such cases exceptions to the general rule should be made, of course, but the writer has still to read a case that would furnish the basis for the first exception. Judicial decisions overruling prior decisions in the field of constitutional law should, as statutes, have prospective operation. The courts should set their faces against retroactivity here as unrelentingly as they have against such effect in legislation. Retroactive effect should be the rare exception; more so even than it is in the cases dealt with in this chapter.[49]

[47] Jones v. McGrath, 16 P. (2d) 853 (Okla. 1932).

[48] In Hanchett Bond Co. v. Morris, 143 Okla. 110, 287 Pac. 1025 (1930), the court could put the parties in their previous position, so that no injury would result from setting aside the order of the court.

[49] On the general subject of this paper see especially Larremore, Stare Decisis and Contractual Rights, 22 Harv. L. Rev. 182 (1909); Boudin, Problem of Stare Decisis in Constitutional Theory, 8 N. Y. L. Q. Rev. 589 (1931); note, The Effect of an Overruling Decision upon Acts Done in Reliance upon the Decision Overruled, 29 Harv. L. Rev. 80 (1915). A cursory statement of the problem will be found in Kocourek, Retrospective Decisions and Stare Decisis, 17 Am. B. A. J. 180 (1931). See also note, 42 Yale L. J. 779 (1933).

Chapter VIII

GOVERNMENT BONDS AND PRIVATE PROMISES UNDER UNCONSTITUTIONAL STATUTES *

A study of the law of promises made under or in reliance upon an unconstitutional statute is in a sense a study in the field of mistake of law. The rules on mistake of law have been formulated to apply to situations involving payments, but to make an agreement to pay is only one step removed from payment. The rules applicable to payments made under invalid statutes are considered elsewhere,[1] and the question to be dealt with here is whether promises to pay or to repay are enforceable if made under such statutes. In a later chapter will be considered the problems connected with promises that have been made in reliance upon a statute after the statute has been declared to be valid by judicial decision but have not been entirely executed before such declaration of invalidity.

Cases involving promises made under unconstitutional statutes may be classified in different ways, but the classification that seems of most significance to the writer in this connection is that based on the parties to the agreement. One individual may promise another that he will perform some act, or he may promise the government that he will do the same thing. The government, on the other hand, may promise an individual that it will perform some act or observe a particular course of conduct. In all these instances the parties, whether individual persons or governmental units, may have in mind existing statutes when entering into agreements. These statutes may subsequently be declared unconstitutional, and the promissor may feel that such a declaration has so altered his situation that he wishes to defend against an attempt to enforce the promise. May he successfully do so, or may the government successfully do so?

I. PROMISES MADE BY ONE INDIVIDUAL TO ANOTHER

Agreements under this heading may be of various types; they may be adoption agreements or agreements to pay for services

* This chapter originally appeared in 17 Iowa L. Rev. (1931).
[1] Payments and mistake of law under unconstitutional statutes are considered in Chapter 9 as are also executed contracts involving payments.

rendered, or they may take the form of bonds, such as appeal bonds, attachment bonds, or materialmen's bonds.

In Albring v. Ward [2] an adoption agreement had been entered into in conformity with a statute governing proceedings for the adoption of minor children. The articles of adoption, signed by the parent and by the adopting parent, provided that the child was to be treated as an heir at law on the death of the latter. The child lived with its foster parents for seventeen years, at the end of which period she established her own home. Upon the death of her foster father she brought an action to establish her right to a share in the estate. The statute under which the adoption had taken place had been declared invalid in another case, and in this case the question was whether the contract should be enforced. The Michigan court refused to enforce it, holding that the agreement was not one for the conveyance of land and that it was not independent of the statute, since it was clearly made in pursuance of it. The action was dismissed.

In Hubbard v. Martin [3] the Tennessee court refused to interfere by equitable decree with an action at law to enforce a promissory note given by a regular judge of one of the inferior courts to a temporary appointee because the former had "drawn the amount of his salary in advance from the treasurer" and the treasurer refused to pay the temporary appointee. The salary of the latter was to be deducted from that of the regular judge, according to the statutory provision governing the appointment of temporary judges. Prior to the time that the action to enforce the note was instituted, the statute under which the temporary judge had been selected and under which he had performed his duties was declared unconstitutional. The regular judge defended against the action by pleading the invalidity of the statute and at the same time sought equitable relief against further prosecution of the recovery action. The prayer for injunctive relief was denied, and presumably the action at law was carried through to completion. The majority of the court thought that, though the temporary judge had a "right in conscience" to receive the cash that the regular judge had paid him, he

[2] 137 Mich. 352, 100 N. W. 609 (1904). When the legitimation proceedings depend entirely upon statute, in the absence of any agreement between the parties, the proceedings will fail if the statute upon which they depend is declared unconstitutional. Lieber v. Heil, 32 S. W. (2d) 792 (Mo. St. L. App. 1930), the statute having been declared invalid in another case because of a defective title.

[3] 8 Yerg. 498 (Tenn. 1835). Cases dealing with recovery for services performed for the government are dealt with in Chapter 9. See this statement in Woodward, Quasi Contracts, 56, note 1: "It is a curious fact that the rule appears to be confined to cases of money paid, although cases of services rendered or goods delivered under mistake of law are in principle undistinguishable."

had no right "in law" to it, but that since the note had been given voluntarily and with full knowledge of all the facts, equity should not interfere with its collection. The opinion intimates that the temporary appointee would have been unable to recover for his services had there been no express promise to pay by the regular judge.

Appeal and attachment bonds have often been enforced despite the invalidity of the statute requiring them. In Daniels v. Tearney [4] the Supreme Court of the United States refused to permit the obligor to defend against an action on an attachment bond given in compliance with an unconstitutional statute, basing the decision on the principle of estoppel and preventing him by the use of that doctrine from assailing the validity of the statute. The opinion emphasized the benefits received by the obligor, and the unfairness of permitting him to accept the benefits accruing from the transaction and then subsequently permitting him to escape the obligations assumed by him therein. The same rule has been applied with respect to sureties,[5] although there is also authority to the contrary.[6]

Other courts, while reaching a conclusion similar to that arrived at in the Tearney case, have done so on other grounds and have denied the applicability of the doctrine of estoppel to this type of case. Thus the Nebraska court based its decision on the ground that the bond could be supported as an obligation independent of the statute, because the obligor had received what he had contracted for, sufficient consideration for the promise having been furnished thereby.[7] In this particular case the obligor had been able to retain possession of the property in dispute pending the appeal, and had in addition obtained a trial of the case in the appellate court. This was all that he had bargained for, and the bargain did not depend upon the statute, nor did the obligation arise from it. The promise was the source of the obligation, and was supported by the benefits received.

With respect to the doctrine of estoppel the Nebraska court

[4] 102 U. S. 415, 26 L. Ed. 187 (1880).

[5] McVey v. Peddie, 69 Neb. 525, 96 N. W. 166 (1903).

[6] On bond for stay of execution, Reay v. Butler, 118 Cal. 115, 50 Pac. 375 (1897).

[7] United States Fidelity & Guaranty Co. v. Ettenheimer, 70 Neb. 147, 79 N. W. 652 (1903), reversing, on rehearing, the decision in the same case in 70 Neb. 144, 97 N. W. 227 (1903). See also Stevenson v. Morgan, 67 Neb. 207, 93 N. W. 180 (1903); State ex rel. Cantwell v. Stark, 75 Mo. 566 (1882). Cf. Caffrey v. Dudgeon, 38 Ind. 512 (1872), action on replevin bond for amount beyond the jurisdiction of the justices of peace to exact, holding the bond not enforceable. This case is distinguished in the opinion in Stevenson v. Morgan, *supra*, on the ground that a jurisdictional limit is in the nature of a prohibition so far as sums in excess thereof are concerned, and that therefore the exaction of a bond for this greater sum is more positively prohibited than are bonds required in accordance with an invalid statute.

stated its belief that this doctrine could not be utilized to compel performance of promises given in accordance with an invalid statute, because both parties would, according to that reasoning, have equally valid claims to the benefits of the doctrine, so that nothing would be accomplished by permitting its use. The true basis on which to rest the decision, according to this court, was the benefit received by the obligor in support of his promise, the statute being left entirely out of view. Accordingly the court distinguished those cases in which the only ground for supporting the promise is the statute. The court thought that in them a different result should be reached.

That this view is adhered to by other courts appears from the West Virginia decision in Love v. McCoy,[8] in which it was held that an election contest bond given in compliance with an unconstitutional statute could not be enforced, no benefits having been obtained by the defendant.

All these cases either assume or explicitly state that the bonds involved in them could not be enforced as statutory obligations alone. As stated in Daniels v. Tearney,

The bond, as a statutory instrument, cannot have more validity than the statute which prescribed it as a means of giving effect to the statute in the way it was intended to operate. To hold the bond valid as a statutory bond, and the statute void, would be an inversion of reason.[9]

This statement assumes, of course, that the statute when declared invalid would be of no effect whatever in the disposition of the case.[10] Perhaps it is not without significance that in most of these cases justice was better served by enforcing the obligations therein involved, and that the invalidity of the statute did not prevent the courts from sustaining their enforcement on other grounds. In the one case in which enforcement was denied, the election bond case, the plaintiff was forced to pay his own costs in the case, not an unusual situation. The only criticism that can be directed at this decision is that the plaintiff did not obtain the advantage intended for him by the legislature, namely, the advantage resulting from limiting the number of contestants by the requirement that they give bond.

Materialmen's and contractors' bonds exacted in conformity with unconstitutional statutes may be enforced as common law obligations if they contain no reference to the statute and if they could

[8] 81 W. Va. 478, 94 S. E. 954 (1918).
[9] 102 U. S. 415, at 419.
[10] See the exposition of the various views as to the effect of unconstitutionality in Chapter 1.

have been exacted by the obligee in the absence of the statute. All courts seem agreed that, to be enforceable as a common law obligation, a bond must have some consideration to support it and must have been entered into voluntarily.

That a bond is given pursuant to an invalid statute is not in itself sufficient to render it void.[11] But if it recites expressly that it is given "in pursuance of" a designated statute, referring to the statute by section number or name, the court will be more hesitant to uphold it, because it feels that a bond given under such circumstances is not given voluntarily; that the statute furnishes the only compulsion in the situation; and that if the parties had known the statute to be invalid, the bond would not have been required or given. Courts still stressing the factor of consideration in such instruments can, of course, reason that the statute is void because unconstitutional, and that the situation is to be treated as though the obligor could have obtained whatever privilege he did obtain by executing the bond without actually doing so, and that therefore no consideration to support the bond can be made out.[12] The recital that the agreement is to be construed as a common law bond as to some of the parties has been held to indicate that as to the other parties the bond should be held to be statutory.[13]

Other courts are slower to presume that the parties would not have required or given the bond had they known at the time of the transaction that the statute was invalid. These courts require, before defeating recovery on the bond, that the obligor show that it was given solely in reliance on the statute.[14] Courts embracing this view

[11] See dictum in People's Lumber Co. v. Gillard, 136 Cal. 55, 68 Pac. 576 (1902). Most of the cases assume or state this in passing.

[12] Shaunessy v. American Surety Co., 138 Cal. 543, 69 Pac. 250 (1903), not referring in the opinion to the Gillard case, *supra*, note 11, but involving the same section of the same statute as that involved in that case. The language of the Shaunessy case seems at first reading to be contradictory to that in the Gillard case, but it is perhaps not so, nor is the decision itself in contradiction of the dictum in the latter case. But the case of Martin v. McCabe, 21 Cal. App. 658, 132 Pac. 606 (1923), seems to hold that the Gillard case is no longer law in California, although the court admits that the two cases are technically distinguishable. See also Roystone Co. v. Darling, 171 Cal. App. 526, 154 Pac. 15 (1916).

See also Montague & Co. v. Furness, 145 Cal. 205, 78 Pac. 640 (1904), holding a bond invalid on the authority of the previous California cases. The same statute was involved in this case as that in the cases reviewed *supra*. See Coburn v. Townsend, 103 Cal. 223, 37 Pac. 203 (1894), bond by person seeking to condemn land. The obligee had apparently been compensated for his loss of possession of the land, so that to permit recovery on the bond would have been unfair.

[13] Martin v. McCabe, *supra*, note 12.

[14] Southern Surety Co. v. Nalle & Co., 242 S. W. 197 (Tex. Com. App., sec. A., 1922). See People, for use of Houghton v. Newberry, 152 Mich. 292, 116 N. W. 419 (1908), holding bond enforceable although the officer requiring it exceeded his

reason that the contracting parties are free to require bonds for their protection or security in the absence of statute, and they presume that obligees will ordinarily do so to protect their interests, the practice being common in certain types of commercial transactions.

These two attitudes, when translated into views of the effect of an unconstitutional statute, resolve themselves into two divergent positions: one that the invalid statute should not be given sufficient effect to furnish consideration for the agreement, the other that it should be given such effect. To give this latter effect to the statute more often doubtless produces results consonant with the intent and understanding of the parties to the agreement, both parties normally intending that the transaction include provision for security. To make this security or obligation a loss or a windfall, as the case may be, in consequence of a judicial decision on the constitutionality of a statute seems to inject too great a factor of uncertainty into an already uncertain field of the law. A mistake in legislative and private judgment as to the validity of a statute should not result in so unjust a penalty on the obligee, nor in such good fortune to the obligor.

If it is clearly intended in an agreement that payment under it shall be made in accordance with a decision as to constitutionality, payment must be so made, even though the court later overrules the decision referred to and even though the action on the contract to recover the payment is brought subsequent to the overruling decision.[15]

The change in the rule as to legal tender notes brought about by the Legal Tender cases[16] raised this type of question. The courts were relatively strict in holding parties to the evident intent of their agreements.[17] They held also that the obligations were not discharged merely because the tender in paper money had been rejected, after Hepburn v. Griswold, though that was exactly what the obligor was permitted to do after the Legal Tender cases.[18]

If, however, the contract did not refer to any specific mode of payment nor to any particular decision or state of the law, payment in paper money was deemed a satisfaction of a mortgage if the ac-

statutory authority. Contra, Leona, etc., Co. v. Roberts, 62 Tex. 615 (1884), holding bond invalid which had been exacted by governor in excess of statutory authority. See Brown v. Am. Surety Co., 110 Okla. 253, 237 Pac. 594 (1925), state gave bond under mistaken idea that statute applied, held not good as common law obligation.

[15] Woodruff v. Woodruff, 52 N.Y. 53 (1873).
[16] 12 Wall. 457, 20 L. Ed. 287 (U.S. 1870), overruling Hepburn v. Griswold, 8 Wall. 603, 19 L. Ed. 513 (U.S. 1868). See, for recovery of payments, Chapter 9.
[17] Harris v. Jex, 55 N.Y. 421 (1875); Crain v. McGoon, 86 Ill. 431 (1877).
[18] Supra, note 16.

tion was brought after the Legal Tender cases and the mortgage had been made before the decision in Hepburn v. Griswold.[19]

Care should be taken to distinguish these cases, since they do not hold nor do they imply that if payment in gold had been contracted for, gold would have to be paid after the Legal Tender cases. Gold would not have to be paid even though specifically called for, if Congress had forbidden it, it being of the very essence of the power involved in these cases that Congress could override such provisions in contracts and make paper money legal tender, dollar for dollar, there being, of course, no express restriction on federal power to impair contracts. Due process alone would furnish such a restriction, and in view of the doctrine of emergency power under due process, and the basis of the Legal Tender decision, no restriction upon the federal government can be made out in this connection. The cases here discussed turned on the fact that Congress had not required acceptance of paper money, dollar for dollar, and for that reason they are not in point in determining the validity of the gold clause repeal of 1933.

Notes given in renewal of old notes and accepted as such prior to Hepburn v. Griswold, if gold was by mutual consent thought to be the basis of exchange but was not expressly so stated, were held to have been given upon sufficient consideration, even though action to recover upon them was not brought until after the Legal Tender cases, when paper money constituted a satisfaction.[20]

Mistake of law in these cases was not permitted to defeat recovery, but recovery was upon a different basis than that in the minds of the parties when they entered into the agreement. Paper money payment was sufficient, but payment was required even though gold had been thought necessary to satisfy the obligation at the time of the bargain. The agreement was not void. It still remained the basis for recovery, though on a different computation, as a result of legal tender acts. The courts were not all in agreement as to the exact measure to be used in calculating the amount to be paid. Some used the gold basis, others did not.

II. GOVERNMENT BONDS AND PROMISES

An individual who loans money to the government ordinarily does so by purchasing a bond. The transaction constitutes a loan by him to the government, the bond being a piece of paper upon which is printed what to the purchaser appears to be a promise that

---

[19] Stockton v. Dundee Mfg. Co., 22 N. J. Eq. 56 (1871). See People ex rel. Chrystal v. Cook, 44 Cal. 639 (1872).

[20] Proctor v. Heaton, 114 Ind. 250, 15 N. E. 23 (1887).

the government will repay the loan at a specified time. May the purchaser enforce the promise to repay the loan if the statute authorizing the issuance of the bond (or, to phrase it differently, authorizing the government to borrow the money) is declared unconstitutional in the interval between the issuance of the bond and the time recovery of the loan is attempted. The mistake in such a case is a mistake as to the legal power of the city or other governmental unit to borrow the money or, to state it more accurately, perhaps, a mistake as to the validity of the statute authorizing the borrowing, or under which the loan was understood to have been made.

The rule is, in the federal courts and apparently in all the state courts, that an action on the bond itself will be defeated if the bond has been issued under a statute declared unconstitutional subsequent to its issuance and prior to the termination of the action.[21] Recovery will be defeated most certainly if the bond refers to the invalid statute in express language,[22] but the same result will be reached if the complaint alleges that it was issued under a designated statute and that statute is declared invalid in the action for recovery.[23] A faint suggestion is found in one case that the bond might be supported if all the provisions of another existing valid statute had been complied with,[24] but it is extremely doubtful whether this should be taken to afford any encouragement to the bondholder in those few cases in which the rule might apply, because apparently in none of the numerous bond cases has a decision turned on this point.

[21] An occasional dictum suggests that recovery would be permitted if the city still retained the money, but there is no decisional authority for this statement. For such a dictum see Newburgh Sav. Bk. v. Town of Woodbury, 173 N. Y. 55, 65 N. E. 858 (1903). See also Whitney v. Hillsborough County, 99 Fla. 628, 127 So. 486 (1930). The cases involving the relation between federal and state courts in so far as the obligation of contracts clause of the federal constitution is concerned are not considered here. They will be considered in another chapter which will deal with the general problem of the effect of judicial decision as to the constitutionality of a statute. The only problem considered at this point is that concerning the effect of bond issues under invalid statutes in the absence of judicial decision prior to the time of issuance.

[22] Central Branch U. P. R. R. v. Smith, 23 Kan. 525 (1880): "And when a bond purports on its face to be issued under the authority of a given law, if that law be unconstitutional, every purchaser takes with notice of the invalidity of the bond. Upon this proposition all the courts agree." Brewer, J., at 529. See Whaley v. Gaillard, 21 S. C. 560 (1884). So, too, if constitutional authority is withdrawn before bonds are issued, and bonds recite authority of previous statute. Town of Concord v. Robinson, 121 U. S. 165, 7 Sup. Ct. Rep. 937, 30 L. Ed. 885 (1887).

[23] Commercial Natl. Bk. v. Iola, 2 Dill. 353, Fed. Cas. No. 3061 (C. C. D. Kan. 1873): "The bonds were issued under the authority of this act, and so the declaration alleges. . . . As the only authority for the issue of the bonds in question was an unconstitutional act of the legislature, they are void — void from the beginning. . . ." Dillon, Cir. J., at 355, 364.

[24] See Central Branch U. P. R. R. v. Smith, *supra*, note 22, 23 Kan. at 533.

The rule is the same as to other government promises also, as in the case of paper money issued on the credit of the state, void because constituting bills of credit.[25] So, too, contracts not evidenced by bonds, as, for instance, contracts for public work, if authorized by an invalid statute are treated as null and void.[26]

The question whether the money can be recovered in any type of action not based on the bond will be discussed after an examination of the reasons advanced by the courts for the rule just stated.

The reasons advanced in support of the rule denying recovery are four. 1. A municipality has, it seems, no power to borrow money in the absence of statutory authority. Therefore, if a statute that is declared unconstitutional is null and void and is to be disregarded entirely in the settlement of the case,[27] the decision should be predicated upon the assumption that the loan was obtained without statutory authority.[28] The theory is that there is a total lack of capacity to borrow on the part of the government. For this reason municipal bonds cannot be sustained as common law obligations, a ground sometimes used in sustaining private bonds, as noted earlier in this chapter. One might query in this connection, What is the source of the government's power to retain the money?

2. Each and every person is presumed to know the law, and each and every purchaser of a bond issued by the government is presumed to know whether the statute authorizing the issuance of the particular bonds purchased by him is constitutional or not. Not only is the purchaser presumed to know these things but he is on notice that the statute is unconstitutional, perhaps long before a court declares it to be so, and for this reason cannot be treated by the courts as a bona fide purchaser for value.[29] Since the invalidity of the stat-

---

[25] Bragg v. Tuffts, 49 Ark. 554, 6 S. W. 158 (1887).

[26] Plattsmouth v. Murphy, 74 Neb. 749, 105 N. W. 293 (1905).

[27] See the discussion of this void ab initio view referred to *supra*, note 10.

[28] Mayor v. Ray, 19 Wall. 468, 22 L. Ed. 164 (U. S. 1874), is the case generally cited for the proposition that a municipality is without power to issue bonds in the absence of constitutional or statutory authority. Duke v. Brown, 96 N. C. 127, 1 S. E. 873 (1887), seems to approve this view, and in that case recovery was denied on bonds issued under an invalid statute.

[29] Ryan v. Lynch, 68 Ill. 160 (1873). Cf. Town of Rochester v. Alfred Bank, 13 Wis. 483 (1861), bonds issued before statute authorizing them took effect; Ogden v. Davies, 102 U. S. 634, 26 L. Ed. 263 (1880), in both of which the courts held that the bondholder had notice of the statutory requirements which were conditions precedent to the issuance of valid bonds. In Town of Rochester v. Alfred Bank, *supra,* the court said, "For the reason that the nature of the defect in the original execution and issue of the bonds is such that there can in law be no innocent holders of them." See also Duke v. Brown, *supra,* note 28, where the court said, at 130, ". . . and parties taking such securities under a statute which ignores the restraint, cannot occupy the position of innocent purchasers" (speaking of bonds under invalid statute).

ute has the effect of completely wiping out the legal basis for the loan transaction, and the purchaser has been on notice that the statute is invalid, he is presumed to have known at the time of his purchase that the bond was a "scrap of paper" without any legal obligation whatever, and, having known this, he must be treated as taking the bond subject to all legal defects and defenses available against it.[30] The nonsense of this reasoning needs no elucidation.

3. The unconstitutionality of the statute authorizing the issuance of bonds is to be treated as a positive prohibition against the loan. This seems to be true whether there is actually a positive constitutional debt limit, or whether the statute is unconstitutional for other reasons.[31] Concerning the hardship of the bond decisions on the purchaser, and the obligation that the courts feel to enforce constitutional rules governing municipal or other governmental loan practices and policies, the Missouri court has said:

> While loss to the holder of a bond issued under a void law would necessarily result, it should not be forgotten that to enforce the payment of such bonds by striking down the organic law would inflict a severe blow on good government and entail a greater loss on the community at large than mere pecuniary sacrifice. While it is the duty of the courts to employ all the appliances and agencies provided for that purpose, to compel the payment of all obligations which are recognized as legal, it is equally their duty to prevent the use of any of them in the enforcement of any obligation which is illegal and void. While it would be unjust not to give force and effect to a valid contract, it would be equally unjust to give effect to a contract which the law pronounces void, either because not allowed or forbidden to be made.[32]

4. The fact that the government receives the money, and spends it, and presumably obtains the benefits normally derived therefrom does not serve as a basis for utilizing the doctrine of estoppel against the government, thereby permitting the purchaser to recover, be-

[30] Central Branch U. P. R. R. v. Smith, *supra*, note 22; Commercial Natl. Bk. v. Iola, *supra*, note 23, Webb v. Lafayette County, 67 Mo. 354 (1878); Loeb v. Columbia Twp., 91 Fed. 37 (C. C. Ohio 1899); Board of Commrs. of Oxford v. Union Bk. of Richmond, 96 Fed. 293 (C. C. A. 4th 1899); Deland v. Platte County, 54 Fed. 823 (C. C. Mo. 1890), cert. denied 155 U. S. 221, 15 Sup. Ct. Rep. 82, 39 L. Ed. 128 (1894); Cohen v. City of Henderson, 182 Ky. 658, 207 S. W. 4 (1918); Wittowsky v. Board of Jackson County, 150 N. C. 90, 63 S. E. 275 (1908). In Ruchs v. Town of Athens, 91 Tenn. 20, 18 S. W. 400 (1891), the court said, at 21, "It was his duty to ascertain — First, is there a legal corporation? and, second, has it power to issue the bonds proposed to be sold? He must, at his peril, determine both questions for himself."

[31] Morton v. Nevada, 41 Fed. 582 (C. C. Mo. 1890), was a case involving bonds issued in excess of a debt limit. See also, on debt limits, Litchfield v. Ballou, 114 U. S. 190, 5 Sup. Ct. Rep. 820, 29 L. Ed. 132 (1885).

[32] Webb v. Lafayette County, *supra*, note 30, at 370.

cause the government cannot be estopped to use as a defense the invalidity of the statute in question. With respect to the inapplicability of the theory of estoppel in these cases the Supreme Court of the United States stated, in the case of Town of South Ottawa v. Perkins:

There can be no estoppel in the way of ascertaining the existence of a law. That which purports to be a law of a state is a law, or it is not a law, according as the truth of the fact may be, and not according to the shifting circumstances of parties. It would be an intolerable state of things if a document purporting to be an act of the legislature could thus be a law in another case and for another party; a law today, and not a law tomorrow; a law in one place, and not a law in another in the same state.[33]

Yet, as every reader of recent Supreme Court decisions knows, this is exactly the pass to which the court has come in some types of cases.[34] Another case phrases much the same view in the following statement:

A corporation may sometimes be estopped from showing its own wrongful acts done under a valid law; but there is no such thing as a void enactment being made valid by estoppel. . . . The law never had any validity, and no acts done under it can infuse life into it, nor create any estoppel upon the municipality.[35]

And again, "The law is good or bad, constitutional or not, at the time it is signed and approved." [36]

In accordance with this reasoning a bill to collect an assessment to raise money with which to pay bonds issued under an invalid law will fail, despite the fact that the lands to be assessed were especially benefited by the improvements made possible by the sale of the bonds.[37] That the taxpayers sit by and watch the bonds being issued without protest has been held insufficient to create an estoppel against the township issuing them.[38] If, on the other hand, the

[33] 94 U. S. 260, 264, 24 L. Ed. 154 (1876). On this problem see Dillon, Municipal Corporations (5th ed., 1911), Chapter 20, particularly secs. 946, 948, 961.

[34] This is particularly true of decisions declaring state statutes invalid because of a conflict with congressional control over interstate commerce or because of the due process clause of the fourteenth amendment. In these cases it is now frequently stated that a statute is invalid as to certain persons situated so as to be unjustly discriminated against by the statute, but that the statute is valid as to other persons not so situated.

[35] Central Branch U. P. R. R. Co. v. Smith, supra, note 22, at 531.

[36] 23 Kan. at 531.

[37] O'Brien v. Wheelock, 184 U. S. 450, 22 Sup. Ct. Rep. 354, 46 L. Ed. 636 (1902). That receipt of benefit, and silence, will not prevent the owner from assailing the validity of the assessment law, see the cases in 9 A. L. R. at 764–65. There are a few cases to the contrary.

[38] Counterman v. Dublin Twp., 8 Ohio St. 517 (1882).

bondholder delays in pressing his claim, he may be met with the bar of estoppel and defeated by it, if no other defense is available.[39]

Two cases remain to receive individual consideration because of the departure from the majority rule in the court's reasoning or decision.

The Kentucky rule is that mistake of law between private individuals may be relieved against,[40] and this rule is adhered to in that state in bond cases also, but the action rests on an equitable basis, not on the validity of the bond. Two cases will illustrate the Kentucky doctrine.

In City of Henderson v. Redman,[41] one R sold a lot to Y, who offered some bonds issued by the City of Henderson in part payment for the lot. Subsequent to R's acceptance of the bonds, the statute under which they had been issued was declared unconstitutional. R then brought suit against Y for the face value of the bonds on the theory that they were void and therefore constituted no payment to him for the lot. Y answered that R had constructive notice of the defect in the bonds, and also cross-petitioned against the city, asking judgment against it in the event that R should prevail against him. The bonds had not been indorsed by Y and were payable to bearer.

The court permitted Y to recover against the city. The bonds were branded as scraps of paper that should be treated as though they had never been issued or delivered. The parties here had dealt with one another under mutual mistake of law. The plaintiff was under no duty or compulsion to pay, and for that reason the case should not be treated as falling within the reasoning of the tax cases, which in Kentucky are exceptions to the local mistake of law rule,[42] recovery in tax cases normally not being permitted. The plaintiff received no consideration, and was entitled to recover the payment for which only scraps of paper had been received.

The second case is that of City of Henderson v. Winstead.[43] Two claims were tried together in this case. Winstead had purchased some bonds issued by the city, the purchase having been made directly from the city. They had been issued under a statute that was declared unconstitutional. Subsequently he brought suit against the city in assumpsit for money had and received. He recovered, the decision resting on broad equitable grounds.

[39] See suggestion in O'Brien v. Wheelock, *supra,* note 37, at 491.
[40] The cases on the Kentucky rule are discussed in Chapter 9.
[41] 185 Ky. 146, 214 S. W. 809 (1919).
[42] See the discussion of the Kentucky rule in Chapter 9.
[43] 185 Ky. 693, 215 S. W. 527 (1919). On remedies, see the annotation in 7 A. R. L. 353, at 365.

The City National Bank of Evansville, Indiana, had also purchased some of these bonds, but had taken them as an assignee from the original purchaser. The bank also brought suit but failed to recover. The court said that the city had received no money from the bank, and consequently an action for money had and received would not lie. The money received by the city came from the original purchaser, not from the bank. There must, apparently, according to this decision, be privity between the parties with relation to the money to be recovered. Since no such privity existed here, the general equitable considerations operative in the Winstead case did not apply.

Action on the bonds themselves would also have failed, according to an intimation by the court, because of the invalidity of the statute creating the obligations evidenced by the bonds. The theory of the court seems to have been that an action could not be maintained on the bond itself if it was authorized by an unconstitutional statute.

This, then, brings us to a consideration of remedies. An action on the bond itself will apparently not lie even in Kentucky, and certainly will fail in all other courts under the general rule as it now stands. Action for money had and received will lie in Kentucky if plaintiff can show that it was his money that was received by the city, but the action will be unsuccessful unless he can show this. This reversion to technicality on the part of the Kentucky court is somewhat puzzling, in view of its reliance on broad equitable principles in establishing its exception to the general rule as to mistake of law. Of course the thing for the bank to do is to see to it that the bond gets back to the hands of the original purchaser and that he brings the action. That might satisfy the technical requirements of the decision just mentioned, although it should not be necessary to resort to this indirection.

Actions relative to bond issues under invalid statutes may arise in various ways. A taxpayer may seek to enjoin the levy or collection of taxes to be used in paying the bonds; [44] an action may be brought to restrain the officers of a municipality from paying the bonds; [45] an action may be brought by the bondholder to collect against the city; an action against the city may be brought for money had and received; or a mandamus may be sought by the

[44] Such actions are frequent and are generally entertained. See, for example, Duke v. Brown, *supra,* note 28.

[45] This type of action is also quite frequently brought. It may be brought by either a taxpayer or some officer or board interested in preventing the illegal payment. See, for example, the action by one officer against another, Missouri River, Ft. Scott & Gulf R. R. v. Commissioners of Miami County, 12 Kan. 182 (1873).

purchaser to compel a disbursing officer to pay him the face value of his bond when the due date arrives.[46]

The actions by the taxpayer will be successful, and will apparently bind all purchasers of the bonds whether they are formally made parties or not,[47] although there is some question on this point.[48] In any event, the usual course will be for courts to consider the disposition of one of the cases as establishing a precedent binding on all other bondholders who are in a similar position with respect to the particular issue involved, so that the result will be much the same as though the rule were formally stated to be that they are bound whether all of them are made parties or not.[49]

The actions on the bonds by the bondholder will, as we have seen, fail everywhere except in Kentucky, and will succeed there only under the circumstances just enumerated in connection with the Winstead and Evansville bank cases. Mandamus will fail, although there is a suggestion in a recent Florida case [50] to the effect that the reason why it will be refused is that an adequate remedy at law exists for the collection of the money. This intimation, however, seems to have been discarded in the opinion rendered after a rehearing. The first opinion stressed the benefits received by the city from the use of the money obtained by it from the sale of the bonds, but the second opinion ignores this element of the argument and stresses the invalidity of the bonds and the inapplicability of mandamus because the city was under no obligation to repay the money borrowed.

Will an action by the bondholders lie against persons to whom the city has paid the money received from the sale of bonds to the plaintiffs? A New York decision refused to permit recovery from them on the ground that it was the city, not the plaintiffs, who had given money to the defendant. For this reason an action for money

[46] In a proceeding to obtain mandamus to compel the officer to certify a levy of taxes to pay bonds, the officer cannot question the constitutionality of the statute authorizing the original issue, if he failed to challenge it in the validating proceedings which occurred subsequent to issue but prior to this application for mandamus. Gowran v. Wood, 171 Ga. 416, 156 S. E. 21 (1930).

[47] See Ryan v. Lynch, 68 Ill. 160 (1873). See Whitney v. Hillsborough County, supra, note 21.

[48] Denver Land Co. v. Moffatt, Tunnel Impr. Dist., 87 Colo. 1, 284 Pac. 339 (1930). See suggestions in Otoe County v. Baldwin, 111 U. S. 1, 4 Sup. Ct. Rep. 265, 28 L. Ed. 331 (1884). If the bondholders were ordered to return the bonds for cancellation, as was done, for instance, in the case of Missouri River, Ft. Scott & Gulf R. R. v. Commissioners, supra, note 45, they would doubtless have to be made parties to the suit.

[49] See the dictum in Whitney v. Hillsborough, supra, note 21, that the bondholders will not be bound, if not parties, by an injunction decree, when the question of recovery on the bonds arises. This is not to be relied upon.

[50] State ex rel. Nuveen v. Greer, 88 Fla. 249, 102 So. 739 (1924).

had and received by the bondholders would fail, on the same theory as that employed in the Evansville case.[51] An action on the bond against the individual would not lie because the latter had not contracted to repay the money. The bond represented the city's, not the individual's, contract to repay the loan.

The void ab initio doctrine is applied with the utmost severity in the bond cases, the courts apparently feeling that it is better for the purchasers to lose their money than for the public to be made to suffer from extravagant borrowing and spending on the part of governmental units. But should the entire burden of enforcing municipal frugality be placed upon the purchasers of bonds? Is it fair that they alone should be charged with the duty of maintaining and enforcing limits on government borrowing?

Several different types of cases should perhaps be distinguished in attempting to answer these questions. There is the case where a specific constitutional debt limit is placed on borrowing. Here there may be some substance to the argument that the purchasers of bonds should bear a portion of the burden of enforcing such restrictions, although one cannot help feeling that the borrowing authorities themselves should have some responsibility in the matter. Nevertheless, this is doubtless the strongest type of case that can be made out for denying relief to purchasers of bonds.

In another type of case the money thus borrowed is to be utilized for a purpose not permitted, according to the view of the courts, by the constitution.

A third possibility is that the statute is invalid because of some defect unrelated to the power of borrowing or the purpose to which the money is to be put, such as a defect in title or other procedural defect.

In the second and third types of cases the bondholder certainly should not be made to bear the whole brunt of the burden. Why would it not be reasonable and fair to hold that if a taxpayer wishes to contest the levy of taxes in these cases, he must do so at a fairly early stage in the proceedings? There are analogies warranting the belief that this could be done in conformity with established legal rules in somewhat similar types of cases.[52]

In this connection attention should be called to the fact that there

---

[51] See Newburgh Sav. Bk. v. Town of Woodbury, *supra,* note 21.

[52] See, for example, the cases holding invalidly organized municipal corporations liable, in Chapter 3. These are the result of judicial reasoning and decision, not of constitution or statute. In these cases much attention is paid to the promptness with which legal action is brought to test the validity of incorporation. Not all of the cases are in agreement, but those holding in favor of liability indicate the possibility of judicial formulation of the rule enforcing payment of bonded obligations.

is no general rule of constitutional law forbidding estoppel to give effect to an unconstitutional statute. There are numerous cases in which courts have held that estoppel can be used, and in which it has been used, to save persons from unjust injuries and losses that would otherwise follow from a strict adherence to the void ab initio doctrine of the effect of an unconstitutional statute. The estoppel doctrine has been used in bond cases where the unconstitutional statute affected the capacity of the borrowing unit because of its connection with the legal existence or nonexistence of the corporation. Why, if a city can be compelled by some courts to pay its bonded obligations in the one case, should it be permitted to escape them in the other?

In the case of a state the situation is, of course, affected by the existing but unfortunate rules relating to the non-suability of the state, but most of the bonds involved in these cases are county, township, city, or special-district bonds, and hence this factor is not operative Granting that the distinction between the three types of cases mentioned above is of some significance, the writer cannot believe that there is any necessary rule of law or any conclusive reason for a policy permitting governmental units otherwise subject to suit to escape their just obligations in the two types of cases, other than express debt limit cases, while private corporate and individual borrowers are compelled to meet similar obligations.

These rules would not be so objectionable if their only results were to cause the bondholders to resort to other means of recovering their money, but the little information the writer has been able to gain on this subject indicates that in the great majority of these cases no recovery is ever effected, and a total loss of the investment, plus attorney's fees, results. The local or state legislative body may in some cases come to the aid of these investors, but they seldom do so, and it is doubtful whether the courts permit them to do so in all states, even though they wish to remedy the injustices resulting from judicial decision.[53]

Certainly the officers of the state concerned in the matter, the officers of the borrowing unit, and the taxpayers of the unit should also bear a portion, and in some cases all, of the burden of enforcing restrictions on borrowing, particularly if a reasonable period elapses after notice has been given to these individuals that a bond issue is pending or has been effected. The formulation of such a rule is not beyond the proper sphere of judges; they have been formulated by courts in analogous cases, and in Kentucky they have virtually been formulated in a limited sense for these very cases.

[53] This is true in cases of private corporations, municipal corporations, and officers.

Every state should remedy the existing situation by statute if the courts will not do so.[54] Would it not be a sensible and workable statutory rule that attacks on a bond issue by either a taxpayer or the city must be made within a specified time prior to their actual issuance for sale, due notice being given to the public that the issue is about to be made? A statute such as that embodied in Section 20 of the County Finance Act of North Carolina passed in 1927 should be on the statute books of every state, and should be made applicable to cities, townships, and other special districts as well as to counties. This statute regulates the issuance of bonds and provides that bond ordinances (and bond statutes should be included) shall be deemed valid in all the courts of the state unless an action to test their validity is brought within thirty days following the first notice by publication of its passage; after the expiration of this period attack on its validity "in any court upon any ground whatever" is barred.[55] The period might be sixty or ninety days, but a fairly short period should be fixed by statute.

One should not be too surprised to learn that the very municipalities and counties escaping these debts have more than paid back the amount saved in increased interest rates on subsequent borrowings.[56] The practice of defending against recovery in these cases may have been not only bad governmental ethics but very poor economy. Certainly the rules of law permitting the defense are of doubtful soundness. They should be remedied immediately in every state.

No consideration will be given in this section to the cases involving bonds valid when originally issued but later declared invalid because of change in judicial opinion as to constitutionality. Such obligations may be enforced against the government under some circumstances.[57]

[54] Some states have statutes forbidding attack on the status of a municipal corporation after a brief period of time. These statutes are constitutional despite the fact that the statute authorizing municipal incorporation is unconstitutional. Loans and bond issues may often be affected by such statutes. So, too, statutes fixing short periods of limitation on actions to recover taxes have been upheld, even though the taxes were authorized and collected by and under invalid statutes. See on these points Chapter 3.

[55] For a discussion of this statute see Kirby v. Board of Commrs. of Person County, 198 N. C. 440, 152 S. E. 165 (1930).

[56] See the examples cited in H. B. Bickner, Washington's Defaulted Bonds Not to Be Redeemed, 16 Nat. Munic. Rev. 493 (1927), showing that "deadbeat" cities pay higher interest rates on subsequent borrowings. Increased borrowing burdens are sometimes reflected in difficulties in disposing of bond issues. See note in 15 Nat. Munic. Rev. 182 (1926).

[57] See Chapter 7. See Willoughby v. Holderness, 62 N. H. 227 (1882).

III. PRIVATE PROMISES TO PAY OR REPAY
THE GOVERNMENT

In striking contrast to the rule exonerating governments from legal responsibility for the repayment of loans is the rule compelling private borrowers to repay money obtained from the government even though the statute authorizing the government to lend them the money is declared unconstitutional.

A promise by an individual to a state to repay a loan in the form of a bill of credit has been held to be unenforceable because it is without consideration, but it should be remembered that bills of credit are specifically prohibited by the federal constitution. The bill itself is forbidden, not only the law authorizing it.[58]

Formal promises by individuals to make payments to the government take various forms. When statutes providing for or requiring such promises have been declared invalid, the question sometimes has subsequently arisen whether the bonds given under these statutes can be enforced.

An early New York case involved a bond given to obtain the discharge of a vessel detained under a wharfage statute, the double wharfage penalty provisions of which were invalid.[59] When suit was brought on the bond to enforce it, the obligor defended on the ground that the statute was invalid; he contended that it should be treated as void and that the bond should be considered as having been given under duress to obtain a privilege that he should have been granted without payment. He was not granted the privilege, without payment, because of the statute. Therefore, having made the promise in order to obtain the privilege, and the statute requiring the payment being unconstitutional, he should be permitted to escape liability on the promise. The court held that the bond was unenforceable.

A recent Illinois decision is in accord with this New York case. An Illinois statute requiring dealers in securities to give bonds before obtaining permission to engage in their business was declared unconstitutional because of the failure of the legislature to furnish a sufficient standard for action on the part of the officer authorized to require the bonds. Suit in the name of the state was brought, in accordance with the statute, against the surety company that had furnished a bond for a dealer in securities, as required by the stat-

[58] Craig v. Missouri, 4 Pet. 410, 7 L. Ed. 903 (U. S. 1830).
[59] Brockman v. Hammill, 43 N. Y. 554 (1871). See the reference to, and discussion of, this case in Stevenson v. Morgan, 67 Neb. 207, 93 N. W. 180 (1903). To be effective the defense of an unconstitutional statute must be raised in the trial court. Vose v. Cockcroft, 44 N. Y. 415 (1871).

ute. The surety company defended on the ground that the bond was unenforceable, being void because of the unconstitutionality of the statute under which it was given. The Supreme Court of Illinois held that the bond could not be enforced,[60] and distinguished this case from those in which estoppel is utilized to prevent persons giving bonds from escaping liability on them, by pointing out that in this case no benefits were received by the individuals giving the bond, whereas in the cases utilizing estoppel benefits had been received. The court said, relative to this point:

. . . the rule which has been announced, that, where the obligor has obtained and availed himself of the benefits to be derived from the execution of the bond, he cannot defeat liability because of the unconstitutionality of the statute, does not apply. That rule requires that a party shall have availed himself, for his own benefit, of an unconstitutional law, but the facts are that the defendant did not and could not avail itself of the statute for its benefit. Without the law, Gettleman and Co. had the right to engage in the business of dealer and broker in securities. It needed no license or permission to do so. The legislature in the passage of the Illinois Securities Law required that such dealers and brokers should procure a license. In the exercise of the police power it had authority to impose such a requirement, but, in attempting to require a bond as a condition precedent to the license, the legislature failed to do so because of its attempted unconstitutional delegation of legislative power in regard to the bond to the secretary of state. This attempted delegation of power being in violation of the constitution, Section 23, is void, and must be eliminated from consideration in the enforcement of the act. The appellant has not induced the appellees, by any action which it has taken or statement which it has made, to believe in the existence of any state of facts and to act upon that belief. . . . It would be a novel idea in the law of estoppel to apply the doctrine to a person who has been guilty of no fraud, simply because under a misapprehension of the law he has treated as legal and valid an act void and open to the inspection of all. The causes of action on the bond are based entirely on Section 23 of the law. That section being void and the defendant being bound by no estoppel or waiver, the appellees have shown no liability of the defendant to them in these actions.

Appeal bonds [61] and contractors' bonds [62] given to the government under invalid statutes are apparently subject to the same rules

[60] People, to Use of Klemmer v. Federal Surety Co., 336 Ill. 472, 168 N. E. 401 (1929).

[61] See Curley v. Town of Marble, 61 Colo. 6, 155 Pac. 334 (1916).

[62] See United States Fidelity & Guaranty Co. v. Henderson County, 276 S. W. 203, 1119 (Tex. Com. App. 1925); City of Cleveland v. Clements Bros., 67 Ohio St. 197, 65 N. E. 885 (1902). See also People ex rel. Rodgers v. Coler, 166 N. Y. 1, 59 N. E. 716 (1901).

as those given by one individual to another.[63] Such bonds are enforced as common law obligations, despite the invalidity of the statute requiring them, if it is possible to find any method of sustaining them. The fact that the section of the statute referred to in the bond is unconstitutional will not be sufficient to invalidate the bond if there is any other section in the statute books under which the bond could have been required and which the parties could have contemplated when executing the instrument.[64] On the other hand, a contractor's bond cannot be enforced against him after it has been canceled by a judicial proceeding even though the statute authorizing the cancellation is unconstitutional.[65] The only way in which the action of the court can be corrected is by appeal from the decree of cancellation.

Byers v. State,[66] an Indiana case, involved a recognizance bond in a bastardy proceeding, the bond having been required under an invalid statute. In denying recovery on the bond the court stated that the bond should be treated as "forbidden by the constitution." The bond was therefore to be treated as positively illegal. The defect in the statute was that it provided for imprisonment in a civil proceeding, not that it required a bond. To treat the exaction of the bond in this case as positively illegal was therefore, according to the court, to give a more direct prohibitory meaning, an interpretation more severe, to the constitutional provision forbidding imprisonment in a civil proceeding than the situation involved in the case justified.

In Cassel v. Scott [67] a bond for observance of the liquor laws had been filed in a county auditor's office. Such a bond is also one to insure personal behavior of a certain type, and is thus much like a bail or recognizance bond. The statute requiring the bond was invalid, and the obligor sought an injunction to prevent the levy of an execution and subsequent sale in accordance with a judgment that had been given on the bond. The injunction was denied. This at first glance would seem to indicate that the court gave effect to the bond despite the invalidity of the statute under which it had been exacted. Such, however, was not the case. What the court decided on this point was that, although the bonds were invalid, the judgment on them had been regularly obtained and could be reversed only upon appeal. The judgment was not void, although the

---

[63] See *supra*, pp. 198–204.
[64] United States Fidelity & Guaranty Co. v. Henderson County, *supra*, note 62.
[65] State v. Arkansas Constr. Co., 201 Ind. 259, 167 N. E. 526 (1929).
[66] 20 Ind. 47 (1863).
[67] 17 Ind. 514 (1861).

bonds were perhaps so, and injunction was not the proper method for correcting the error. The bonds should have been treated as un-enforceable because they lacked consideration, said the court, but to render them unenforceable now it was necessary to appeal from the judgment giving them operative effect. This case is then an authority in support of the position that the bonds were without consideration and unenforceable. In this respect it is in accord with the Byers case.[68]

The weight of authority in bail and recognizance cases is to the contrary, however, and recent cases tend to give effect to bonds for recognizance and bail that have been exacted under invalid statutes. These cases usually involve a situation in which the accused has fled from the state and he or his surety assails the validity of the statute requiring the bond in defense to an action against them by a repre-sentative of the government. Thus in a Louisiana criminal case [69] a bond to insure appearance was given, the accused failed to appear, and suit was brought against the surety. The defense set up the unconstitutionality of the statute under which the proceedings had been held. The court held that the accused could not set up such a claim, being absent from the state under these circumstances, nor could the surety do so, since that would accomplish indirectly the result to be prevented. To hold the bond invalid would by inference be declaring the statute invalid also.

The same result is reached, on the ground that the surety is not the real party in interest, if the accused has posted money with which to indemnify the surety in case of loss on his part.[70] Another reason for denying the surety or the accused the defense of the unconstitu-tionality of the statute is that collateral attack on the validity of a statute should not be encouraged. The action in such a case is on the bond. This action does not establish the guilt or innocence of the accused. The bond recites a promise to pay money upon failure to appear for trial. The accused fails to appear. Action is brought to enforce the promise contained in the bond. Such an action is civil,

[68] A recent case in Indiana which supports this same view, that the judgment stands until changed in the methods provided for by law, is that of State v. Arkansas Constr. Co., 201 Ind. 259, 167 N. E. 526 (1929), where the defendant gave a bond to perform a contract with a county. A subsequent statute authorized the courts to relieve contractors of the obligations of these bonds upon certain showings. A judg-ment giving such relief was entered. The statute was later declared unconstitutional. The county brought suit against the contractor to recover the sums paid out in excess of the amount called for in the original contract. The judgment had never been appealed from. Held, the judgment is conclusive; recovery denied.

[69] State v. Rushing, 49 La. Ann. 909, 22 So. 199 (1899).

[70] Louisiana Society for Prevention of Cruelty to Children v. Moody, 52 La. Ann. 1815, 28 So. 224 (1906).

not criminal, in character. The validity of the statute under which the person is accused can be assailed only in proceedings involving that statute directly.[71] Often the statute requiring the bond is the same one that provides for other proceedings in a criminal case, and its provisions are inseparable. This is not always true, of course, and to this extent such a decision does not cover the entire ground.

In Du Faur v. United States,[72] the accused gave, in addition to a recognizance bond, some real estate as security for his appearance. The bond was forfeited and the money paid into the treasury of the United States. The accused and the surety both assailed the constitutionality of the statute under which the accused was charged with crime. The Supreme Court of the United States affirmed a decision by a lower federal court holding that neither the accused nor the surety could raise the question of constitutionality. The basis for the decision was that the bond contained a contract of record, that it imported verity, and could not be inquired into in such a proceeding.

The tendency, as illustrated by these cases, seems to be for courts to enforce such bonds, though the statute under which criminal charges are preferred and even the statute requiring the bond may have been declared invalid. Perhaps a careful generalization from the decisions as they now stand can be formulated in a series of statements.

1. A bond to release property being detained under an unconstitutional statute or to obtain the privilege of engaging in a business cannot be enforced against the obligor.

2. Appeal and contractors' bonds will be held invalid and unenforceable if they refer specifically to the invalid statute, if there is no other valid section under which the bond could have been required, and if no benefit can be found to support the obligation.

3. A recognizance or bail bond given in compliance with an invalid statute or in connection with a criminal proceeding under an unconstitutional statute may not be enforced in Indiana but will support a judgment in an action to enforce it until corrected on appeal, whereas in Louisiana, Illinois, and the federal courts such bonds may be enforced against either the accused or the sureties.

The first rule, which is perhaps fair enough, is another example of the proper use of the so-called void ab initio doctrine. The majority view set forth in the second one appeals to the writer, because

---

[71] People v. Rubright, 160 Ill. App. 528 (1911), also 241 Ill. 600, 89 N. E. 713 (1909).

[72] 223 U. S. 732, 32 Sup. Ct. Rep. 528, 56 L. Ed. 635 (1912), affirming 187 Fed. 812 (C. C. A. 7th 1911).

he feels that persons accused of crime who fail to keep their promise to appear for trial should not, in addition to escaping — for all ordinary purposes — accountability for their acts, receive judicial approval of their failure to appear. Thus to view a decision giving the accused or surety the advantage of the unconstitutionality of the statute is justified, because, after all, the privilege of bail is a considerable concession on the part of the state, and in the absence of statute permitting it the accused would normally suffer confinement until trial. It is, of course, important that persons should not be confined unfairly or in direct violation of the constitutional provisions relative to bail and criminal procedure, but it is also important that persons accused of crime be subjected to some pressure to insure appearance for trial. The difficulty of apprehending such persons is sufficient to make one feel that, when apprehended, they should at least be present when the time for trial arrives. The time elapsing between apprehension and trial is usually long enough as it is, and the likelihood of subsequent trial, although it is considerable, is lessened by the cumbersome methods of obtaining the return of the accused, by prosecutors' loss of interest in the case, and by the disappearance of witnesses or dimming of memories.

Chapter IX

MISTAKE OF LAW AND UNCONSTITUTIONAL STATUTES : PAYMENTS AND SERVICES

The generally stated rule with respect to the recovery of money paid under mistake of law is that courts will not relieve against such mistake, and that recovery will not be permitted.[1] Statutes have altered or modified the rule in some states, and in a smaller number the courts have refused to follow the "weight of authority."[2]

Certain exceptions to the general rule have also become well established, and are perhaps growing in importance.[3] The rule does not apply to mistakes relating to foreign law, such mistakes being treated as mistakes of fact, not as mistakes of law.[4] However, the rule is still enunciated in nearly every judicial opinion explaining a decision in a case involving mistake of law.

Mistake of law, as that phrase is used in this chapter, primarily refers to the law governing the recovery of payments. This is the rather restricted sense in which it is used in private law, and particularly in quasi contracts and equity. The rules relating to recovery for services rendered are included here also, because they should be compared with rules on payments, and because the two types of situations have much in common; more, perhaps, than writers and courts generally suppose.[5] The recovery of compulsory payments, such as taxes and fines, will not be considered here. They are considered elsewhere.[6]

[1] See Woodward, Recovery of Money Paid under Mistake of Law, 5 Col. L. Rev. 366 (1905); Stadden, Error of Law, 7 Col. L. Rev. 476 (1907); note, 9 Va. L. Rev. 126, 220 (1922); Johnson, Mistake of Law, 18 Cent. L. J. 7 (1884); 3 Williston, Contracts, secs. 1581–83; Smith, Correcting Mistakes of Law in Texas, 9 Tex. L. Rev. 309 (1931).

[2] In Kentucky and Connecticut the general rule is not followed by the courts. For citations to statutes in California, Montana, North Dakota, South Dakota, Oklahoma, Georgia, and Virginia, modifying or abrogating the rule, see 3 Williston, Contracts, sec. 1582; comment, 9 Va. L. Rev. 225 (1922).

[3] For a consideration of these exceptions, see 3 Williston, Contracts, sec. 1581. See this statement in Collier v. Montgomery, 103 Tenn. 716, 54 S. E. 969 (1900): "We are not unmindful of the trend of modern decisions to the effect that mistake of law will in many cases be relieved against, especially where the mistake is mutual."

[4] Keener, Quasi Contracts, 92; note, 30 Mich. L. Rev. 301 (1931).

[5] See Chapter 8 for discussion of mistake of law relating to agreements.

[6] See Chapter 10.

Some cases will be discussed in this chapter that have already been analyzed in connection with reliance on judicial decisions and the law applicable to promises to pay. Most of the cases in this chapter do not deal with reliance on decisions, however, but rather with reliance on statutes themselves, without an intervening judicial decision.

This is really a study in the relations between the rules as to the effect of an unconstitutional statute, the rules as to mistake of law, and the rules as to reliance on judicial decision. The mistake involved in all the cases considered in this chapter is a mistake as to the constitutionality of a statute thought to be applicable by the parties or by the court.

I. PAYMENTS AND SERVICES BY ONE INDIVIDUAL TO ANOTHER

A. PAYMENTS

The case of Doll v. Earle [7] presents an excellent example of payment under a mistake as to the constitutionality of a statute. In that case the parties to a mortgage were apparently misinformed as to the decision reached in the Legal Tender cases; [8] on the theory that Hepburn v. Griswold [9] had been followed, the mortgagor had signed an order authorizing the payment of $985 to the mortgagee. A dispute had arisen between the parties over the exact amount due, and $985 had been deposited in a bank until the outcome of the Legal Tender cases should be known. When the decision of the Supreme Court reversed Hepburn v. Griswold, and the mortgagor learned that he had paid more than he thought he was legally obligated to pay, he brought suit in the state courts to recover the excess. The New York courts decided that recovery should not be permitted, the money having been paid voluntarily and having been paid under a mistake of law, no mistake of fact having entered into the transaction.

In re Dunham [10] also involved a payment in gold, after Hepburn v. Griswold; the court decided that no recovery could be had of the excess in an action brought after the decision of the Legal Tender cases.

Two grounds, as pointed out in connection with the discussion

[7] 59 N. Y. 638 (1874).
[8] 12 Wall. 457, 20 L. Ed. 287 (U. S. 1871). For a discussion of this case, see Warren, The Supreme Court in United States History, Chapter 31, p. 220.
[9] 8 Wall. 603, 19 L. Ed. 513 (U. S. 1869).
[10] 9 Phila. 451, Fed. Cas. No. 4146 (D. C. N. Y. 1872). To the same effect, denying recovery, Troy v. Bland, 58 Ala. 197 (1877).

of the cases resulting from the decision in the Legal Tender cases, are available for the disposition of these cases. One ground is reliance on judicial decision, which the courts seek to protect, and the other, the rule that payments made in mutual mistake of law are not recoverable. "Ignorance of the law" and similar phrases in some of these opinions make it reasonably certain that mistake of law considerations played their part in some decisions here referred to.

In Flower v. Lance [11] the payment in a similar type of case was made under written protest, but in this case also the New York courts refused to permit recovery, despite the mistake and the protest. The payment was made directly by one party to another. The court said in the course of its opinion:

The creditor in demanding gold required nothing but what the law as then declared authorized him to demand, and the plaintiff in paying it only complied with his legal obligation as the courts then construed it. But if there was no legal right on the part of the plaintiff to pay it, and payment in gold was made under a mistake of law, the plaintiff cannot recall it. If he voluntarily yielded to the claim, and there was no duress of person or of goods, or fraud on the part of the creditor, the payment concludes him; and he could not avoid the force or effect of the act of payment, as an admission, or reserve the right to draw the matter into controversy thereafter by paying under protest. The act of payment was voluntary, and if he intended to litigate the right, he was bound at the time to take his position and resist the demand made upon him.[12]

The result of this decision is, therefore, that a payment is not involuntary merely because it is made under written protest. Statutes in some states have adopted this rule,[13] and the decision itself on this point is in accord with that in the tax recovery cases. Statutes have occasionally changed the rule as to the effect of protest in the tax cases. These decisions, leaving the payment on the gold basis undisturbed, doubtless met with general favor among New York creditors, but one cannot be so sure that a Nebraska or Kansas court would at that time have reached a similar result.

Unconstitutional sales taxes have sometimes presented difficult situations. A tax on gasoline or cider, for example, of two cents a gallon for each gallon produced and sold within the state will in the ordinary case be passed on from producer to retailer and thence to consumer. Let us assume that the producer pays the tax to the government but that the taxing statute is unconstitutional, and that

[11] 59 N. Y. 603 (1874).
[12] 59 N. Y. at 610.
[13] Filing a protest at the time of payment does not change the rule. Ga. Code (1911), sec. 4317.

because it is believed to be unconstitutional the tax is paid under protest. May the retailer recover from the producer the two-cent addition to the purchase price?

In Kansas the retailer was permitted to deduct this amount when suit was brought against him for the price of the goods.[14] Cases in the District of Columbia[15] and New York[16] have refused, however, to permit retailers to recover such amounts paid in accordance with an administrative order that was not supported by the taxing statutes. The latter cases emphasized the fact that the tax was imposed upon the producer, not upon the retailer. The government had not asked the retailer to pay the tax. The producer paid the tax for himself, not for the retailer, and for that reason the producer was under no trust relationship to the retailer when he recovered the tax that the government had collected illegally. No duress or undue confidence had entered into the transaction and the retailer had made the payment under a pure mistake of law. The fact that all cider or gasoline producers added the tax to the price of their product and that unless the retailer paid it he would have to forego selling these products in his place of business, was perhaps a form of commercial coercion, said the court, but it was not sufficient to constitute legal duress nor to render the payment involuntary. The courts said that neither equity nor law would aid the retailer. A different result would of course have been attained had there been an express agreement to repay the amount of the tax in case of recovery from the government.

These cases illustrate the difference between the position of the retailer who pays his bill on time and the one who waits to see whether the taxing statute is upheld or not before paying for his goods. At first glance the penalty for prompt payment seems distressingly high. But the policy of waiting also creates difficulties. If the retailer is permitted to recover in these cases the question of the rights of the consumers would immediately arise and it is difficult to make sure that those who really "paid the tax" (the consumers) would eventually receive the refund. This difficulty may furnish the basis for an argument that can be utilized with equal plausibility against permitting recovery by the producer when he attempts to get back the tax from the government, and some courts have denied him recovery on this ground.[17]

[14] Sinclair Refining Co. v. Rosier, 104 Kan. 719, 180 Pac. 807 (1919).

[15] Heckman & Co. v. I. S. Dawes & Son Co., 12 F. (2d) 154, 56 App. D. C. 213 (C. A. A. D. of C. 1926). See Cent. Transfer Co. v. Commercial Co., 45 F. (2d), 400 (E. D. Mo. 1930), consumer interest too remote to get injunction against distributor to test tax statute.

[16] Kastner v. Duff-Mott Co., 125 Misc. Rep. 886, 213 N. Y. S. 128 (1925).

[17] See Chapter 10.

The argument that the producer should be permitted to recover because the taxes are "imposed upon *him*" is certainly unconvincing when one considers that the reason for "imposing" the tax on him instead of on someone else is that it is easier to collect it by so doing. If recovery is to be granted or denied upon principles of equity in these cases, as the courts say it should, the equities are as strong against recovery by the producer as against recovery by the retailer. Either recovery should be open all the way down the line to the consumer, or it should be denied all the way down and the government should keep the taxes in question.

The converse of these tax cases is suggested by the case wherein a gasoline dealer paid a tax at the rate fixed by an existing statute instead of at a higher rate fixed by a later statute thought not to be in effect because of a veto by the governor. The veto was declared unconstitutional and ineffective, but in an action by the government to recover the higher rate the gasoline dealer was protected in his reliance upon the supposed veto, and the action failed.[18]

Every state should require that adequate bond be given by the distributor to insure refund by him to the real taxpaying consumer before he is given any refund. Such a statute is constitutional.

Another type of situation in which a payment may be made under mistake of law is illustrated by a Washington case.[19] A shareholder in a bank had paid an assessment against him in pursuance of a statute that perhaps was unconstitutional, although the court had not specifically decided that it was invalid. The assessment was illegal, however, because made in excess of the statutory authority of the officers exacting it. A period of one year elapsed before the shareholder brought suit to recover the payment; the bank had, in the meantime, contracted new debts. The Washington court, though it indicated that the payment should be considered involuntary, denied recovery, emphasizing the accrual of rights of third parties during the year elapsing between the time of payment and the time of the initiation of the action. In the course of its opinion the court suggested that it would favor a rule permitting recovery in the ordinary mistake of law case if the payment were involuntary and no third party's rights had intervened. California has recently held that no recovery will be granted where through mutual mistake a shareholder paid an assessment on his bank stock, no duress being shown. Enforcement was by a statutory suit if payment was refused. No

---

[18] Texas Co. v. Arizona, 31 Ariz. 485, 254 Pac. 1060 (1927). A statute such as that suggested in the next paragraph in the text was held valid in United States v. Jefferson Elec. Mfg. Co., 54 Sup. Ct. Rep. 443 (1934).

[19] Duke v. Force, 120 Wash. 599, 208 Pac. 67 (1922).

suit had been started when plaintiff paid his assessment in this case.[20]

In St. Louis & San Francisco Railway v. Evans & Howard Fire Brick Company [21] the railroad company sought to condemn certain land owned by the defendant. The statute under which the proceedings were instituted provided that the company could acquire possession of the land by paying money into court to cover whatever damages the court on appeal might assess against it as just compensation, in case the company thought the damages too high. The owner of the land assailed the constitutionality of the statute, and, in addition, apparently contended that the railroad company should not be permitted to recover the money paid into court nor to retain possession of the land. In response to this contention the Missouri court said:

But granting that the *whole* statute on the subject under consideration is constitutionally invalid, what then? Are the rights of the plaintiff to be sacrificed on the altar of mistake? Is it to suffer because it has in all confidence relied on the validity of a statute with whose terms and provisions it has made literal and exact compliance? I hold not. To hold differently would make the statute itself *a pitfall and a snare.* It seems to have been thought that the plaintiff, having paid its money into court for the owner, having filed its exceptions to the exorbitancy of the damages assessed against it, and then taken possession of the land in compliance with the statute under the belief that its exceptions would be heard, and that the court, doing what right and justice would require, would so reduce the unwarranted amount assessed that it would fall within the limits of "just compensation" is in some way *estopped* from asserting its rights as expounded in the statute and in the constitution. It is sufficient to say that if the statute be invalid "the doctrine of estoppel is totally inadmissible in the case." [22]

In another Missouri case [23] the former owner of a parcel of land that had been sold for delinquent taxes sought to redeem the land in compliance with a statute that turned out to be unconstitutional. The statute under which he would have proceeded, had he known that the latter statute was invalid, required a greater sum for redemption than did the invalid statute, and before he could comply with the earlier valid statute the period for redemption specified in

[20] Campbell v. Rainey, 16 P. (2d) 310 (Cal. App. 1932).
[21] 85 Mo. 307 (1884).
[22] 85 Mo. at 334.
[23] Harney v. Charles, 45 Mo. 157 (1869). When the legitimation proceedings depend entirely upon statute, in the absence of any agreement between the parties, the proceedings will fail if the statute upon which they depend is declared unconstitutional. Lieber v. Heil, 32 S. W. (2d) 792 (Mo. St. L. App. 1930), the statute having been declared invalid in another case because of a defective title.

that statute expired. The court permitted him to bring the additional sum into court and obtain possession of the land, saying in the course of its opinion:

I know this action appears to conflict with the maxim *ignorantia legis, etc.* Everyone is presumed to know not only the statutes and common law, but also what acts are constitutional and what are not — a matter which so often embarrasses the courts. It would not do to adopt any other rule. And yet where can we find a more equitable exception? Especially when we consider that the delay beyond the two years given him to redeem by the old statute was caused in part by the action of the court.[24]

If the court itself was mistaken as to the constitutionality of the redemption statute under which plaintiff first acted, it seemed only fair to the court to permit redemption under the valid statute under which action should have been taken. This case is, in a sense, a tax payment case, but it is included here because of its close bearing on the problem under discussion. Courts have not always been so just in cases involving claims rather than payments,[25] although at times this same rule has been applied.[26]

The purchasers of land at a tax sale that had been confirmed by the court were permitted to recover the purchase price of the land from the clerk of court, who still held the money, on the ground that the statute authorizing the sale was invalid; that all the parties to the original proceeding were before the court; and that none of them had altered their position to their detriment as a result of the sale.[27] The court emphasized the fact that the purchase price could be returned without prejudice to the rights of other interested parties. To have refused recovery would have meant that the purchasers would have been given a title, the validity of which would probably have been contested in a lawsuit. To permit them to recover meant that the bondholders at whose instance the land was sold for taxes could not recover on their bonds in this proceeding. Between these two conflicting interests the court favored those of the purchasers. The rule that the judicial confirmation of the sale cannot be attacked collaterally was held to be inapplicable because the confirming court totally lacked jurisdiction, the statute being unconstitutional and void.[28] Equity could be accomplished here by overturning the

---

[24] 45 Mo. at 159.

[25] Robinson v. Robbins Dry Dock Co., 238 N. Y. 271, 144 N. E. 579 (1923), writ of error denied, 271 U. S. 649, 46 Sup. Ct. Rep. 636, 70 L. Ed. 1131 (1924).

[26] Texas Co. v. Arizona, *supra*, note 18; Chapter 10.

[27] Hanchett Bond Co. v. Morris, 143 Okla. 110, 287 Pac. 1025 (1930).

[28] See State v. Arkansas Constr. Co., 201 Ind. 259, 167 N. E. 526 (1929). And the Oklahoma court has decided that in the absence of such equitable considerations

judgment. The rule that recovery of a payment will be permitted even though made under a mistake of law if equitable considerations justify it is illustrated by this decision. The bondholders in this case will, presumably, eventually collect the money due on the bonds, because the invalidity of the statute authorizing the foreclosure of the tax liens did not affect the validity of the bond-issuing statute itself.

B. Services

May a person who pays another for services performed under an invalid statute requiring such payment recover it? On the other hand, may the person performing the services compel payment for his services? Most of the cases dealing with the problem of recovery for services rendered under an invalid statute concern situations in which the services are performed for some governmental unit, but a Tennessee case is perhaps at least suggestive of the attitude that might be taken by courts in a situation involving only private individuals.

In this case [29] a judge of one of the courts of general trial jurisdiction certified to the governor that he was ill and temporarily unable to perform the duties of his office. A statute provided that the governor could, in such a situation, appoint a temporary judge, whose compensation should be deducted from that of the disabled judge. The appointment was made and the appointee performed the duties of the office, but the regular judge had "drawn the amount of his salary in advance from the treasurer" so that the latter refused to make any payments to the temporary officer. Finally the regular judge paid a portion of the amount due and gave his note in payment of the remainder. The next event of importance was that the Tennessee court held the statute under which these proceedings had taken place to be unconstitutional.

The note had not been paid, and an action was brought to enforce its payment. The maker thereupon sought an injunction to prevent its enforcement, on the theory that the note was not a binding obligation because of the invalidity of the statute providing for the appointment and payment of the temporary judge. The prayer

the rule against collateral attack applies. See Jones v. McGrath, 16 P. (2d) 853 (Okla. 1932), denying collateral attack on tax sale confirmed by court under statute later held invalid.

[29] Hubbard v. Martin, 8 Yerg. 498 (Tenn. 1835). Cases dealing with recovery for services performed for the government are dealt with *infra*, p. 239. See this statement in Woodward, Quasi Contracts, 56, note 1: "It is a curious fact that the rule appears to be confined to cases of money paid, although cases of services rendered or goods delivered under mistake of law are in principle undistinguishable."

for an injunction was denied, and presumably the action at law was carried through to completion. The court said that the temporary judge had "a right in conscience to receive the money," although he had no right in law to it. The note had been given voluntarily and with full knowledge of all the facts. Therefore a court of equity could not enjoin the collection of the note. A vigorous dissent from the majority opinion contended that since the statute was void, the obligation of the note was not effective and should not be enforced.

On the other hand, the court intimated that the regular judge could not recover the amount paid in cash. The answers suggested by this opinion are, therefore, that if the services are paid for, the payment may not be recovered; if a promise to pay for them is made, the promise will be enforced; at least a court will not interfere with its enforcement through the ordinary legal methods; and, finally, that the person performing the service could not, in the absence of such a promise, compel in an action at law the payment of the compensation specified in the statute. Whether any quasi contractual relief would be permitted is doubtful, because it was the state rather than the disabled judge who received the benefit of the temporary appointee's services.

Crigler v. Shepler,[30] a case that has been considered in connection with reliance upon judicial decision, should also be mentioned here. In it services were rendered which both employer and employee thought to be legal because a judicial decision had held the prohibitory statute to be invalid. Later the statute was revived as a result of congressional action permitting the state to exercise the power provided for in the statute. An action was brought to recover for the services performed during the time when they could be performed legally, but the court denied recovery. This case is severely criticized in the chapter dealing with reliance, and it should be noted here that the decision turned on the effect of the decision and the subsequent revival of the statute rather than on any rule on mistake of law, but it is clear that the result is the same as it would have been if strict mistake-of-law rules on payment had been applied to services. But, the mistake having been mutual, the services having been rendered in good faith, and the employer having received a benefit therefrom, recovery should have been permitted under the exception often made in payments cases, even though the case involved services.

An interesting group of Indiana and Ohio cases[31] present the

[30] 79 Kan. 834, 101 Pac. 619 (1909).
[31] Thompson v. Bronk, 126 Mich. 455, 85 N. W. 1084 (1901); Patterson v. Crawford, 12 Ind. 241 (1859); Patterson v. Prior, 12 Ind. 440 (1862).

problem of recovery for services very suggestively, although illegality rather than unconstitutionality caused the mistake. Under an
illegal contract entered into between the defendant employer and
the prison warden, plaintiffs worked for the defendant. The defendant paid the warden the stipulated sum. When released from
prison, plaintiffs sued the employer to recover for their services.
The Ohio court denied recovery, saying that quantum meruit would
not lie, the employer not being responsible for the mistake and having paid once, that no agreement to pay plaintiffs could be implied.[32] The contract here called for a price fixed at so much per
day. The court relied on this point considerably to differentiate Patterson v. Crawford,[33] the Indiana case, where recovery was allowed
against the lessee. There the contract called for the services of all
prisoners, which meant all lawful prisoners. Plaintiff having been
unlawfully treated as a prisoner was not covered by the contract, so
he could sue the employer (lessee) for services performed for him,
benefit presumably having been conferred thereby. A similar result
was reached in the second of the Indiana cases.[34] The problem of
the liability of the warden is dealt with in the chapter on officer's
liability.

It is difficult to make any generalizations from the cases considered thus far because in each of them the court seems to have been
influenced by the equities of the particular situation, the term "equities" being used in its more general sense of fairness and justice in a
specific case.

In the gold payment cases the courts refused to relieve from
mistake of law, and in so doing they perhaps reflected the general
opinion of an important and influential group of persons in the
community and in addition enforced what was perhaps the intention of the parties at the time the mortgage was executed, the legal
tender acts not being law at that time. It also ignored the protest
under which payment was made in the latter case.

As to recovery of money paid as part of the purchase price, which
included illegal taxes subsequently recovered by the vendor, the rule
remains to be established, but by analogy the general mistake-of-law
rule will perhaps be applied if the court permits the vendor to recover the tax in the first place. This analogy is not sound, and it is to
be hoped that it will not be followed.

In the Washington assessment case the court seemed disposed to
follow the opposite rule and to permit recovery of the payment that

[32] Thompson v. Bronk, *supra*, note 31.
[33] *Supra*, note 31.
[34] Patterson v. Prior, *supra*, note 31.

had been made under an invalid statute. It curbed that disposition, however, because of the intervention of the rights of third parties, thus for the sake of justice refusing to follow a rule that when generally stated seems to be opposed to the mistake-of-law rule. Recovery of the payment was denied, but not because it had been made under mistake of law. This case is not an authority in favor of the general rule as to mistake of law; it is rather an exception, or an authority to the contrary. It illustrates how a court, starting from a rule diametrically opposed to general rule, can reach a result, by exception, consonant with the general rule as to mistake of law. Perhaps the real explanation of this case is to be found in the feeling of the court that the payment was not really voluntary but was made only because the statute required it and provided means for enforcing that requirement. When the statute was declared invalid this element of compulsion was removed, and the court might well feel that if the shareholder had known at the time of his payment that it was invalid he would not have made the payment. On that ground, viewed from the standpoint of the shareholder, the statute should be declared void ab initio and his payment returned to him. With this view the court would apparently have agreed had it not been for the rights of intervening creditors. This is not so different from the rules applied in cases where promises have been entered into in reliance on, or because of, statutes that are subsequently declared unconstitutional.

The eminent domain and tax redemption cases will doubtless meet with the approval of most persons interested in the settlement of cases in accordance with prevailing ideas of fairness and justice rather than in accordance with general rules, and they both illustrate that courts are often ready to interfere with the operation of the general rule as to mistake of law, and to permit the recovery of money or property lost, or thought lost, through mistake of law. On the other hand, one can sympathize with the Tennessee court's suggestion that payments made to the temporary judge for services rendered in accordance with an invalid statute could not be recovered. The result of the Kansas case on services is less desirable, however, although it conforms with other service cases and also with strict rules on payment.

The only significant generalization possible from these fragments is that in this type of case the courts tend to follow that rule of law, or exception, which permits the most equitable disposition of the particular case before the court. The situations presented to courts in this field of the law are very likely to make a strong appeal for the application of equitable considerations. For those preferring a rule

these cases may perhaps be said to support the principle that payments made under an unconstitutional statute may not be recovered
unless some consideration of equity causes the court to make an
exception and permit recovery. Some courts are more ready than
others to give effect to these equitable considerations.

II. DONATIONS TO, AND PERFORMANCE OF SERVICES FOR, THE GOVERNMENT

Donations to the government and the performance of services for
the government may be voluntary or involuntary. The former are
normally voluntary, from the standpoint of the courts. Taxes are
excluded from this discussion, since they are to be discussed separately. Services, also, with few well-defined exceptions, are normally
voluntary.

A. DONATIONS TO THE GOVERNMENT

Suppose that John Blank, a citizen of means who wishes to aid a
municipal program for the establishment of public playgrounds,
offers the municipal authorities a designated sum of money for use
in carrying out the program, on condition that the municipality
contribute an equivalent sum for the same purpose. Suppose, further, that the municipal authorities accept the offer and make provisions for raising the municipality's share. Mr. Blank thereupon pays
into the city treasury the sum pledged in his offer. Subsequent to
the receipt of the money by the city another citizen institutes an
action to restrain the officers of the municipality from levying taxes
for playground purposes, and succeeds in persuading the courts of
the state to declare invalid the statute authorizing the city to levy the
tax and establish the playgrounds. Then, to make a final supposition — and municipal ethics in some instances seem to indicate that
the supposition is not an impossible one — let us suppose that the
city decides to use Mr. Blank's donation as far as it will go in the
establishment of playgrounds. May the donor recover the money
from the city if his action is brought before the money is actually
expended?

The Wisconsin court held, in a case similar to the one just supposed (a case involving a road-building project), that Mr. Blank
could recover the amount of his donation and that the action for
recovery was properly brought against the municipality instead of
against the officers to whom the money had originally been paid,
because the city's acts of dominion over the money showed that the
city claimed to possess it.[35] The result would doubtless have been

[35] Conway v. Town of Grand Chute, 162 Wis. 172, 155 N. W. 953 (1916).

the same if the money had been expended for playgrounds had the city spent it after its return had been demanded or an action for its recovery had been instituted. Estoppel might intervene to defeat recovery of the money, however, if Mr. Blank had stood by and allowed the donation to be used without protesting at the time, even though the statute authorizing the town to proceed had subsequently been declared invalid. On these latter points there is no direct authority, but these answers to them are suggested by decisions in analogous, though not identical, situations.

B. Services Performed for the Government

No recovery is permitted for services performed for the government if the statute authorizing the work to be done is declared unconstitutional before compensation has been received by the person performing the services.

An undersheriff brought suit against a board of county commissioners for services performed in pursuance of an invalid statute. He failed to recover.[36] An engineer who conducted a survey of a drainage project was refused compensation on the ground that the statute authorizing the work and providing for payment was invalid. He brought an action to obtain the salary he believed to be due him under the statute, but was unsuccessful.[37] Another, suing upon certificates issued in payment for services, was denied recovery because the statute authorizing the work was invalid, but recovery was permitted for work done preliminary to the project so authorized.[38] A person who had caught gophers in order to obtain a county bounty provided for by law received nothing for his efforts,[39] the law being held invalid, like those in the preceding cases. In this case the court said in the course of its opinion that "whatever labor was done or services performed for the county . . . pursuant to the reward offered which was authorized in the body of the said law" could not be recovered upon the ground that the county received a benefit for which it justly ought to pay, because there was a total lack of capacity in the board of commissioners to incur any obligation of the kind mentioned. A New York case suggests the rule that no recovery can be obtained for printing done for the government under an invalid act.[40]

[36] Gustafson v. Bd. of County Commrs., 88 Kan. 335, 128 Pac. 186 (1912).
[37] Gove v. Murray County, 147 Minn. 24, 179 N. W. 569 (1920).
[38] Filbert v. Ark. & Mo. Highway Dist., 2 F. (2d) 114 (D. C. Ark. 1924).
[39] Felix v. Wallace County, 62 Kan. 832, 62 Pac. 667 (1900). Also Teeple v. Wayne County, 23 Pa. Co. Ct. 361 (1900), mink bounty.
[40] People ex rel. McSpedon v. Haws, 12 Abb. Prac. 70 (N. Y. 1861); People ex rel. Commrs. of Records, 11 Abb. Prac. 114 (N. Y. 1860).

That recovery is denied in these cases may not mean that in every instance the person rendering the service will remain uncompensated for his labor, but in many cases it means just that, and in practically all cases it means that he will be forced to wait for his salary for a period ranging from a few months to several years, and that he will be put to considerable expense in recovering it. Curative legislation does not always remedy these injustices, and when it does attempt to do so, it often fails to take account of these additional expenses and the long period of time elapsing before the claim is settled.[41]

Statutes providing for increased salaries are occasionally held invalid. Should a person who has performed the duties of an office under such a statute recover compensation at the increased rate or at the rate provided for by the previous statute? A petition for a writ of mandamus to compel payment at an increased rate in such a case was denied by the Georgia court.[42] Such a decision ignores the fact that the duties may have been performed in reliance on the statute and in innocent ignorance of its invalidity, although it is true that in many instances the duties of the office would not have been performed in reliance on the increased rate provided for by the unconstitutional law. If the invalid statute is treated as void, recovery under the previous statute will be permitted, although this result might be affected in some cases by questions arising out of the effect of the invalidity of an amendatory statute as compared with the effect of the invalidity of a new statute expressly repealing the existing law.[43]

In Smith v. Chickasaw County [44] a clerk of court brought suit to recover compensation for himself and his deputy. A salary statute had been superseded by a fee statute, and the clerk and deputy had contracted to divide certain specified fees, while others were to be retained in full by the deputy. The salary statute had authorized the clerk to fix the salary of the deputy, subject to a stipulation as to the maximum that might be paid. The sum due the deputy under the new statute was less than the maximum fixed by the old law.

[41] In the Gove case, *supra*, note 37, practically ten years elapsed before compensation was recovered.

[42] Clark v. Hammond, 134 Ga. 792, 68 S. E. 600 (1910). For a later development in this situation see Hammond v. Clark, 136 Ga. 313, 71 S. E. 479 (1911). See State v. Lewis, 69 Ohio St. 202, 69 N. E. 132 (1903), officer granted mandamus to obtain fee rate when invalid salary statute had replaced fee rate. State ex rel. Allison v. Garver, 66 Ohio St. 555, 64 N. E. 573 (1902); Roberts v. Roane County, 160 Tenn. 109, 23 S. W. (2d) 239 (1929).

[43] For a consideration of the problems arising out of invalid amendatory statutes, see Chapter 11.

[44] 156 Miss. 171, 125 So. 96 (1929).

The new, or fee, statute was declared unconstitutional, and the court permitted the clerk to recover compensation under the first, or salary, statute, deducting such fees as he had received. The fee statute was entirely eliminated from consideration so far as the compensation of the clerk was concerned. The deduction of fees received might have been accomplished even though they had not been received under the new statute, their deduction being sustainable on equitable grounds and perhaps on the theory that an officer is entitled only to such compensation as is fixed by law.

As to the compensation of the deputy, the court said that the clerk could not recover for him anything more than he had received under the agreement between them. The deputy had received what he had contracted for; he was entitled to no more, even if what he had received was less than it might have been under the salary statute.

The upshot of this decision seems to be that the clerk, whose salary was fixed by the salary statute, was entitled to receive the amounts specified in that statute, the invalid fee statute being eliminated though the moneys received under it were deducted from the amount due. The deputy, whose salary was fixed not by the statute but by agreement under the statute, received, on the other hand, the amount fixed by the agreement, despite the fact that the agreement was entered into in reliance on the unconstitutional fee statute. The deputy's salary, it should be observed, was not fixed by the old salary statute either but by the clerk, in accordance with a maximum limit, so the only gain that might have accrued to him from a decision applying the old statute to him would have been the difference between the amount fixed by the clerk under the old statute and that agreed upon by the two officers under the invalid new statute. Certain difficulties might have been encountered in applying the old statute; if the clerk had not had this particular deputy under the old statute, the only applicable standard existing under the old statute might have been the maximum sum permitted under it, which might or might not have been the amount that would have been fixed by the clerk, although presumably the two figures would generally coincide. The distinction between the two cases seems, then, to be sound.

Another case in which the statute containing specified amounts to be paid as compensation was superseded by one providing that compensation should be fixed by contract is that of Collier v. Montgomery County.[45] In this case, as in the Chickasaw County case,

[45] 103 Tenn. 716, 54 S. W. 989 (1900).

the second statute was held unconstitutional, but, as in that case, the contract entered into under the invalid statute was held to be the proper measure of the compensation to be received by the officer prior to the time when the statute was declared invalid. The officer was not permitted either to obtain a cancellation of the contract or an accounting of the moneys received which would under the old fee statute have gone to him. The contract had been entered into voluntarily, the mistake as to the constitutionality of the statute had been mutual, the agreement had been observed for several years, a valid consideration for the contract existed, the contract had been executed in large part, and the officer had received the benefits of the agreement without complaint. All these factors were stressed by the court, and the doctrine of estoppel was invoked against the plaintiff officer. The court also emphasized the difficulty of obtaining an accurate accounting in view of the inadequate records that had been kept of the moneys received. In the light of all these factors the court felt it proper to treat the parties in accordance with the expressed legislative will up to the time when the statute was held invalid. A South Carolina decision denies recovery to a sheriff at the new rate of an invalid statute providing rates for boarding prisoners, and holds him to the old rate of the prior valid statute, although board had been furnished in reliance upon the new law; but no evidence of an improvement in the quality of table fare appears.[46]

The rules applicable to de facto officers and claims for their services, which are considered elsewhere, need not be considered at this point.

Mention should be made, however, of the type of case in which a contractor performs services for a government, receiving in return a tax bill that can be enforced against persons receiving benefits from the services. This often happens in connection with public improvements, the costs of which are assessed against property owners who benefit therefrom. May the property owner escape payment for the improvement on the ground that the statute authorizing the work or creating the district is invalid? One taxpayer, seeking cancellation of a tax bill on this ground, failed to escape payment, the court emphasizing the receipt of benefits as the basis for invoking estoppel against him.[47] He had sat by and watched the improve-

[46] Dean v. Spartenburg County, 59 S. C. 110, 37 S. E. 226 (1900).
[47] St. Louis Malleable Casting Co. v. Prendergast Constr. Co., 260 U. S. 469, 43 Sup. Ct. Rep. 178, 67 L. Ed. 351 (1922). But getting benefits of improvements does not usually estop the owner of land from assailing the validity of the assessment statute, providing he did not sign the petition asking for the improvement. 9 A. L. R. 651, 763 (annotation). Also Wendt v. Berry, 154 Ky. 586, 157 S. W. 1115 (1913); Thomas v. State ex rel. Gilbert, 76 Ohio St. 341, 81 N. E. 437 (1907).

ments and had received the benefits accruing from them; it was then too late to assail the proceedings. In one sense such a controversy is between the contractor and the taxpayer; in another it is between the government and the taxpayer. That the result attained by the court is fair, from whatever angle it is viewed, seems clear. Not all courts agree with this decision, however, many cases to the contrary being in the books.

III. RECOVERY BY GOVERNMENT OF PAYMENTS TO OFFICERS AND PRIVATE INDIVIDUALS

Some courts hold that payments made by the government to private individuals under invalid statutes can be recovered by the government, whereas others hold that the same rule applies to this type of case as applies to cases involving private individuals only.[48]

Perhaps most courts would agree with the Alabama court, which held in State v. Clements [49] that the government could not recover money paid out by an officer in obedience to a writ of mandamus, despite a subsequent decision that the statute under which the payment was made was unconstitutional.

Minnesota and Arkansas have decisions permitting the government to recover loans that have been made to private individuals under an invalid statute.

The state of Minnesota at one time loaned money to counties to be advanced to farmers as loans for the purchase of seed grain. The statute provided for the collection of the loan by the county, but the county was responsible to the state for the repayment of the loan, irrespective of repayment to the county by the farmer. To give security to the county the statute created a lien in favor of the county on grain raised by the farmer obtaining the loan. The statute providing for these loans was assailed by a debtor farmer in a proceeding instituted by a creditor of the farmer. The creditor sought to attach grain held by a third party, alleging that it belonged to the farmer. The county intervened, asserting a prior claim to the grain. The court held that the farmer could not assail the validity of the statute under which he had obtained the loan, and that the state, not the county, should be the intervening party, because the ordinary

---

[48] For cases dealing with private individuals see *supra,* pp. 222–32. In general on recovery by government, see Levitt, The Recovery of Money Paid out by Government Officials through Mistake of Law or Fact, 9 Iowa L. Bull. 225 (1924); 63 A. L. R. 1345, 1354 (annotation). (1) The federal government permits recovery, (2) the states are divided, (3) some of the states permitting cities to recover refuse to do so if the city has paid out the money in a proprietary capacity.

[49] 217 Ala. 685, 117 So. 296 (1928). See Sudbury v. Board, 157 Ind. 446, 62 N. E. 45 (1901).

presumption in favor of the regular performance of official duties in accordance with statute could not be indulged when the statute under which the duties were to be performed was unconstitutional. The statute was treated as unconstitutional so far as parties to the action were concerned, but as to the farmer it was treated as valid.[50] Another method of stating the result of this case is to say that despite the invalidity of the statute authorizing the loan the state was permitted to recover the money advanced by the county to the farmer.

In Town of Luxora v. Jonesboro, etc., R. R.[51] a city had donated money to a public utility company in accordance with an invalid ordinance. The city brought suit to recover the amount of the donation and succeeded, the court holding that the ordinance, being unconstitutional, had no binding effect upon the city and that such a payment was ultra vires the corporate powers of the city.

In accord with these two cases is a Virginia case[52] involving the recovery of a parcel of land traded by the state to a private individual. The statute which was declared unconstitutional in this case authorized the state fish commissioner to deed to the plaintiff certain state lands in exchange for some of plaintiff's land. Subsequent to the exchange the legislature instructed the attorney-general to institute proceedings to regain for the state the lands so deeded. The latter had, in the meantime, made some improvements on the land and had prepared it for the uses to which he wished to put it. The state recovered the land, the court consoling the plaintiff with the following statement:

If, relying upon the act, . . . Ellinger has in good faith expended money, it may be that he has some ground upon which to appeal to the General Assembly to be reimbursed, but upon that aspect of the case we are not sufficiently advised to entertain an opinion, and it would be beyond our province in any event to give expression to it. The General Assembly, with full knowledge of all the attending circumstances, will doubtless do whatever good faith and fair dealing shall dictate.[53]

The government may not only lend money to or make trades of property with private individuals but may make refunds of taxes. Suppose that the statute authorizing the refund is unconstitutional. May the payment be recovered by the government?

An Iowa case[54] answers this question in the negative. The re-

[50] Deering & Co. v. Peterson, 75 Minn. 118, 77 N. W. 568 (1898).
[51] 83 Ark. 275, 203 S. W. 605 (1907).
[52] Ellinger v. Commonwealth, 102 Va. 100, 45 S. E. 807 (1903). See also Peters v. Broward, 222 U. S. 483, 32 Sup. Ct. Rep. 122, 56 L. Ed. 1178 (1912).
[53] 102 Va. at 106.
[54] Adair County v. Johnston, 160 Iowa 683, 142 N. W. 210 (1913).

fund was made voluntarily and without protest. The county need not have refunded the money, said the court, but having done so it was in the same position as the taxpayer before the refund and could not recover the payment. "The same rule that would prevent the defendant from recovering of the county now estops the county from recovering of the defendant."

Payments in the form of salaries are sometimes made under unconstitutional statutes by the government to its officers. Sometimes a statute increasing the rate of compensation is invalid. A decision and some dicta indicate that recovery will perhaps be permitted in such cases,[55] although such a holding would be based not on any implied contract to repay but rather upon some theory of official payment, without authority, which did not bind the government.[56] In one case at least, however, a court has recognized that good faith and mutual mistake of law will so operate as to estop the government from demanding the return of money paid to an officer under an invalid statute.[57] Recovery of double the amount of the excess salary paid to county officers by the governing board was denied in a statutory action brought by a taxpayer on behalf of the public, good-faith payment being shown and the statute being held not to apply to such payments.[58] Whether a legislative act validating payments by the government under invalid statutes is constitutional will be considered in Chapter XI.[59]

The cases dealing with recovery of payments made by the government to a private individual or officer are not in harmony, some courts permitting recovery and others refusing to permit it.

IV. RECOVERY OF PAYMENTS MADE BY ONE GOVERNMENTAL UNIT TO ANOTHER

Kentucky has held that its rule respecting mistake of law between private parties obtains as to payments made by one governmental agency to another. Such payments may be recovered from the branch of the government to whom they were made by mistake.[60]

[55] Sudbury v. Board, 157 Ind. 446, 62 N. E. 45 (1901); Ellis v. Board of State Auditors, 107 Mich. 528, 65 N. W. 577 (1895).

[56] Hammond v. Clark, 136 Ga. 313, 71 S. E. 479 (1911).

[57] Roberts v. Roane County, 160 Tenn. 109, 23 S. W. (2d) 239 (1929).

[58] Wade v. Bd. of Commrs., 17 P. (2d) 691 (Okla. 1932).

[59] As to the return of taxes by invalid statute, cured by subsequent statute, see Calderwood v. Schlitz Brewing Co., 107 Minn. 465, 121 N. W. 221 (1909). For a study of curative legislation and validating legislation and the effect of an unconstitutional statute, see Chapter 11.

[60] Bd. of Trustees of Public Library v. Bd. of Education, 25 Ky. L. Rep. 341, 75 S. W. 225 (1903). On this subject see the annotation in 63 A. L. R. 1346.

In applying the void ab initio doctrine to this situation the Kentucky court said: "The legal status of the parties is the same as if the act had not been passed, for, so far as it authorized a diversion of the taxes levied for such school purposes to another purpose, it was a nullity." [61] The court explained in its opinion that no consideration for the payment had been shown, that plaintiff had no right to make the payment, and that defendant had no right to receive it. The payment had been made under a "pure" mistake of law on both sides, and recovery should therefore be permitted.

Will the same rule be applied in other jurisdictions which hold that, as between taxpayers and officers, taxes may not be recovered, and that, as between private individuals, no relief will be granted against mistake of law? In Illinois the rule seems to be the same as in Kentucky with respect to taxes, but different as to mistake of law between private individuals. But as between two governmental agencies the Illinois court has permitted recovery of payments made under invalid statutes. [62]

In commenting on, and following, the view of Justice Field in Norton v. Shelby County, [63] the Illinois court said: "There being no question of wrongful intention on the part of anyone in connection with this transaction, the unconstitutional statute must be eliminated from all consideration." The city had received the money that rightfully belonged to the township and must therefore return it. This is an intelligent use of the void ab initio doctrine.

Both these cases permit recovery of money paid by one government to another under a mistake as to the constitutionality of a statute. This is true irrespective of the rules followed in the state with respect to mistake of law between private individuals.

In the Illinois case the court refused, however, to permit the recovery of interest because of the presence of good faith and the absence of any tort, the invalid statute having, according to the court, been an "apparent authority" for the receipt of the money. As to the interest the invalid statute was given some effect, while as to the principal no effect was given to it.

[61] 25 Ky. L. Rep. at 342.
[62] Bd. of Highway Commrs. v. Bloomington, 253 Ill. 176, 97 N. E. 285 (1911).
[63] 118 U. S. 425, 6 Sup. Ct. Rep. 1121, 30 L. Ed. 178 (1886).

Chapter X

THE RECOVERY OF UNCONSTITUTIONAL TAXES *

State and national court reports contain hundreds of cases on taxation every year, and in them some tax statutes are declared unconstitutional almost as a matter of course. Not long ago the Supreme Court of the United States declared unconstitutional the provisions of state inheritance statutes under which millions of dollars had been collected.[1] Some of these taxes were paid many years ago; others have been paid very recently. Many other instances of invalid taxing statutes that remained on the books for many years before they were declared unconstitutional will occur to those familiar with the tax laws of this country.

Sometimes refunds are made to recompense those subjected to the illegal levies, but more often neither refund nor recovery is permitted. There is no tradition in the United States requiring that taxes be refunded or repaid if illegally collected, and the law has made only stumbling progress in setting up such a requirement.

A taxpayer called upon to pay a tax unconstitutionally imposed upon him may be interested either in (1) preventing the collection of the tax or (2) in recovering it after he has paid it. Inasmuch as the subject of tax recovery is affected to some extent by the rules governing attempts to prevent collection, the latter will be considered first.

I. PREVENTIVE MEASURES

In treating preventive measures from the standpoint of their effect on recovery, we may put aside the possibility of preventive administrative relief, because courts are likely,[2] although not cer-

---

* This chapter appeared in somewhat briefer form in 45 Harv. L. Rev. 501 (1932).

[1] Farmers' Loan & Trust Co. v. Minnesota, 280 U. S. 204, 50 Sup. Ct. Rep. 98, 74 L. Ed. 371 (1930); Baldwin v. Missouri, 281 U. S. 586, 50 Sup. Ct. Rep. 436, 74 L. Ed. 1056 (1930). Some of the cases considered in this chapter refer to illegal rather than unconstitutional taxes, but they have been included only because in certain instances they illustrate similar or contrasting rules as applied to the two categories. Most of the cases involve unconstitutional levies.

[2] Nelson v. First Natl. Bk., 42 F. (2d) 30 (C. C. A. 8th 1930); Hodgins v. Board of County Commrs., 123 Kan. 246, 255 Pac. 46 (1927); Smith v. Boston, 194 Mass. 31, 79 N. E. 786 (1907); Blanchard v. City of Detroit, 253 Mich. 491,

tain,[3] to hold that administrative remedies need not be sought if a taxing statute is invalid or the tax is otherwise void. The legal weapons available to the taxpayer are, then, the injunction and the declaratory judgment.

About thirty states have the declaratory judgment, and it should, unless restricted unduly by judicial interpretation [4] or by express statutes governing tax remedies, afford a simple and expeditious method of testing the validity of a taxing statute. In many of the states, however, it is not available, and in many of those in which it has been adopted, its possibilities have not been fully realized. This means that injunction is still, in many jurisdictions, the only hope of obtaining preventive judicial relief.

The federal courts are forbidden by statute to enjoin the collection of federal taxes,[5] but they have interpreted this to permit an injunction if the tax is in the nature of a penalty [6] or if preponderating equitable considerations favor it.[7] The statute has also been evaded occasionally in the case of corporate taxpayers by having a shareholder petition for an order restraining the corporate officers from paying the tax, on the ground that the taxing statute is in-

235 N. W. 230 (1931). See also Hattiesburg v. New Orleans & N. E. R. R., 141 Miss. 497, 106 So. 749 (1926). For statutes embodying this rule, see N. D. Comp. Laws (1913), sec. 2241; Wash. Comp. Stat. (Remington, 1922), sec. 955. For discussion see Stason, Judicial Review of Tax Errors — Effect of Failure to Resort to Administrative Remedies, 28 Mich. L. Rev. 637 (1930).

[3] A claim for refund is necessary before the federal courts will entertain a suit for the recovery of certain federal taxes. Pacific Mut. Life Ins. Co. v. United States, 44 F. (2d) 887 (Ct. Cl. 1930). But the federal courts do not always adhere to the same rule when state taxes are involved, although some cases tend to apply the same rule to both types of cases. See Pender County v. Garysburg, 50 F. (2d) 732 (C. C. A. 4th 1931). State courts sometimes require exhausting administrative remedies first. See Bell County Coke & Impr. Co. v. Pineville, 19 Ky. L. Rep. 789, 42 S. W. 92 (1897).

[4] Some courts have taken the view that a declaration should not be given in disputes involving the invalidity of taxing statutes, because their validity could be settled when proceedings were instituted to collect the tax. This reasoning would not apply to instances of summary action to collect, and will doubtless be relaxed as the bench and bar become more accustomed to the use of the declaratory judgment. See Borchard, The Declaratory Judgment — A Needed Procedural Reform, 28 Yale L. J. 1, 105, 114 (1918); Judicial Relief for Peril and Insecurity, 45 Harv. L. Rev. 793 (1932); and The Declaratory Judgment.

[5] "No suit for the purpose of restraining the assessment or collection of any tax shall be maintained in any court." 26 U. S. C., sec. 154 (1926). See note, 44 Harv. L. Rev. 1221 (1931).

[6] Lipke v. Lederer, 259 U. S. 557, 42 Sup. Ct. Rep. 549, 66 L. Ed. 1061 (1922).

[7] E. g., Peerless Woolen Mills v. Rose, 28 F. (2d) 661 (C. C. A. 5th 1928) (collection by distraint enjoined during pendency of appeal to Board of Tax Appeals). For a discussion of these cases and this statute, see Graham v. Dupont, 262 U. S. 234, 43 Sup. Ct. Rep. 567, 67 L. Ed. 965 (1923); note, 38 Yale L. J. 122 (1928); 4 Pomeroy, Equity Jurisprudence (2d ed., 1919), sec. 1849. The Supreme Court seems to have been influenced somewhat in its interpretation of this statute by the conceptions developed in connection with 28 U. S. C., sec. 384 (1926). See note 9.

valid.[8] The federal courts may, however, enjoin the collection of
state taxes unless the state law provides for a "plain, adequate, and
complete remedy . . . at law,"[9] even though the state statutes [10]
expressly forbid the state courts to enjoin the collection of state
taxes.[11] Injunctions by the federal courts will issue if no refund law
is applicable,[12] and even if one is applicable it must be adequate.
An empty treasury and many outstanding refund warrants will
justify injunctive relief.[13] States wishing to avoid the interference of
federal injunction in the state tax field must, therefore, provide a
really adequate system of tax refunds or recovery.[14]

A few states specifically authorize the use of the injunction in tax
cases,[15] whereas in others its use in certain types of cases is impliedly
authorized.[16] But statutes authorizing or regulating the use of injunctions in revenue cases usually refer to illegal taxes and practically never to unconstitutional taxes or taxing statutes; and the
statutes of very few states have defined the term "illegal taxes" to

[8] Pollock v. Farmers' Loan & Trust Co., 157 U. S. 429, 15 Sup. Ct. Rep. 673, 39
L. Ed. 759 (1895).

[9] 28 U. S. C., sec. 384 (1926): "Suits in equity shall not be sustained in any court
of the United States in any case where a plain, adequate, and complete remedy may
be had at law." The remedy must be adequate in a federal court. See 37 Yale L. J.
378 (1928); 38 *id*. 122 (1928). On this statute see Hopkins v. Southern Cal. Tel.
Co., 275 U. S. 393, 48 Sup. Ct. Rep. 180, 72 L. Ed. 329 (1928); Dawson v. Kentucky Distilleries & Warehouse Co., 255 U. S. 288, 41 Sup. Ct. Rep. 272, 65 L. Ed.
638 (1921) (both enjoining state taxing authorities); Henrietta Mills v. Rutherford
County, 281 U. S. 121, 50 Sup. Ct. Rep. 270, 74 L. Ed. 737 (1930); Port Angeles
Western R. R. v. Clallam County, 44 F. (2d) 28 (C. C. A. 9th 1930) (both denying injunctive relief). See also Mathews v. Rodgers, 284 U. S. 521, 52 Sup. Ct. Rep.
217, 76 L. Ed. 447 (1932); Stratton v. St. L. & S. W. Ry., 284 U. S. 530, 52 Sup.
Ct. Rep. 222, 76 L. Ed. 465 (1932).

[10] Ariz. Code (Struckmeyer, 1928), sec. 3186; Ky. Stat. (Carroll, 1930), secs.
4214a-6, 4214b-8 (certain license taxes "on any ground"); S. C. Civ. Code (1922),
sec. 511; S. D. Rev. Code (1919), sec. 6826.

[11] Taylor v. Louisville & N. R. R., 88 Fed. 350 (C. C. A. 6th 1898); Freund, Administrative Powers over Persons and Property, 239 (1928).

[12] Graniteville Mfg. Co. v. Query, 44 F. (2d) 64 (D. C. S. C. 1930).

[13] Stewart Dry Goods Co. v. Lewis, 53 Sup. Ct. Rep. 68 (1933).

[14] See Field, Memorandum on Some Recent Decisions Relating to the Restraint
and Recovery of Illegal Taxes in Iowa, 16 Iowa L. Rev. 381 (1931).

[15] Ark. Dig. Stat. (Crawford & Moses, 1921), sec. 5786 ("illegal or unauthorized
taxes"); Minn. Stat. (Mason, 1927), sec. 2069 (levy in "excess of amount authorized
by law" irrespective of adequacy of legal remedy); Miss. Code Ann. (Hemming-
way, 1927), secs. 304–06; Wyo. Comp. Stat. Ann. (1920), secs. 6302–06. See also
the statutory method of challenging taxes by court action, in Fla. Comp. Laws
(1927), sec. 5082.

[16] Mont. Rev. Code (Choate, 1921), sec. 2268 (but see First Natl. Bank v. Sanders County, 85 Mont. 450 (1929); Neb. Comp. Stat. (1929), sec. 77-1923; Ohio
Gen. Code (Page, 1931), sec. 12075; Utah Comp. Laws (1917), sec. 6093; Wash.
Comp. Stat. (Remington, 1922), sec. 955. Okla. Comp. Stat. Ann. (Bunn, 1921),
sec. 420, authorizing injunction, has apparently been modified by secs. 9970–71. See
Duling v. First Natl. Bank of Weleetka, 71 Okla. 98, 175 Pac. 554 (1918); Carpenter v. Shaw, 280 U. S. 363, 50 Sup. Ct. Rep. 121, 74 L. Ed. 478 (1930).

include taxes unauthorized by any law.[17] Only under the void ab initio theory of the effect of an unconstitutional statute [18] can taxes levied under invalid statutes be brought within this definition. Courts have tended to define illegal taxes as something more than merely irregular taxes; they have often refused to grant an injunction to restrain the collection of the latter when they might have been willing to restrain the collection of the former.[19]

Statutes sometimes forbid the use of injunction in tax cases, and such a prohibition is valid if action to recover the tax can be brought after it has been paid.[20]

In the absence of statute, and many states are without statutes on this subject, the law with respect to the issuance of injunctions in tax cases is in "hopeless confusion." [21] This is often true within a single jurisdiction. Some courts are slow to interfere and insist on the presence of very clear equitable grounds before acting; others are much more ready to restrain the revenue-collecting officers and require only a flimsy showing of conventional grounds of equity jurisdiction.

The existence of an adequate remedy at law is usually, but not always, sufficient to deprive the petitioner of injunctive relief.[22] As to what constitutes an adequate remedy at law, courts differ. Thus, injunctive relief may be denied by some courts on the ground that the taxes, if paid, can be recovered in a subsequent action. Whether the recovery statute permits the recovery of interest is seldom a factor, although a few recent cases have emphasized this as an important item.[23]

That the anticipated legal remedy is not always as adequate as the taxpayer is led to think appears from a situation that arose in

[17] E. g., Mich. Comp. Laws (1929), sec. 3469, subd. 1.

[18] For a summary of the various views of the effect of an unconstitutional statute, see Chapter 1.

[19] The following Iowa cases illustrate the distinction between irregular and illegal taxes; the latter are treated as void, and are therefore enjoinable; the former are not: Conway v. Younkin, 28 Iowa 295 (1869); First Natl. Bank v. Anderson, 196 Iowa 587, 192 N. W. 6 (1923), rev. on other grounds, 269 U. S. 341, 46 Sup. Ct. Rep. 135, 70 L. Ed. 295 (1926); Franklin Motor Co. v. Alber, 196 Iowa 88, 194 N. W. 297 (1923); Lamont Sav. Bank v. Luther, 200 Iowa 180, 204 N. W. 430 (1925); Wilcox v. Miner, 201 Iowa 476, 205 N. W. 847 (1926).

[20] Casco Co. v. Thurston County, 163 Wash. 666, 2 Pac. (2d) 677 (1931).

[21] 4 Cooley, Taxation (4th ed., 1924), secs. 1640–69. For ambiguities under statutes, see N. C. Code Ann. (Michie, 1931), secs. 858, 7880 (157), 7880 (189), 7979.

[22] 4 Cooley, Taxation, sec. 1647, note 74. Injunctive relief is often denied where taxes can be collected only by suit. Wall v. Borgen, 152 Minn. 106, 188 N. W. 159 (1922). But injunction lies even in these jurisdictions if enforcement provisions are drastic. Fairley v. Duluth, 150 Minn. 374, 185 N. W. 390 (1921).

[23] Hopkins v. Southern Cal. Tel. Co., supra, note 9; Educational Films Corp. v. Ward, 282 U. S. 379, 51 Sup. Ct. Rep. 170, 75 L. Ed. 400 (1931); Nutt v. Ellerbee, 56 F. (2d) 1058 (D. C. S. D. 1932).

Indiana a few years ago. A federal district court refused to enjoin the collection of a state tax because the statutory provision permitted recovery by action in the state courts; some months later the taxpayer was turned out of the state courts empty-handed because the statutes did not cover his case.[24] All that remains to complete the picture of confusion is for a court to refuse to enjoin collection because of the adequacy of the legal remedy, and then for the same court to refuse to entertain an action for recovery on the ground that an injunction should have been sought.

The situation involved in Brinkerhoff-Faris Trust and Savings Co. v. Hill [25] was almost as bad as this. In that case a taxpayer, alleging systematic discrimination in assessment, sought to enjoin collection. The decisional law in the state had, for six years, been that the tax commission had no power to correct discriminations of this kind, and the commission had regularly refused to entertain applications for such corrections. The injunction was denied on the ground that the tax commission had this power, and that the taxpayer should have applied for this administrative remedy before seeking an injunction. When the taxpayer turned to the commission, he found that the period fixed by statute for presenting applications had expired and that it was too late for him to obtain the administrative relief to which the court had referred him. The Supreme Court of the United States decided, however, that this was too much of an imposition upon the taxpayer. Thus it may be that some relief from the present confusion will be found by utilizing the fourteenth amendment to extend federal supervision over the adequacy of the taxpayer's remedy. It should, in fairness, be pointed out in this connection that suits for recovery of taxes are not often barred merely on the ground that injunctive relief has not previously been sought.[26]

The adequacy of the legal means of recovering taxes is, then, important not only for the taxpayer who has already paid his tax and is seeking to recover it but also for the one who is seeking to prevent collection in the first instance. With reference to recovery, the states can be divided into two groups, depending on whether they provide for recovery under a statutory system or leave the subject as at common law.

II. TAX REFUNDS

Legislation for the return or the recovery of taxes has usually provided for one or more of four different types of procedure.

[24] Spring Valley Coal Co. v. State, 198 Ind. 620, 154 N. E. 380 (1926).
[25] 281 U. S. 673, 50 Sup. Ct. Rep. 451, 74 L. Ed. 1107 (1930).
[26] Salthouse v. Board of County Commrs., 115 Kan. 668, 224 Pac. 70 (1924); St. Johns Elec. Co. v. City of St. Augustine, 81 Fla. 588, 88 So. 387 (1921).

1. The legislature may provide for the refundment of specifically mentioned illegal taxes, without providing for the return of all illegal or unconstitutional taxes. Such statutes have been enacted at various times by both the federal and state governments.[27] In some states specific constitutional provisions require that refunds of this character must be made by general, not by special, law,[28] but a provision forbidding refund by private act of money *lawfully* paid into the treasury has been held not to apply to the return of taxes *unlawfully* paid into the treasury.[29]

2. Administrative refunds are sometimes provided for by statute. But it is difficult, in some instances, to tell whether statutes governing administrative correction of errors in assessment and levy, and providing for administrative refunds of illegally exacted taxes, apply to taxes collected under invalid statutes.[30] Some courts construe such statutes quite narrowly against the taxpayer.[31] For instance, in Kentucky, a statute providing that "when it shall appear to the auditor that money has been paid into the treasury for taxes when no such taxes were in fact due, he shall issue his warrant on the treasury for such money so improperly paid, in behalf of the person who paid the same" [32] has been held to afford the taxpayer no relief.[33] The decision, however, has been partially corrected by subsequent legislative enactment.[34]

The constitutionality of statutes providing for tax refunds has sometimes been questioned. However, they have been sustained even when they cover taxes paid voluntarily and without protest.[35] A

[27] Examples of such statutes can be found in Colo. Comp. Laws (1921), sec. 7513; Ind. Ann. Stat. (Burns, 1926), sec. 14,380; Wis. Laws (1929), Chapter 365; Fla. Gen. Laws (1929), Chapters 14, 542. That such statutes are valid, even though not limited to taxes paid under duress or protest, see Smith v. Tennessee Coal, Iron & R. R., 192 Ala. 129, 68 So. 865 (1915); Commercial Natl. Bank v. Board of Supervisors, 168 Iowa 501, 150 N. W. 704 (1915). See also Minneapolis Brewing Co. v. Bagley, 142 Minn. 16, 170 N. W. 704 (1919).

[28] Ky. Const., sec. 59 (14), "to refund money legally paid into the state treasury."

[29] Commonwealth v. Ferries Co., 120 Va. 827, 92 S. E. 804 (1917), construing Va. Const., sec. 63, cl. 9.

[30] For example of such statutes, see Ga. Code Ann. (Michie, 1926), secs. 1102–04; Ind. Ann. Stat. (Burns, 1926), secs. 14,251, 14,376–79; Md. Ann. Code (Bagby, 1924), sec. 10.

[31] Security Natl. Bank v. Twinde, 52 S. D. 352, 217 N. W. 542 (1928), construing S. D. Comp. Laws (1929), sec. 6813. Some courts construe these statutes more favorably to the taxpayer. Brenner v. Los Angeles, 160 Cal. 72, 116 Pac. 397 (1911).

[32] Ky. Stat. (Carroll, 1930), sec. 162. For a discussion and summary of the cases arising under this statute, see Craig v. Security Producing & Distilling Co., 189 Ky. 565, 225 S. W. 729 (1920); Craig v. Renaker, 201 Ky. 576, 257 S. W. 1018 (1923); Coleman v. Inland Gas Corp., 231 Ky. 637, 21 S. W. (2d) 1030 (1929).

[33] Coleman v. Inland Gas Corp., *supra*, note 32.

[34] Ky. Stat. (Carroll, 1930), secs. 4214a-6, 4214b-8.

[35] Commonwealth v. Ferries Co., *supra*, note 29; People ex rel. Eckerson v. Board

municipality may make provision for the return of illegally collected taxes under its power to pay its debts, even in the absence of an authorizing statute.[36]

3. Courts of claims have been established in a few states and in the national government, and in a number of states general trial or other courts have been given claims jurisdiction. Such jurisdiction is usually restricted to cases involving claims arising out of contract, and the tendency has been to construe this jurisdiction narrowly.

Claims for illegally collected taxes have been treated as coming within the phrase "implied contract," which is sometimes covered by the statute, on the theory that the government is under an obligation to return money held by it to which it is not entitled in good conscience,[37] but this view is not accepted by all courts.[38] Express grants of jurisdiction over claims arising out of illegal tax collections may, of course, be made to designated courts,[39] and the United States Court of Claims can entertain this type of claim on the ground that it involves an act of Congress,[40] although if the court wished to be very technical it might apply the void ab initio doctrine and hold that the statute never had any legal existence and that therefore it was not "involved" in the case.

Another type of statute which at first glance might seem to offer some hope to the taxpayer is that authorizing the presentation of claims against counties or other local governmental units to the governing board, provision being made at the same time for the allowance of such claims by these boards. But unless there is a specific provision to that effect, these statutes do not cover claims

of Education, 126 App. Div. 414, 110 N. Y. S. 769 (1908); Adams v. Board of Supervisors, 154 N. Y. 619, 49 N. E. 144 (1898).

[36] Blum Co. v. Town of Hastings, 76 Fla. 7, 79 So. 442 (1918). State constitutional provisions sometimes constitute a bar to a refund of money paid into the treasury, because such moneys can be paid out only by appropriation. Thus, for example, money illegally exacted as rental for a lease could not be returned by judicial order, mandamus being denied. McAdoo Petroleum Corp. v. Pankey, 35 N. M. 246, 294 Pac. 322 (1930). Funds which have not been covered into the treasury are not so treated, however, and if they are held "in suspension" or placed in funds devoted to specific purposes, recovery by judicial order may be effected.

[37] Ford Motor Co. v. State, 59 N. D. 792, 231 N. W. 883 (1930); Welsbach v. State, 206 Cal. 556, 275 Pac. 436 (1929). But cf. Sinclair, Owens & Brown v. State, 69 N. C. 47 1873) ($50 held too small to invoke claims jurisdiction of Supreme Court).

[38] Spring Valley Coal Co. v. State, *supra,* note 24; Flower v. State, 143 App. Div. 871, 128 N. Y. S. 208 (1911).

[39] United States v. Hvoslef, 237 U. S. 1, 35 Sup. Ct. Rep. 459, 59 L. Ed. 813 (1915); Van Antwerp v. New York, 218 N. Y. 422, 113 N. E. 497 (1916).

[40] Dooley v. United States, 182 U. S. 222, 21 Sup. Ct. Rep. 762, 45 L. Ed. 1074 (1901). The Court of Customs and Patent Appeals hears many tax cases, and section 516 of the Tariff Act of 1930 provides an interesting series of remedies. See T. D. 46,124, and Baltimore Daily Record, Feb. 24, 1933, p. 5.

arising out of the payment of taxes levied under an invalid statute,[41] nor those arising out of illegal tax collections generally.[42]

4. An increasing number of states are providing by statute for suits against designated officers or governments to recover illegally collected taxes. These statutes are not always as comprehensive as they should be, but a number of states have now satisfactorily covered this subject.

Some states require that payment of the tax be made before questions touching its legality can be raised, and such statutes are strictly construed by some courts.[43] Provisions for administrative refunds do not exclude court actions unless they specifically so provide.[44]

Under these statutes actions to recover taxes are generally brought in the general trial courts,[45] although in some cases the probate courts are designated.[46] Administrative officers are authorized to make the refunds upon receipt of a certificate or copy of the judgment of the particular court.[47] Appeals on questions involving the constitutionality or application of the recovery statute may be taken as in other cases.[48] Judgments of the inferior court may not be assailed collaterally if no appeal has been taken within the time permitted by statute, even though a mistake may have been made as to the constitutionality of a statute.[49] The Supreme Court of the United States has indicated that it will not interfere with this rule forbidding collateral attack,[50] although the rule is perhaps to be confined to *final* decrees or judgments,[51] and it is very doubtful

[41] Boyer Bros. v. Board of Commrs., 87 Colo. 275, 288 Pac. 408 (1930).

[42] Bradley v. City of Eau Claire, 56 Wis. 168, 14 N. W. 10 (1882); White v. Smith, 117 Ala. 232, 23 So. 525 (1897); contra, Bibbins v. Clark & Co., 90 Iowa 230, 57 N. W. 884, 59 N. W. 290 (1894).

[43] See Cent. Trust Co. v. Howard, 275 Mass. 153, 175 N. E. 461 (1931).

[44] Blanchard v. Detroit, 253 Mich. 491, 235 N. W. 230 (1931). See Shriver v. Woodbine Sav. Bk., 285 U. S. 467, 52 Sup. Ct. Rep. 430, 76 L. Ed. 884 (1932).

[45] Mont. Rev. Code (Choate, 1921), sec. 2269; Ohio Gen. Code (Page, 1931), secs. 5398, 12,075; Wyo. Comp. Stat. Ann. (1920), secs. 6302–06. See also Ariz. Code (Struckmeyer, 1928), sec. 3136; Iowa Code (1927), sec. 7396 (inheritance taxes); S. D. Comp. Laws (1929), sec. 6826.

[46] Ala. Code (Michie, 1928), secs. 3142–46; Mo. Rev. Stat. (1929), sec. 9981.

[47] N. Y. Cons. Laws (Cahill, 1930), Chapter 61, sec. 296; N. D. Comp. Laws (Supp. 1925), sec. 2346b-11; S. C. Civ. Code (1922), sec. 511; Colo. Ann. Stat. (Mills, 1930), sec. 6343. In the absence of court action, some states require the administrative officer to obtain the certificate from a law officer, such as the attorney-general. See, as to legacy and succession taxes, Mass. Gen. Laws (1921), Chapter 58, sec. 27.

[48] Blan v. Hollywood Realty Co., 218 Ala. 1, 118 So. 257 (1927).

[49] Beck v. State, 196 Wis. 242, 219 N. W. 197 (1928), cert. denied, 278 U. S. 639, 49 Sup. Ct. Rep. 34, 73 L. Ed. 555 (1928); cf. Hanchett Bond Co. v. Morris, 143 Okla. 110, 287 Pac. 1025 (1930).

[50] Manley v. Park, 187 U. S. 547, 23 Sup. Ct. Rep. 208, 47 L. Ed. 296 (1903).

[51] Manley v. Park involved a final judgment.

whether this "hands off" policy would be followed in the case of temporary orders, such as those entered under inheritance tax statutes, ordering tentative payment or deposit of securities.[52]

New York, Iowa, and Mississippi have held that recovery statutes applying to taxes "erroneously or illegally" paid or to taxes for stamps "erroneously affixed" permit the recovery of illegal or unconstitutional taxes.[53] Arkansas, on the other hand, has held that taxes paid under an invalid statute may not be recovered under a statute relating to taxes "erroneously assessed," but that only illegal taxes may be recovered under this provision.[54]

The courts of those states that have statutes permitting recovery of money paid under mistake of law are not favorably disposed toward the extension of these statutes to cover taxes,[55] although recovery may be permitted under them if taxes are expressly mentioned.[56]

The tendency to construe tax recovery statutes narrowly against the taxpayer is also illustrated by decisions restricting recovery to particular kinds of taxes, such as property, local, or state taxes, as the case may be, even though the statutes do not state that no other

[52] A decision handed down by a New York surrogate, refusing to vacate an order fixing a maximum tax and ordering a deposit of bonds as security, is unsatisfactory. See In re Burrough's Estate, 137 Misc. Rep. 844, 244 N. Y. S. 640 (1930). The problem in this type of case is, of course, whether the bonds shall be returned immediately, if the tax is presumably invalid under the Farmers' Loan & Trust case, or whether the taxpayer must wait until the contingency occurs before getting back the bonds. It is inconceivable that the bonds would be retained permanently by the state when the taxes which they were to secure could never be collected. In re Muir's Estate, 139 Misc. Rep. 434, 248 N. Y. S. 143 (1931), is a more convincing decision, in view of the time involved, and visualizes the possibility of not collecting the tax when the contingency occurs.

[53] Matter of O'Berry, 179 N. Y. 285, 72 N. E. 109 (1904); People ex rel. Noyes v. Sohmer, 81 Misc. Rep. 522, 143 N. Y. S. 475, 159 App. Div. 929 (1913), same 210 N. Y. 619, 104 N. E. 1138 (1914); Commercial Natl. Bank v. Board of Supervisors, *supra*, note 27; Pearl River County v. Lacey Lumber Co., 124 Miss. 85, 86 So. 755 (1920); Boyer Bros. v. Board of Commrs., *supra*, note 41. So, too, "wrongfully or illegally collected." See Security Natl. Bank v. Twinde, *supra*, note 31. Under U. S. Rev. Stat., sec. 3220, "erroneously or illegally" was assumed to include unconstitutionally collected taxes. See Chesebrough v. United States, 192 U. S. 253, 24 Sup. Ct. Rep. 262, 48 L. Ed. 432 (1904).

[54] Walton v. Arkansas County, 153 Ark. 285, 239 S. W. 1054 (1922).

[55] Simpson v. New Orleans, 133 La. 384, 63 So. 57 (1913) (construing La. Civ. Code, Merrick, 1925, sec. 2301); Wingerter v. City and County of San Francisco, 134 Cal. 547, 66 Pac. 730 (1901); cf. Factors & Traders' Ins. Co. v. New Orleans, 25 La. Ann. 454 (1873) (holding, on rehearing, that a "natural" obligation to pay taxes existed under an invalid law); Dupre v. City of Opelousas, 161 La. 272, 108 So. 479 (1926) (construing La. Rev. Code of Prac., Marr, 1927, art. 18). On secs. 2301, 2302, and 2303 of the Code, see also State ex rel. Newgass v. New Orleans, 38 La. Ann. 119 (1886); Sims v. Village of Mer Rouge, 141 La. 91, 74 So. 706 (1917).

[56] Norwood v. Goldsmith, 168 Ala. 224, 53 So. 84 (1910); Ga. Code Ann. (Michie, 1926), sec. 4317.

taxes are to be included.[57] The liberal interpretation customary in the application of remedial legislation has not been characteristic of the courts' attitude toward tax recovery statutes. Some restrictions, of course, are justifiable — for instance, the denial of relief for trivial irregularities in the assessment, levy, or collection, and the requirement that it be shown that the tax was not equitably due.[58]

The party against whom the action must be brought varies. It may be the state, county, city, or other territorial subdivision of the state for whom the tax was collected.[59] Or the statute may provide for suit against the collecting officer, and may or may not make satisfactory provision for paying the judgment if the taxpayer is successful. In Michigan, however, action against the officer is expressly forbidden.[60] When a judgment has been obtained in accordance with the statutory provision, mandamus will lie to compel the designated disbursing officer to make the proper payment.[61]

The substantive rules of relief thus far considered have all assumed legislative intervention in aid of the taxpayer. If the statute expressly covers his case, and if he complies exactly with it, return of his payment may be obtained. Sometimes these statutes dispense with the common law requirements of protest and payment under compulsion.[62] The statute in such a case furnishes the only standard with which the taxpayer can be held to comply. Previously existing common law remedies are not taken away merely because of a recovery statute; but the statute may, and sometimes does, provide that the statutory remedy shall be exclusive.[63] It has been decided, however, that, so far as citizens of other states are concerned, even a state statute of this kind cannot cut off the common law remedy against the tax collector, if such nonresidents wish to pursue this remedy in the federal courts.[64]

[57] O'Brien v. County of Colusa, 67 Cal. 503, 8 Pac. 37 (1885); Spring Valley Coal Co. v. State, *supra*, note 24; see Prescott v. City of Memphis, 154 Tenn. 462, 285 S. W. 587 (1926). On construction of statutes see note, 94 Am. St. Rep. 439 (1904).

[58] Board of Commrs. v. Armstrong, 91 Ind. 528 (1883); Carton v. Board of Commrs., 10 Wyo. 416, 69 Pac. 1013 (1902).

[59] See the elaborate provisions for joining parties in Wyo. Comp. Stat. Ann. (1920), secs. 6302–06. See also for statutes governing suit, Mont. Rev. Code (Choate, 1921), sec. 2269; Ohio Gen. Code (Page, 1931), secs. 5398, 12,075; Neb. Comp. Stat. (1929), sec. 77-1923, Part 2.

[60] Mich. Comp. Laws (1929), sec. 3748.

[61] Allgood v. Sloss-Sheffield Steel & Iron Co., 196 Ala. 500, 71 So. 724 (1916); Blan v. Hollywood Realty Co., *supra*, note 48.

[62] Freund, *supra*, note 11, at 567; Miss. Code Ann. (1930), sec. 3276. See Adams v. Board of Supervisors, *supra*, note 35; 3 Cooley, Taxation (4th ed., 1924), sec. 1278.

[63] S. C. Civ. Code (1922), sec. 513; Utah Comp. Laws (1917), sec. 6096. See Bank of Holyrood v. Kottmann, 132 Kan. 593, 296 Pac. 357 (1931).

[64] International Paper Co. v. Burrill, 260 Fed. 664 (D. Mass. 1919).

III. TAX RECOVERY

The generally stated rule in the absence of statute is that illegally collected taxes may not be recovered unless they are paid under compulsion and under protest.[65] It should be noted that a similar doctrine is applicable to payments made under compulsion in transactions between private parties.[66] The rule applies to taxes generally,[67] including special assessments[68] and illegal, as well as unconstitutional, taxes.[69] This rule covers taxes paid under statutes imposing taxes directly and statutes providing for the organization of taxing units.[70]

The Georgia court stated the attitude of many courts when it said that three elements are essential and must concur to maintain an action to recover an illegal tax payment: (1) the tax must have been collected without authority; (2) the money must have been received by the government; (3) payment must have been under duress.[71] Protest is not stressed as an essential; nor is it essential in the cases involving payments made under duress by one private individual to another.[72]

Little attention has been given in judicial opinions to the question whether the rule should be the same in tax cases as it is in cases of dealings between private individuals.[73] Courts have been unwilling to formulate different rules for the two types of situations, and although some of them manifest a disposition to be more lenient toward the taxpayer than toward the ordinary payer because of the inequality of the parties, the majority of courts are anything but lenient toward him.[74]

[65] See notes (1927), 48 A. L. R. 1381; 74 A. L. R. 1301 (1931). A leading case dealing with illegally, though not unconstitutionally, collected taxes, is Elliott v. Swartwout, 10 Pet. 137, 9 L. Ed. 373 (U. S. 1836). Indirect recovery, as by set-off, is not permitted either. See a recent case discussing this rule, State v. Canfield Oil Co., 34 Ohio App. 267, 171 N. E. 111 (1930); note, 41 A. L. R. 1110 (1926). But see N. C. Code Ann. (Michie, 1927), sec. 7880 (157) (tax due is debt for purposes of set-off).

[66] See Keener, Quasi Contracts (1893), Chapter 10; Chapter 9.

[67] No recovery: Commissioners of Town of Thomson v. Norris, 62 Ga. 538 (1879). Recovery: Matheson v. Town of Mazomanie, 20 Wis. 191 (1865); Fecheimer Bros. & Co. v. Louisville, 84 Ky. 306, 2 S. W. 65 (1886). See Board of Council of Harrodsburg v. Renfro, 22 Ky. L. Rep. 806, 58 S. W. 795 (1900).

[68] Dexter v. Boston, 176 Mass. 247, 57 N. E. 379 (1900); Natl. Rockland Bank v. Boston, 296 Fed. 743 (D. Mass. 1924).

[69] Elliott v. Swartwout, 10 Pet. 137, 9 L. Ed. 373 (U. S. 1836).

[70] Couch v. Kansas City, 120 Mo. 436, 30 S. W. 117 (1895). See Chapter 3.

[71] First Natl. Bk. of Americus v. Mayor, 68 Ga. 119, 122 (1881).

[72] Cf. Doll v. Earle, 59 N. Y. 638 (1874); Flower v. Lance, 59 N. Y. 603 (1875); Ga. Code Ann. (Michie, 1926), sec. 4317.

[73] Chicago v. Klinkert, 94 Ill. App. 524 (1900); Gould v. Board of Commrs., 76 Minn. 379, 79 N. W. 303 (1899).

[74] In re Burrough's Estate, 137 Misc. Rep. 844, 853, 244 N. Y. S. 640, 646

Several reasons have been advanced in support of the rule denying recovery of taxes paid voluntarily and without protest.

A. The Plaintiff Should Have Resisted Payment of the Tax

This does not ordinarily mean forcible physical resistance (although one may have some doubts on this score after reading the cases on voluntary payment) but that the plaintiff has invoked preventive or defensive relief at some earlier stage.[75] Not all courts deny recovery on this ground,[76] nor on the ground that administrative remedies should first have been exhausted,[77] but with respect to the latter some courts take a different view.[78] Whether this argument should be considered weighty depends largely upon the effectiveness of such injunctive, declaratory, or defensive relief as is available. No general appraisal of the soundness of this reason can be made, therefore, without examining for each particular jurisdiction the status of these remedies. It is certainly true that preventive relief is so grudgingly given in some jurisdictions that to deny recovery on this ground would be most unfair.

B. Ignorance of the Law Not a Ground for Relief

As stated by the Iowa court, "the principle upon which courts refuse to relieve mistakes in law is, we suppose, the fact that the law presumes every man to be cognizant not only of what are its provisions in force, but how far they are valid and operative." [79] A much more satisfactory and frank statement of the attitude of the courts on this subject would be for them to say that they deem it inadvisable to afford relief in mistake-of-law cases even though the parties are ignorant of the law, as they generally are. Recovery is not denied on the basis of a person's ignorance or cognizance of the law. People are deemed ignorant of the law in these cases, and recovery is denied because of some actual or fancied reason of logic, precedent, or policy. Obviously, if a person *actually knew* that he

(1930), cites four cases of payments between private individuals to support a tax decision. But in Kentucky where recovery is allowed for mistake of law generally, recovery of taxes is permitted more readily than in most states. Spalding v. City of Lebanon, 156 Ky. 37, 160 S. W. 751 (1913); and cases cited note 80, *infra.*

[75] First Natl. Bank of Americus v. Mayor, 68 Ga. 119, 124 (1881); Braddock Iron Mining Co. v. Erskine, 155 Minn. 70, 192 N. W. 193 (1923).

[76] See cases cited in note 26, *supra.*

[77] Brenner v. Los Angeles, 160 Cal. 72, 116 Pac. 397 (1911); Aetna Ins. Co. v. City of New York, 153 N. Y. 331, 47 N. E. 593 (1897); Second Natl. Bank v. New York, 213 N. Y. 457, 107 N. E. 1039 (1915).

[78] Clarke v. County of Stearns, 66 Minn. 304, 69 N. W. 25 (1896).

[79] Kraft v. City of Keokuk, 14 Iowa 86, 87 (1862). See also Yates v. Royal Ins. Co., 200 Ill. 202, 206, 65 N. E. 726, 728 (1902).

was paying an illegal tax and nevertheless paid it without protest or compulsion, recovery would be denied.[80]

C. Only an Exercise of Legislative Power Can Authorize Repayment of Money Paid into Treasury

According to this view the courts cannot by judgment or decree order the payment of money from the treasury.[81] What a court is really saying when it adopts this reasoning is that it cannot grant recovery because it does not have the power finally to enforce judgment. This is true in case of action against the state without its consent, but it is not true if the action is against the collecting officer, unless the case is of such a nature that the court would hold it to be in substance an action against the state. If the money had not been covered into the treasury, action to recover it from a special fund would lie.[82]

This reasoning does not apply to actions against a local governmental unit. Judgments against these units are constantly being rendered, and even in the absence of a statute authorizing the action, the rendition of such a judgment is not considered a legislative act appropriating money from the municipal treasury.

D. Taxpayer Has Received the Benefits from the Government's Expenditure of Tax Money

According to one opinion a tax is

intended for immediate expenditure for the common good, and it would be unjust to require its repayment after it had been thus, in whole or in part, properly expended, which would often be the case if suit could be brought for its recovery without notice having been given at the time of payment; and there would be no bar against its insidious spring but the statute of limitations.[83]

This refers, of course, to that general benefit which every taxpayer receives from the maintenance of government.

A more direct benefit is illustrated in the license cases. Thus, in a liquor license case, one court said that "the great fact on which

[80] Bruner v. Stanton, 102 Ky. 459, 43 S. W. 411 (1897); Fecheimer Bros. & Co. v. Louisville, *supra*, note 67; cf. Garrison v. Tillinghast, 18 Cal. 404 (1861); Tripler v. City of New York, 125 N. Y. 617, 26 N. E. 721 (1891).

[81] Minneapolis Brewing Co. v. Village of Bagley, 142 Minn. 16, 170 N. W. 704 (1919); cf. McAdoo Petroleum Corp. v. Pankey, 35 N. M. 246, 294 Pac. 322 (1930).

[82] The courts tend to attach some importance to the fact of actually "covering" the money into the treasury. See McAdoo Petroleum Corp. v. Pankey, *supra*, note 81.

[83] Borough of Allentown v. Saeger, 20 Pa. St. 421 (1853). This case involved an illegal tax. See also Laredo v. Lowry, 4 Willson Tex. Civ. Cas. Ct. App. 320, 20 S. W. 89 (1892).

this case turns, in our judgment, is that Norris voluntarily paid the license to retail liquors, acted under it, and got the consideration in full for which it was paid." [84] Similarly, the Ohio court said that the plaintiff had "enjoyed the monopoly which these illegal ordinances were calculated to afford; and it is fair to presume, as in all such cases, that he has got back the money paid for his licenses from his customers, in the increased price of his commodities." [85] The immunity from prosecution enjoyed during the license period has also been stressed as a reason for denying relief in these cases.[86]

A more difficult situation arises if only a portion of the license period has expired when the licensing statute is declared invalid. Kentucky, under its general policy of permitting recovery of money paid under mutual mistake of law, would very likely permit the recovery of the amount of the payment apportionable to the unexpired term.[87] Recovery of part of the license money has been permitted where the statute was valid when the license was granted but was rendered invalid by a subsequent constitutional amendment.[88] Neither the void ab initio doctrine as to the effect of an invalid statute nor the usual doctrine concerning mistake of law is applicable in such a case. Recovery can therefore be permitted on the general equitable ground that it would be unfair for the government to keep the money when it had disabled itself from continuing the privilege granted to the licensee. The same result could be obtained in the case of a license granted under a statute declared invalid during the license period if the void ab initio doctrine were not applied. But the same factors of policy which cause courts to apply that doctrine in other cases would perhaps influence some courts to deny relief in this type of case, and such factors would be tucked under such phrases as "voluntary payment" or "paid without protest."

E. Taxpayer Only Nominally the Real Payer and Refuses to Refund Money to Those from Whom He Collected It

Recovery has been denied by some courts because the taxpayer had collected the amount of the tax from his customers and had manifested no intention of refunding it, or because it appeared im-

[84] Commissioners of Town of Thomson v. Norris, 62 Ga. 538, 541 (1879).

[85] Mays v. Cincinnati, 1 Ohio St. 269, 279 (1853); cf. Washington v. Barber, 5 Cranch C. C. 157, Fed. Cas. No. 17,224 (D. C. 1837).

[86] Kraft v. City of Keokuk, 14 Iowa 86 (1862).

[87] Spalding v. City of Lebanon, *supra*, note 74, seems to be a case permitting recovery of the payment for the unexpired period. For a discussion of many of the cases, pro and con, see Blum Co. v. Hastings, 76 Fla. 7, 79 So. 442 (1918).

[88] Allsman v. Oklahoma City, 21 Okla. 142, 95 Pac. 468 (1908).

practicable to refund it even if recovery from the government had been permitted.[89] When the facts warrant its application, this rule is fair, especially since the customer would be unable to recover in an action against the merchant, because of the general mistake-of-law rule.[90] His only opportunity to avoid paying the amount of the tax is to delay payment of the purchase price until the taxing statute is declared invalid, and then to get a set-off equal to the amount of the tax.[91] To formally protest and take a receipt for sales taxes would be too inconvenient even if the law permitted recovery of payments made with these formalities. In New York the taxpayer has been permitted to recover where he could be treated as the agent of the customer (the taxpayer being a broker), and was under a legal obligation to pay the amount over.[92] Banks and corporations are sometimes permitted to sue to recover taxes paid on behalf of shareholders when by law the bank is under a duty to pay the tax and retain a portion of dividends for that purpose.[93]

F. To Permit Recovery Would Disrupt Governmental Finance

This view is expressed in an early South Carolina case in which it is said that to encourage such actions "would be to remove the sense of security for past transactions, and to let loose a great deal of treacherous litigation" after the money had been expended on the assumption that it was lawfully acquired.[94] No doubt security for past transactions is as important in dealings between the government and the individual as between private parties. This objection could be removed, in large part, by proper budget arrangements, but at best it is a difficult problem in those states in which one or two collecting units disburse tax money to five or ten spending authorities. In the absence of a statutory system, however, and as things now stand in many jurisdictions, this reason for discouraging tax recovery actions is not to be dismissed lightly.

Opposed to this general view is the statement found in an Ohio opinion that "indeed, it would be difficult to find substantial reason for holding that one who observed the forms of the statute by paying his money into the treasury, should be left in a worse condition

[89] Standard Oil Co. v. Bollinger, 337 Ill. 353, 169 N.E. 236 (1929).

[90] See the discussion of these cases in Chapter 9. See the interesting discussion in Central Transfer Co. v. Commercial Oil Co., 45 F. (2d) 400 (E.D. Mo. 1930), denying injunctive relief to gasoline distributor who added tax to purchase price. See criticism of case in 31 Col. L. Rev. 888 (1931).

[91] Sinclair Ref. Co. v. Rosier, 104 Kan. 719, 180 Pac. 807 (1919).

[92] Van Antwerp v. New York, supra, note 39.

[93] Security Natl. Bk. v. Young, 55 F. (2d) 616 (C.C.A. 8th 1932).

[94] Robinson v. City of Charleston, 2 Rich. L. 317 (S.C. 1846); Coleman v. Inland Gas Corp., supra, note 32; Gould v. Board of Commrs., supra, note 73.

than one who treated the act at all times as a mere nullity." This opinion, it should be noted, does not state the rule for Ohio either, for Ohio follows the general common law rule unless it is abrogated by statute.[95]

Assuming that a tax has been paid under protest and under compulsion, action to recover it may, in the absence of statute, be brought by the taxpayer against the officer to whom the payment was made.[96] This action may take the form of a suit in equity to enjoin payment over to the government.[97] It may also be an action on the officer's bond,[98] or one for money had and received.[99] The officer is responsible in some states whether he retains the money or not, although there is great confusion in the cases as to the effect of payment over to the government.[100] Courts that disregard such payments argue that the officer committed the wrong; he, therefore, is to be held liable. The protest made at the time of payment is said to constitute notice to the officer that he should retain the money.[101] If he pays it over under such circumstances he does so at his own risk.

The federal government and some of the states have statutes compelling the officer to turn into the treasury any moneys collected by him.[102] Under these statutes [103] the officer's responsibility to the taxpayer is not always clear, although the moral obligation of the government to reimburse him may be.

[95] Catoir v. Watterson, 39 Ohio St. 319, 320 (1882).
[96] Scottish Union & Natl. Ins. Co. v. Herriott, 109 Iowa 606, 80 N. W. 665 (1899); White River Lumber Co. v. Elliott, 146 Ark. 551, 226 S. W. 164 (1920); note 48 A. L. R. 1395 (1927); Chapter 5. Payment to an agent of the defendant officer is sufficient to impose liability on the principal. International Paper Co. v. Burrill, 260 Fed. 664 (D. Mass. 1919).
[97] Standard Oil Co. v. Bollinger, *supra*, note 89.
[98] The Sonoma County Tax case, 13 Fed. 789 (C. C. D. Cal. 1882).
[99] Toy Natl. Bank v. Nelson, 38 F. (2d) 261 (D. C. N. D. Iowa 1930).
[100] See discussion in Elliott v. Swartwout, 10 Pet. 137, 9 L. Ed. 373 (U. S. 1836); International Paper Co. v. Burrill, *supra*, note 64; First Natl. Bank v. Norris, 113 Ark. 138, 167 S. W. 1104 (1914), note 11 L. R. A. (N. S.) 1104 (1908); 3 Cooley, Taxation (4th ed., 1924), sec. 1299.
[101] Tyler v. Dane County, 289 Fed. 843 (W. D. Wis. 1923). Some statutes provide that the officer shall retain the money until the dispute is settled. Neb. Comp. Stat., secs. 77-1923, 6018–19 (1929); Okla. Comp. Stat. Ann., secs. 9970–71 (Bunn, 1921).
[102] Massachusetts enacted such a statute as early as 1854. Mass. Acts and Res. 1854, Chapter 17. For the development of the federal law on this point see Freund, *supra*, note 11, at 242 et seq. See Ill. Rev. Stats. (Cahill, 1927), Chapter 127b, par. 35, officer to hold money 30 days if paid under protest, commented upon in Roxana Petroleum Corp. v. Bollinger, 54 F. (2d) 296 (C. C. A. 7th 1931).
[103] The reason for such statutes is quaintly expressed in Town of Cahaba v. Burnett, 34 Ala. 400, 404 (1859): "regarding the money as his own, he might be induced to adopt a style of living, or to dispense benefactions, not justified by his fortune." They guard also against too great delay in the receipt of the money by the government.

When statutory provision is made for actions against collecting officers, it is important that some means be clearly provided for substituting successors in office as defendants in case of the death of the original defendant.[104] Otherwise provisions for payment out of the treasury may be ineffective.[105]

Action need not be brought against the officer but may, as previously indicated, be brought against the city or county for whom the officer acted.[106] But the taxpayer must choose between the two. He cannot sue both in independent actions.[107] In an action against the municipality, it is not necessary to join the collecting officer, for he is merely the defendant's agent.[108] On this theory the municipality could not plead in defense that the officer still retained the money, and there is some authority for this view.[109] In Iowa, however, mandamus to compel a refund by the officer is said to be the proper course in such a case.[110] And on the agency theory it is difficult to explain the New York holding that the city is liable despite the fact that the collector is neither appointed nor controlled by the city.[111] Furthermore, Texas apparently holds that, if the taxes were for the use of another governmental unit, the city is not liable even though its officers made the collections.[112]

One case permits suit to be brought for an accounting and for recovery of unexpended balance after the project has been abandoned for which the tax was collected.[113]

The city cannot plead that it has expended the money for public improvements nor, in many states, that it has paid it over to some other governmental agency.[114] Neither is it a valid defense that the

[104] For statutes in which this is done, see Ala. Code (Michie, 1928), sec. 3144; Ky. Stat. (Carroll, 1930), secs. 4214a-6, 4214b-8.

[105] Smietanka v. Indiana Steel Co., 257 U.S. 1, 42 Sup. Ct. Rep. 1, 66 L. Ed. 99 (1921). See the discussion of this case in Freund, supra, note 11, at 567–68.

[106] Tyler v. Dane County, supra, note 101; St. Johns Elec. Co. v. City of St. Augustine, supra, note 26; International Paper Co. v. Burrill, supra, note 64. See also Scottish Union & Natl. Ins. Co. v. Herriott, supra, note 96.

[107] Ware v. Percival, 61 Me. 391 (1873); Raleigh v. Salt Lake City, 17 Utah 130, 53 Pac. 574 (1898).

[108] Salthouse v. Board of Commrs., 115 Kan. 668, 224 Pac. 70 (1924). See the Wyoming statutes cited note 59, supra, for provisions on joining government and officers.

[109] County of Galveston v. Galveston Gas Co., 72 Tex. 509, 10 S.W. 583 (1889). (no proof of payment over required); Bank v. New York, 43 N.Y. 184 (1870) (payment over presumed).

[110] Eyerly v. Jasper County, 72 Iowa 149, 33 N.W. 609 (1887).

[111] Bank v. New York, supra, note 109.

[112] County of Galveston v. Galveston Gas Co., supra, note 109.

[113] New Smyrna Inlet Dist. v. Esch, 103 Fla. 24, 137 So. 1, 138 So. 49 (1931).

[114] Pearl River County v. Lacey Lumber Co., 124 Miss. 85, 86 So. 755 (1921); Ward v. Commissioners of Love County, 253 U.S. 17, 40 Sup. Ct. Rep. 419, 64 L. Ed. 751 (1920); Hodgins v. Board of County Commrs., supra, note 2.

city has exceeded its constitutional debt limit, inasmuch as an obligation to repay illegally collected taxes is said not to be within the meaning of the term "debt" as it is used in such constitutional provisions.[115]

The state, in the absence of statute, is not liable to suit in either the state [116] or the federal [117] courts. But a state may consent to suit in its own courts and also, it appears, in the federal courts; but it may confine its consent to actions in the state courts alone.[118] In Tyler v. Dane County,[119] a distinction was drawn between an action against the treasurer in his official capacity and one against him in his individual capacity. The court suggested that if the judgment would have to be paid out of public funds the suit should be considered as prohibited by the eleventh amendment, because it would then be against him in his official representative capacity. On the other hand, it has been suggested that if the taxing statute is unconstitutional, the "stripping doctrine" should apply, that is, the officer would be treated as a private individual acting without the authority or protection of law.[120] Thus, if personal property has been seized for taxes under an invalid statute, it may be recovered from the officer in an action of detinue, and this is not considered an action against the state or against the officer in his official capacity.[121]

With respect to the period of limitations during which tax recovery actions must be brought, the tendency is to make it short.[122] Some statutes provide for as short a period as thirty days. Others

[115] Thomas v. Burlington, 69 Iowa 140, 28 N.W. 480 (1886).

[116] Lord & Polk v. State Board of Agriculture, 111 N.C. 135, 15 S.E. 1032 (1892).

[117] Hans v. Louisiana, 134 U.S. 1, 10 Sup. Ct. Rep. 504, 33 L. Ed. 842 (1890); Tyler v. Dane County, supra, note 101. In Scottish Union & Natl. Ins. Co. v. Herriott, supra, note 96, a demurrer was filed by the officer in his official capacity, and it was sustained. On the eleventh amendment see Hyneman, Judicial Interpretation of the Eleventh Amendment, 2 Ind. L. J. 371 (1927).

[118] Smith v. Reeves, 178 U.S. 436, 20 Sup. Ct. Rep. 919, 44 L. Ed. 1140 (1900).

[119] Supra, note 101. On the "stripping doctrine" see Bonnett v. Vallier, 136 Wis. 193, 116 N.W. 885 (1908); Chapter 5.

[120] Scottish Union Natl. Ins. Co. v. Herriott, supra, note 96.

[121] Poindexter v. Greenhow, 114 U.S. 270, 5 Sup. Ct. Rep. 903, 962, 29 L. Ed. 185 (1884).

[122] Ala. Code (Michie, 1928), sec. 3146 (6 years); Iowa Code (1927), sec. 7396 (5 years); Ky. Stat. (Carroll, 1930), secs. 4214a-6, 4214b-8 (2 years, license taxes); N.Y. Cons. Laws (Cahill, 1930), sec. 296-3 (3 years after judgment entered, application must be made for refund); N.C. Code Ann. (Michie, 1927), sec. 7979 (90 days after payment); R.I. Gen. Laws (1929), Chapter 1355, sec. 24 (2 years, inheritance taxes); S.C. Civ. Code (1922), sec. 511 (30 days); S.D. Comp. Laws (1929), sec. 6826 (30 days); Wyo. Comp. Stat. Ann. (1920), sec. 6302-6 (1 year). See the statute cited and discussed in Natl. Rockland Bank v. Boston, 296 Fed. 743 (D. Mass. 1924). Some inheritance tax statutes provide that no recovery can be obtained after the estate has been closed and final decrees entered. See Kan. Rev. Stat. Ann. (1923), sec. 79-1517.

allow six years, but much shorter periods are usual.[123] And even though the period of limitations may not have expired, recovery may be barred by laches.[124] But recent federal court opinions indicate that if the tax payment is made under compulsion, the state may not too severely restrict the period during which actions to recover may be instituted.[125]

The cause of action accrues immediately upon payment of the tax; no demand for the return of the tax need be made unless required by statute.[126] Accordingly, the period of limitations begins to run immediately, not when the statute is declared unconstitutional, although the illegality of the tax may not have been previously recognized.[127] Statutes of limitations governing actions on contract are not applicable, since there is no contract, express or implied, to repay the taxes, according to some courts.[128]

The problem of interest is one that has been solved by statute in some states,[129] but in many no statutes govern the subject. Moreover, those states that do have interest statutes do not always extend them to all kinds of taxes.[130] In the absence of statute the "weight of authority" is perhaps on the side of recovery of interest,[131] although the authorities are divided.[132]

Once the taxpayer recovers his payment he may, ordinarily, feel that he is safe.[133] But the federal rule is apparently that the govern-

---

[123] City of Okmulgee v. Jones, 146 Okla. 116, 293 Pac. 1053 (1930).

[124] Laches will bar at common law. See Allgood v. Sloss-Sheffield Steel & Iron Co., *supra*, note 61; cf. Evans v. Steele, 125 Tenn. 483, 145 S. W. 162 (1911).

[125] Sneed v. Schaffer Oil & Refining Co., 35 F. (2d) 21 (C. C. A. 8th 1929) (thirty days insufficient); see Carpenter v. Shaw, 280 U. S. 363, 50 Sup. Ct. Rep. 121, 74 L. Ed. 478 (1930); Security Natl. Bk. v. Young, 55 F. (2d) 616 (C. C. A. 8th 1932), thirty days too short; contra, Blackwell v. City of Gastonia, 181 N. C. 378, 107 S. E. 218 (1921).

[126] Rath v. Chicago, 207 Ill. App. 117 (1917); see Corwin Inv. Co. v. White, 166 Wash. 195, 6 Pac. (2d) 607 (1932); 3 Cooley, Taxation (4th ed., 1924), sec. 1301, notes 30, 31. But see the statute in Nebraska, requiring a written demand. Neb. Comp. Stat. (1929), sec. 77-1923, Part 2.

[127] Sperry Hutchinson Co. v. Mattson, 64 Utah 214, 228 Pac. 755 (1924); Salthouse v. Board of Commrs., *supra*, note 108; 3 Cooley, Taxation (4th ed., 1924), sec. 1304.

[128] Rath v. Chicago, *supra*, note 126. Compare cases cited in notes 37, 38, *supra*. But see Corwin Inv. Co. v. White, 166 Wash. 195, 6 Pac. (2d) 607 (1932), applying statute of limitations on implied contracts not in writing.

[129] See Colo. Ann. Stat. (Mills, 1930), sec. 6343 (10%); Ky. Stat. (Carroll, 1930), secs. 4214a-6, 4214b-8.

[130] S. D. Comp. Laws (1929), secs. 6793, 6813, 6821, 6826; Ky. Stat. (Carroll, 1930), secs. 4214a-6, 4214b-8.

[131] See the discussion of this question in Chicago, St. P. & M. Ry. v. Mundt, 56 S. D. 530, 229 N. W. 394 (1930).

[132] See note, 57 A. L. R. 357 (1928).

[133] Adair County v. Johnston, 160 Iowa 683, 142 N. W. 210 (1896); Graves County v. First Natl. Bank, 108 Ky. 194, 56 S. W. 16 (1900).

ment may reclaim the tax refund if its return was effected by a mistake of law.[134] A taxpayer is also protected against collection of taxes for the period paid for, if he made his payment in reliance upon judicial decision [135] or a governor's veto.[136]

The rule that taxes paid under protest and under compulsion may be recovered even in the absence of statute was formulated by the state courts without reference to any federal constitutional provision, but the opinions in Ward v. Commissioners of Love County [137] and in Carpenter v. Shaw [138] indicate that it might have been forced upon them in time if they had not formulated it themselves. In the first case the Supreme Court held that no state statutory authority is necessary for the recovery of an illegal tax paid under compulsion. The opinion bases the obligation to repay taxes collected under duress on the due process clause of the fourteenth amendment. The opinion in the Carpenter case goes somewhat further and states that "a denial by a state court of a recovery of taxes exacted in violation of the law or constitution of the United States by compulsion is itself in contravention of the fourteenth Amendment." In both these cases an independent federal question was presented (the taxation of Indian lands), and they do not go so far as to hold that an inadequate recovery system is in itself a violation of the federal constitution, but for cases of duress such a remedial system may soon be required under the fourteenth amendment. The recent trend toward the extension of federal judicial supervision over the adequacy of state remedies for arbitrary tax procedures will very likely develop to include supervision over the adequacy of remedies for the recovery of unconstitutional and illegal taxes generally.[139] The reliance placed in these opinions on the due process clause makes this seem the more probable.

A state court has been able to defeat recovery of the tax by defining a state recovery statute in such a manner as to call the statute constitutional for recovery purposes, overruling an earlier interpretation of it which had been held to render it unconstitutional by the Supreme Court of the United States.[140] The recovery statute

---

[134] United States v. Standard Spring Mfg. Co., 23 F. (2d) 495 (D. C. Minn. 1927).

[135] Phila. v. Ridge Ave. Ry., 142 Pa. 484, 21 Atl. 982 (1891).

[136] Texas Co. v. Arizona, 21 Ariz. 485, 254 Pac. 1060 (1927).

[137] 253 U. S. 17, 40 Sup. Ct. Rep. 419, 64 L. Ed. 751 (1920).

[138] 280 U. S. 363, 50 Sup. Ct. Rep. 121, 74 L. Ed. 478 (1930).

[139] See also Sneed v. Schaffer Oil Co., *supra*, note 125. See the statement of the Kentucky Court of Appeals in Coleman v. Inland Gas Corp., *supra*, note 32, that no federal question is involved if the payment is voluntary. This does not necessarily mean that the definition of what constituted a voluntary payment is a non-federal question although that court indicates that it would so regard it.

[140] Sloan v. Commonwealth, 253 Mass. 529, 149 N. E. 407 (1925).

applied to unconstitutional taxes. The court said that the taxing statute had been interpreted in such a way as to make it unconstitutional. The new interpretation made it constitutional. This seems clearly to merit the intervention of the federal courts.

IV. PROTEST AND DURESS

It will be remembered that the rule is that in the absence of statute recovery will be permitted if the taxes have been paid (1) under protest and (2) under compulsion. Each of these conditions will now be considered separately.

A. PROTEST

Protest may be made a prerequisite by statute,[141] but it may also be dispensed with,[142] as has been done in the case of some federal taxes.[143] Some courts hold protest to be necessary unless expressly dispensed with by statute;[144] others dispense with it unless it is expressly required by statute.[145]

Some statutes require written protests,[146] but unless this is the case an oral protest is sufficient, though decisions permitting recovery on oral protests are not numerous.[147] If the statute requires that the protest be written, apparently the taxpayer himself must write it; a memorandum of protest written out by a clerk in the collector's office is insufficient if the clerk is under orders from the collector to make such memoranda as part of the routine office work.[148]

The protest must be specific enough to enable the collector and the court to know that payment was resisted because the tax was

[141] Natl. Rockland Bank v. Boston, *supra,* note 122, discussing Mass. Gen. Laws (1921), Chapter 60, sec. 98; Sperry Hutchinson Co. v. Mattson, 64 Utah 214, 228 Pac. 755 (1924). See Ky. Stat. (Carroll, 1930), secs. 4214a-6, 4214b-8; Kan. Rev. Stat. Ann. (Supp. 1930), sec. 79-2005; Mont. Rev. Code (Choate, 1921), sec. 2269; Neb. Comp. Stat. (1929), sec. 77-1923; Utah Comp. Laws (1917), sec. 6094. See 3 Cooley, Taxation (4th ed., 1924), sec. 2585.

[142] Ala. Code (Michie, 1928), sec. 3143; Iowa Code (1927), sec. 7235; Miss. Code Ann. (1930), sec. 8270; Whyte v. State, 63 Cal. App. 1292, 294 Pac. 417 (1930).

[143] See discussion in Freund, *supra,* note 11, sec. 266; Hyatt Roller Bearing Co. v. United States, 43 F. (2d) 1008 (Ct. Cl. 1930). On protest generally, see note, 64 A. L. R. 26 (1929).

[144] Union Land & Timber Co. v. Pearl River County, 141 Miss. 131, 106 So. 277 (1925); accord, Blackwell v. City of Gastonia, 181 N. C. 378, 107 S. E. 218 (1921).

[145] Smith v. Tennessee Coal, Iron & R. R., *supra,* note 27. See Commercial Natl. Bank v. Board of Supervisors, *supra,* note 27.

[146] Kan. Rev. Stat. Ann. (Supp. 1930), sec. 79-2005; N. C. Code Ann. (Michie, 1931), sec. 7979; Neb. Comp. Stat. (1929), sec. 77-1923.

[147] For example, in Chicago v. Klinkert, *supra,* note 73; Salthouse v. Board of Commrs., *supra,* note 26.

[148] Knowles v. Boston, 129 Mass. 551 (1880). But protest written by taxpayer after conference with collector may be sufficient. Corwin Inv. Co. v. White, 166 Wash. 195, 6 Pac. (2d) 607 (1932).

thought to be illegal or invalid.[149] Statutes may require certain specifications in the protest,[150] but the exact sections of the statute thought to be defective need not be identified,[151] and some courts hold that the basis of the alleged unconstitutionality of a taxing statute need not be specified, although if the protest specifies illegality the grounds upon which illegality is charged must be stated.[152] Designation of specific amounts is not required. Nor need the grounds be specified if the officer knows from repeated conversations what the objections are.[153]

An early Minnesota case indicates that the protest should recite the particular type of compulsion under which the tax was paid — for example, that it was made to avoid the sacrifice of property rights of a certain kind.[154] A recent Kansas statute is extremely severe in its protest stipulations, requiring not only that it be written and that it state the grounds for objection to the tax but also that it recite the particular facts and portions of the statutes complained of and, finally, that the exact portion of the tax protested be identified.[155]

There seems to be no agreement as to the function of a protest. A Michigan opinion states that its principal object is "to warn the officer not to pay over the money." [156] It has been said also to constitute notice of the illegality of the tax.[157] Thus an application for a refund made nineteen months after payment of the tax is not to be considered a protest.[158]

Ordinarily the absence of protest is not conclusive evidence that

[149] Hattiesburg v. New Orleans & N. E. Ry., *supra*, note 2. The federal rule as to claims is strict. "The precise ground upon which the refund is demanded must be stated in the application to the commissioner." Williams & Co. v. United States, 46 F. (2d) 155, 157 (E. D. N. Y. 1930).

[150] Mich. Comp. Laws (1929), sec. 4049; S. D. Comp. Laws (1929), sec. 6826; R. I. Gen. Laws (1929), Chapter 1355 (inheritance taxes).

[151] Catoir v. Watterson, 38 Ohio St. 319 (1882). However, in Railroad v. Commissioners, 98 U. S. 541, 25 L. Ed. 196 (1878), the protest was held insufficient because it was too general. The court intimated that the protest should specify in what respect the statute is illegal, and also what property was involved.

[152] See Pearl River County v. Lacey Lumber Co., *supra*, note 53. (The protest need not specify that the statute is unconstitutional, for the proceeding is "void.")

[153] Home Tel. & Tel. Co. v. Los Angeles, 40 Cal. App. 492, 181 Pac. 100 (1919).

[154] Smith v. Schroeder, 15 Minn. 35 (1870). See the comment on this case in State ex rel. McCardy v. Nelson, 41 Minn. 25, 42 N. W. 548 (1889). See also Railroad v. Commrs., 98 U. S. 541, 25 L. Ed. 196 (1878).

[155] Kan. Rev. Stat. Ann. (Supp. 1930), sec. 79-2005.

[156] First Natl. Bank of Sturgis v. Watkins, 21 Mich. 483, 490 (1870). See also Dennison Mfg. Co. v. Wright, 156 Ga. 789, 120 S. E. 111 (1923).

[157] Detroit v. Martin, 34 Mich. 170, 177 (1876); Railroad v. Commissioners, 98 U. S. 541, 25 L. Ed. 196 (1878).

[158] Chesebrough v. United States, 192 U. S. 253, 24 Sup. Ct. Rep. 262, 48 L. Ed. 432 (1904).

the payment was voluntary, although the Illinois Court of Appeals said in one case that inasmuch as the tax was paid without protest, "the payment was voluntary . . . notwithstanding the presence of duress." [159] Protest alone, on the other hand, is insufficient to render a payment involuntary. To write a letter explaining that the enclosed check is "deposited" with the collector "under protest" and "reserving all rights under the law" and to write "paid under protest" on the tax receipt is not sufficient for recovery.[160] And an oral protest that "I told him I did not like to pay the money, but I reckoned I would have to" was held insufficient by the Indiana court to render the payment involuntary.[161] Other cases are in accord.[162] Protest is effective, however, if it is clearly stated and is accompanied by a notice of suit to recover the tax for which a receipt has been given, recognizing the protest.[163]

Protest may be a determining factor in border-line cases, and it is often, though not always, of great value in determining whether the taxpayer believed the tax to be illegal.[164] In many instances a protest that is specific and vigorous lends an air of honest dispute to a transaction between the collector and taxpayer. But there can be no doubt that the courts have been wise in refusing, in the absence of statute, to permit recovery on the basis of protest alone, because the practice of encouraging taxpayers to protest "on general principles" should not be fostered unless some systematic statutory provision has been made for accumulating funds from which to make tax refunds. Protest should be of some value, but in the absence of some such statutory method as prevails in the federal income tax administration, it should not be determinative.

[159] Rath v. City of Chicago, 207 Ill. App. 117, 122 (1917); accord, Standard Oil Co. v. Bollinger, *supra*, note 89. See Arizona Eastern Ry. v. Graham County, 20 Ariz. 257, 179 Pac. 959 (1919); Asp v. Canyon County, 43 Idaho 560, 256 Pac. 92 (1927). No protest held to show voluntary payment in Pac. Finance Co. v. Spokane County, 15 P. (2d) 652 (Wash. 1932).

[160] Steffen v. State, 19 S. D. 314, 103 N. W. 44 (1905). But see Corwin Inv. Co. v. White, 166 Wash. 195, 6 Pac. (2d) 607 (1932).

[161] Edinburg v. Hackney, 54 Ind. 83 (1876).

[162] Chesebrough v. United States, 192 U. S. 253, 24 Sup. Ct. Rep. 262, 48 L. Ed. 432 (1904); Spring Valley Coal Co. v. State, *supra*, note 24; Hoke v. Atlanta, 107 Ga. 416, 33 S. E. 412 (1899); Union Pac. Ry. v. Board of Commrs., 98 U. S. 541, 25 L. Ed. 196 (1878); Oceanic Steam Nav. Co. v. Tappan, 16 Blatchf. 296, Fed. Cas. No. 10,405 (S. D. N. Y. 1879); Brumagin v. Tillinghast, 18 Cal. 265 (1861); Cook County v. Fairbank, 222 Ill. 578, 78 N. E. 895 (1906); Beck v. State, *supra*, note 49.

[163] Ward v. First Natl. Bk., 142 So. 93 (Ala. 1932).

[164] Sinclair, Owens & Brown v. State, 69 N. C. 47 (1873) (protest tends to make payment look involuntary); Koewing v. Town of West Orange, 89 N. J. L. 539, 99 Atl. 203 (1916) ("may be taken into account"); see Shane v. St. Paul, 26 Minn. 543, 6 N. W. 349 (1880).

B. Compulsion

Compulsion, to be effective, according to some courts, must not only have been brought to bear by the defendant officer but must have been brought to bear upon the plaintiff personally. Thus an employer of traveling salesmen cannot recover license taxes paid on their behalf. The payment is regarded as voluntary because the threatened prosecution was against the salesmen, not against the employer.[165] The compulsion must also, as just noted, have been exercised by the officer collecting or receiving the tax. Payments made to state officers cannot, under this view, be recovered by proving that the federal officers subjected the plaintiff to duress.[166]

The state courts have, on the whole, been more strict in their definition of what is necessary to constitute an involuntary payment than have the federal courts,[167] and it is likely that if the Supreme Court of the United States should enter this field, it would tend to compel some relaxation by the state courts of their previous tests of what constitutes an involuntary payment.

The question whether a payment is compulsory or not is decided by the courts themselves in the great majority of states, but Illinois apparently leaves the question to the jury.[168] As involuntary payment means something different in "the law" from what it does in lay language, and because it is desirable that there be more uniform adherence to standards in the field of governmental finance than can be expected from juries, it is more satisfactory to have judges determine this question.

The following summary of decisions in the more typical situations presented to the courts will illustrate the present state of the law on, and the attitude of judges toward, the problem of defining involuntary payments.

1. The unconstitutional taxing statute alone is not sufficient to make a payment compulsory.[169] An individual will not "be heard

[165] Noyes v. State, 46 Wis. 250, 1 N. W. 1 (1879). No assignment was averred, and the court intimated that a valid claim might have been made out had the statement of facts been less vague. Compare Aetna Ins. Co. v. City of New York, 153 N. Y. 331, 47 N. E. 593 (1897), with Mayor v. Hussey, 67 Md. 112, 9 Atl. 19 (1887) (payment by corporation for shareholder).

[166] Taylor v. Board of Health, 31 Pa. St. 73, 76 (1855); see also Garrison v. Tillinghast, *supra,* note 80; Chesebrough v. United States, 192 U. S. 253, 24 Sup. Ct. Rep. 262, 48 L. Ed. 432 (1904).

[167] See the opinion in Ward v. Commrs. of Love County, 253 U. S. 17, 40 Sup. Ct. Rep. 419, 64 L. Ed. 751 (1920); Atchison, Topeka & Santa Fe Ry. v. O'Connor, 223 U. S. 280, 32 Sup. Ct. Rep. 216, 56 L. Ed. 432 (1912).

[168] Harvey & Boyd v. Town of Olney, 42 Ill. 336 (1866); Chicago v. Klinkert, *supra,* note 73.

[169] Yates v. Royal Ins. Co., *supra,* note 79; Board of Education v. Toennigs, 297 Ill. 469, 130 N. E. 758 (1921).

to say that he was coerced to do that which he believed the law required of him" even though what he thought to be a law turned out to be invalid.[170]

2. Payment made in ignorance of the illegality of the tax is likewise voluntary, whether the illegality is due to the invalidity of the statute [171] or to other causes.[172]

3. Payment made to avoid expense and inconvenience is voluntary,[173] provided the burden or penalty is not too heavy. Payments made to obtain discounts fall within this rule.[174] No duress is present if payment of a tax is made as a part of the sales price and the payment is merely protested.[175]

4. Protest, taken alone, does not prove compulsion.[176]

5. That a payment was made without first seeking administrative relief is not conclusive that it was voluntary,[177] but it has been suggested that payment made after an unsuccessful attempt to obtain judicial relief is to be considered as involuntary.[178]

6. A mere notice that a tax is overdue is not coercion,[179] but Vermont has held that if the notice states that a distress warrant will issue if the tax becomes overdue, the rule is different.[180] The issuance of a tax warrant is not such compulsion as will justify recovery; [181] nor is a threat to issue a distress warrant ordinarily

[170] Town of Ligonier v. Ackerman, 46 Ind. 552, 559 (1874).

[171] Carr v. City of Memphis, 22 F. (2d) 678 (C. C. A. 6th 1927); Prescott v. City of Memphis, *supra*, note 57.

[172] Gould v. Board of Commrs., *supra*, note 73; 3 Cooley, Taxation (4th ed., 1924), sec. 1294, note 85. See Security Natl. Bk. v. Young, 55 F. (2d) 616 (C. C. A. 8th 1932).

[173] Spring Valley Coal Co. v. State, *supra*, note 24; Falvey v. Board of County Commrs., 76 Minn. 257, 79 N. W. 302 (1899).

[174] Beck v. State, *supra*, note 49; Bush v. City of Beloit, 105 Kan. 79, 181 Pac. 615 (1919); Lee v. Templeton, 13 Gray 476 (Mass. 1859); see note, 41 L. R. A. (N. S.) 175 (1913); contra, Stowe v. Town of Stowe, 70 Vt. 609, 41 Atl. 1024 (1898). In Morris v. Baltimore, 5 Gill. 244 (Md. 1847), payment was made to obtain discount, but the court did not consider this aspect of the case. On payment to avoid interest, see Morris v. New Haven, 78 Conn. 673, 63 Atl. 123 (1906).

[175] Roxana Petroleum Corp. v. Bollinger, 54 F. (2d) 296 (C. C. A. 7th 1932).

[176] See cases in note 162, *supra;* 2 Cooley, Taxation (4th ed., 1924), sec. 1299, note 1. See Security Natl. Bk. v. Young, *supra*, note 172.

[177] Home Tel. & Tel. Co. v. Los Angeles, *supra*, note 153; Salthouse v. Board of County Commrs., *supra*, note 26. Cf. cases cited in notes 76, 77, 78, *supra*. It has been suggested that payment is voluntary if made before suit, where suit is the only method of enforcing the tax. Braddock Iron Mining Co. v. Erskine, 155 Minn. 70, 192 N. W. 193 (1923).

[178] Coleman v. Inland Gas Corp., *supra*, note 32.

[179] Russell v. New Haven, 51 Conn. 259 (1883).

[180] Stowe v. Town of Stowe, *supra*, note 174. See Bank v. Kottmann, *supra*, note 63.

[181] First Natl. Bank of Sturgis v. Watkins, *supra*, note 156; Salthouse v. Board of County Commrs., *supra*, note 26; Dunnell Mfg. Co. v. Newell, 15 R. I. 233, 2 Atl. 766 (1886) (warrant including authorization for distress).

sufficient.[182] If, however, steps are taken to execute the distress warrant, the owner of the property may pay the tax with some assurance that he has been subjected to the requisite legal compulsion.[183]

The Kansas court has well said: "This court long ago reached the conclusion that it was not necessary that the sheriff should be knocking at the door with a tax warrant in his hand before the harassed taxpayer could pay a tax illegally levied and contest the validity." [184]

The existence of summary methods of tax collection creates a presumption in the minds of some courts in favor of the taxpayer, it being thought less likely that he has been coerced if the state must institute criminal or civil proceedings.[185] In the latter situation he can defend himself when formal action is instituted, but in the former he has no such opportunity. If acts to be taken by an administrative officer precedent to the institution of suit have not been taken, payment is deemed voluntary.[186] The size of the penalty is also an important factor. Recently a penalty of 18 per cent has been held high enough to be coercive.[187]

7. To allege that a tax was paid to avoid a possible cloud on title from an anticipated seizure of property is insufficient,[188] and some courts presume that such payments are voluntary if there are no further allegations.[189]

The advertising of property for sale for taxes due under an invalid statute is not compulsion,[190] because neither the sale, nor a

[182] Union Natl. Bank of New York v. Mayer, 51 N. Y. 638 (1872); see Mayor v. Lefferman, 4 Gill. 425, 436 (Md. 1846): "Menace of an impending distress warrant would not render it a payment by commission."

[183] Railroad v. Commrs., 98 U. S. 541, 25 L. Ed. 196 (1878), holding that since no steps had been taken to execute the warrant the payment was voluntary; Atwell v. Zeluff, 26 Mich. 118 (1872).

[184] First Natl. Bk. v. Board of Commrs., 134 Kan. 781, 8 P. (2d) 312 (1932).

[185] Atchison, Topeka & Santa Fe Ry. v. O'Connor, 223 U. S. 280, 32 Sup. Ct. Rep. 216, 56 L. Ed. 436 (1912); Jackson v. Town of Union, 82 Conn. 266, 73 Atl. 773 (1909); Eaton v. Noyes, 76 N. H. 52, 78 Atl. 1080 (1911); Brunson v. Levee Dist., 107 Ark. 24, 153 S. W. 828 (1913); Maxwell v. County of San Luis Obispo, 71 Cal. 466, 12 Pac. 484 (1886). See Braddock Iron Mining Co. v. Erskine, *supra*, note 177.

[186] Oceanic Steam Nav. Co. v. Tappan, *supra*, note 162.

[187] Ward v. Commrs. of Love County, 253 U. S. 17, 40 Sup. Ct. Rep. 419, 64 L. Ed. 751 (1920). See also Oceanic Steam Nav. Co. v. Tappan, *supra*, note 162; Sneed v. Schaffer Oil & Refining Co., 35 F. (2d) 21 (C. C. A. 8th 1929); Beck v. State, *supra*, note 49.

[188] First Natl. Bank of Americus v. Mayor, *supra*, note 71.

[189] Jenks v. Lima Township, 17 Ind. 326 (1861).

[190] San Francisco & North Pac. R. R. v. Dinwiddie, 13 Fed. 789 (C. C. Cal. 1882). See the comment, narrowing the California rule followed in this case, in Home Tel. & Tel. Co. v. Los Angeles, *supra*, note 153; cf. Bakersfield Fuel & Oil Co. v. Kern County, 144 Cal. 148, 77 Pac. 892 (1904).

conveyance under it, could create any cloud on the title.[191] The Supreme Court of Michigan has held that even if seizure were threatened, payment would be voluntary, because the taxpayer should know that a sale of property for a tax imposed by an unconstitutional statute could not create a cloud on title.[192] Other decisions take a more realistic view of the situation and hold that for all practical purposes a cloud on title is created under such circumstances, as the owner quickly learns if he attempts to sell the property.[193] This view is adopted in the more recent cases.[194] A recent Michigan decision holds, in accord with this trend, that a tax which is a lien on the property, by force of statute, may be paid without protest and recovered by court action, because the payment is involuntary.[195]

A different rule has been suggested with respect to personal property,[196] because of the ease with which it can be carried off by the collector. But little judicial support has been given this distinction, and properly so, for fixity of location is no test of whether one may be ousted from possession.[197]

8. Threatened loss of business privileges, such as the loss of a license, for instance, is now ordinarily held to render payments compulsory unless they are made without protest and without actual compulsion.[198] Foreign corporations frequently pay taxes because of threatened loss of the privilege of carrying on business in the state, and in view of the heavy statutory penalties [199] usually accom-

[191] 13 Fed. at 790.

[192] Detroit v. Martin, 34 Mich. 170 (1876); accord, Barrett v. Cambridge, 10 Allen 48 (Mass. 1865); Murphy v. Wilmington, 6 Houst. 108 (Del. 1880); Heywood v. City of Buffalo, 14 N. Y. 534 (1856); Lamborn v. County Commrs., 97 U. S. 181, 24 L. Ed. 926 (1877); The Sonoma County Tax case, 13 Fed. 789 (C. C. D. Cal. 1882).

[193] Whitney v. City of Port Huron, 88 Mich. 268, 50 N. W. 316 (1891). See, on statutory lien for taxes, Thompson v. City of Detroit, 114 Mich. 502, 72 N. W. 320 (1897); Underwood Typewriter Co. v. Chamberlain, 92 Conn. 199, 102 Atl. 600 (1917).

[194] White River Lumber Co. v. Elliott, 146 Ark. 551, 226 S. W. 164 (1920); Tyler v. Dane County, 289 Fed. 843 (W. D. Wis. 1923); Underwood Typewriter Co. v. Chamberlain, *supra,* note 193.

[195] Blanchard v. City of Detroit, 253 Mich. 491, 235 N. W. 230 (1931).

[196] Boyer Bros. v. Board of Commrs., *supra,* note 41.

[197] See Keener, Quasi Contracts, 425 (1893), Chapter 9.

[198] 3 Cooley, Taxation (4th ed., 1924), secs. 1283, 1288; Hartford Fire Ins. Co. v. Jordan, 168 Cal. 270, 142 Pac. 839 (1914); Duke v. Force, 120 Wash. 599, 620, 621, 208 Pac. 68, 69 (1922).

[199] American Mfg. Co. v. St. Louis, 270 Mo. 40, 192 S. W. 402 (1917); Ratterman v. American Exp. Co., 49 Ohio St. 608, 32 N. E. 754 (1892); Gaar, Scott & Co. v. Shannon, 223 U. S. 468, 32 Sup. Ct. Rep. 236, 56 L. Ed. 510 (1912); see Scottish Union & Natl. Ins. Co. v. Herriott, 109 Iowa 606, 610, 80 N. W. 665, 667 (1899). In Yates v. Royal Ins. Co., *supra,* note 79, it was held that no recovery would be permitted when the plaintiff was ignorant of any constitutional defect in the

panying this threat, many of their payments are held to be involuntary.[200]

A tax is apparently involuntary if it is paid by a foreign corporation to save its contracts from being treated as unenforceable by the state courts.[201]

9. Service and privilege fees present various types of situations. Payment made in order to probate an estate has been held involuntary [202] on the ground that, to prevent delay of the settlement of the estate, the administrator should be free to pay under protest and recover.[203] This rule also applies to the recording of deeds; [204] and the availability of mandamus to compel the officer to file the document without exacting the fee does not place the case outside its operation.[205] It has been held, though the soundness of the holding is doubtful, that payment of a stamp tax was voluntary even though the stamp was necessary for the admissibility of an instrument as evidence.[206] Recovery of a fee exacted for having one's name printed on a primary ballot has been permitted where there was not enough time before the election date to permit the institution of special proceedings to compel the entry without fee.[207]

Pennsylvania holds to be voluntary the fees paid to obtain the entry of immigrants; [208] Massachusetts has taken a contrary view.[209] Recovery of a twenty-five dollar trademark registration fee was denied by the United States Court of Claims, but the case turned

statute at the time of payment. The court seemed to feel that making payment a condition precedent to doing business in the state was insufficient.

[200] There is some reason to believe that this alone would not be sufficient to serve as a basis for recovery. See Yates v. Royal Ins. Co., *supra*, note 79. Laredo v. Loury, 4 Willson Tex. Civ. Cas. Ct. App. 320, 20 S. W. 89 (1892), is distinguishable from the cases cited *supra*, note 199, in that the licensee had recouped himself out of collections from customers.

[201] Whyte v. State, 110 Cal. App. 314, 294 Pac. 417 (1931).

[202] Trower v. City & County of San Francisco, 152 Cal. 479, 92 Pac. 1025 (1907); Mearkle v. Board of Commrs., 44 Minn. 546, 47 N. W. 165 (1890); Cook County v. Fairbank, *supra*, note 162; Malin v. La Moure County, 27 N. D. 140, 145 N. W. 582 (1914); Adams v. Board of Supervisors, 154 N. Y. 619, 49 N. E. 144 (1898) (suggestion that payment by executor to facilitate sale of property in estate is involuntary).

[203] Mearkle v. Board of Commrs., *supra*, note 202. See also Diocese of Fargo v. Cass County, 28 N. D. 209, 148 N. W. 541 (1914).

[204] State ex rel. McCardy v. Nelson, 41 Minn. 25, 42 N. W. 548 (1889); Oakland Cemetery Assn. v. Ramsey County, 98 Minn. 404, 108 N. W. 857, 109 N. W. 237 (1906); cf. Smith v. Shroeder, 15 Minn. 35 (1870); Chesebrough v. United States, 192 U. S. 253, 24 Sup. Ct. Rep. 262, 48 L. Ed. 432 (1904).

[205] Lewis v. City & County of San Francisco, 2 Cal. App. 112, 115, 82 Pac. 1106 (1905).

[206] Garrison v. Tillinghast, *supra*, note 80.

[207] Johnson v. Grand Forks County, 16 N. D. 363, 113 N. W. 1071 (1907).

[208] Taylor v. Board of Health, *supra*, note 166.

[209] Cunningham v. Munroe, 15 Gray 471 (Mass. 1860).

largely on the absence of statutory authority upon which to predicate recovery.[210]

10. Threats of arrest, especially if conviction of the crime for which the arrest is made carries with it heavy penalties, have been held to constitute compulsion,[211] but some courts are much slower than others to follow this rule in actual application.[212] They emphasize the opportunity available to the taxpayer to obtain injunctive relief,[213] or they explain that payment made in ignorance of law cannot be recovered.[214] The courts are divided as to whether, in the absence of threats to enforce them, ordinary criminal penalties constitute compulsion.[215]

11. Payments made pursuant to court order have seldom been challenged as compulsory, but litigation on this point is almost certain to arise under those inheritance tax statutes that provide for the deposit of securities or the provisional payment of taxes, pending the happening of a contingency before which the tax cannot be determined finally. When such a statute is declared unconstitutional, the depositors will doubtless wish to obtain their securities or payments. There seems to be no authority on this point, but a New York case contains a remote suggestion that payment in pursuance of a judicial order is compulsory,[216] and this suggestion will probably be developed to the point of permitting recovery of deposits and payments made under such circumstances.

V. CONCLUSION

The courts should not be criticized too severely for their attitude toward tax recovery actions. No doubt they have been influenced by their knowledge of some taxpayers and their ways. The situation is unsatisfactory, nevertheless, and legislation is necessary to correct it.

Statutes should provide either for the liberal use of injunctions

[210] Woodman's case, 15 Ct. Cl. 541 (U. S. 1879).

[211] Home Tel. & Tel. Co. v. Los Angeles, *supra*, note 153; Atchison, Topeka & Santa Fe Ry. v. O'Connor, 223 U. S. 280, 32 Sup. Ct. Rep. 216, 56 L. Ed. 436 (1912); Rath v. City of Chicago, *supra*, note 159; Chicago v. Klinkert, *supra*, note 73; Walsh v. Denver, 11 Colo. App. 523, 53 Pac. 458 (1898); Dennison Mfg. Co. v. Wright, *supra*, note 156; Eslow v. City of Albion, 153 Mich. 720, 117 N. W. 328 (1908); Mayor v. Wicks, 16 Del. (2 Marvel) 297, 43 Atl. 173 (1896).

[212] Maxwell v. County of San Luis Obispo, 71 Cal. 466, 12 Pac. 484 (1886); Spring Valley Coal Co. v. State, *supra*, note 24.

[213] Michel Brewing Co. v. State, 19 S. D. 302, 103 N. W. 40 (1905).

[214] Tatum v. Town of Trenton, 85 Ga. 468, 11 S. E. 705 (1890).

[215] Standard Oil Co. v. Bollinger, *supra*, note 89; Beck v. State, *supra*, note 49; City of Savannah v. Southern Stevedoring Co., 36 Ga. App. 526, 137 S. E. 123 (1927) (no compulsion); contra, St. Johns Elec. Co. v. City of St. Augustine, *supra*, note 26.

[216] See Tripler v. City of New York, 125 N. Y. 617, 626, 26 N. E. 721, 727 (1891).

to test the validity of taxes before they have been collected, permitting little opportunity for complaint if this remedy is not utilized, or for a reasonable period of limitations following payment, during which action can be instituted to recover the tax.

The advantage of the injunction is that the tax will not be collected if it is illegal, and the question of illegality will be settled early. The disadvantage is that if the tax is held to be invalid, the government will be deprived of an expected source of revenue, and, as a result, government finance may be disrupted. Certainly if the injunctive method is adopted, the statute should embody the rule now followed by some courts, that taxes are not to be restrained if they are authorized by *any existing valid statute* [217] or if they are legally assessed, levied, and collected under any valid statute.

A system of recovery after payment may be the preferable alternative, provided that the use of injunctions is specifically authorized in case of very summary collection and in case of irreparable damage in the strict sense. Under such a system the period of limitations should be short — one or, at most, two years. The statute would of course require, subject to the exceptions that have been noted, the payment of the tax when it is due if administrative remedies for its abatement had failed.

The problem of providing a satisfactory system of tax recovery in the states is much more difficult than it is in the national government. In many states the county collects the greatest part of the taxes for the state and also for the other governmental subdivisions. In providing for the accumulation of a fund from which tax refunds should be made, care must therefore be taken to insure contributions by each governmental unit for which the county collects the tax. After the fund has been established, deficits due to refunds of taxes collected for a particular unit can be taken care of by proper deductions from taxes collected for that unit during the succeeding taxing year.

This fund should be administered by the county financial authorities, and claims for refunds up to a given amount — five hundred dollars, for example — should be presented to the designated county authorities, regardless of the subdivision for which the county may have collected the money. Such claims should be presented to the governing officer or board of the county, but should not be allowed without a certificate from the tax-collecting officer showing that the whole of the amount claimed had been paid. Claims amounting to

[217] Reynolds v. Hall, 154 Ga. 623, 114 S. E. 891 (1922); Bemis Bag Co. v. Louisiana Tax Comm., 158 La. 1, 103 So. 337 (1925).

more than five hundred dollars should be handled by regular action in the local court of general trial jurisdiction, or in an administrative court if there is one.

Taxes paid directly to the state government, and taxes and license fees paid directly to local governmental units, should be governed in a similar manner, except that the fund should be a city fund or a state fund, as the case may be, and the action, where court action is required for large claims, should be against the officer or his successor in charge of the fund, not against the government. This will prevent the difficulties arising out of immunity from suit or the death of the officer.

The requirements of protest and compulsion should be dispensed with, but specific statutory provisions should be made to deny refunds to nominal taxpayers who have in reality collected the tax from customers by adding the amount of the tax to the price of the goods, at least wherever it seems difficult or impossible to administer a system of refund by him in turn to his customers.

If a general administrative court is established in a state, it should have jurisdiction over all claims against all units of government; with a few exceptions all claims arising out of taxation should be settled in such courts, if they are to be settled by courts at all, and as suggested earlier larger claims should be settled in courts. So far as possible, judgments should be against a single fund, as in the case of government liability generally, discussed in an earlier chapter. Experience already available would make contributions to such a fund approach an actuarial basis soon after the adoption of such a plan.

The law of tax recovery has little in it to support the void ab initio view of the effect of an unconstitutional statute. Under this view the government collects a tax without any legal power to do so if the law is unconstitutional. But as in the cases of payments generally, courts hold that other doctrines operate to deny relief to the person paying out money in accordance with such a statute. Effect is given to an invalid statute in the tax cases; sufficient effect to permit the government to retain the money, and sufficient effect to deny the taxpayer any recovery. Protest and duress are the words that the courts use in these cases to give effect to people's actions under invalid statutes in the field of taxation. Here as in so many other instances effect is given to the invalid statute not directly but by making use of other established rules of law that seem at first thought to have no relation to the question of the effect of an invalid statute.

A Note on the Recovery of Fines

The cases involving the question whether a fine imposed and paid under an unconstitutional statute can be recovered are in conflict and confusion. Sometimes the rule is stated to be that unconstitutionally imposed fines may be recovered, if their payment is involuntary, fines thus being treated the same as taxes.

Definitions of "voluntary payment" are as confusing in this branch of the law as in that of taxation. In Smith v. Hutchinson,[1] in which the plaintiff had paid a fine to avoid a jail sentence, the court held the payment to be voluntary because the plaintiff had paid the fine instead of appealing the case to a higher court. Some mention was made of the failure of the plaintiff to protest against the payment, but it is not clear whether the court had in mind the filing of a formal protest or the request for an appeal.

In Bailey v. Town of Paullina[2] recovery was denied to an assignee of a claim for a fine on the ground that it was not shown that the person paying the fine did so *because* of his arrest. The court emphasized the fact that no formal argument against the validity of the statute had been made at the trial, and stated that the accused had paid the fine because he believed it to be constitutionally imposed.

The federal courts seem to be equally severe in applying the rules denying recovery. In United States v. Gettinger,[3] a plea of nole contendere was entered, in a prosecution for the violation of the Lever Act, undertaking to "waive any and all claims which I now have or hereafter may have to any and all fines which the court may see fit to impose upon me upon such plea, except in the event that the so-called Lever Act under which said indictment is founded shall be declared unconstitutional by the Supreme Court of the United States." A fine was imposed by the court, paid to the clerk, and turned over to the treasury of the United States. Subsequently the Lever Act was held to be invalid, and the lower court set aside the judgment of conviction. Plaintiff brought assumpsit to recover the amount of the fine. He failed to recover, because the Supreme Court was unable to find a contract on the part of the United States to return the fine.

In Blumenthal v. United States[4] a federal district court in California held that a fine imposed under the Lever Act could not be recovered in the district court sitting as a court of claims. The in-

[1] 8 Rich. Law 260 (S. C. 1855).
[2] 69 Iowa 463, 29 N. W. 418 (1886).
[3] 272 U. S. 734, 47 Sup. Ct., Rep. 276, 71 L. Ed. 499 (1927).
[4] 4 F. (2d) 808 (D. C. S. D. Cal. 1925).

validity of the statute had not been raised in the trial, and the fine had been paid without protest. Such a payment was held not to create an implied contract under the Tucker Act.

The Circuit Court of Appeals for the Seventh Circuit, however, held in United States v. Rothstein [5] that a judgment of a district court, sitting as a court of claims, for the recovery of a fine paid under an invalid statute was proper. The contention was made in argument that the district court, sitting as a court of claims, could not vacate its judgment after the term of court had expired. It was held, however, that the judgment could be vacated, and the fine returned.

To recover a fine, if recovery is permitted, it must apparently have been paid by the person suing to recover it. Payment by a surety, even though the surety recouped itself from the plaintiff, will not furnish the basis for an action to recover, if it is brought by the accused person.[6]

[5] 187 Fed. 268, 109 C. C. A. 521 (C. C. A. 7th 1911).
[6] Curley v. Town of Marble, 61 Colo. 6, 155 Pac. 334 (1916).

Chapter XI

AMENDATORY, VALIDATING, CURATIVE, AND REMEDIAL MEASURES

How to make the legislation effective again is naturally one of the questions that arises when a statute is declared unconstitutional, if there is a strong demand that it be continued. Proposals to amend the statute suggest themselves; constitutional amendments to remove obstacles or to grant new powers are occasionally resorted to; federal legislation to remove restrictions upon state legislation has often been attempted; and in other instances curative and validating legislation has been enacted. All of these will be considered in this chapter. In addition, some attention will be paid to the problem of the effect of unconstitutional amendments to statutes, a problem suggested by that involving the legislative attempt to amend the invalid law.

I. AMENDMENTS TO INVALID STATUTES

In passing, reference should be made here to a type of decision holding a statute unconstitutional that has the effect of making the statute valid. The point is illustrated by a California decision denouncing a statutory discrimination against nonresidents. The effect of this decision was not to make the statute ineffective, as one might expect upon first thought, but to make it applicable to residents and nonresidents alike.[1] Such a decision, declaring unconstitutional the restriction embodied in the statute, removes the restriction (so far as application by the courts is concerned) and leaves the law valid. Nice distinctions are drawn in this type of case, and if the statute imposes a burden upon nonresidents, it is said to be unconstitutional and unenforceable.[2]

In cases such as this California one, no amendment is required to make the statute good; the decision does that.

Amendment should be distinguished from re-enactment. Legislatures have in some instances enacted the identical law again after

[1] Quon Ham Wah Co. v. Industrial Accident Comm., 184 Cal. 26, 192 Pac. 1021 (1920).

[2] See the distinction drawn in the opinion in Quon Ham Wah Co. v. Industrial Accident Comm., *supra*, note 1, between that case and Spraigue v. Thompson, 118 U. S. 90, 6 Sup. Ct. Rep. 988, 30 L. Ed. 115 (1886), wherein the statute was said to be invalid because of a discriminatory burden on the nonresident.

it has been declared invalid, but under the principle of stare decisis such a statute will be declared invalid again.[3]

The discussion in this section of the rules relating to legislative amendment of an unconstitutional statute will assume that amendments of this kind are not prohibited by any express constitutional provision, such as that against special legislation which is found in the constitutions of several of the states.[4] Amendatory statutes, as here discussed, will be deemed to be valid on all other grounds, unless otherwise stated, leaving only one question, namely, whether the legislature can amend an invalid act, the only constitutional question being whether such an amendment is within legislative power in so far as the effect of judicial decision declaring a statute unconstitutional is concerned. Under this explanation should be placed the cases in which the courts hold that a bad title cannot be amended by reference to the title only, if the constitution forbids such amendments.[5] Some of these cases contain discussions which are misleading, dealing as they do with the question as though it involved only the amendability of an invalid statute. This, of course, is not the problem in this group of cases,[6] the problem being whether defective titles can be amended in a certain way, such as by reference, under constitutional provisions governing amendment.

Reference to partial unconstitutionality has been made from time to time throughout the discussion in the preceding chapters, and some attention has been paid to the varieties of partial unconstitutionality referred to in the opinions. The statement is often made that partially unconstitutional statutes may be amended so as to make the invalid portion valid. This statement in its most common form seems to refer to what might be called "sectional unconstitutionality," that is, the invalidity of a particular section of a statute containing more than one section, or the invalidity of some part of

[3] See facts and decision of Cary v. Simpson, 239 Ky. 381, 39 S. W. (2d) 668 (1931).

[4] On special legislation as it concerns this problem, see Kimball v. Town of Rosendale, 42 Wis. 407 (1877). On the general problem of this section, see 60 L. R. A. 564 (annotation), 1 L. R. A. N. S. 431 (annotation); 4 Am. and Eng. Cas. 920 (annotation). See, on vested rights not to be disturbed by curative act, Smith v. Cameron, 123 Or. 501, 262 Pac. 946 (1928).

[5] Teeple v. Wayne County, 23 Pa. County Ct. 361 (1900); Shear v. Potter County, 9 Pa. Dist. Ct. Rep. 289 (1899); McLaughlin v. Summit Hill Borough, 224 Pa. St. 425, 73 Atl. 975 (1909). See also Allison v. Corker, 67 N. J. L. 596, 52 Atl. 362 (1902). See for example of other procedural rules sometimes found in state constitution governing legislative work, State v. Corbett, 61 Ark. 226, 32 S. W. 686 (1895).

[6] See the following statement from Teeple v. Wayne County, supra, note 5: "If the main stock were alive and only the top were affected this engrafting process might give it new life. The transfusion of blood may save a dying patient but a dead one cannot be resurrected by such process. The original act never was a law."

a single section.[7] One court has said, with respect to partial unconstitutionality:

There is a marked difference in regard to the amendment of an act which is void in its entirety and one that is only void in part, or when one section of an act is in conflict with the constitution of the state and the remaining sections are in harmony therewith. When the entire act is void there is nothing to amend, while it is otherwise when there is only one section or a part of one section sought to be amended, as in the case at bar. In the latter case the amendment may be made to any part of the section, or by substituting an entire new section in lieu thereof, provided the act when amended does not embrace a purpose outside its title, and inconsistent with the provisions remaining unrepealed.[8]

An unconstitutional statute may be saved by reference, in a later statute, without having been re-enacted by the legislature.[9] The theory upon which such reference is said to save the act is that it has been incorporated into the later act by the reference. The reference need not always be specific; it is sufficient that the legislative intent to incorporate it in later legislation is clear.[10] An interesting situation is presented by Ex parte Young,[11] wherein an ordinance expressly mentioned the section of the statute in pursuance of which it was adopted. The statute was held invalid. The court decided that the ordinance was valid, nevertheless, if the power to enact such an ordinance could be established without reference to the statute, and that the mistaken and unnecessary recital of the section of the statute referred to was not fatal to the ordinance. Reference to a list of powers contained in an invalid statute has been permitted, when the legislature wished to transfer the powers therein enumerated to another officer.[12] The theory of this decision is stated in the following quotation from the opinion:

. . . the act of 1855 . . . referred to these acts, not for the purpose of giving them validity as they stood, but for the purpose of divesting these acts of their supposed unconstitutional features, and lodging the same

[7] Lynch v. Murphy, 119 Mo. 163, 24 S. W. 774 (1893). See Central R. R. v. Bd. of Assessors, 75 N. J. L. 771, 69 Atl. 239 (1907). Also 60 L. R. A. 564 (annotation), Part II.

[8] 119 Mo. at 173. See also Sweet v. Syracuse, 129 N. Y. 316, 10 N. E. 1081 (1891); Hill v. American Book Co., 171 Ark. 427, 285 S. W. 20 (1926).

[9] Range Co. v. Carver, 118 N. C. 328, 24 S. E. 352 (1896). See also Atty. Gen. v. Joy, 55 Mich. 94, 20 N. W. 806 (1884); Water Commrs. v. Curtis, 87 Conn. 506, 89 Atl. 189 (1913).

[10] Atty. Gen. v. Joy, *supra*, note 9. Mere inclusion in a later code, without re-enactment and without reference in any later act, does not suffice to save it. Mayor v. Williams, 124 Md. 502, 92 Atl. 1066 (1915). Presumably a legislative enactment of such a code would be sufficient.

[11] 154 Cal. 317, 97 Pac. 822 (1908).

[12] People v. Bircham, 12 Cal. 50 (1859).

power in different hands. This is not to validate void acts, but to make acts, void because the powers were misplaced, valid for the future, by placing these powers in constitutional hands.[13]

In accordance with the reasoning in these decisions it has also been held that reference to districts created by an invalid law for other purposes than those originally intended in the invalid statute is permissible.[14]

Another group of cases often included in citations pro and con on the question whether an invalid statute can be amended, which do not bear on that question directly, is the group involving repeal. It is settled that an invalid part of a statute may be repealed. If the statute is then left in a form and with a substance that is otherwise constitutional, the repeal is effective.[15] This result is reached even though a statute provides that a repeal shall not revive the former act.[16] With the repeal may be coupled a substitute section or statute, and the two accomplish the repeal of the invalid section and the enactment of a new law.[17] On this the following passage merits quotation:

> The legislature of this state has a plenary law-making power within the territorial limits of this state, either to enact new laws or repeal old laws, unless prohibited by the constitution of the United States or the constitution of this state. But it is said a void act is no law, and the power to repeal does not reach it. It is evident, however, that this argument ignores the fact that unconstitutional enactments are sometimes spread upon our statute books and are obeyed by the people and the officers of the law, and are usually clothed with the semblance at least of valid laws. They stand unchallenged sometimes for years, and then present the gravest questions for the determination of the courts. Now, when placed upon the statute books by the action of the legislature, why should not the same governmental agency remove them from the statutes and prevent them from becoming snares and pitfalls to the people of the state.
>
> Surely it needs no argument to demonstrate that the legislature has the power to see that nothing shall deface our statute books that is not a law. It is of supreme importance to the administration of justice in our courts that the people should obey the processes of our courts and that no doubt should exist as to the rightfulness of the sessions they hold. Under our system a court can only be held at the time and place appointed by law and the most direful consequences might ensue if the

[13] 12 Cal. at 55.

[14] Mortland v. Christian, 23 Vrooman 52, 20 Atl. 673 (N. J. L. 1896).

[15] American Uniform Co. v. Commonwealth, 237 Mass. 42, 129 N. E. 622 (1921). See State v. Field, 119 Mo. 593, 24 S. W. 752 (1893).

[16] Lawton Spinning Co. v. Commonwealth, 232 Mass. 28, 121 N. E. 518 (1919).

[17] State v. Field, *supra*, note 15. See State ex rel. Dawes v. Bailey, 56 Kan. 81, 42 Pac. 373 (1895).

judges and officers of the law were to meet and pass upon the personal and property rights of our citizens at times or places unauthorized by law.

Now the relator says the act of February 14 was unconstitutional, but upon its face it essayed to fix the times for holding courts in the fifteenth judicial circuit of this state, a large and populous district, and yet when the legislature also discovers the truth, as relator sees it, and deems it a matter of simple justice that its own improvident action shall not mislead the judge and officers of the court in that circuit and solemnly declares according to the forms prescribed by the constitution that the said act of February 14 is not and shall not be considered and obeyed as a law of this state, they are met with the objection that they cannot repeal a void act. The bare statement of the proposition furnishes its own refutation. Certainly the legislature may purge the statute books of any matter not lawfully there. To deny it this power is to ascribe to it a most dishonoring impotence and a disregard of the analogies of the law.

A judgment or decree of a court, though formal, is void if the court had no jurisdiction over the subject matter or the persons of the parties; and may be disregarded even in collateral proceedings, but courts do not on this account hesitate to set aside and declare such judgments void, when their attention is called to them. On the contrary, they regard it a plain duty to set aside such judgments. Cole v. Cole, 3 Mo. App. 571; Cole v. Cole, 4 C. L. Journal 64.

So when an act of the legislature is void for failure to observe some constitutional prerequisite, nothing could be more appropriate than for the legislature to remove the act at once from a place among the valid laws of the state and by an apt reference call attention to its repeal and at the same time enact a valid law on the same subject in its stead. It is not an attempt to resuscitate the void act, nor to build upon it as a foundation. It is a simple declaration that in future it is not to be regarded. The power to repeal a law has been held to involve the power to abrogate a bill in its progress before it becomes a law. Bank v. Commonwealth, 26 Pa. St. 446.

Likewise, the cases in which invalid statutes have been re-enacted, the invalid portions having been omitted, are not to be grouped with those involving amendment of an invalid statute. Such re-enactment, with or without repeal,[18] or with or without amendment, is valid if the constitutional rules of legislative procedure have not been transgressed thereby.[19] This should be so, because the new enactment is to be judged as a separate statute, and

[18] Keystone State T. & T. Co. v. Ridley Park Borough, 28 Pa. Super. Ct. 635 (1905).

[19] State ex rel. Richards v. Cincinnati, 52 Ohio St. 419, 40 N. E. 508 (1895); Polk v. Booker, 112 Ark. 101, 165 S. W. 262 (1914); State v. Silver Bow Ref. Co., 78 Mont. 1, 252 Pac. 301 (1926). See also Pederson v. Patterson, 124 Or. 105, 258 Pac. 204 (1928); People v. Stout, 23 Barb. 349 (N. Y. 1856).

not in the light of previous statutes, so far as its validity is concerned; it should stand on its own merits, divorced from any question of the invalidity of the former statute, or any part of it.

In Swanson v. Dolezal [20] the Nebraska court held that a statute phrased in terms "cumulative and supplementary" to an invalid statute was ineffective, and lacked curative force. But if, as was done in New York, the supplementary act had included a re-enactment of the defective statute, with the invalid portion omitted, or with the form corrected, if that was the defect, the new statute would have been rendered valid, in accordance with the general rule governing the re-enactment of invalid statutes.[21]

Thus narrowed, the cases involving amendment, without re-enactment, will be considered. The leading case sustaining legislative power to cure a statute by such an amendment, other constitutional requirements being satisfied, is Allison v. Corker.[22] The importance of the opinion in this case requires that it be set forth in some detail. The court said:

> But I am prepared to go farther and hold that an unconstitutional statute is nevertheless a statute — that is, a legislative act. Such a statute is commonly spoken of as void. I should prefer to call it unenforceable because in conflict with a paramount law. If properly to be called void, it is only so with reference to claims based upon it. . . . The function of the judicial department, with respect to legislation deemed unconstitutional, is not exercised *in rem*, but always *in personam*. The Supreme Court cannot set aside a statute as it can an ordinance. It simply ignores statutes deemed unconstitutional. For many purposes an unconstitutional statute may influence judicial judgment, where, for example, under color of it, private or public action has been taken. An unconstitutional statute is not merely blank paper. The solemn act of the legislature is a fact to be reckoned with. Nowhere has power been vested to expunge it or remove it from its proper place among statutes.

Some other decisions and dicta follow this same rule.[23] In another New Jersey case,[24] the court stated: "It clearly was not necessary, in accomplishing this result, to repeal the whole corporation act, and re-enact it with the changed provisions. The method adopted was the usual and, as I think, the proper one."

[20] 114 Neb. 540, 208 N. W. 639 (1926). Also Allison v. Corker, 67 N. J. L. 596, 52 Atl. 362 (1902).
[21] Smith v. State Board of Medical Examiners, 172 Ga. 106, 157 S. E. 268 (1931); Clay v. Buchanan, 162 Tenn. 204, 36 S. W. (2d) 91 (1931).
[22] *Supra,* note 20.
[23] State, McLorinan v. Ryno, 49 N. J. L. 603, 10 Atl. 189 (1887); State ex rel. Salter v. McDonald, 121 Minn. 207, 141 N. W. 110 (1913). See City of Beatrice v. Masslich, 108 Fed. 743 (C. C. A. 8th 1901); Columbia Wire Co. v. Boyce, 104 Fed. 172 (C. C. A. 7th 1900); Jordan v. Griffin, 131 Ga. 487, 62 S. E. 673 (1908).
[24] State, Trenton Iron Co., Prosecutor v. Yard, 42 N. J. L. 357 (1880).

Some writers have sought to distinguish from the preceding cases sustaining amendment those in which the amendment removed some part, or supplied some necessary element, to make the statute valid. The opinions of some courts tend to make a distinction between an amendment which, for example, provides for notice to certain parties, such notice being required by the constitutional provision, as interpreted by the court, and an amendment which seeks to change the statute so as to make it in substance a permissible exercise of legislative power. Such opinions stress the competence of the legislature over the general subject sought to be covered by the statute, and differentiate the case in which this is present from the one in which the legislature does not have general competence to deal with it, on the assumption that an amendment could validate it, nevertheless, if the effect of a judicial decision holding it invalid is not to render it void in the sense of the "blank paper" concept. In the decision rendered in Ross v. Board of Supervisors [25] the Iowa court said:

. . . that the legislature may by amendment cure a constitutional defect in a statute the main purpose of which is within the scope of legislative power and give such amendment retroactive effect upon cases already begun and pending is expressly held by this court in Ferry v. Campbell.

The statement of the same court in the case cited in this quotation is as follows:

A re-enactment of the whole statute was unnecessary. The amendatory act simply removed an impediment to the enforcement of the tax, and, when that impediment was removed, the original act was effectual, and capable of enforcement by proceedings had under the new act.[26]

And also:

While it is true that the original act was unconstitutional, because it did not provide for notice, that defect has now been cured, and we must decide the case on appeal in the light of the law as it now exists.[27]

Similarly, in an eminent domain case, the Florida court speaks of the earlier statute as "merely invalid and inoperative" until the six-man jury was replaced by a jury of twelve.[28] Discriminations rendering the statute invalid may be removed by amendment to make

[25] Ross v. Bd. of Supers., 128 Iowa 427, 104 N. W. 506 (1905).
[26] Ferry v. Campbell, 110 Iowa 290, 81 N. W. 604 (1900), the quotation being from 110 Iowa at 301.
[27] 110 Iowa at 300.
[28] Jacksonville, Tampa and Key West Ry. v. Adams, 33 Fla. 608, 15 So. 257 (1894). See State v. McCall, 162 La. 471, 110 So. 723 (1926); Edalgo v. So. Ry., 129 Ga. 258, 58 S. E. 846 (1907).

it valid.[29] An Indiana case phrases it in a slightly different manner when it speaks of extending the statute to all objects to which it constitutionally ought to extend.[30]

One of the more recent cases of this type is that of Dwyer v. Volmer Trucking Corporation.[31] A statute of 1924 enacted by the New Jersey legislature failed to provide for the necessary notice in service of process as required by the Supreme Court of the United States. The statute was held invalid in the federal Supreme Court. In 1927 the New Jersey legislature amended the statute to cure the defect indicated in the Supreme Court opinion. The statute thereupon was applied by the New Jersey court to a case which had arisen in the interval between its enactment and the declaration of its invalidity, on the theory that it was amended so as to make it valid and, there being no vested rights involved, should be applied retroactively. The following statement in the opinion of the court indicates the essential basis of the decision:

> That decision did not act as a repealer of the statute of 1924, but merely pointed out the constitutional defect existing in the legislative enactment, and decided that the defect tainted the validity thereof and prevented its enforcement, leaving it, however, free to the sovereign power of the state to cure the evil by enacting proper legislation to that end.

We may now turn to the authority directly holding that an act, or a part of it, which is invalid cannot be amended so as to make it valid. The reason for these holdings is briefly stated by the Indiana court in Cowley v. Town of Rushville: [32]

> For, if the latter act . . . was unconstitutional and void, it is clear that the act . . . amendatory of the former act must also be unconstitutional and void; for a valid law cannot be enacted by amending an invalid and void law.

With this reasoning no quarrel can be raised if the premises upon which it is based be admitted. The court says that an amendment cannot make a law valid if it is invalid and void. The question to be settled is whether an invalid law is also void. The courts who agree with the Indiana court, and those making the distinction referred to

[29] People v. De Blaay, 137 Mich. 402, 100 N. W. 598 (1904).

[30] Walsh v. State ex rel. Soules, 142 Ind. 357, 41 N. E. 65 (1895).

[31] 105 N. J. L. 518, 146 Atl. 685 (1929); accord, Rubin v. Goldberg, 9 N. J. Misc. 460, 154 Atl. 535 (1931); Paris Mountain Water Co. v. Greenville, 110 S. C. 36, 96 S. E. 545 (1918).

[32] 60 Ind. 327 (1878); accord, Igoe v. State, 14 Ind. 239 (1860); Keane v. Remy, 201 Ind. 286, 168 N. E. 10 (1929); City of Plattsmouth v. Murphy, 74 Neb. 749, 105 N. W. 293 (1905); Dean v. Spartanburg County, 59 S. C. 110, 37 S. E. 226 (1900); State v. Long, 132 La. 170, 61 So. 154 (1913); Ex parte Bockhorn,

in discussing the cases differentiating invalidity in substance from invalidity of extent as to object, proceed upon the assumption that invalidity equals legal nonexistence. That is, for purposes of amendment the void ab initio doctrine is applied. Nothing can be amended that does not exist, runs the argument. Thus is hidden the problem to be solved, namely, whether anything exists to be amended. Courts holding that a repeal of the invalid act is effective must assume that something does exist. Courts holding with the Indiana court treat the question as similar to one involving the amendment of a repealed statute. A number of cases hold that such statutes cannot be amended.[33] Another type of case sometimes referred to in these opinions is that in which a law that was to have taken effect upon the happening of a specified event never went into effect because the event never occurred. Such a statute apparently cannot be amended.[34]

Reason and policy both dictate that amendments to invalid statutes should be permitted if they are not expressly prohibited by the constitution, and, so far as the writer knows, no state constitution at present contains such a prohibitory provision. This is not to say that the invalid statute should be held to be constitutional *merely* because of its amendment. If, as amended, it is still unconstitutional, it should be declared to be so. Nor does it mean that the procedural requirements of the constitution for accomplishing such an amendment should be relaxed by judicial decision. That they should be changed is clear to most students of legislation, but that does not mean that they should be changed by decision. In most states proper methods for accomplishing such changes exist in the constitutional amendment machinery.

When a statute is declared unconstitutional, either in part or in its entirety, an amendment should be permitted to make it valid if an amendment can make it so. On no score should the void ab initio view as to the effect of a judicial decision upon the existence

---

62 Tex. Cr. 651, 138 S. W. 706 (1911). See Pederson v. Patterson, 124 Or. 105, 258 Pac. 204 (1928); People v. Stout, 23 Barb. 349 (N. Y. 1856). An amendment of an invalid law may not be amended. Copeland v. Sheridan, 152 Ind. 101, 51 N. E. 474 (1899).

[33] State v. Wheeler, 172 Ind. 578, 89 N. E. 1 (1909); Lampkin v. Pike, 115 Ga. 827, 42 S. E. 213 (1902). But if the new amendment is a complete act in itself, it is not invalid merely because it amends a repealed act. Some courts treat this as a contrary view to that expressed in the cases cited above in this note. This technically is not true. Am. Fidelity Co. v. State, 128 Md. 50, 97 Atl. 12 (1916); Commonwealth ex rel. Richmond v. Chesapeake & Ohio Ry., 118 Va. 261, 87 S. E. 622 (1916). A statute providing that a repealed act could not be amended has been interpreted to permit the amendment of an unconstitutional statute. State v. Silver Bow Ref. Co., 78 Mont. 1, 252 Pac. 301 (1926).

[34] See People v. Onahan, 170 Ill. 449, 48 N. E. 1003 (1897).

of a statute be permitted to extend to such cases as these. The concern of the court should end when by constitutional means a statute is made constitutional. Nothing besides an erroneous statement of the general effect of a declaration of unconstitutionality has ever been adduced by the courts to support a decision that such amendments are ineffective, and nothing else can be adduced in support of them. To give such a general application to the void ab initio doctrine is to give it the status of express constitutional prohibition for this purpose. As stated repeatedly throughout this study, there are cases in which the void ab initio doctrine is properly applied, but this is not one of them. This class of cases illustrates most strikingly the undesirable results that can flow from a blind adherence to dogma, without analysis of its theoretical or practical foundations. All that can be said for the cases that hold to the void ab initio theory in connection with this problem is that they have been decided, and that they constitute indefensibly bad law, which the courts themselves can and should correct.

Legislatures should, to be sure, consider carefully each statute that has been declared unconstitutional and decide whether they wish to continue it in force. Those that cannot be continued in force by amendment or by re-enactment should be repealed. Those that can be continued and that the legislature wishes to continue should be permitted by the courts to be continued if, as remarked previously, no express constitutional provision dealing with form, procedure, or substance stands in the way of it. But the failure of the legislature to repeal statutes promptly should not affect judgment on the methods used to continue laws in force when it wishes to do so. To formulate a rule of law that the legislature must re-enact the statute or repeal, amend, and re-enact the statute to make it valid, when the constitution does not require it, is to make the courts the formulators of the rules of legislative procedure.

The problem raised by later constitutional amendments which render invalid laws valid if the constitutional amendment is construed to have a retroactive effect involves somewhat different considerations, and will be dealt with in a subsequent section.

II. EFFECT OF AN INVALID AMENDATORY
OR REPEALING STATUTE

This question will be dealt with at this point because it is naturally suggested by the preceding discussion, being the converse of the problem presented there.

The rule is general that an unconstitutional amendment to a

valid statute is of no effect, the statute being left in force just as though the amendment had not been enacted.[35] An unconstitutional statute seeking to repeal a statute is also ineffective, if it can be said that the legislature meant to leave the prior act in force if the new one were declared invalid.[36] An invalid repealing act does repeal a prior valid statute, however, if it is shown to the satisfaction of the court that the legislature meant to repeal it in any event and meant the new statute to be a complete substitute for the old one.[37]

The law upon this question of the effect of a repealing statute has sometimes been stated by writers and commentators to be in a state of confusion, the courts being divided as to the proper rule to be applied. Some courts are said to hold that a repealing act if invalid has no legal force whatever, others that such acts have the effect of a repeal. The cases do not support such a statement. All courts are apparently willing to hold that a repealing statute is ineffective if it is invalid and no other facts are present to complicate the question. All courts also seem willing to hold that such acts do repeal prior statutes if from the four corners of the statute, or from any other recognized source of interpretative rule, it is clear that the legislature meant to repeal the prior statute in any event. Nothing turns upon whether the repeal be express,[38] merely an inconsistent re-

---

[35] To cite the numerous cases on this point would be superfluous. They are collected in the Century and Decennial Digests under the appropriate sections under the title "Statutes." Random examples are: In re Cullinan, 97 App. Div. 122, 89 N. Y. S. 683 (1904); State v. Donato, 127 La. 393, 53 So. 662 (1910); Bissett v. Pioneer Irrig. Dist., 21 Idaho 98, 120 Pac. 461 (1912).

[36] People v. De Blaay, 137 Mich. 402, 100 N. W. 598 (1904); Williams v. State, 81 N. H. 341, 125 Atl. 661 (1924); Patapsco Guano Co. v. Bd. of Agriculture, 171 U. S. 345, 18 Sup. Ct. Rep. 862, 43 L. Ed. 191 (1897); In re Rafferty, 1 Wash. 382, 25 Pac. 465 (1890); State v. Luscher, 157 Minn. 192, 195 N. W. 914 (1923); State v. Edmondson, 89 Ohio St. 351, 106 N. E. 41 (1913); Rippinger v. Niederst, 317 Ill. 264, 148 N. E. 7 (1925); State v. Ehr, 57 N. D. 310, 221 N. W. 883 (1928). People v. Butler Foundry Co., 201 Ill. 236, 66 N. E. 349 (1903); Allen v. Raleigh, 181 N. C. 453, 107 S. E. 462 (1921); Fesler v. Brayton, 145 Ind. 71, 44 N. E. 37 (1896); Childs v. Shower, 18 Iowa 261 (1865); City of Portland v. Coffey, 67 Or. 507, 135 Pac. 358 (1913); Nevada v. Hallock, 14 Nev. 202 (1879). See the discussion in comment, 32 Col. L. Rev. 534 (1932). The cases on this point are also legion.

[37] Harvey v. Commonwealth, 20 Fed. 411 (C. C. Va. 1884); Ely v. Thompson, 3 A. K. Marsh. 70 (Ky. 1830); Blankenship v. St. L. R. R., 160 Mo. App. 631, 142 S. W. 471 (1912); In re Medley, 134 U. S. 160, 10 Sup. Ct. Rep. 384, 33 L. Ed. 835 (1890); Childs v. Shower, 18 Iowa 261 (1865). The cases in note 36, deciding that no repeal had taken place, by their reasoning sustain this position, those cases merely showing that the legislature had not intended to repeal. See recent case note, 17 Minn. L. Rev. 322 (1933).

[38] The cases usually say that there is no presumption of repeal if no express repeal is included in the statute, but that should not be understood to mean that if the intent be clear such failure to have an express repeal will never be interpreted to show an intent to repeal, although it would probably be so interpreted in the normal case.

peal [39] (that is, "all laws inconsistent with the provisions of this act are hereby repealed"), or whether the repealing provision be a separate section or an integral part of the repealing statute.[40] Of course, the ordinary rules on separability and partial unconstitutionality still govern, but if the repealing section is invalid — either on the merits or because integrally bound up with the substitute statute — it is nevertheless effective to repeal prior statutes if that is clearly the legislative intent, and is ineffective to accomplish such a repeal if such an intention is not clear. Courts may not agree on the interpretation of certain operative facts present in a given case; some tend to hold that legislative intent to repeal at all costs is clear, whereas in the same sort of case other courts may hold that no such intention has been shown. There is no clear distinction whereby courts and cases can be classified on this score, and it is believed that the particular cases, of which there are a great many, are decided on the facts of the case rather than in accordance with rule.

This curious, but nevertheless sensible and practical rule, giving sufficient effect to an invalid statute to permit it to accomplish what the legislature meant it to accomplish, is not without support from other branches of the law. As indicated elsewhere, invalid statutes have, under various circumstances, been taken to be effective expressions of legislative intention.[41]

This use of a qualification of the ab initio doctrine when good reason for introducing the qualification exists, the doctrine being left to operate in the normal case, is to be commended.

Those desiring more generality and certainty in legal rule will doubtless object that to leave it to judicial interpretation to determine what had been the legislative intention with respect to the old statute is to leave the law in a state of confusion. In this instance, however, much may be gained by permitting some elasticity in the application of the rule; *grave questions of policy* may be involved in the particular case if a general rigid rule be applied that invalidates entirely, and leaves without any legal effect, every unconstitutional repealing statute. Subsequent legislative sessions may cure the defect, but in the meantime it may be important that the statute previously existing be left in force, or that no statute be permitted

[39] An "inconsistent repeal" was held effective to repeal a prior statute although the repealing statute was held invalid, in In re Medley, *supra,* note 37.

[40] See People v. Fox, 294 Ill. 263, 128 N. E. 505 (1925); Equitable Guarantee & Trust Co. v. Donahue, 19 Del. 191, 49 Atl. 372 (1901); State v. Wardell, 153 Mo. 319, 54 S. W. 574 (1899).

[41] Bentley v. State Bd. of Medical Examiners, 152 Ga. 836, 111 S. E. 379 (1921), invalid statute gives legislative intent to exclude certain remedies. See Claybrook v. State, 164 Tenn. 440, 51 S. W. (2d) 499 (1932), defendant not guilty of manslaughter under repealed act though repealing act invalid. See Chapter 1.

to exist until the legislature has again expressed its will. While in the normal case the writer would favor the rule that invalid amendments or repeals are ineffective, still he favors the qualification introduced by the courts, because of the large element which policy and discretion may play in exceptional cases in this field of the law.

III. EFFECT OF CONGRESSIONAL ACTION REMOVING OBSTACLE TO STATE EXERCISE OF POWER

A situation that occasionally arises in a federal system, such as the American system, is that in which a state statute is declared invalid because it is in conflict with national law. As in interstate commerce, this conflict may arise because of the existence of positive statute law enacted by Congress, or it may result from inaction by Congress, silence on the part of Congress being taken to mean that neither state nor national occupation of the field is deemed desirable. Subsequently the field may be occupied by Congress, or may be occupied by the state because of congressional grant of permission to do so. May the statute be revived by congressional action without subsequent re-enactment by the state legislature?

The rule to be derived from the cases seems pretty clearly to be that such statutes may be revived in this manner unless they have been declared invalid under state constitutional provisions. An analysis of the cases in the several fields in which cases of this type have arisen will make clear the significance of this rule.

The situation has arisen several times in connection with interstate commerce. Federal and state cases have agreed that no re-enactment of the state statute is required if Congress has permitted the state to occupy the field previously denied to the states by Supreme Court decision.[42]

As was said in one case, state statutes thus declared invalid are not really declared *unconstitutional* but are declared to be *unenforceable* because of conflict with congressional power. Therefore the void ab initio doctrine should not be applied in these cases. The United States Supreme Court, when it declared the state law invalid, was said to have "in legal effect declared [that] its extension

[42] In re Rahrer, 140 U.S. 545, 11 Sup. Ct. Rep. 865, 35 L. Ed. 572 (1891); In re Van Vliet, 43 Fed. 761 (C.C. Ark. 1890); In re Spickler, 43 Fed. 653 (C.C. S.D. Iowa 1890); State v. Adams Express Co., 219 Fed. 794 (C.C.A. 4th 1915); McCollum v. McConnaughy, 141 Iowa 172, 119 N.W. 539 (1909); State v. U.S. Express Co., 164 Iowa 112, 145 N.W. 451 (1914); State ex rel. Bartlett v. Fraser, 1 N.D. 425, 48 N.W. 343 (1890); Storace v. Rossi, 69 N.C. 363, 37 Atl. 1109 (1897). See Tinker v. State, 90 Ala. 638, 8 So. 814 (1891); Commonwealth v. Calhane, 154 Mass. 115, 27 N.E. 881 (1890).

or application to liquor in the original packages, . . . in the absence of congressional sanction, was unconstitutional." [43] But, as said by this same court: "A statute is neither unconstitutional nor void for not containing an exception or qualification which the law will imply. Its operation will be restrained within constitutional limits, but the act itself will not be declared void." The statute not being unconstitutional in the sense of being void ab initio, it could be revived in its original form by congressional action permitting the state to apply the statute to articles previously held not subject to state control because such control interfered with interstate commerce. This is the theory of all of the interstate commerce cases on this point examined by the writer. Some cases, such as Atkinson v. Southern Express Company,[44] are sometimes cited to the contrary, but in that instance the state court had held the statute invalid because it was contrary to the state constitution as well as being in conflict with federal power. This being true, the case is to be grouped with those deciding that invalid statutes cannot be amended or revived by subsequent constitutional amendments or later legislative action in the state, and merely extends that principle to apply to a case where congressional action was held ineffective to cure a state constitutional defect in a statute.

Blair v. Ostrander [45] applies the rule that re-enactment is not required where Congress has removed the barrier limiting an invalid state statute providing that liens on land located within the county were binding only if filed in the county, Congress having later provided that federal courts should recognize liens in accordance with the rules of state law.

Bankruptcy cases have also involved this question. The theory of state and national power over bankruptcy seems to be that the states may enact laws covering the field, subject to some limitations, if Congress has not occupied the field. When Congress does enact a federal bankruptcy statute, state laws in conflict therewith are suspended from operation. They are not repealed by the federal statute but are suspended, and when Congress repeals its own statute, leaving the field unregulated, the courts have held that the state statutes again apply without re-enactment by state legislative bodies.[46]

National bank taxation by states has raised similar problems.

[43] In re Van Vliet, *supra*, note 42, at 765.
[44] 94 S. C. 444, 78 S. E. 516 (1913). This is also the explanation for Corbin v. McConnell, 71 N. H. 350, 52 Atl. 447 (1902).
[45] 109 Iowa 204, 80 N. W. 330 (1899). See Bank v. Clark, 55 Kan. 219, 40 Pac. 270 (1895), question raised but not decided.
[46] Tua v. Carriere, 117 U. S. 201, 6 Sup. Ct. Rep. 565, 29 L. Ed. 855 (1885); In re Wright, 95 Fed. 807 (D. C. Mass. 1899).

Here, too, the rule seems clear that if Congress permits, as it has permitted, state taxation of shares of stock in national banks, states may levy such a tax, subject to the restrictions prescribed by congressional statute. Suppose a state law is held to exceed these restrictions and subsequently Congress amends the federal statute so as to permit the tax hitherto declared invalid. Re-enactment should not be necessary here, either, to render such state statutes enforceable if Congress has permitted taxes of this kind. This is the rule, likewise, when a state taxes lands granted to railroads by the federal government, a later statute having removed the federal immunity from state taxes.[47] But, as in the interstate commerce cases, these state laws must be re-enacted if they have been held to be invalid because they are in conflict with state constitutional provisions as well as in conflict with the permissive federal statute. This is the explanation of a case like Stockyards National Bank v. Baumann.[48]

These cases seem to support the formulation of the rule of law stated at the beginning of this section.

IV. EFFECT ON INVALID STATUTE OF SUBSEQUENT CONSTITUTIONAL AMENDMENT

A more difficult but perfectly feasible method of removing constitutional obstacles from the path of statutes or of enlarging legislative powers is the constitutional amendment or, if need be, constitutional revision.

Several instances of the use of this method will occur to those familiar with our legal or constitutional history. The sixteenth amendment to the constitution of the United States is traceable to the decision by the Supreme Court of the United States in Pollock v. Farmers' Loan and Trust Company.[49] In New York[50] and Ohio[51] constitutional changes have also been made because of judicial decisions, the change in the former resulting from the decision in the famous Ives case.[52]

Some have thought that courts should incline toward the view that in case of doubt the statute should be declared unconstitutional,

[47] Cent. Pac. R. R. v. Nevada, 162 U. S. 512, 16 Sup. Ct. Rep. 885, 40 L. Ed. 1057 (1895).
[48] Stockyards Natl. Bk. v. Bauman, 5 F. (2d) 905 (C. C. A. 8th 1925). Also Cent. Natl. Bk. v. Sutherland, 113 Neb. 126, 202 N. W. 428 (1925).
[49] Pollock v. Farmers' Loan & Trust Co., 157 U. S. 429, 15 Sup. Ct. Rep. 912, 39 L. Ed. 1108 (1895).
[50] See N. Y. Const., Art. 10, sec. 19.
[51] F. R. Aumann. The Course of Judicial Review in the State of Ohio, 25 Am. Pol. Sci. Rev. 367, at 373, note 27 (1931). See Ohio Const., Art. 1, sec. 19a.
[52] Ives v. South Buffalo Ry., 201 N. Y. 271, 94 N. E. 431 (1911).

in order that proponents of the law may test the popular demand for it by amending the constitution so as to remove the doubt as to constitutionality. To require such a showing of popular support is said to furnish an educational impetus to the proponents of the measure that is desirable in popular government.[53] Many doubtless feel, however, that the difficulties normally attendant upon constitutional amendment in many of the states as well as in the national government put too great an impediment in the way of the realization of popular will through legislative action.[54]

A new constitution or a constitutional amendment may, of course, expressly recognize existing statutes, or doubtless even expressly validate statutes that have been declared unconstitutional under the former constitution or the constitution as it stood prior to amendment.[55] The constituent power presumably would extend to recognition of invalid acts even under the void ab initio theory, since that doctrine is not a limitation upon the power to make constitutions but rather upon legislative power. So, too, the converse is true; the statutes valid under the old constitution but prohibited under the new would be invalid.[56] The more difficult questions arise when the new constitution or the new constitutional provision does not expressly state whether existing statutes are to be perpetuated, or whether statutes invalid under the constitution prior to its amendment are revived without re-enactment by the legislature.

The cases are not harmonious in their answers to this question, and the opinions and decisions must be examined to make the divergences clear.

State ex rel. Stevenson v. Tufly,[57] a Nevada case, is much cited in this connection. In it a mandamus was sought to compel the investment of certain funds in accordance with the provisions of a statute that had previously been declared unconstitutional but which, because of a constitutional amendment, was alleged to be in effect despite the lack of re-enactment by the legislature. No new

[53] This is not the attitude expressed by courts, for they usually say that the presumption, in case of doubt, is in favor of the statute, not against it. See Cushman, Constitutional Decisions by a Bare Majority of the Court, 19 Mich. L. Rev. 771 (1921).

[54] Despite current complaint as to the ease with which the constitution of the United States can be amended, the fact remains that it is relatively difficult to amend it. The Child Labor Amendment is evidence of this, for at the time of its submission considerable support was mustered for it. It did not become the twentieth amendment, however.

[55] Henry v. State, 26 Ark. 527 (1871).

[56] Cock v. Stewart, 85 Mo. 575 (1885). See the interesting case of Durr v. Commonwealth, 3 Pa. Co. Ct. Rep. 525 (1887), statute valid prior to amendment, but repealed before amendment to constitution, may not be revived by repeal of repeal.

[57] 20 Nev. 427, 22 Pac. 1024 (1890). See State v. Tufly, 20 Nev. 427 (1897).

statute had been enacted on the subject. Mandamus was denied, the court stating that the statute could not be revitalized without legislative action. Strictly viewed, the constitutional amendment here involved gave the legislature only the power to enact such statutes and did not expressly affect prior or existing acts, nor was it meant to be self-executing. From this point of view the court could have decided that the petition for mandamus should be denied because the amendment had no retroactive effect and was, according to its express wording, intended to have none, and no new legislation had been adopted. According to some views of the nature of precedent and the technique of judicial decision, this is all that the case definitely settled. The Nevada court, in its opinion, however, expressed itself clearly on the effect of a constitutional amendment upon a prior invalid statute: "The act being void, no subsequent adoption of an amendment to the constitution, authorizing the legislature to provide for such investment, would have the effect to infuse life into a thing that never had any existence. . . ." [58]

That the Nevada court took this expression of opinion seriously is clear from a later case in which the court stated that the doctrine would apply to a case wherein the statute had not been judicially declared unconstitutional prior to the adoption of the constitutional amendment, but was declared so in the case arising subsequent to its adoption.[59] The constitutionality of the statute, under this opinion, is to be tested as of the time of its enactment.

A group of California cases turns more clearly on the intention and phraseology of the amendment, the court holding that it should not be so applied as to revive city charter provisions previously held invalid because inconsistent with state statute unless the words of the amendment unmistakably indicated that it should be so extended.[60]

Dewar v. People,[61] another case often referred to in this connection, is in accord with the California case; the Michigan court said in the course of its opinion that "the meaning of the charter is the same today that it was when adopted, and it cannot be affected and enlarged by any subsequent change of the constitution." Other Michigan cases agree with this position.[62]

---

[58] 20 Nev. at 429.

[59] Comstock Mill & Mining Co. v. Allen, 21 Nev. 325, 31 Pac. 434 (1892).

[60] Ex parte Sweetman, 5 Cal. App. 577, 90 Pac. 1069 (1907); Banaz v. Smith, 133 Cal. 102, 65 Pac. 309 (1901); Fleming v. Hance, 153 Cal. 162, 94 Pac. 620 (1908); Ex parte Sparks, 120 Cal. 395, 52 Pac. 715 (1898).

[61] 40 Mich. 401 (1879). See also Mount Pleasant v. Vancise, 43 Mich. 361, 5 N. W. 378 (1880).

[62] Seneca Mining Co. v. Secretary of State, 82 Mich. 573, 47 N. W. 25 (1890); DuHam v. Wilson, 53 Mich. 392, 19 N. W. 112 (1884).

In Oregon it was held that an eminent domain statute was not revived by a constitutional amendment adopted after the statute had been declared invalid; [63] similar decisions were rendered with respect to changes in the jurisdiction of certain courts in Louisiana [64] and Nebraska.[65] In the Nebraska case particular emphasis was laid on the void ab initio doctrine, and much was made of the "smitten at birth" type of argument. In Newberry v. United States [66] the court said in passing that the seventeenth amendment did not validate a statute enacted prior to its adoption. A later Louisiana case distinguishes cases like Pratt v. Allen [67] from the typical case of constitutional amendment subsequent to the enactment of an invalid statute by saying that if the legislature actually has power to enact the statute, it may do so in anticipation of constitutional change, making it take effect upon the occurrence of a certain and defined event, but that if the legislature does not have the power to enact the statute in the first instance, such a statute, whether declared invalid or not prior to the constitutional change, cannot be validated by the change when it is made, so long as the statute was not enacted with reference to the likelihood of the change.[68] Other cases have taken the same position as that of Pratt v. Allen and sustained statutes enacted in anticipation of the constitutional change, on the ground that legislative power existed to enact the statute.[69] A dictum in a Missouri case says that an amendment to the federal constitution does not have the effect of reviving a state statute that was invalid under the federal constitution at the time of its enactment.[70]

Turning to the cases usually cited as holding a subsequent constitutional amendment to have validated statutes which were invalid prior to the change, it must be conceded that several of them are difficult, if not impossible, to explain on the theory that, as a matter of interpretation, the amendment was intended to validate them. Some of the cases are explicable on this ground, but others are not.

Cobb v. Cohron [71] was a case involving statutes prescribing procedure for the trial of election cases in certain general trial courts, the legislature having the power to regulate the procedure in election disputes but not to give these courts jurisdiction over such

[63] Smith v. Cameron, 123 Or. 501, 262 Pac. 946 (1928).
[64] Mayor v. Blackburn, 27 La. Ann. 544 (1877).
[65] Whetstone v. Slonaker, 110 Neb. 343, 193 N. W. 749 (1923).
[66] 256 U. S. 232, 41 Sup. Ct. Rep. 469, 65 L. Ed. 913 (1921).
[67] 13 Conn. 119 (1839).
[68] Etchison Drilling Co. v. Flournoy, 131 La. 442, 59 So. 867 (1912).
[69] Galveston, B. & C. N. G. Ry. v. Gross, 47 Tex. 428 (1877).
[70] In re Graves, 325 Mo. 888, 30 S. W. (2d) 149 (1930).
[71] 26 S. W. 846 (Tex. Civ. App. 1894).

cases. Constitutional amendment later gave the power to these courts to try such cases. This amendment was held to validate the statute without re-enactment. In a sense this case is distinguishable from the jurisdictional and other cases hitherto discussed in that the amendment directly removed the obstacle to the validity of the statute rather than giving the legislature power to do so. In another sense it is in conflict with those cases, because the court did not stress this point in its opinion.

Other cases take this same view, that the constitutional removal of obstacles blocking portions of the legislative program expressed in the statute validates the entire act,[72] but the holdings are not unequivocal. In one of these cases, a civil service statute which had applied to a department to which it could 'not apply under the constitution as it stood at the time of the enactment was rendered valid by a constitutional amendment permitting all departments to be subjected to such legislation; the court emphasized the general power of the legislature to enact the law and insisted that the statute had not been declared *invalid* but merely *inapplicable* to this department. The basis for this inapplicability having been removed, it became applicable, because it was valid as applied to other departments.[73]

Hammond v. Clark,[74] declaring that a constitutional amendment cured an officer salary statute, and Fontenot v. Young,[75] giving effect to a statute invalid at the time of enactment because of the retroactive force of the amendment, are more difficult to harmonize with the doctrine of the cases described earlier.

Constitutional amendments curing or validating acts done, such as bonds issued, in reliance on invalid statutes, have been held to reach acts as well as statutes, and so far as acts rather than statutes are involved in these cases, can be validated because the doctrine of void ab initio has not been applied to acts done, as it has been to statutes.[76]

Most of the cases on the subject of this section can be said to be in harmony in actual decision; some writers have sought to explain them by saying that the element of interpretation, based upon the

[72] State ex rel. Marr v. Luther, 56 Minn. 156, 57 N. W. 464 (1894); People ex rel. McClelland v. Roberts, 148 N. Y. 360, 42 N. E. 1082 (1896).

[73] People ex rel. McClelland v. Roberts, *supra*, note 72.

[74] 136 Ga. 313, 71 S. E. 479 (1911).

[75] 128 La. 20, 54 So. 408 (1911). See also Beaudrot v. Murphy, 53 S. C. 118, 30 S. E. 825 (1898).

[76] Blake v. People, 109 Ill. 504, 31 N. E. 123 (1884); Hutchinson v. Patching, 126 S. W. 1107 (Tex. 1910), reversed on another point, 103 Tex. 497, 129 S. W. 603 (1910); Badger-Louisiana Land Co. v. Estopinal, 143 La. 775, 79 So. 339 (1918). See Hammond v. Clark, 136 Ga. 313, 71 S. E. 479 (1911).

intention of those framing the constitutional amendment, whether expressed or derived from surrounding circumstances, is decisive.[77] Power to pass the law has also been stressed, its existence being taken to mean that constitutional change could validate it. Few of the cases thoroughly discuss the theory involved in the question. It is clear, nevertheless, that some of the opinions proceed upon the assumption that the void ab initio doctrine is conclusive here, as it is with some courts in cases involving legislative amendment of the invalid statute. Others assume that it is not conclusive.

It should be clear that, as stated earlier in this section, the void ab initio doctrine is not conclusive. The constituent power may call a spade a spade, or it may call a spade a hoe, and a hoe it will be thereafter, so far as law is concerned. So those making or changing constitutions may revive an invalid statute by saying that it is revived, if anyone authorized to do so can find any trace of what the provisions of the statute were. The problem then is, What shall be the rule when there is no evident intention to revive any particular act?

It is submitted that the rule should be that in the absence of evident intent, to revive a prior invalid statute, the statue should be deemed not to have been revived. Most of the decisions support this rule; the few that do not proceed upon an erroneous assumption as to the scope of the doctrine of void ab initio. Constitutional amendments are relatively formal acts, and, as compared with statutes, less frequently made. Considerable periods of time elapse between the enactment of particular statutes and subsequent constitutional amendments upon the same subject, unless as occasionally happens, the statute is enacted in anticipation of the amendment. Normally the amendment should not do more than grant power, if an exercise of governmental power is contemplated; the legislature, which will be the legislative body in the usual case, should work out the details. Such a grant of power should be taken to mean that the amendment did not directly, as a self-executing instrument, affect prior invalid statutes upon the subject. The only rule of interpretation which should be stressed here, and which is incorporated in the rule as it is stated above, should be that intention to revive must be expressed in so many words before the courts will consider that result to have been achieved without legislative re-enactment.

This position is in perfect harmony with that advocated in the first section of this chapter. The two positions deal with two phases of the problem. The first deals with legislative power to amend in-

[77] 38 L. R. A. N. S. 78 (annotation).

valid statutes, if by such an amendment the statute could be rendered generally valid; the second deals with constitutional amendment and leaves to the legislature the power to determine whether the statute should be put into operation again, in the absence of specific constitutional provision on the subject. In both, the matter is left with the legislature, the ordinary law-making body.

A real difference exists between a legislative amendment to remove a defect in an invalid statute and a constitutional amendment. For the legislature to do this is an ordinary legislative function. It is part of what we think of as legislative work. Constitutional amendments, on the other hand, are seldom designed to act directly, in a self-executing manner, upon prior statutes, with a view to validating them. They are more properly designed to give or restrict power or to declare general policy, the exercise of the power in detail being left to the legislature. Unless a clear intention exists to vary the normal situation, the legislature should be the organ to act upon the question whether now, after power has been given it, the prior invalid act is desired, and if it is, it should so signify.

When constitutional amendments validate or cure acts done rather than statutes previously enacted, they are usually so expressed as to affect those acts directly; often the legislature is without power to act in a curative manner, and it is not thought desirable to give to it broad general powers to validate such acts. Such validating amendments differ from those discussed in the preceding paragraph in that they usually refer to specific acts done, whereas power-giving amendments commonly are phrased in more general terms.

V. CURATIVE, VALIDATING, AND COMPENSATORY ACTS

Thus far the remedial devices considered for overcoming defects in, or results of, unconstitutionality have dealt with changes in the statutes themselves or in the constitution. No clear line divides curative from validating statutes, although technically such a distinction can be drawn; in this section they will be considered together as methods for rectifying an unsatisfactory situation sometimes resulting from the invalidity of statutes and the acts done in reliance upon them. They seek to operate, in the usual case, upon persons or acts or situations or things rather than directly upon the invalid statutes themselves. Compensatory statutes may authorize money payments which are thought to be due, on ethical or moral grounds, but which could not be paid under the invalid statute.

Curative acts often encounter constitutional obstacles of their own, and it is not easy to clear all the constitutional hurdles in the path of such enactments. The separation of powers may prove a stumbling block, and care must be taken that the judgment of the court is not reversed, because courts are jealous of their judicial power, and probably very properly so in this type of case.[78]

Care must also be taken to see that the special legislation prohibitions included in many state constitutions are not violated, but courts have rendered this task less difficult because of their lenient attitude toward curative laws which are really special in character.[79] But a special act held invalid as such cannot be rendered valid by another act which is special.[80] A statute "validating" an invalid statute is ineffective.[81]

Other constitutional difficulties will be considered as they are presented by special cases, such as those involving the disturbance of vested rights or taxation for a public purpose. No specific restraints seem to have been placed upon acts curing or validating acts done in reliance upon unconstitutional statutes so far as the problem of capacity alone is concerned, but the generalization is often found in textbooks and judicial opinions that a curative or validating statute, if otherwise valid, is valid if the legislature could have done in the original defective statute what it seeks to do in the curative law. This statement is a very general one which furnishes little more than a general guide to the law on this subject, so far as unconstitutional statutes are concerned.

An interesting method of avoiding some of the injustices resulting from a strict application of the void ab initio doctrine in constitutional law is illustrated in Robinson v. Robins Dry Dock and Repair Company.[82] In that case a widow had relied upon a workmen's compensation statute instead of bringing an action for loss occasioned by the death of her husband; when the remedy afforded under the compensation statute was taken away because of the invalidity of that statute, she found that the period of limitations had run upon the right of action accruing under the personal injury statute. The legislature extended the time for the institution of such actions, and this extension was upheld by the New York Court of Appeals. The court narrowly restricted the decision, but nevertheless upheld the legislative extension of the period of limitations.

[78] Preveslin v. Derby & Ansonia Development Company, 112 Conn. 129, 151 Atl. 518 (1930); Bartlett v. Ohio, 73 Ohio St. 54, 75 N. E. 939 (1905); Richards v. Rote, 68 Pa. St. 248 (1871).

[79] State ex rel. Oblinger v. Spaude, 37 Minn. 322, 34 N. W. 164 (1887); State ex rel. Board of Education v. Minneapolis, 97 Minn. 402, 106 N. W. 477 (1906); City of Redlands v. Brook, 151 Cal. 474, 91 Pac. 150 (1907).

[80] Bartlett v. Ohio, supra, note 78.

[81] Roberts v. Roane County, 160 Tenn. 109, 23 S. W. (2d) 239 (1929).

[82] 238 N. Y. 271, 144 N. E. 579 (1924).

An earlier New York decision foreshadowed the New York law, in holding that the legislature might authorize an action against a town for the building of a bridge, despite the fact that action would not otherwise have been entertained against the town because of the absence of certain requisite formalities in the proceedings for the authorization of the structure.[83]

A number of cases have involved the power of the legislature to validate payments that should not have been made because of defective authority in the governmental unit making the payment, or directly to compensate for work or services rendered in reliance on invalid statutes. Other aspects of these cases have been considered in connection with various subjects dealt with in preceding chapters. Felix v. Wallace County,[84] a Kansas case, presented the question whether certificates to pay bounties could be "legalized" by statute after the authorizing statute had been declared invalid. The court held that no recovery could be had upon the certificates. The opinion distinguishes between legalization of the certificates and legalization of the act of the county board in issuing them. The latter might constitutionally have been done, intimated the court, but a legalization of the certificates themselves is insufficient to show that the legislature recognized a moral obligation and wished to satisfy it.

Taxes are apparently sustained in New York on the ground of moral obligation in cases where the money is used to pay for services rendered under contracts made by officers selected under invalid statutes.[85] In one of these cases the court said:

Conceding the act of 1855 to be unconstitutional, and all contracts under it to be invalid, it does not follow that the legislature might not, adjudging the services to be performed under the act to be valuable to the county, direct their payment absolutely, and cause a tax to be levied for that purpose.[86]

A Pennsylvania decision holds that a statute providing that where a county contracted for work but could not pay for it because it lacked the power to make the contract — the authorizing statute being invalid — "such contract is made valid and binding on such county" and to be paid for at the contract price, is constitutional and it is unnecessary first to enact a valid law authorizing the contract

[83] Wrought Iron Bridge Company v. Town of Attica, 119 N. Y. 204, 23 N. E. 542 (1890).
[84] 62 Kan. 832, 62 Pac. 887 (1900).
[85] People ex rel. McSpedon v. Haws, 12 Abb. Prac. 70 (N. Y. 1861); People ex rel. Commrs. of Records, 11 Abb. Prac. 114 (N. Y. 1860).
[86] People ex rel. Commrs. of Public Records, *supra*, note 85, at 121.

before validating the contract in this manner.[87] Emphasis was placed in the opinion upon the fact that the legislature might have authorized the contract in the first instance, but that it failed to do so in a constitutionally valid statutory form. The moral obligation created by reliance upon the statute was held to be sufficient to support the validating act, and thus to validate it was not a loan of public money to a private person.

An important California case is in agreement with this Pennsylvania decision in holding that the legislature may authorize payment for services performed for an unconstitutionally organized district, because to do so is not violative of the constitutional provision that public money shall not be paid except by express authority of law. This obligation, said the court, was created under a "law" as that term is used in the popular sense in this portion of the constitution, and inasmuch as the action was taken before the statute had been declared invalid, sufficient effect should be given to that popular acceptance of the word to create a moral obligation upon which to predicate a legislative act authorizing the payment of the obligation thus incurred.[88] In the course of the opinion the court said that

an unconstitutional statute is not always and for all purposes a nullity, so far as the rights of a citizen are concerned. After a citizen has dealt with the state under circumstances like those shown here . . . the legislature is not prohibited . . . from authorizing the payment to him of such reasonable sums as shall to it seem proper.[89]

Express denial was made by the court of the doctrine that an invalid statute is always and for all purposes absolutely void.

Another case of interest and significance in this group is Minnesota Sugar Company v. Iverson.[90] In this case the Minnesota court held that a bounty due under an invalid statute could not be legalized by subsequent statute. The reasoning is set forth at some length because of its significance.

That the legislature is without authority to appropriate money or to provide for the imposition of a tax, except for a public purpose, has again

[87] Kennedy v. Meyer, 259 Pa. St. 306, 103 Atl. 44 (1918). The court said, 259 Pa. St. at 320: "The theory upon which curative acts of the nature of the one now before us have been sustained is briefly this: where the legislature has power to enact the substance of a matter covered by a statute which has been declared void because unconstitutional in form . . . it may subsequently ratify and make legal anything done under the prior void legislation which it might previously have authorized in due form."

[88] Miller v. Dunn, 72 Cal. 462, 14 Pac. 27 (1887).

[89] 72 Cal. at 469.

[90] 91 Minn. 30, 97 N. W. 454 (1903).

and again been held by this court; and it would seem to be self-evident that if it cannot provide for the imposition of a tax, except for a public purpose, it cannot appropriate money for such purpose, the direct result being the imposition of a tax to replenish the treasury.[91]

And again:

It has again and again been held that an unconstitutional statute is simply a statute in form, is not a law, and under every circumstance or condition lacks the force of law, and further, that it is of no more saving effect to justify action taken under it than as though it had never been enacted. A moral obligation upon the part of the state must have something more substantial than legislation obnoxious to the fundamental law to rest upon — something more for a foundation or a starting point than a statute which is itself immoral. A moral obligation can never be deemed to rest upon the people of the state to discharge a contract made by the legislature in direct violation of the constitution, and no such obligation can be predicated upon the act in question.[92]

The fallacy of this argument should be clear to the careful student. The moral obligation resulting in such situations as those referred to in the preceding paragraphs is predicated upon a number of elements, not upon a single one; in no case is it predicated upon an unconstitutional statute alone. The fact that people acted in reliance upon the statute is an important factor in these cases; that the court feels that they were entitled to rely upon it under all the circumstances is another; and that the condition resulting from this fair reliance is one justifying equitable claims is a third. The court may hold that an invalid statute is void ab initio. When it does so, it holds that the statute is to be treated as though it had never been enacted, but that does not mean that the *fact* must necessarily be ignored that the statute books carried what looked like a statute, and that people acted as though it were a statute. This *fact* is one of the elements that go into the new situation, and this new situation may be such that legislation recognizing it is valid. But, as noted in the opening chapter, the void ab initio view does not admit even the *fact* of a statute. The reasoning of the Minnesota court is logically without flaw if one assumes as a premise what is not true, namely, that the only factor present in such situations is the invalid statute. Further evidence is here presented of the power of words to control the reason of men, and even of judges.

Michigan Sugar Company v. Auditor General [93] is distinguish-

---

[91] 91 Minn. at 37.

[92] 91 Minn. at 40.

[93] 124 Mich. 674, 83 N. W. 625 (1900). See also State ex rel. Garrett v. Froelich, 118 Wis. 131, 94 N. W. 50 (1903).

able from the Minnesota decision; while the tenor of the opinion leads one to believe that the court sympathized with the viewpoint of the Minnesota court, mandamus was properly refused, no appropriations having been made for the payment of the bounties.

United States v. Realty Company [94] contains a dictum expressing the opinion that a sufficient moral obligation is created to support a bounty law when persons claiming the bounty have relied upon a bounty statute held to be invalid, providing, of course, that it has not been declared invalid prior to the reliance referred to.

The weight of reason is with the cases opposed to the Minnesota case, but the courts must be recognized to be divided. And yet the Minnesota court said, in a dictum, that taxes collected under an invalid statute could be returned by legislative act.[95] The two positions are difficult to reconcile.

In studying the cases of attempted validation of invalid tax levies or assessments, the general rules enunciated in the opening paragraphs of this section are illustrated very nicely. A tax cannot be validated if as a result of the validation it still suffers from a constitutional defect, such as non-uniformity.[96] The only way to cure a non-uniform tax is to make it uniform. So, too, an act that "legalized, ratified, validated, and confirmed" taxes, and thereby sought to cut off the right of the taxpayer to test their validity after he had initiated an action for that purpose, is invalid.[97] But if the curative act or the validating act supplies sufficient corrective remedy, the assessment may be upheld even though the levy has been invalid originally.[98]

Where benefits have been received as the result of public improvements constructed under an invalid statute, the legislature has been held to have the power to provide for the assessment of benefits against the benefiting owners, and if this assessment is free from constitutional objection on the merits, it is valid so far as validation is concerned. In a leading case, the court said:

The work having been done under void authority, and the property owners having received the benefits of the street improvements, the legislature had the clear right to legalize what it might previously have

[94] 163 U. S. 427, 16 Sup. Ct. Rep. 1120, 41 L. Ed. 215 (1896). Cf. Guthrie Natl. Bk. v. Guthrie, 173 U. S. 528, 19 Sup. Ct. Rep. 513, 43 L. Ed. 796 (1899), statute sustained which validated obligation incurred by group of people as in municipal organization, when in law they were not yet a municipality.

[95] Minneapolis Brewing Company v. Bagley, 142 Minn. 16, 170 N. W. 704 (1919).

[96] People v. Lynch, 51 Cal. 15 (1875).

[97] New Smyrna Inlet Dist. v. Esch, 103 Fla. 24, 137 So. 1, 138 So. 49 (1931). See also Smith Bros. v. Williams, 100 Fla. 642, 126 So. 367 (1930).

[98] Blake v. People, 109 Ill. 504 (1884).

ordered. That the legislature has the power to pass such remedial legislation is settled by abundant authority.[99]

Note particularly that here no validating or curative legislation was attempted; nothing more was done than to provide for the assessments where public improvements had been done under invalid laws. The underlying theory of such a decision as this is of course that of the moral obligation referred to in the preceding cases. The United States Supreme Court has held in accord with the preceding case.[100] A tax imposed to pay off bonds issued under an invalid statute because the people were said to have shown a desire that the aid be given to the project for which the bond issue was floated, having approved the issue at a popular election, has been upheld, although an act validating the bonds themselves would have been invalid.[101] The purpose being public, the tax was valid. The legislature could have done this itself originally. An early New York case sustains an act authorizing notice and assessment on the same basis as that which had taken place under an invalid statute, notice having been unconstitutionally omitted in the first proceeding.[102]

With respect to the possibility of curing defects in bond issues, the Florida court has said:

The legislature, in view of organic limitations upon the subject, being without power to authorize the bond issue, the act . . . purporting to validate the bonds is of course ineffectual.[103]

The Supreme Court of the United States said, in Beloit v. Morgan:

Whenever it has been presented, the ruling has been that in cases of bonds issued by municipal corporations, under a statute upon the subject, ratification by the legislature is in all respects equivalent to original authority, and cures all defects of power, if such defects existed, and all irregularities in its execution.[104]

But that court has also held that bonds cannot be validated if they could not have been validly issued when originally issued.[105] The

[99] Donley v. Pittsburgh, 147 Pa. St. 348, 350, 23 Atl. 394 (1892).

[100] Spencer v. Merchant, 125 U.S. 345, 8 Sup. Ct. Rep. 921, 31 L. Ed. 763 (1887).

[101] State ex rel. C. C. & C. Ry. v. Whitesides, 30 S.C. 579, 9 S.E. 661 (1888). See the discussion in City of Ottawa v. Hulse, 332 Ill. 286, 163 N.E. 685 (1928).

[102] Lang v. Kiendl, 27 Hun 66 (N.Y. 1882). That re-assessments may be ordered, when first ones were invalid, see City of Chester v. Black, 132 Pa. St. 568, 19 Atl. 276 (1890).

[103] State ex rel. Nuveen v. Greer, 88 Fla. 249, 102 So. 739 (1924). See discussion in Kunkle v. Town of Franklin, 13 Minn. 127 (1868), sustaining validation of bonds issued without authority.

[104] 7 Wall. 619, 19 L. Ed. 205 (U.S. 1868).

[105] See discussions in Katzenberger v. City of Aberdeen, 121 U.S. 172, 7 Sup. Ct. Rep. 947, 30 L. Ed. 911 (1886); Lewis v. City of Shreveport, 108 U.S. 282, 2 Sup. Ct. Rep. 634, 27 L. Ed. 728 (1882).

New York court has held that legislation may not validate a bond issue so as to make it a debt against the town if the issue is invalid originally, unless the validating act can supply the constitutional defect and does so.[106] This doctrine was carried so far by one of the lower courts of New York state that ratification of the issue could not save an officer from personal liability on the bonds when he had issued them without first calling an election which he knew to be necessary, because to remove his liability would be violative of the contracts clause of the federal constitution.[107] According to a Florida decision,[108] bonds, though not subject to validation, may, if invalid, nevertheless be paid off by new taxes or by a new valid bond issue, providing, of course, that the bonds could originally have been validly issued.

A statute validating and curing a bond issue and proceedings in the organization of an electric district was held to be ineffectual in Anderson v. Lehmukuhl,[109] the court stressing the fact that the law was special and that no moral obligation existed to support it. The court intimated that a curative act might have been effective here if it had been properly formulated, but gave no clue as to the method to be employed. Presumably the only thing that would have saved the situation would have been for the validating statute to have validated the evidences of indebtedness themselves, on the theory that there was a moral obligation to support the later statute because of popular reliance upon the earlier defective proceedings and issues. A Minnesota case, however, differs from the New York cases mentioned above; it upheld a statute providing that warrants issued under an invalid act "shall become a lawful indebtedness of such county" and outlined the procedure for taxation to provide the necessary funds with which to pay the warrants.[110] Here, too, equitable obligation was stressed by the court as being sufficient to support the statute.

The proper and heartening use that some courts make of the doctrine of moral obligation to sustain validating or curative acts seeking to impose financial honesty upon the government is illustrated by this statement from an opinion:

It follows that the treasury warrants in suit are not only not receivable for taxes, but they are not even legal obligations of the state. Nothing herein, however, must be construed into an expression of opinion that

[106] Horton v. Town of Thompson, 71 N. Y. 513 (1877). See the discussion in People ex rel. D. W. & P. R. R. v. Batchellor, 53 N. Y. 128 (1873).
[107] Hardenburgh v. Van Keuren, 16 Hun 17 (N. Y. 1878).
[108] Cheney v. Jones, 14 Fla. 587 (1874) at 614.
[109] 119 Neb. 451, 229 N. W. 773 (1930).
[110] State ex rel. Skyllingstad v. Gunn, 92 Minn. 436, 100 N. W. 97 (1904).

no moral obligation rests upon the legislature to provide for them. The majority of claims upon which they are issued are as meritorious as the salaries of the present state officers. And the holder of the warrants ought to be considered as the equitable assignee, pro tanto, of the claims and subrogated to all the rights and equities of the original claimants.[111]

The general rule with respect to the validation of bond issues seems to be, then, that such issues may not be validated unless the curative act also contains something that renders the issue valid, and that if this remedy is not furnished by the curative act the cure fails, under the general rule referred to earlier in this section: that if originally invalid, subsequent legislation cannot make it valid, if the defect is one of capacity. Some courts, however, permit the recognition of a moral obligation upon which may be predicated the imposition of taxes or new bond issues to satisfy the original invalid obligation, while others refuse to permit such a moral obligation to be raised. Curative acts are valid as to bonds, if the curative act itself furnishes the missing element in the original statute, such as notice or hearing.

Reference has been made earlier to the cases involving the validation of cities and corporations, and their acts and proceedings and fiscal obligations, done under invalid statutory authorization. It will be remembered that the line was drawn in some of the cases between recognizing the acts done under the statute and validating the corporations and proceedings themselves, and that some courts were willing to permit the recognition of facts, such as existing bonds or cities, and permit their validation, in effect, but refused to permit acts that sought directly to legalize the proceedings.[112]

Some courts permit the type of statute that expressly legalizes defective incorporation, as such, without drawing such distinctions.[113] A Texas case upheld a statute providing that school districts organized under invalid laws "are hereby in all things validated" and "all acts" of the governing boards "are hereby in all things ratified, confirmed, and validated." [114] Other cases are in accord with this view.[115]

In Ohio, on the other hand, a statute was declared invalid which, with respect to invalidly organized school districts, provided that

[111] Henry v. State, *supra*, note 55.

[112] See Chapter 3. An attempt to cure the statute often fails, as in Anderson v. Lehmkuhl, 119 Neb. 451, 229 N. W. 773 (1930).

[113] State ex rel. Lee v. Thief River Falls, 76 Minn. 15, 78 N. W. 867 (1899).

[114] Pyote Ind. School Dist. v. Dyer, 34 S. W. (2d) 578 (Tex. Comm. App., sec. A. 1931).

[115] Lyford Ind. School Dist. v. Williams Ind. School Dist., 34 S. W. (2d) 854 (Tex. Comm. App., sec. A. 1931).

the districts "shall . . . continue to be and remain and be recognized and regarded as legal special school districts." Also, provision was made that "any school district . . . which has been established by a vote of the people in accordance with any act of the General Assembly or which has been established by a general or local act . . . shall constitute a school district . . . to be styled a special school district." [116] This, the court held, constituted a special law and, furthermore, a violation of the separation of powers. For, said the court, "it is well settled that the legislature cannot annul, reverse, or modify a judgment of a court already rendered, nor require the courts to treat as valid laws those which are unconstitutional."

A New York decision permits the validation of proceedings taken under an invalid statute in the organization of a private corporation. [117]

Here, as throughout this subject, the courts divide, some being much slower than others to permit curative and validating statutes to pass the gauntlet of constitutional provisions. The only safe thing for a legislature to do in the case of defectively authorized municipal corporations is to recognize the facts of the situation and treat them as facts rather than to refer to the proceedings and organizations as such, because in that way alone can they be certain that they will not run counter to the void ab initio doctrine. None of the courts apparently have thus far refused to permit legislation to recognize a group of people living together with the forms of governmental organization and to call that group whatever name the legislature will call it, and give to it directly, or by such classification or reference, whatever powers it will, providing that by so doing no other provision of the constitution has been transgressed.

One cannot help being struck with the difficulties that beset the path of remedial legislation of the various types discussed in this chapter. Courts may be expected to recognize more clearly in the future the nature of the theory underlying the creation and recognition of the doctrine of moral obligation. Also, more leeway is to be expected in permitting legislatures to at least refer to acts done under the supposed authority of statute, so that direct validation of proceedings and cities may be as effective as to validate them by saying that all groups of people who attempted to become cities but failed shall now be called cities and be treated as such. The tax and bond cases are somewhat more satisfactory. Direct imposition of the tax itself by curative act has accomplished much in this field, and

[116] Bartlett v. Ohio, 73 Ohio St. 54, 75 N. E. 939 (1905).
[117] People v. Newburgh Plank Road Co., 86 N. Y. 1 (1881).

has been generally upheld. The limitation on all these cases still persists, and properly so, that if the curative act does not aid in removing some original defect or supply some lack of power in the legislature itself, then such attempts are ineffectual. This results from the theory of constitutional limitations itself, and is no more true of curative laws than of the original laws themselves. But the void ab initio theory should not be given the force of express constitutional provision, because it is not that, but only a theory of the effect of decision.

Chapter XII

JUDICIAL REVIEW AS AN INSTRUMENT OF GOVERNMENT

I. INTRODUCTION

A study of the effect of an unconstitutional statute or of decisions on constitutionality is a study of one phase of the operation of judicial review. Some observations upon judicial review as a device of government rather than as a purely legal doctrine may therefore not be amiss, although they should be taken as suggestive fragments only, pending further studies that will furnish more reliable data and generalizations.

Three phases of judicial review suggest themselves when the doctrine is viewed as an instrument of government: (1) its function in a federal system in enforcing the constitutional distribution of powers territorially; (2) its function in any given unit of government in preserving the constitutional separation of powers between departments; (3) its function in adjusting relations between government and the individual, as an instrument for enforcing constitutional guarantees of individual rights.

1) Judicial review in a federal system. — The rôle of judicial review in the United States as an instrument of federalism has been pointed out by many commentators. Professor Westel W. Willoughby, in his *Constitutional Law,* has emphasized this phase of judicial review by the very organization of the materials in the first volume of his work; in doing so he has influenced other writers and teachers and has again drawn attention to the place of the Supreme Court in our federal system, a place which that court itself has usually remembered in the decision of cases.

From the standpoint of federalism, judicial review of both legislative and administrative acts is a method of enforcing constitutional limitations upon the national government in its relations with the states, upon the states in their relations with the national government, and upon the states in their relations with each other. It serves a somewhat similar function in the states, being utilized to some extent to interpret and apply the rules governing the relations between the state governments and their subdivisions, such as counties and cities. In a general sense it is common to speak of the state governments as being unitary in character; but inasmuch as a number of state constitutions include constitutional guarantees protecting local units of government in the possession of certain powers and functions, judicial review serves also to maintain the constitutional boundaries of power fixed for state and local governments in their relations to each other.

2) Judicial review and the separation of powers. — The constitutional doctrine of the separation of powers has likewise given to judicial review a political significance, because the operations of, and demands upon, government are such that deviations from the doctrine are often attempted and are frequently necessary. Whether the case involves one or the other, it may be brought to the judiciary for settlement, although the great majority of disputes between departments never reach the stage of formal legal litigation, being settled by surrender or compromise on the part of one or more of the departments concerned. But occasionally judicial aid in settling the dispute is invoked, and when it is, it is politically significant.

3) Judicial review to protect private rights. — Less attention will be paid here to the use of judicial review to enforce constitutional limitations upon government in favor of the individual, because while it is a political device or technique, it has come to partake, in a sense, of a more strictly legal rule or doctrine, being applied by the courts more as are the usual rules of law, in the settlement of disputes between private parties. Something will be said upon this problem, but it has been so fully covered by previous writers, and so little has been said of the other two uses of judicial review, that the latter will receive the major portion of the space in this chapter.

II. DEFECTS IN THE OPERATION OF JUDICIAL REVIEW

A. PRIVATE LITIGANTS

One of the most striking facts about judicial review as an instrument of government is that many constitutional problems of government, and problems of the relations between the units and departments thereof, are raised, formulated, and presented to courts by private litigants. Private parties often raise constitutional issues of governmental power that are not primarily concerned with individual rights; issues that really concern governments, not individuals; that concern the distributions of governmental power rather than the exercise of an excess of such power against the individual.

In this practice lies one of the chief weaknesses of judicial review as it is exercised in the state and federal courts.

The national government sometimes brings a legal action against a state. Sometimes that government sues as a proprietor, as in the cases involving its territories; at other times it sues to defend its political powers or to restrain the states from crossing the constitutional boundaries fixed for them. The states are at a disadvantage in this relationship because they may not sue the national government, although they may be sued by it. This is an indefensible rule, the result of a failure to understand that to permit such suits is no disparagement of the constitutional position of the national government, but is only necessary when judicial settlement takes the place of non-legal modes of settling political disputes between members of a federal system. The states must, therefore, rely upon private individuals to present their interests in restraining the national government from overstepping constitutional limitations upon the latter government.

Many cases are presented by private parties on the one side and representatives of a governmental division on the other, often where the issues are primarily intergovernmental or interdepartmental and only incidentally involve the relation of the individual to the government.

Governments exercise little or no control over private parties in such instances, and although the legal representatives of affected governments may, upon application, be permitted to appear in a case, frequently no such leave is requested. Cases are therefore not infrequently decided with only one of the affected governments officially represented.

It should be remembered that under our system of judicial review the public or private nature of the question involved is not always divulged by a glance at the record of a legal action. The names of the parties of record often give practically no clue to the real parties to the action. Some requirement that courts must notify interested governments or departments when questions are raised in litigation which, to judge from the records alone, appear to have no relation to these public bodies would do much to aid in the proper presentation of the issues involved.

Cases between the states more commonly show the states, as governmental units, as official parties of record, but this is not an invariable rule.

Numerous instances can be cited that duplicate the situation presented recently in one of the states, wherein the legislature enacted a congressional redistricting act, which was vetoed by the governor. In the arguments on the constitutionality of this act the attorney-general represented the legislature and a private volunteer represented the governor.[1] Several objections to this practice readily suggest themselves.

1) Public nature of controversy not clear. — One effect is that it almost certainly obscures, to some extent, the essentially public nature of many of the constitutional controversies presented to courts for decision; if the public nature of the question is made clear, to have it so formulated as to make it seem one between a private individual and a government, instead of one between governments or departments. This in turn accounts in part, though not completely, for the surprising private-law technique that often appears in, and dominates, decisions and opinions in the field of public law, in the state and federal courts. The setting and spirit of the case is essentially that of a private litigation.

An interesting example of this is to be found in the case in which a private individual sues to have a tax law declared invalid because it is contrary to the inspection clause of the constitution of the United States. The rule stated in the constitution is that if the tax is excessive, the excess shall go to the treasury of the United States.[2] In a number of instances taxes have been declared to be excessive under this rule, but the excess has not gone into the national treasury. It is pretty clear that in some of these cases the national government did not know of the excess, although the Supreme Court of the United States declared the tax to be excessive. Nothing on the record shows that the law officers of the national government were ever notified that the case was pending.[3]

There are, of course, many constitutional questions which are properly raised and formulated by private parties, as in cases under bills of rights. But the group of cases referred to here is that in which, for example, state laws are challenged by individuals not acting in a public or official capacity, on the ground that the power exercised by the state belongs to the national government. The practice that permits this to be done has the result of making all persons, collectively or individually, the proper representatives of either government, without any necessary supervision or control over the parties by the government so represented.

This doctrine that any person may represent the government is the converse of the theory of popular sovereignty. Not only does

[1] State ex rel. Smiley v. Holm, 285 U. S. 355, 52 Sup. Ct. Rep. 397, 76 L. Ed. 795 (1932).

[2] Constitution of the United States, Art. I, sec. 10.

[3] Phipps v. Cleveland Ref. Co., 261 U. S. 449, 43 Sup. Ct. Rep. 418, 67 L. Ed. 739 (1923).

the government represent the people but every citizen may represent the government. To carry this theory to such absurd lengths produces undesirable results. It tends to overemphasize the interest of the individual and to minimize that of the politically organized group, in the constitutional distribution of governmental power and the maintenance of such a distribution. It also tends to make all constitutional questions seem primarily to involve excess of governmental authority, supposedly to the disadvantage of the individual. It reflects the legal rules applicable to persons rather than the political principles applicable to government. It is evidence of the influence of the individualistic private law of the past century, in the American philosophy of government. To make of almost every constitutional problem a problem of individual rights is going too far for effective government and for effective use of judicial review in government.

It should also be remembered that in some instances certain groups of individuals are interested in having no governmental action whatever on the subject, that is, in having the field left open to anarchy or, as it is more nicely phrased, open to individual initiative without the fetters of governmental regulation.

2) Private individuals control presentation of questions. — Another defect in this practice of permitting private parties to take the initiative in raising questions of constitutional power is that it leaves to the whim of the individual the determination of the time when such questions shall be raised and settled. There is no way of compelling private parties to initiate a suit to challenge or defend state or national legislative action, and private parties cannot always be depended upon to do so merely because the public welfare dictates that it should be done, and done quickly. Usually private parties do not take action until private interests are affected adversely.

The cases are legion in which courts have been called upon to determine questions of constitutional power long after the power has been asserted, long after it has been exercised, and long after large groups of the public have acquiesced in, and conformed their lives or business practices to, the exercise of the power. A statute may be declared valid or invalid a few days or weeks after its enactment, but more often some months slip by before the question is determined; in numerous instances several years have elapsed; and in a few cases from twenty-five to fifty years have passed before the question has been raised and settled. It took a long time, for instance, to determine whether a national protective tariff law was valid. Half a century elapsed before the Tenure of Office Act was declared invalid. No great public or private damage was done in either instance by the long delay, but that would not have been the case if the tariff act had been declared invalid. Bond and tax statutes are examples of laws under which great injury may be inflicted by a delay in deciding upon constitutionality. The laws declared invalid in Farmers' Loan and Trust Company v. Minnesota [4] are in point. Other examples will be found in the preceding chapters. Long delay sometimes means that the courts are practically powerless to declare a statute invalid because of the hardships resulting from such a decision.

Sometimes courts refuse to declare a statute unconstitutional when the exercise of power has gone unchallenged for so long; on the other hand, courts sometimes feel bound to hold the statute invalid if it seems clear to them that it is so. Judicial regrets are often very explicitly stated in such opinions, and not infrequently suggestions for rectifying the resulting situation. Difficult questions are raised by these decisions, such as those of the retroactivity of the effect of the decision, and the status of those who in good faith have relied upon the statute for so many years.

To the contention that public policy is sometimes better served by delay in the settlement of some of these constitutional questions, the answer is that, if this is really true, the courts can easily invoke the doctrine of political questions to avoid the responsibility for deciding the question at all. This class of cases is quite small, however, and normally more is to be gained by an early than by a delayed decision, if judicial review is accepted as a principle.

It is only natural that private persons should wait until their private interests are affected and that cases are likely to be presented in terms of individual rights rather than in terms of the relation of one department to another.

Governments themselves are not sufficiently ready to raise and have determined questions of constitutional power. Law officers of the government could contribute something here by giving more recognition to the public benefits to be derived from an early determination of many of these questions, and they should not wait, as they now so commonly do, for some private interest to be affected before presenting the issue to a court. The adoption of the Declaratory Judgment Act should facilitate this, and if any doubt exists about the authority to do this, the Act should be amended so as to remove it.

[4] 280 U.S. 204, 50 Sup. Ct. Rep. 98, 74 L. Ed. 371 (1930). See also First Natl. Bk. of Boston v. Maine, 284 U.S. 312, 52 Sup. Ct. Rep. 174, 76 L. Ed. 313 (1932). See the long delay in reviewing land office rules, H. L. McClintock, The Administrative Determination of Public Land Controversies, 9 Minn. L. Rev. 420 (1925).

3) Rules on parties narrowly interpreted. — The whole matter is complicated by the rules applied in determining whether particular parties of record are the proper ones in a given case. The rules governing the raising of constitutional questions have been relatively liberal, but some surprising exceptions to this generalization exist. If private parties are to be permitted to represent governments in these questions, if they are to carry the burden of presenting and formulating constitutional issues for judicial decision, then the rules as to who may raise a constitutional question should be very liberal indeed. Membership in the politically organized community should be sufficient for this purpose, if this is to be the theory upon which the practice is to be justified. The rules as they now exist require an unjustified showing of personal interest in a strictly private-law sense. The writer does not believe that private individuals alone should be permitted to obtain a determination of such public questions, but if they are to be relied upon to obtain such determination, it should be made easy for them to do so.

Under this system not even all cases of governmental invasion of constitutionally guaranteed individual rights are always raised, even though private persons be injured, if the parties do not know the source of the injury, do not know their legal rights, or are too poor to assert them.

4) Conflict of governmental and private interests. — Still another difficulty resulting from private representation of government in this field is the divergence in interests which sometimes exists between the government and the self-appointed representative acting for it. An individual may, for example, by failing to appeal a case, really embarrass a government considerably in its work, if the decision be adverse to its claims, and may conclude a governmental unit for a long time for all practical purposes, and the case may have been very badly managed in the lower court, from the standpoint of the government. Appeal rights may be lost by the lapse of time, and decisions not appealed from are conclusive upon the parties under the doctrine of res adjudicata, and have the force of precedent, under the doctrine of stare decisis, and although a case may later be carried to the highest court and a different decision obtained, much confusion and injury may have been occasioned by the earlier decision in the inferior court. Not all important constitutional questions are appealed simultaneously to the highest courts, as students of law and government know too well. Friendly suits sometimes result in a judicial decision on a question which both parties are in fact interested in having decided the same way.

B. Judicial Review and Legislation

A second striking fact about judicial review is that it exercises so little preventive influence upon the course of legislators and administrators. By this it is not meant that judicial review is never heeded, for it is sometimes, and at times it seems an insuperable obstacle to reform and progress to those whose programs have encountered its rebuffs. But it must be clear, nevertheless, to those familiar with the work of government that it is astonishing that judicial review should exercise so slight a restraint as it does upon governments and departments, when the whole of the work of government is considered. What is meant by the first sentence of this paragraph is that years of judicial review have not influenced legislatures sufficiently to keep them from enacting thousands of invalid statutes.

That the many decisions on constitutional questions in state and national courts have not prevented the enactment of other invalid acts must be clear to those who read current decisions. Courts are constantly being called upon to declare laws unconstitutional that should have been known to be invalid from a study of previous decisions. The numerous special and local laws upon the books of the states whose constitutions prohibit such laws are well known to the careful student of local government. These laws illustrate not only the ineffectiveness of the deterrent supplied by judicial review but also the unsatisfactory situation prevailing in some fields dependent upon private initiative to challenge invalid statutes. Private or local initiative procured the enactment of practically all these laws, and the very groups upon whom judicial review depends to raise constitutional questions as to their validity are interested in permitting them to go unchallenged.

The frequent failure of legislative bodies to give more than perfunctory heed to judicial decisions is not limited to decisions involving relationships between territorial units of government. It extends to the field of interdepartmental relations as well. For example, the Minnesota statute book still contains several statutes identical in form and substance with one declared invalid because it unconstitutionally narrowed the appointing power of the state governor.[5] These statutes are clearly invalid so long as the state Supreme Court does not change its mind and overrule its decision on this point, a possibility that did not, however, play an important part in the legislative decision with respect to the statutes still on the books. The

[5] State ex rel. Childs v. Griffin, 69 Minn. 311, 72 N. W. 117 (1897), and Minn. Stat. (Mason's, 1927), secs. 5395, 5757, 5846-21.

result of this carelessness on the part of the legislatures is that almost every general compilation of statutes contains numerous statutes that have been enacted subsequent to, and in violation of, decisions certainly applicable to them. It is perhaps perfectly permissible and proper practice for a legislative body to enact a statute that seems clearly to be invalid under existing decisions if it does so in the hope that these decisions will be overruled. But it is not proper to enact such laws because of indifference, carelessness, or ignorance.

Professor Emmett L. Bennett, who has recently analyzed a general election code enacted by the legislature of Ohio, has shown how many simple constitutional prohibitions and decisions can be violated by a legislature in any comprehensive act.[6] He points out clearly how the greater number of these mistakes in the statute could have been corrected or eliminated had the legislation been drafted with the skill, care, and knowledge that are available and necessary in the drafting of bills.

Some of these invalid statutes are clearly invalid and were believed by many of the legislators to be so, but were enacted because of political pressure or public demand. Many others have been and are enacted because they are not known to be invalid.

Several reasons for the failure of judicial review to act as a satisfactory preventive device come to mind upon reflection.

1) Delay. — Judicial review does not operate until considerable time has elapsed subsequent to the enactment of the statute or the promulgation of the regulation made by the executive authority. Advisory opinions to the legislature or to the executive have never been considered a proper part of judicial review in this country unless specific constitutional authorization for them could be found. So strongly is this idea entrenched in the judicial mind that the United States Supreme Court has only recently freed itself from serious doubts about the constitutionality of the declaratory judgment, which is in reality quite a different device.[7] The unfortunate results flowing from this restriction imposed on judicial review by doctrinal tradition have, of course, no necessary connection with the basic theory of the doctrine, but in operation the connection is clear and, as it now stands, is unfortunate in so far as preventive remedial work is concerned.

2) Furnishes insufficient standards for legislation. — The technique of judicial review furnishes too uncertain a standard for legislatures and administrators, because it operates through the decision

---

[6] 30 Ohio L. Rep. 127 (1930): "Should Constitutions Be Forgot?"
[7] Nashville, C. & St. L. Ry. v. Wallace, 53 Sup. Ct. Rep. 345 (U. S. 1933).

of individual cases and does not establish general rules. Statutes are not declared unconstitutional in general; constitutional provisions are not interpreted in general; and administrative regulations are not passed upon in general. Judicial review suffers, from this point of view, because it furnishes so little of generality or rule. The task of formulating generalizations is left to the legislature, to the administrator charged with executing the laws, to the citizen charged with adapting his conduct to conform to the laws, and to the courts later settling subsequent disputes involving similar, but not identical, situations or disputes. The difficulties that have vexed the administrative rate-making bodies in the public utility field have arisen in large part from the failure of the Supreme Court to lay down sufficiently explicit and comprehensive rules on this subject.[8] Judicial decisions under our practice and theory concern particular situations, particular parties, particular statutes, and particular constitutional provisions. These situations and parties, when added to the influence of procedural rules on the merits of the case, exert a powerful influence upon the court and its judgment as to constitutionality and as to the nature of unconstitutionality, its scope and effect. It must inevitably be true, also, that when stare decisis is not the inflexible rule (and it is not in constitutional matters), and decisions are overruled, or statutes are held valid as to Smith, but invalid as to Jones, very little certain guide and standard is furnished to legislative bodies. Legislatures are to be pardoned somewhat, perhaps, for their bewildered statements as to their own powers.

The lack of precision in fixing the scope of constitutional decisions as precedents is made the more vexing by uncertainty and lack of agreement among courts and scholars as to the theory whereby to explain what is done by judicial decision in formulating rules or principles. Sometimes a court holds strictly to the theory that a judicial decision goes no further than just what the words say and that only decisions, not opinions, are included. At other times the same courts hold that the spirit, or theory, of the decision, as evidenced by the opinion, taken together with the procedural and factual situation, is controlling. What should be said theoretically and practically of an opinion that overrules earlier *opinions,* or an opinion that overrules earlier opinions as to the future but applies them for the present to the case before the court, the decisions and opinions that the court in this very case overrules?[9] Such a procedure

[8] Clay, Regulation of Public Utilities, Chapters 3, 4.

[9] See the history of this series of cases in Great Northern Ry. v. Sunburst Oil and Ref. Co., 53 Sup. Ct. Rep. 145 (U. S. 1932).

may be eminently sound, but it certainly creates difficult problems in the operation of the technique of judicial review. It may be that there is nothing inherent in judicial review as a doctrine or theory to bring about this result, but it is certain that in practice it does not furnish a sufficient standard for prediction to answer a need felt by every legislative body and a growing number of administrators. One familiar with current constitutional decisions need think only of the fields of due process, interstate commerce, and taxation, as they are dealt with in state and federal courts, for examples to bear out this assertion. The problem of generalization so much emphasized by Professor Herman Oliphant and others is doubly important and difficult in the constitutional field, where nice legal distinctions reflect varying factors of religious, economic, racial, social, or political influence, in addition to the doctrinal influence of law itself as a system of thought or analysis.

No one is more keenly aware than is the writer of the dangers inherent in too much emphasis upon generalization in law, and especially of generalizations in advance in those branches of law dealing with government. Shocking examples of the stultifying effects of such generalization come to the mind of every student of constitutional law. But the fact remains that, taking the problems of legislation and administration as a whole, a real need exists for more of a guide than judicial review now furnishes. The lack of such a guide often results in as much inaction where action is necessary as would result from greater generalization; moreover, many mistakes and injuries could be eliminated if the constitutional rules and courses were more clearly charted. Finally, questions of improper constitutional restraints upon governmental powers, or upon the powers of any department, or the lack of necessary power in any branch of the government would be much more clearly presented, with the result that changes in the constitution itself would be the more easy to achieve.

Something could be done to correct this defect, in part at least. A legislative drafting and reference bureau properly organized, staffed, and equipped, and a permanent statutory reviser with an adequate staff, preferably in connection with the drafting office, would do something to correct the existing situation. The legislature should receive, at every session, a report on the state of legislation then on the books; how decisions seem to have affected it; what alternatives are available to the legislature in connection with resulting problems; and what results are likely to flow from failure of the legislature to act or from positive action along any of the alternative lines suggested. Some suggestions should be included also to indicate what would be likely to happen if, in the absence of further legislative action, courts apply the various legal rules and doctrines giving or denying effect to invalid statutes, and the decisions on them, and what would be the status of persons or governments who acted in reliance upon either decision or statute or both. Such an organization and such information are minimum essentials, a first step, in any program looking toward intelligent action by legislatures on problems of legislation created by the operation of judicial review.

Information of this type alone is not sufficient, however; new or corrective legislation must be drafted with a knowledge of the pitfalls into which the best-intentioned measures may fall. The need for expert drafting is always great, in any case, in the legislative process, but in the United States it is especially so, whenever a constitutional problem is presented in connection with proposed enactments.

In America lawyers have generally been overrepresented in legislative bodies, and until recently they drafted most of our legislation. This has been the case even with bills originating outside the legislature. The mediocrity of much of the legislative product, so far as form and constitutionality are concerned, is conclusive proof that to be trained for the practice of law does not guarantee an ability to draft bills. It would be almost inconceivable, did one not know the character of legal education in the United States, that legislative bodies with so many lawyers in them could contrive to do so badly. Lawyers have in the past been fitted for private practice, not public service, and persons familiar with the statute books and legislative processes need not be told of the difference between the skills involved in the practice of law and the art of legislation.

It is not advocated that the expert should replace the legislator in the work of legislation. It is simply urged that lawyers who are legislators realize that they are lawyers and legislators, not expert draftsmen; the legislature must retain the power to decide whether it wishes to repeal or not; whether it wishes to amend or not; whether it wishes to enact a law believed by it to be constitutional or not. These are questions of policy, and the legislature should decide them. But a legislature should act intelligently, knowing what it is doing. Such a service as has been suggested above would insure such action to a limited extent, at least. To be sure, freedom of legislative choice would be somewhat restricted, for knowledge always has its restrictive aspect, but the writer still believes that some of the restraints implicit in knowledge are desirable.

The suggestions submitted in the preceding paragraphs are not cure-alls; they are aids, not remedies, but if judicial review is to operate with a reasonable degree of effectiveness, such steps are essential.

Attention should be directed at this point to the fact that the uncertainty in judicial review sometimes has the effect, noted earlier, of restraining legislatures from enacting legislation that is likely to be, or almost certain to be, constitutional. It is this phase of judicial review that has received so much attention from persons interested in the improvement or change of government in this country. It is of the gravest concern. Legislators are often able to evade their responsibility for enacting laws desired by the public, or groups of the public, by hiding under the cloak of unconstitutionality when actually they are interested in the defeat of the proposal on social, economic, or political grounds. Opponents invariably levy the charge of unconstitutionality against proposed legislation, and often with great effect.[10]

A most unfortunate result of judicial review as it is practiced in this country is the effect it has had upon the legislative consideration of bills. No person familiar with congressional or state legislative work can fail to be impressed with the undue amount of time spent in legislative and committee proceedings upon questions of constitutionality. The result is that the real issues involved in proposed legislation tend to be obscured and not enough attention is given to the policy involved. This must, of course, always be true to some extent of legislative work in a government having judicial review, but the situation could be materially improved by the adoption of some of the suggestions made in this chapter.

One of the difficulties in the system of judicial review that has developed in connection with legislative practice is that legislatures pursue no uniform policy with respect to statutes that have been declared unconstitutional. This is partly due to a weakness in the legislative branch of government, but it is partly the fault of the judiciary. Sometimes such statutes are amended and re-enacted in a form that is valid; others are repealed; still others are not dealt with by legislative action for a long time. There are instances where legislatures have re-enacted the identical statute again at the next succeeding session, probably in the hope that the court will change its mind. Instances so bald as this are not numerous, but they have occurred.[11] Sometimes legislative inaction with reference to such

[10] See comment on this point in Clay, Regulation of Public Utilities, 103, and Smith, Growth and Decadence of Constitutional Government, 59.

[11] The writer has found a few instances of re-enactment without change, but it is difficult to tell whether they are intentionally so or the result of inadvertence.

laws is merely inadvertent; occasionally one suspects that it is the result of a hope that the judicial mind will change. It is almost impossible, as matters now stand, to keep statutory compilations sufficiently abreast of judicial work to make them reliable and accurate. This situation is not altogether the fault of the legislature; it is the result in part of the loose manner in which constitutionality and the different degrees of constitutionality are pronounced by the courts.

The task of the reviser or compiler is difficult. In the case of compilations that are not official and do not have the force of law, there is no uniformity of practice respecting the tests that shall govern the inclusion or exclusion of condemned statutes or sections of statutes. Nor have the courts done anything to aid them in their work. When the compilation is official and is given the stamp of legislative approval, the problem is simplified but not eliminated. There still remains the problem of determining whether the statute has been declared invalid in its entirety, as to all persons and objects to which it purports to apply; whether it has been declared invalid in part only; whether the partial invalidity is as to a section or as to a particular purpose or class of persons; whether the section declared invalid should be omitted and the other sections included, or whether the whole act falls with the section; the courts often fail to indicate the exact scope of their decision.

C. Judicial Review as a Supervisory Agent

A weakness in judicial review in its application to the federal system is that judicial review is ineffective to regulate governmental relationships because it does not function continuously as an instrument of supervision. Administrative supervision is much more effective than judicial review in adjusting and enforcing territorial distributions of power provided for in the constitution. The inadequacy of judicial review arises not only from the lack of preventive influence, as suggested earlier in this chapter, but from the nature of judicial review itself. It is essentially sporadic; and other existing rules of law permit the states, without resorting to the gross forms of evasion and revolt that have taken place at various stages of our constitutional history, to avoid legally and constitutionally the supervisory effects of judicial review of state administrative and legislative acts by the national courts.

For example, in 1923 the congressional law for the District of Columbia establishing a minimum wage for women and minors was declared invalid, in so far as it applied to women, by the Supreme Court of the United States.[12] Some state statutes thought to come within the sphere of that opinion were not declared unconstitutional until 1927. So, too, many states collected inheritance taxes on shares of stock in corporations for a year or more after Farmers' Loan and Trust Company v. Minnesota,[13] although such shares were later held to come within the rule of the Minnesota case.[14] But there are more glaring instances than these of the ineffective operation of judicial review as a control over the members of a federal system.

In one case a public utility company was restrained from recovering a reasonable rate from its customers, although the lower-than-reasonable rate imposed upon the company by state authorities and courts had been declared to be too low by the federal courts.[15] This denial of what the federal courts said the company was entitled to was accomplished not by a show of insubordination on the part of state courts but by the application of the rule that protest is necessary in mistake-of-law recoveries involving payments or services.

A Massachusetts tax statute was held to be unconstitutional, as applied to foreign corporations, by the Supreme Court of the United States. The Massachusetts courts had previously held the statute constitutional and the tax had been paid, on the theory that it could be recovered under a tax recovery statute permitting the recovery of taxes collected under an unconstitutional statute. In the action to recover the tax the Massachusetts court changed its construction of the original taxing law and overruled the earlier decision in which the law had been construed so as to require foreign corporations to pay the tax. Now the court construed the tax law so as to *exclude* such corporations from its operation. The overruling decision, on the declaratory theory of judicial decision, operated retrospectively so as to eliminate the earlier erroneous decision, not only leaving the tax law constitutional as now construed but leaving it valid from the beginning. The result was, of course, to deny to the taxpayer recovery of the tax paid, even though the Supreme Court of the United States had held it invalid, because the tax had not been paid under an unconstitutional statute, as that phrase was used in the state tax recovery statute.[16] This decision would probably have been reversed had it been brought before the federal courts under due process,

[12] Adkins v. Children's Hospital, 261 U. S. 525, 43 Sup. Ct. Rep. 394, 67 L. Ed. 785 (1923). See Donham v. West-Nelson Mfg. Co., 273 U. S. 657, 47 Sup. Ct. Rep. 343, 71 L. Ed. 825 (1927).

[13] *Supra,* note 4.

[14] See First Natl. Bk. of Boston v. Maine, *supra,* note 4.

[15] Chapter 7, note 33.

[16] Sloan v. Commonwealth, 253 Mass. 529, 149 N. E. 407 (1925).

although recent federal decisions were not then available to indicate the developing policy of extending that clause to cover tax recovery law.[17]

Such devious reasoning as that employed by the Massachusetts court is not always resorted to by state courts in denying recovery of taxes unconstitutionally exacted. More often it is sufficient to defeat recovery to show that the tax was paid under a decision by a state court holding the statute valid. The court had jurisdiction over the persons and subject, and its decision is final unless it is appealed from to a federal court. A judgment given by a court of competent jurisdiction, unappealed from, cannot later be assailed even if the statute involved is subsequently declared unconstitutional in another case, and payments made in accordance with such a judgment may not be recovered.[18]

The effect of such rules as this is to encourage litigiousness on the part of the taxpayer and to force appeals to the Supreme Court of the United States itself in every case of this kind involving a new taxing statute. In fact, as pointed out elsewhere,[19] the only way to avoid injustices resulting from tax remedy law as it now exists is for the taxpayer to seek preventive relief wherever possible. Only a decent remedial system will obviate the injustices. In any event, the present system is unfair to the small taxpayer who cannot afford to press his suit to the last appeal. The small taxpayer thus pays — with some grumbling, it is true, but he pays — while the larger one resists payment more often, although not so often as he might, because in some cases political expediency dictates payment instead of resistance.[20]

An interesting study in federal-state relations and the effect of judicial review is to be found in an Illinois case.[21] A national bank had asked permission of the proper state officers to engage in certain types of trust work. The Illinois courts had sustained the refusal of the state officers. No appeal to the federal courts was taken from the state court decision. The decision had turned upon the interpretation to be given a section of a federal statute and upon the validity of the section as interpreted. Later the same question was raised in a case in another state, and on appeal the Supreme Court of the

---

[17] See the discussion in Chapter 10.

[18] See Chapter 10. Beck v. State, 196 Wis. 242, 219 N. W. 197 (1928).

[19] See the opening paragraphs of Chapter 10.

[20] To the writer's personal knowledge, some cities in Minnesota are collecting certain types of taxes which both taxpayers and municipal authorities know and agree are invalid under existing decisions. Several states have been collecting taxes on the shares of stock in national banks, under informal compromises, the taxing being invalid under Supreme Court decisions.

[21] People ex rel. Bank v. Russell, 283 Ill. 520, 119 N. E. 617 (1918).

United States upheld the validity of the federal statute and so interpreted it as to give power to the national banks to engage in such services. Now the same national bank in Illinois that had previously been denied the power to conduct such business requested the proper officer to issue a certificate of authority to do so. Upon his refusal to do so, the bank asked for a writ of mandamus to compel its issuance. The state courts refused the writ, saying that the earlier state decision was binding, not having been appealed from, and could now not be attacked. The following statement makes clear the state court's position:

The reason given by the relator for bringing the same suit again is that since our decision in the case when it was before us the first time the Supreme Court of the United States has considered the same questions on writ of error to the Supreme Court of Michigan (National Bank of Bay City v. Fellows, 37 Sup. Ct. Rep. 734), and in an opinion filed June 11, 1917, sustained the validity of section 11k of the Federal Reserve Act and the power of the Federal Reserve Board under said act to clothe a national bank with authority to act as trustee, executor, or administrator, and it is, in substance, contended that we should disregard or ignore our former judgment in this case and award the peremptory writ. We willingly and cheerfully yield obedience to the authority of decisions of the United States Supreme Court when we have any liberty of choice in the matter, but we do not understand that in this case we have the power to adopt the view of the United States Supreme Court and render a judgment granting the relief prayed. If that court had been asked to review our decision it would have had the power to reverse and set it aside, but we do not understand the reversal of the judgment of the Supreme Court of Michigan in any way disturbed or affected the conclusiveness of the judgment of this court as a bar to a second suit between the same parties on the same cause of action. Under the decisions of the Supreme Court of the United States our judgment was erroneous, but the conclusiveness of a judgment upon the parties to it does not depend upon whether it is erroneous. (Case v. Beauregard, 101 U.S. 688.) Although it may be based upon unsound principles, it is binding on the parties and on the court rendering it unless reversed or set aside, and it is unaffected by the fact that in another case another court has rendered a different judgment upon the same issues of law or fact. We do not understand that we have the power to entertain, hear, and determine this case so long as our judgment in the same case rendered at a former term is in full force and effect. For these reasons we feel compelled to deny the writ.[22]

A decade ago Massachusetts declared its opposition to the rule of valuation in public utilities laid down by the Supreme Court of the

[22] 283 Ill. at 523.

United States, and this opposition has been successfully maintained for many years.[23]

The converse of this situation should also be mentioned. Not only do states sometimes escape the constitutional controls sought to be placed upon them with the sanction of judicial review but because of uncertainty they sometimes go much farther than the federal courts intended they should and hold state legislative enactments to be invalid on the ground that they are contrary to the constitution of the United States when in reality such enactments would, so far as one can tell, have been held by the federal courts to be valid exercises of state power.[24]

Problems of federal-state relations are also complicated by the anomalous situation existing with respect to concurrent powers of state and national governments. As in interstate commerce or bankruptcy, the theory is that states may occupy at least a portion of the regulatory field in the absence of conflicting national statutes. But the state laws may not occupy the field if the national government has done so in such a manner as to indicate its desire that the states be ousted from it.

What happens to exercises of state power under such circumstances? The theory is said to be that state laws are *suspended* from operation. The courts often speak of these laws as being unconstitutional, but they are not unconstitutional in the sense in which an ex post facto law is unconstitutional. They do not violate the constitutional prohibition directly, but they violate the principle that a congressional act is superior, if it is within the field of valid federal power, and is superior by virtue of its constitutional status.

This theory of suspension is different from the strict void ab initio doctrine and from any of the other theories of the effect of unconstitutionality. Suspended laws are inoperative only, not by virtue of judicial action but by virtue of congressional action; and congressional action, not judicial action, may again bring them back to life. Congressional withdrawal from the field at a subsequent date may serve to revive the state law, without re-enactment by the state legislature, unless the statute has been held to be invalid because it is in conflict with the state constitution, and unless, of course, it has been repealed.

[23] This has been true despite the decision in Worcester Elec. Light Co. v. Atwill, 23 F. (2d) 891 (D. C. Mass. 1927), the companies having dropped the case after obtaining a decision favorable to them.

[24] Compare Dairs v. Farmers' Cooperative Equity Co., 262 U. S. 312, 42 Sup. Ct. Rep. 556, 67 L. Ed. 996 (1923), statute invalid permitting suit to be brought against carrier in Minnesota, having only soliciting agent there, on injury occurring outside of Minnesota; Gamble Robinson Co. v. Pa. R. R., 157 Minn. 306, 196 N. W. 266 (1923), where plaintiff lived in state of Minnesota.

It is in connection with this field of the law that interest attaches to the rule that congress may evidence its intention to occupy the field even though the federal statute be invalid.[25]

Finally, judicial review has been deficient because so little attention has been paid by the courts to the development of sound rules on the legal effect of unconstitutional statutes and the legal effect of a decision as to constitutionality. The preceding chapters should convince most readers that these rules have been developed in a somewhat haphazard manner. Courts and writers seem never to have set for themselves the task of formulating a system of rules on the effect of unconstitutional statutes. Numerous rules dealing with this subject now exist, as the decisions cited in this book illustrate, but too little attention has been paid by legislatures, courts, and framers of constitutions to the adequacy of these rules or to the way in which they operate and the results they bring about. That judicial review is intimately connected with and affected by these rules should be clear. To have exercised the power of judicial review with so little attention to the legal rules that have come into play through the exercise of the power is to have been doctrinaire where doctrine should have been tempered by the practical considerations of the commercial and social and political world.

The present operation of judicial review is not without some advantages, however, both in the field of governmental and in private relations. Its chief advantage, it seems clear, is that it permits of great freedom and elasticity in the joints of the federal body politic.

Under a system of case-to-case review states are permitted to experiment in matters of government. Questions and doubts as to the scope of a Supreme Court decision may enable the state to continue using the condemned practice for a considerable time if it meets with general local or community approval. In any event, delay in appeals and in having collateral issues determined usually give the state time to make its institutions and practices conform to the constitutional requirements as these are interpreted by the courts. For example, the state mortgage moratoria laws of 1932 and 1933 were, if upheld by state courts, in operation during the spring and summer of 1933 and during most of the autumn also, because not until the October term did the Supreme Court pass upon them. The friends of state and local self-government have much to thank the courts for, although they seem not to know it.

Administrative supervision in a federal government would be much more effective, judged from the standpoint of uniformity and lack of deviation from rule, than judicial supervision. There would

[25] See Chapter 1, note 18.

also be greater certainty and a more unbroken continuity of policy and rule. But flexibility can be achieved by administration only to a limited extent, if the institution is an old or a large one and the procedures are relatively formal, as they tend to be. Administrative controls and supervision impose a strait jacket much more than does judicial review. Judicial control of administration can become fairly effective, as it has in France, although it never actually achieves the effectiveness that it gives the illusion of having reached.[26]

D. JUDICIAL REVIEW AND PRIVATE RIGHTS

For many of the same reasons given above, judicial review fails also to provide a really secure basis for safeguarding individual rights guaranteed by constitutions. This is not to say that judicial review is not of some, or even of great, value as a method of enforcing constitutional guarantees of private rights. But its effectiveness in this respect is limited. Here also its failure to afford preventive measures is significant. With a constitutional doctrine of governmental immunity for wrongs are coupled, in some instances, the delay and common law damage requirements of judicial relief — more important, perhaps, in personal rights cases than in cases of governmental power. Also, in this class of cases, the case-to-case nature of the exercise of judicial review is a weakening factor in its effectiveness, because general rule is important in freedom of speech, for example. Freedom to speak when there is the will to speak is worth more than later assurances that the freedom to speak is constitutionally guaranteed and the enforced silence an error. The will and time to speak having passed, the value of the right, both to the individual and to society, has been reduced greatly. So, too, it is small, though of course of some, comfort to know that habeas corpus will free one if he can afford to pay for it, because incarceration is unconstitutional. It may be that these are unavoidable occurrences in the operation of government, but it seems clear that judicial review itself could be more effective than it is at present as a method of sanctioning constitutional guarantees of individual rights. Under present rules and practices one man may be in prison for five years under an invalid law, and another who has committed identical acts under the same set of statutes, and with the same courts, may not be imprisoned for a day.

III. CONCLUSION

If judicial review is to be retained as a method of intergovernmental control, private parties should not be permitted to present or

[26] See Sharp, The French Civil Service, 68–75.

formulate the issues or disputes or the problems of constitutional power, unless an excess of authority is involved, and then not as between governmental units or departments, but as between government as a whole and the individual. In other words, the rules as to the proper parties to raise constitutional questions before the courts in this class of cases should be narrowed greatly. If private parties are to be permitted to continue their present rôle in this respect the rules as to proper parties should be broadened materially.

In the field involving relations of the government to the individual, the rules on proper parties should be relaxed so as to make of judicial review a more effective safeguard of individual rights.

In any event, the rules should be changed, by decision where change can be accomplished that way, by constitutional change if not, so as to give to judicial review more extensive advisory and preventive possibilities. This should be done in both classes of cases alluded to above.

Much would be gained also if judicial opinions were either eliminated or improved. To eliminate them would simplify somewhat the problem of generalization and would decrease their use as a basis of prediction.

To improve the opinion would require more specific statement on the part of the courts as to the scope of the decision. This would tend to give decisional status to judicial opinion, and likewise would aid in the process of prediction. More stress should be laid in opinions, if they are to be retained, on the rule-establishing function of judicial decision and opinion. Common denominators of agreed doctrine only should appear in majority opinions. When decisions are overruled, more explicit statement is necessary as to *what* is being overruled, and *why,* and *how much* is being changed, and what the rules with respect to retroactivity are to be.

The present ridiculous judicial practice of saying that the statute is invalid, "and we so hold," and then with a shrug of the judicial shoulder informing the parties and the country that "as to all the things connected herewith that you now need to know, and to which we could give an answer, this court says nothing," should cease.

The courts, if they are to continue to share in the work of government, must modify the American limitations upon, and theories of, the nature and function of judicial decision, and the rôle of the courts in a system of judicial review. A real responsibility is theirs, under such a system, and technical restrictions (increasing, it seems) tending to obscure their real rôle and permitting them to evade the serious governmental task of making it operate intelligently, as an institution of government, should be either relaxed or discarded altogether.

If we are to have judicial review, let us have it, and let us have it in such fashion as to give us more of its possible benefits. Growing governmental power and increasing administrative activity mean that judicial review will need to develop, not that it should be restricted. Those who now clamor for more restricted judicial review may be defending the fort and losing the country. The battleground of judicial review is already changing from the field of legislation to that of administration, and lawyers, judges, and political scientists should realize it if they do not do so now.

The technique of judicial review can be improved. It has real possibilities as an instrument of government. But its present utility is rapidly decreasing, just as many practices are less effective today than they were when they were devised for more simple governments and governmental tasks. The pity of it is that we are now going to have a vital governmental need for it, in a much-improved form, and the likelihood is great that as we come to need it in an expanded and improved form we are about to limit it positively, or to limit it in effect, by retaining traditional restrictions upon its use and effect.

A first step in such an improvement would be a careful statement or restatement of the rules on the effect of unconstitutional statutes, and the effect of decisions on constitutionality. If courts cannot do this satisfactorily, legislatures may wish to attempt it,[27] and if legislatures are not permitted to do it, the framers of new constitutions will have to do it.[28] The preceding chapters are intended to be of aid in carrying out such a program.

[27] There is probably little that can be accomplished by legislative declarations concerning the proper scope of the effect of a judicial decision on unconstitutionality. Such a declaration as that included in the National Industrial Recovery Act is likely to be ineffective. The doctrine of judicial review is a judicial doctrine and can be controlled by the judiciary itself, or the constitution, but not by statute. The courts may follow it, and accept such a declaration as evidence that this rule should be followed in the cases arising under this statute. The judges, however, must decide for themselves whether any given case or any given statute is such as to call for the application of the void ab initio, the presumption that the law is invalid, or the partial invalidity rules of the effect of a decision that a statute is unconstitutional. This is a part of the doctrine of judicial review as that doctrine has developed during the past century. Legislative declarations of this kind may or may not have any effect; they are advisory only.

[28] Since this was written Professor J. A. C. Grant has explained in an interesting note in 28 Am. Pol. Sci. Rev. 670 (1934) how some of the weaknesses of judicial review were corrected in the Austrian constitution preceding the changes of 1934. Most of the Austrian modifications were improvements upon American practice.

TABLE OF CASES

GENERAL INDEX

Accrual, of cause of action, in tax cases, 259

Action, cause of, and res adjudicata, 158–60; time of accrual, 259

Acts, compensatory, 294–304; curative and validating, 294–304

Administrative relief, in taxes, and duress, 265

Adoption agreements, 199

Advertising, of property for sale in tax cases as duress, 266

Affidavit, *see* Complaint

Amendment, constitutional, effect of, on prior statute, 288; distinguished from re-enactment, 274; invalid, 283; of invalid statute, 279–83

Appeal bonds, 200

Arrest, duress in tax payment, 269; false, 133–35

Attachment bonds, 200

Attack, collateral, on judgment, 152–56; on title to office, *see* Officers; on cities, *see* Municipal corporations

Attorney-general, in quo warranto, 77

Aumann, on judicial review in Ohio, 288

Bail, bonds for, 218–19

Ballantine, on de facto corporations, 38, 42

Bank, forgery of notes of, 34; organized under invalid statute, note to, 16

Bankruptcy, effect of national act on state law, 287

Benefits, as reason for denying recovery of taxes, 253

Bennett, on judicial review as guide to legislature, 313

Bickner, on defaulted bonds, 214

Bill drafting, improvement needed, 315

Bonds, appeal, 200; attachment, 200; in bail cases, 218; in reliance on invalid statutes, 189–90; in reliance on decisions, 189

Bonds, government, 204–15; and mistake of law, 209; reasons for denying recovery, 206–08; criticism of rule denying recovery, 212–14; remedies on, 210–12; under invalid statutes, 198; title to office questioned in recovery, 90

Bonds, private, under decisions, 192; to government, 215–20

Borchard, on declaratory judgments, 147, 243

Boudin, on judicial review and stare decisis, 162, 197

Building and loan associations, corporate existence assailed, 30

Canfield, on de facto corporations, 38

Carpenter, on de facto corporations, 22

Case-to-case method of decision, 6

Cause of action in tax recovery, when accruing, 259

City, donation by, 238; liability for acts of officer, 144

Civil cases, reliance on decision, 187–91; and res adjudicata, 155; testing title of judges in, 94

Claims, courts of, in tax refund cases, 247

Clark, on de facto corporations, 26, 39, 40, 43

Clay, on Massachusetts evasion of Supreme Court decision in utility rates, 314

Clerks, court, title of, tested in civil cases, 100; in criminal cases, 105

Cloud on title, tax paid to avoid, 266

Collateral attack, on judgment, 152

Common law, technique of, in judicial review, 318–26

Compensation, for injuries under invalid statute, 294–304; of de facto officers, 108

Complaint, liability for making, 135; by private person, 137

Compulsion, *see* Duress

Concurrent powers: suspension of state powers, 286–88

Congressional action, effect on state law, 286; intent of, as evidenced by invalid act, 5

Considerations, in contracts, 198–204

Constitutional amendment, as method of changing rule of a decision, 288; effect on prior statute, 288

Constitutional government, ideal of, 10–11

Constitutional limitations, judicial review in enforcing, 305–26

Constitutions, written, early supremacy over legislation, 10

Contested elections, and res adjudicata, 156

Contracts, obligation of, and stare decisis, 189; under unconstitutional statutes, 198–204; title to office questioned in suits on, 90; to pay government, 215–20; reliance on decision, 187

Cooley, on taxation, 244, 256, 261, 267;

351